Regulating Information Asymmetry in the Residential Real Estate Market

This book conducts a detailed examination of the current form of the Hong Kong residential property regulatory system: the 2013 *Residential Properties (First-hand Sales) Ordinance* (Cap 621). The author sheds light on how the legislation promotes a number of values including information symmetry, consumer protection, the free market and business efficacy. It provides a detailed account of how this regulatory mechanism has evolved over the past three decades to catch unconscionable sales tactics (such as selective information and/or misrepresentation of location, size, completion date and past transactions) and monitor sales practices in order to protect the interests of stakeholders in this ever-changing first-hand residential property market.

The book breaks down this complicated subject matter by focusing a number of chapters each on a specific attribute of the residential property on sale. It then examines the various channels through which the information is communicated to the prospective buyer, and discusses misrepresentation of the key information in sales of residential properties as criminal liability. The tension between consumer's rights on one hand and the pursuit of free market principles on the other is but one example of the conflicting values thoroughly discussed in the book, others include superstition vs. modernization and clarity vs. flexibility.

Aimed at those with an interest in consumer protection and transparency-oriented legislation in commercialized real estate transactions, this book seeks to provide an in-depth discussion of the latest trends and directions of travel.

Devin S. Lin, PhD researches on Construction Law and Property Law and is now teaching in the Southwest University of Political Science and Law, China.

T0384151

Routledge Studies in International Real Estate

The Routledge Studies in International Real Estate series presents a forum for the presentation of academic research into international real estate issues. Books in the series are broad in their conceptual scope and reflect an inter-disciplinary approach to Real Estate as an academic discipline.

Regulating Information Asymmetry in the Residential Real Estate Market

The Hong Kong Experience

Devin S. Lin

Routledge
Taylor & Francis Group

LONDON AND NEW YORK

First published 2018
by Routledge
2 Park Square, Milton Park, Abingdon, Oxon OX14 4RN

and by Routledge
605 Third Avenue, New York, NY 10017

First issued in paperback 2020

Routledge is an imprint of the Taylor & Francis Group, an informa business

British Library Cataloguing-in-Publication Data
A catalogue record for this book is available from the British Library

Library of Congress Cataloging in Publication Data
Names: Lin, Devin S.Title: Regulating information asymmetry in the
residential real estate market : the Hong Kong experience / Devin S. Lin.
Description: Abingdon, Oxon [UK] ; New York : Routledge, 2017. |
Series: Routledge studies in international real estate | Includes
bibliographical references and index.
Identifiers: LCCN 2016055543| ISBN 9781138231399 (hardback : alk.
paper) | ISBN 9781315315409 (ebook : alk. paper)
Subjects: LCSH: Real estate business--Law and legislation--China--Hong
Kong. | Vendors and purchasers--China--Hong Kong. | Residential real
estate--China--Hong Kong. | Land grants--Law and legislation--China--
Hong Kong.
Classification: LCC KNQ9317 .L56 2017 | DDC 343.5125/025--dc23
LC record available at https://lccn.loc.gov/2016055543

ISBN 13: 978-0-367-73610-1 (pbk)
ISBN 13: 978-1-138-23139-9 (hbk)

Typeset in Times New Roman
by Saxon Graphics Ltd, Derby

Dedicated to Professor Tang Lieying. Ph.D,
my mother, who inspired me to become a legal researcher

Contents

Illustrations

Figures

Tables

Maps

Preface

The sale of residential flats before completion of their physical construction has a history of more than half a century in Hong Kong. It has been a feature of the housing market and a cornerstone of the economy for decades. Unfortunately, because buyers have no actual property to inspect before signing to buy and must rely on the seller for information, it has been a source of complaint and scene of crafty practices for almost as long. The Hong Kong government has made repeated efforts to moderate certain of those practices, relying on administrative measures, negotiated self-regulation and ultimately on legislation.

Dr. Devin Lin's admirable book traces the history of these governmental efforts and the difficulties that they encountered. The text describes the questionable tactics employed by developers and estate agents in marketing uncompleted developments. The book is the product of years of research during which Dr. Lin visited numerous new developments. He personally observed the sales tactics that he describes. He collected, inspected and compared countless brochures and other commercial literature and spoke to dozens of participants in the market.

The Residential Properties (First-hand Sales) Ordinance was eventually enacted in June 2012. This legislation includes several provisions for which Dr. Lin had been advocating. In this book he describes its complex provisions in a systematic way and casts a critical eye on how the Ordinance is working. He provides a thoughtful, distinctive, independent voice in the debate about an effective regulatory regime. Those interested in off-the-plan sales will read this account with interest and profit.

Malcolm Merry
University of Hong Kong

The Residential Properties (Firsthand Sales) Ordinance (Cap 621) can be downloaded from the homepage of the Sales of First-hand Residential Properties Authority, The Government of the Hong Kong Special Administrative Region at http://www.srpa.gov.hk/en/ordinance.html

Acknowledgement

It was in 2008 that I started the research on the sale of uncompleted first-hand residential properties in Hong Kong at the University of Hong Kong, under the supervision of Professor Alice Lee and Professor S. H. Goo. Despite the protracted local debate and early systematic studies on the regulatory regime (perhaps best represented by the 1991 *Study on the Disclosure of Information to Prospective Purchasers of Uncompleted Unit* by the Consumer Council and the 1995 *Report on Description of Flats on Sale* by the Law Reform Commission of Hong Kong), the regime of control based on the Lands Department Consent Scheme had not changed much before 2007. The year 2008 marked the beginning of extensive reform by the Hong Kong government within the framework of the Consent Scheme to tackle information asymmetry and unconscionable sales practices in the sale of first-hand residential properties. The magnitude of the issue and the pressing need for a solution led to heated debates in 2010 on potential legislation. By the end of that year, the Steering Committee on Regulation of Sale of First-hand Residential Properties by Legislation had been established by the then Chief Executive, Dr Donald Tsang. One year later, in November 2011, the government completed the draft of the *Residential Properties (First-hand Sales) Bill*, based on the Steering Committee's deliberation over the provisions of the new law. After a three-month consultation period, the revised Bill was introduced in the Legislative Council in March 2012. It took another four months of legislative debate and deliberation before the *Residential Properties (First-hand Sales) Ordinance* (Cap 621) was finally published in the *Gazette* on 6 July 2012. Four months later, in October 2012, I obtained my Ph.D with a thesis discussing this new piece of legislation. In April 2013, the *Ordinance* entered into force and the Sales of First-hand Residential Properties Authority was set up to implement the *Ordinance*.

This book provides the very first systematic and comprehensive academic discussion and examination of the function of the new regulatory regime and the implementation of the new legislation by the Sales of First-hand Residential Properties Authority since April 2013. The year 2016 saw the first successful prosecutions under the *Ordinance* against three vendors of first-hand residential properties, in respect of the sale of *Ocean One* in 2013, the sale of *Graces* (a phase in the development of *Providence Bay*) in 2013, and the sale of *Full Art Court* in 2014. At the time of writing, almost four years have passed since the enactment of the *Ordinance*, during which time the new regulatory regime centred on this unique piece of legislation has proven its effectiveness in promoting transparency in the first-hand residential property sector.

Much has happened in the sector over the last nine years (2008–2016), and it is now a pertinent juncture for a timely academic review of these developments, sharing with the world Hong Kong's innovative experience in creating a transparent and efficient residential property market. I have been fortunate to witness the lead-up to Hong Kong's unprecedented legislation to promote information disclosure and regulate misleading sales practices in the property sector, while carrying out my research at the very frontiers of this area of law, with the guidance and encouragement of the following mentors, colleagues and friends.

First, my sincerest expression of appreciation goes to my primary Ph.D supervisor Professor Alice Lee, Associate Dean of the Faculty of Law, for her unparalleled supervision from 2008 to 2012. I can never thank Professor Lee enough for her confidence in me and my research from the very beginning. Professor Lee played an instrumental role in inspiring my research topic and has guided me since through a transformative process, with four years of continuous attention and innovative coaching – from the drafting of the very first research proposal on the topic (submitted in January 2008) to the revision of the thesis (submitted in October 2012). I hope this book can reflect to some extent the elegance and clarity of her works. The very first piece of academic work I have read in this area was the joint paper by Professor Lee and Professor Goo. Professor Lee took me to the University of Macau in December 2008 when she presented the joint paper at an international conference.

I would also like to extend my sincere gratitude to my co-supervisor Professor S. H. Goo, Professor of Law at the University of Hong Kong, who started the pioneering research project on regulating off-plan sales in Hong Kong, for the research topic and supervision. It was my tremendous honour to join him and Professor Lee in the research, and I am greatly indebted to them for their continuous encouragement and inspiration, through their helpful ideas, comments, guidance and advice in discussing the issues, focus and methodology of my research. Professor Goo's 2010 paper published in The Conveyancer and Property Lawyer, which studies the effectiveness of the Consent Scheme before its 2010 reform and shaped the subsequent regulations and legislation, served as one of my early inspirations for studying the evolution of the regulatory regime. I am particularly grateful to Professor Goo for his introduction to Professor Malcolm Merry and his support for my lecture entitled 'New Rules for Sales of Uncompleted Flats' in *Law Lectures for Practitioners 2010*. It was also through Professor Goo's introduction that I became acquainted with Dr Martin Dixon of the University of Cambridge and Professor Roger Smith of the University of Oxford in 2011, both of whom have further influenced my research on land law.

I would like to express my deep appreciation to Professor Malcolm Merry of the University of Hong Kong, for his guidance in the writing process and for his detailed comments on the many drafts of this book. In 2010 I was introduced by Professor Merry to Ms Teresa Wong of the Legal Advisory and Conveyancing

Office in the Lands Department, whose answers to my questions led me to a deeper understanding of the regulatory regime, especially the numerous administrative measures first introduced to the Consent Scheme in June 2010 to enhance transparency. As a major breakthrough, on 30 September 2010 I delivered my first lecture on the new measures introduced to the Consent Scheme on June 2010 in the *Law Lectures for Practitioners 2010*; the manuscript of the lecture was written under the edition of Professor Merry. In March 2012, I attended the *Modern Study in Property Law 2012* at the University of Southampton with Professor Merry and presented a paper in the postgraduate research student's conference which now forms part of Chapter 4 of this book. I am fortunate to have the continuous attention and guidance of Professor Merry after graduating from the University of Hong Kong. My writing has been heavily influenced by his works in this area, particularly his 2008 conference paper delivered at the HKU-NUS-SMU Symposium in Singapore, which provided a detailed analysis on the sale, financing, construction of uncompleted residential flats in Hong Kong from a purchasing consumer's perspective.

My gratitude is also extended to Professor Philip Britton, whom I met through the introduction of Dr Leslie Turano Taylor and Dr John Barber during my visit to the King's College London School of Law (as it then was) in the spring of 2011, when he was chairing the Centre of Construction Law. Professor Britton has been guiding me in my studies and research on UK construction law and consumer protection law since then and continues to advise me on parallel UK issues. His works on UK construction law is a model of leading scholarship in this fast-moving area of law. I have benefited immensely from Professor Britton's comments on the final draft of this book, in particular his update on the latest developments in consumer protection legislation in the UK.

I wish to thank His Honour Judge Humphrey Lloyd QC for publishing the article on legislating floor numbers in Hong Kong (now part of Chapter 7 of this book) in the *International Construction Law Review* in 2015, and to Mr Andrew Burr for two co-related publications in the *Construction Law Journal* in 2013 and 2014, which have now become part of Chapter 3 and Chapter 4 respectively.

I would also like to thank Professor K. W. Chau of the Faculty of Architecture, the University of Hong Kong for his comments and suggestions on my thesis, based on his profound understanding of the real estate market in Hong Kong. I am indebted to Dr Arthur McInnis for his guidance on my studies and research on Hong Kong construction law and his comments on the final draft of this book. Furthermore, I deeply value the comments from Mr Matthew Bell of the University of Melbourne and other members of the Society of Construction Law Australia.

Throughout the winding path to completing this research, I have had the pleasure of growing with and learning from two outstanding peers and young scholars in property and construction law: Dr Louise Cheung of the University of Southampton, and Mr Mathias Cheung, Barrister at Atkin Chambers, who was recently awarded first Prize by the Society of Construction Law UK for his 2015 Hudson Prize paper on liquidated damages and penalty clauses. I owe both of them a debt of gratitude for their unfailing support and insightful observations.

I wish to express my great appreciation to Miss Lucy Yen of Yen, Yu & Co., Solicitors, for all her encouragement and strong support over the years. She has provided me with encouragement and guidance since we met each other in 2008.

I would also like to offer my special thanks to Miss Coria Cheng and Miss Gloria Wong of Faculty of Law of the University of Hong Kong and Miss Betty Lam of Lui Che Woo Law Library for their kind help.

For the publication of this book, I am greatly indebted to Mr Ed Needle of Taylor & Francis for his guidance and advice. Mr Needle suggested the title of this book, *Regulating Information Asymmetry in the Residential Real Estate Market*, after reading the first draft, which perfectly summarizes the gist of my work. I thank Mr Matthew Turpie and Mr Scott Oakley of Taylor & Francis for all their patience, encouragement and professional help in editing this book, which has enabled me to include in this edition of the book the discussion on the sales of *Ocean One*, *Graces* as well as the Court of Appeal decision in *Yang Dandan v Hong Kong Resort Co. Ltd* [2016] HKEC 1722. And I thank Miss Lisa Sharp for her assistance and help in the production of this book.

Although I can never emphasize enough the support and contribution by the people mentioned above, all omissions and mistakes remain my sole responsibility.

For this special period of my life, I have had the privilege and honour to receive the guidance and training on matters outside my research from three extraordinary entrepreneurs: Mr Desmond Cheung of Interior Contract International Ltd, Mr Derek Chong of Oceanarch International Co. and Mr Daniel Wong. Their wisdom has transformed my understanding of the construction industry, the commercial world and life in general, and this has also been critical to the successful and timely completion of my research.

As this is my first book on a legal subject, I take the opportunity to thank the following prominent scholars who have been helping me in my legal studies and research: Professor Zhang Xianchu, Professor Fu Hualing, Professor Albert Chen, Professor Johannes Chan, Professor Michael Wilkinson, and Professor Rick Glofcheski of the University of Hong Kong; Professor Kelvin Low of the Singapore Management University; and Professor Chen Li of Fudan University.

I am blessed to have had the incredible companionship of Mr Yury Elsov and my brother Mr Tang Linyao along the journey. Last, I would like to acknowledge the support of my parents – I can never thank my father, Professor Lin Yiquan, enough for his wisdom and encouragement, and I am forever indebted to my mother, Professor Tang Lieying of the Southwest University of Political Science and Law, for her love and support. Her pioneering writing and nationwide publications on Chinese civil law and property law are the greatest source of inspiration for my legal studies and research. I dedicate this book to her.

Devin Lin
11 January 2017

1 Introduction

The ground-breaking Hong Kong approach

Consumer protection is a fascinating subject that has remained on the fringe of property law and construction law for too long. With the fast development in the private real estate market worldwide in recent years, these two seemingly remote disciplines start to interact with each other. Malcolm Merry (2008) recorded the very beginning of an emerging awareness among flat purchasers of their status as consumers in the 1980s when property became big business in Hong Kong and the corresponding request for government control to promote fair practice in the sale and purchase of flats as follows:

> They became more discriminating and realized that as customers they had a choice and as consumers they had, or ought to have, rights. It was no longer enough for the government just to make sure that the flats were built. Buyers expected to be protected from the sharp practices of developers and their agents.

This phenomenon suggests the connection point between consumer protection law and property law may be administrative or legislative regulation for protection of consumer rights in the transaction of properties, perhaps in particular first-hand residential properties, which aims to provide purchaser-consumers with access to relevant and important information regarding the residential property on sale. In the absence of mandatory regulation, much of this information can be hidden by the vendor, who may not otherwise be obliged to disclose important details under the common law doctrine *caveat emptor*.

On the other hand, government control is a much-discussed topic for property law and construction law. The degree of government control in regulating sales of commercial properties is a subject of much debate in different jurisdictions. The central goal of government regulation in respect of property transaction – in Hong Kong and elsewhere – is to promote a market that is efficient and transparent for consumers. A couple of years ago, it was considered that there was a serious lack of comprehensive and effective laws and regulations in the sale of residential flats in Hong Kong; it was then suggested that an appropriate regulatory system in the sector must balance market efficiency, consumer protection and developers' interests (Goo 2010). Merry (2008) expressed a similar view when he concluded that the government regulation then 'is generally effective to ensure that the flats are built and delivered to purchasers and that adequate arrangements are made for the management and administration of the building thereafter but that it is deficient in promoting fair practice in the sale and purchase of the flats on sale'.

As a general principle, government regulation in the property market should be balanced between two values: firstly, the value of a transparent, efficient market where both the vendor and the purchaser are equally able to access key information regarding the property on sale; and secondly, the interests of the free market, where the details of the transaction should mainly be subject to the contract agreed and entered into freely by the vendor and the purchaser. At the same time, the vendor shall enjoy certain rights as the owner of the property, i.e. *the freedom to dispose of her property* and *the freedom not to sell*.

In any jurisdiction where the value of the property is subject to market evaluation, the amount of money involved in the sale of any residential property tends to be significant for an ordinary purchaser. The damage the purchaser will suffer if the development is not completed, is delayed in its completion, is defective or is of a smaller size than promised, or if the vendor is not a qualified vendor of the property (i.e., with a defective title, without the qualification to sell at all, or without the qualification to sell before completion of construction), will be too great to recover in a short period of time. Some observers argue that the non-equal footing bargaining power between purchasers and developers further manifests the need of government to protect the interests of the general public in first-hand property sales (Chan et al. 2015). Indeed, it is both the unequal position between the vendor and the purchaser and the risk the purchaser is taking in entering into the agreement for sale and purchase that require the intervention of the government to oversee the transaction. The question then becomes one of the degree of regulation.

Hong Kong has been known as the world's freest economy. The Special Administrative Region of People's Republic of China ranks No. 1 in the 2016 Index of Economic Freedom. Quite remarkably, the Index scored Hong Kong 97.4 out of 100 in terms of business freedom under the category of regulatory efficiency (Miller and Kim 2016).[1] How should the sales of residential properties be regulated in the world's freest economy?

The sale practices were loosely regulated until the last decade of the twentieth century; but the need for consumer protection in this field of activity was firstly discussed by the Consumer Council in 1977 (CC 2014) and systematically studied in 1989 (CC 1991). With the growing concern of consumer rights in property transactions, the regulation has steadily increased since June 2010 (Lin 2012). It was pointed out in 2010 that the Hong Kong Government should strike a balance between market efficiency and consumer protection on the one hand, and developers' interests and the fear of government intervention in the market on the other hand (Goo 2010).

Then, in 2012, Hong Kong passed a new piece of legislation that arguably represents the strictest regulation over sales of first-hand residential properties in the world.

For Hong Kong Special Administrative Region (HKSAR), the enactment of the *Residential Properties (First-hand Sales) Ordinance* (Cap 621) (hereafter the *Ordinance*) in 2012 represents a milestone in a decade-long process of constructing a transparent and efficient first-hand residential real estate market in the region. The process can claim its beginning as early as the 1960s, when the first case of incompletion occurred in the region's earliest off-plan sales (i.e., *the Peony House Incident*). The incident triggered the first efforts of government intervention and led to the introduction of the Consent Scheme in 1969 (Fan 2005). The Scheme exhibited an awareness of higher degree of consumer protection in the 1990s where the focus of government monitoring gradually shifted to information disclosure. The process has been accelerated since the first decade of the millennium with a growing request for frank and accurate information disclosure in the market. After rounds of development where more and more substantive measures were introduced to the Consent Scheme from June 2010, the need for consolidating all the rules in the form of one legislation emerged. Finally, the Bill drafted by the Transport and Housing Bureau passed the legislature after three readings and a number of amendments in 2012. The *Ordinance* came into full effect on 29 April 2013.

As such, seemingly paradoxically to its pursuit of business freedom, Hong Kong has passed a law to standardize sale practices of first-hand residential properties. Although the new legislation mainly operates on the acts of developers (some of its provisions apply to real estate agents too), the law is grounded in the need for consumer protection in the residential real estate market. It has placed the value of constructing a transparent, efficient market over the value of maintaining a free market with minimum government intervention. In other words, Hong Kong has given its unequivocal answer in giving priority to consumer protection and the construction of a transparent and efficient market at the costs of strong government intervention with substantive aggressive regulation over a market in which there has been a high degree of business freedom.[2]

Such preference is evident in the legislative purpose of the *Ordinance*: i.e., *to enhance the transparency and fairness of the sales arrangements and transactions of first-hand residential properties and consumer protection, and provide a level playing field for vendors of first-hand residential properties* (LC 2013). The Sales of First-hand Residential Properties Authority (SRPA) established under section 86 of the *Ordinance* also highlights *transparency* as their core value (SRPA 2013). Thus the meaning of the word *transparency* in the context of sale of property transaction is worthy of exploration.

To start, the word *transparency* in Latin etymology means *being seen through*; therefore in physical science, a transparent object has the property of transmitting light without appreciable scattering; the definition has been metaphorically adopted by social science to 'connote the ability of interested parties to see through otherwise private information' (Schnackenberg 2009).

A recent liberal elaboration on the concept by *Fortune Magazine* suggests that transparency means making the practices, policies, algorithms, and even code, operating data, and future plans available to customers, employees, or business partners – [which] runs counter to traditional business practices (Hagel III and Brown 2014). The standard is probably a bit forward-looking for any traditional business practices including property development business. This is certainly not within the meaning of transparency that is accorded to the *Ordinance*. Yet, it explains the concept in the context of running an enterprise in the twenty-first century.

Transparency is classically defined and most frequently cited as a state of a functional market 'when much is known by many' (Starke 2016). The 'much' which is 'known by many' refers to the information on various aspects of the goods. The concept of transparency is intimately related with provision and disclosure of information in the market. According to Black's Law Dictionary, a transparent market is where all prices and supply information is publicly available. Some even suggest that when transparency relates to information flow from the company to investors, it is simply known as 'full disclosure'.[3] An even more thoughtful definition suggests that transparency is associated with the quality of information a company provides to various stakeholders (Churchwell 2003).

On a more specific level, transparency is recognized, in transactional settings, as the extent to which the seller reveals private information to the consumer (Granados, Gupta and Kauffman 2005). According to Daniel Schwarcz (2014), transparency, broadly construed, involves making relevant information available to consumers. Schwarcz, in his discussion on consumer protection in insurance, further argued that transparency-oriented regulatory strategies promote consumer choice, harness market discipline and ensure regulatory accountability.

Any discussion on market transparency is almost inevitably accompanied with the discussion of a co-related concept: *information asymmetry*. One of the earliest discussions on the concept is the publication of the article 'The Market for "Lemons": Quality Uncertainty and the Market Mechanism' by George A. Akerlof in the *Quarterly Journal of Economics* in 1970. In the article, George, using 'lemon' as a metaphor for defective cars, suggested the high possibility of consequence of adverse selection in a market where sellers have more information than purchasers about product quality. In general, information asymmetry occurs where the seller possesses greater information than the purchaser in regards to the goods of sale. Study on information asymmetry has received enormous attention since the last decade of the twentieth century (Stiglitz 2001); the first milestone was the award of the Sveriges Riksbank Prize in Economic Sciences in Memory of Alfred Nobel (also known as the Nobel Memorial Prize in Economic Sciences) in 1996 to James A. Mirrlees and William Vickrey for their contributions to the economic theory of incentives under asymmetric information.[4] Then in 2001, for their analyses of markets with asymmetric information, the Nobel Memorial Prize in Economic Sciences was awarded to George Akerlof, Michael Spence and Joseph E. Stiglitz.[5] Over the past decades the pervasive effects of information asymmetry in relation to the efficiency of the market as well as the protection of consumer rights have been studied in many contexts (e.g., lending and borrowing, accounting, insurance, sale of second-hand products, etc.), but a systematic study of information asymmetry in the first-hand residential real estate market is comparatively new.

Early research on the Consent Scheme concludes that information asymmetry and irrational behaviour of purchasers caused market failure and lack of consumer protection in sale of off-the-plan properties in Hong Kong (Goo 2010). This is further confirmed by recent research into regulation of the sale of first-hand residential properties suggesting that information asymmetry between purchasers and developers always fails in the market, and the market failure necessitates government regulation (Chan et al. 2015). Accordingly, it was advised that the aim of the regulatory system was to reduce the occurrence of information asymmetry and irrational behaviour of purchasers (Goo 2010).

In the context of residential real estate market, information asymmetry occurs wherever the vendor knows more about the property than the purchaser, which is usually the case. As transparency demands full disclosure of quality information, the existence of information asymmetry undermines the degree of transparency of the market. The occurrence of information asymmetry in the residential real estate market has been a common phenomenon in the major cities of the world. The question is, where does asymmetric information occur in the sale of residential properties and how does that affect the decision of the purchaser?

For a proper understanding of the meaning of transparency in residential real estate market, we need to understand what information a vendor developer shall make available for the sale of first-hand residential properties, for only full and accurate disclosure eliminates information asymmetry. The kinds of information that demand disclosure concern a variety of key aspects of the property on sale and the transaction. In terms of the physical attributes of the residential unit, this includes: the floor area of the property (to be discussed in Chapters 3 and 4); the internal and external dimensions of the property and the fittings, finishes and appliances installed within (to be discussed in Chapter 5); location and environmental features (to be discussed in Chapter 6); in multi-storey developments, the information on the floor the apartment is on (to be discussed in Chapter 7). In terms of the transaction, issues include: the date of completion and lease term of the development (to be discussed in Chapter 8); salient points of the Deed of Mutual Covenants and Land Grant Conditions (to be discussed in Chapter 9); the price of the property (to be discussed in Chapter 10); sales arrangement (to be discussed in Chapter 11); the agreement for sale and purchase and past transaction record (to be discussed in Chapter 12).

With such volume of information needing disclosure in sales of residential properties, the requirement of transparency also concerns the construction of information channels to systematically present the information to prospective purchasers and the public. In the sale of residential properties in Hong Kong, major information channels include sales brochures, advertisements, price lists, registers of transaction, show flats and websites designated by the vendor for the development (to be discussed in Chapter 13).

The *Ordinance* can be conveniently summarized as the law to deal with how the various sorts of information pertaining to the property and the transaction should be disclosed and presented in the various information channels. As its Long Title proclaims:

> [A]n Ordinance to regulate the provision of sales brochures and price lists and the use of show flats in connection with the sale of residential properties in respect of which neither an agreement for sale and purchase nor an assignment has ever been entered into and made, to regulate the viewing of such properties before sale, to regulate the publication of sale arrangements and the execution of agreements for sale and purchase in connection with such properties, to provide for registers of transactions in connection with such properties, to regulate advertisements promoting the sale of such properties, to provide for offences in connection with misrepresentations and dissemination of false or misleading information, and to provide for incidental and connected matters.[6]

Thus if information asymmetry is intentionally caused or recklessly ignored by the vendor and/or the estate agents due to partial disclosure, inaccurate disclosure, untimely disclosure or non-disclosure of the information requested under the *Ordinance*, then the vendor or the estate agents may be committing various offences of the *Ordinance*. In other words, the *Ordinance* aims to enhance transparency by regulating the sales practices of the vendor and estate agents in sale of first-hand residential properties.

Recent developments in consumer protection regulation have given rise to a popular application of a legal term in modern consumer protection law that specifically addresses the selling activities in B2C (business-to-consumer) transactions: that of *commercial practice*, which is defined as any act, omission, course of conduct, representation or commercial communication (including advertising and marketing) by a trader, which is directly connected with the promotion, sale or supply of a product to or from consumers, whether occurring before, during or after a commercial transaction (if any) in relation to a product. Accordingly, a *consumer* is redefined as any individual who in relation to a commercial practice is acting for purposes which are outside of her business.[7] The *UK Consumer Rights Act* (CRA) 2015 further defines a customer as 'an individual acting for purposes that wholly or mainly outside that individual's trade, business, craft or profession'.[8]

The truth is, not all commercial practices are fair. *The Consumer Protection from Unfair Trading Regulations 2008* provides that a commercial practice is unfair if it materially distorts or is likely to materially distort the economic behaviour of the average consumer with regard to the product, or if contravenes the requirements of professional diligence, i.e., the standard of special skill and care which a trader may reasonably be expected to exercise towards consumers which is commensurate with either honest market practice or the general principle of good faith in the trader's field of activity.[9]

It is noteworthy that the *Ordinance* focuses exclusively on commercial practices by the vendor (and on some occasions the estate agents as well) on information disclosure and marketing behaviours (i.e., construction of show flats and release of advertisements). In this regard, the implementation of the *Ordinance* in Hong Kong could also represent the latest and quite substantial development in *promotional marketing law*, a concept that has been discussed in consumer protection law for some time, yet is not officially recognized as a dedicated body of law (Circus 2011).

Misleading and aggressive commercial practices by either the vendor or the estate agents occur in sales of both new and second-hand residential properties in Hong Kong. However, the *Ordinance* only applies to the sale of first-hand residential properties. To better understand the scope of the *Ordinance*, we need to take a close look at the real estate market of Hong Kong.

The residential real estate market in Hong Kong

Types of housing in Hong Kong

Hong Kong is internationally renowned for its modern architecture and expansive skyline. According to *Emporis* (a worldwide information provider who runs the world's largest and most comprehensive database of skyscrapers[10] and high-rise buildings[11]), Hong Kong outnumbers any other city in the world in terms of the number of skyscrapers and high-rise buildings (Emporis 2016).[12] On the land mass of 1,104 km², where only a portion of about 200 km² flat land are estimated to be available for construction,[13] lies one of the world's most vibrant and expensive property markets.

Broadly speaking, three types of residential properties are sold and purchased in the local real estate market: (i) private housing (or in Chinese, 私人樓宇); (ii) the New Territories Exempted Houses (NTEHs, or in Chinese, 丁屋); (iii) flats built by Hong Kong Housing Authority under the Home Ownership Scheme (HOS Flats, or in Chinese 居屋); this category includes flats built by private developers in agreement with the Housing Authority under the Private Sector Participation Scheme.[14]

The following statistical table by Hong Kong Housing Authority shows that by the year 2014, 45.7 per cent of the city's population lived in private permanent housing, 29.1 per cent in public rental housing, and 16.5 per cent in subsidized housing (HKHA 2015).

Table 1.1 Population by Type of Housing, 2004, 2009 and 2014 by Hong Kong Housing Authority (2015)

	%		
	2004	*2009*	*2014*
Public permanent housing	49.0	47.1	45.7
Rental housing	30.5	29.2	29.1
Subsidised sale flats	18.5	17.9	16.5
Private permanent housing	50.2	52.2	53.8
Temporary housing	0.8	0.7	0.6

Private housing

Private housing refers to housing estates developed by private developers. Main sources of land supply for private housing include: (i) Government residential sites sold to developers by the Lands Department; (ii) Railway sites under the exclusive development right of the Mass Transit Railway Corporation; (iii) Urban Renewal Authority (URA) sites sold to developers for redevelopment; and (iv) privately owned sites with planning approval for residential use for which requisite lease modifications have been executed with government (LC 2011).[15]

The first modern private housing estate in Hong Kong – *The Mei Foo Sun Chuen* – was built between 1965 and 1978 in eight phases. The estate, believed to be the largest residential estate in the world up till today, contains 99 residential buildings accommodating 13,149 apartments. Since then, multi-block housing complexes have been thriving across the territory, with the residential towers growing all the more stately. One of the most notable trends is the tremendous increase in the construction of large housing estates. The development usually bears what could be best described as a *birthday cake* structure, where a number of residential towers erect atop a large multi-storey podium that contains recreational facilities including shopping malls, car-parks, clubhouses and restaurants. In some of these large-scale complex projects, a line of independent houses is built.[16] There are also developments in the New Territories which consist purely of independent houses.[17]

With few exceptions, the lots sold to developers by private landlords or by the Urban Renewal Authority are piecemeal land in the crowded parts of Hong Kong and Kowloon. This is also the case for most new developments in the mountainous parts on the Hong Kong Island. The lot is not usually large enough for housing complexes with multiple residential buildings; instead, a single-block high-rise tower will be built upon, usually with a car-park in the foundation and a clubhouse located either on the ground or top floor of the development.

New Territories Exempted Houses

New Territories Exempted Houses (NTEHs) are village houses built within the boundaries of a list of 642 villages in the New Territories. When the *Buildings Ordinance* (Cap 123) was extended to the New Territories in 1961, the custom that an indigenous male could build in his village a small house for himself or his son upon marriage was upheld. The erection of a house is exempted for building approval provided certain conditions are met (Merry 2011a). One of the conditions is the dimension of the building. The house when constructed should not be more than three floors and should not exceed 27 feet (or 8.23 metres) in height; its roofed-over area should not exceed 700 square feet (or 65.03 square metres).[18] Starting from December 1972, the government began to administer the small house grant via a Small House Policy: every indigenous male villager over 18 years old and who is descended through the male line of a resident in 1898 in one of the 642 listed villages in the New Territories is entitled to a small house grant of 700 square-foot plot of building land by way of application for a free building licence to build a small house on his own land at nil premium, or a private treaty grant of government land, if available, at a concessionary premium (LC 2006). New Territories (NT) Exempted Houses are addressed as *specified NT development* in the *Ordinance*: a development if a certificate of exemption has been issued under section 5(a) of the *Buildings Ordinance (Application to the New Territories) Ordinance* in respect of building works for every building in the development.[19]

To prevent the abuse of the scheme by villagers from cashing in on their eligibility for the small house grants, most New Territories Exempted Houses are granted under a three-year to five-year moratorium on the removal of restriction on alienation in case of a resale of the house to an outsider. 'Alienation' refers to the sale of the house by the grantee to an outsider or a non-indigenous villager within the operative period of the restriction: the grantee has to pay the land premium up to the difference between the market value of the lot at the time of application to remove the alienation and the premium, if any, paid at the time of grant (AC 2002). Hence New Territories Exempted Houses can be purchased and sold in the open market after the restrictive period or after paying off the land premium. In fact, estates of modern independent houses have been built on contiguous village lots assembled by developers, who recruited indigenous males, assisted them to apply for a permission to build on privately owned village land registered in their name (beneficially owned by the entrepreneur) or for concessionary grants of land, then built the house and sold to third parties for benefits. In these cases, the land premiums are ultimately paid by the purchasers (Merry 2011b).

HOS flats

Under the Home Ownership Scheme (*HOS*), the Hong Kong Housing Authority develops and sells HOS flats at a concessionary price on behalf of the government to a specific group of citizens known as green form and white form applicants.[20] Within five years from the date of purchase, purchasers of HOS flats can only resell the flats to public housing tenants or Green Form Certificate holders.[21] The resale of HOS flats in the open market is subject to statutory alienation restrictions including a payment of premium to the Hong Kong Housing Authority.[22] These restrictions separate the HOS secondary market from the rest of second-hand housing market.

The Scheme was suspended in the first decade of the millennium. In his *Policy Address 2011–12*, the then Chief Executive Donald Tsang Yam Kuen[23] announced a new policy for resumption of the Home Ownership Scheme. Under the new policy the government plans to provide more than 17,000 flats over four years from 2016–17 onwards, with an annual production of between 2,500 and 6,500 flats (Tsang 2011).

An uncompleted flat and a presale

Having identified the main sectors in the local residential real estate market, we come to one fascinating phenomenon, the presence of which has been seen in sales of all types of first-hand residential properties in the region. From apartments developed by private developers to HOS units by the Housing Authority and in some cases the commercialized NTEHs in the listed villages in the New Territories, a sale of flats can and does usually start before the construction of the building is completed. To a large extent, flats in Hong Kong are sold *off-plan.*

Generally speaking, an uncompleted flat is a flat, at the time of execution of the agreement for sale and purchase, the construction of which is uncompleted either physically or from the point of law. For flats under the Consent Scheme, it refers to flats to which a certificate of compliance or consent to assign has not yet been granted by the Director of Lands; for flats under the Non-Consent Scheme, a flat is regarded as uncompleted if the occupation permit is yet to be issued by the Building Authority under section 21(2) of the *Buildings Ordinance* (THB 2011). In the case of an HOS flat, the completion certificate has yet to be issued by the Director of Housing (LRC 1995). Since NTEHs are exempted from the application of the *Buildings Ordinance* under section 5 of the *Buildings Ordinance (Application to the New Territories) Ordinance* (Cap 121), an uncompleted NTEH flat may refer to those the agreement for sale and purchase has been executed before completion of the construction of the house.

The *Ordinance* defines an uncompleted development by describing what it is not – a *completed* development. According to the *Ordinance*, a development is a completed development if the occupation permit has been issued in respect of every building in the development; and in the case of a specified New Territories development, a no-objection letter has been issued by the Director of Lands in respect of every building in the development or a certificate of compliance or consent to assign has been issued by the Director of Lands in respect of the development. And a development is an uncompleted development if it is not a completed development.[24] On the other hand, *a completed development pending compliance* is not an uncompleted development: it is a development where an occupation permit has been issued in respect of every building in the development (*completed*) but the conditions of the land grant have not been complied with, so the consent of the Director of Lands for any sale and purchase of residential property has not been granted (*pending compliance*).[25]

A sale of an uncompleted flat is locally known as a *presale.* The sale takes place before the subject of the sale, i.e., the residential unit, is physically constructed. The Chinese word to describe the equitable interests created by the agreement for sale and purchase – '樓花' (*lau fat; literally means the flower(s) out of the developing estates*) – best signifies that the contract is executed at an early stage of the construction of the development. This qualifies an off-plan sale of land as future goods. The practice of off-plan sales (and any subsequent re-sales before the completion of the development) creates a future market sector within the real estate market. The agreement for sale and purchase of uncompleted flats is what is known as a *real forward contract*, which only creates equitable interests based on the transaction price while the assignment of the legal interest is executed in the future. Some studies suggest that presale of uncompleted properties at planning or construction stage by developers has, essentially created a *forward property market* (Lindholm, Gibler and Levainen 2006; Leung, Hui and Seabrooke 2007).

Purchasers of uncompleted flats may benefit from a price difference between the contract price and the market price by the time of completion. Essentially, the sale is a financial means to hedge against future price fluctuations. Developers can secure the upfront capital for the construction and transfer the market risk of the project during the construction period to the purchasers through passing the equitable ownership of the presale properties to the purchasers (Lindholm, Gibler and Levainen 2006; Leung, Hui and Seabrooke 2007). This may explain why presale is a very popular and common practice in the region.

For example, in China, the practice of presale of commercial housing has already been recognized and regulated by a number of national laws in addition to local regulations: a *presale* under Chinese property law is a sale of commercial housing prior to the completion of construction upon the payment of deposit or the contract price by the purchaser to the developer under an agreement to deliver the property on a specified date (Tang 2008).[26] Predictably, it will be the dominating way residential properties are sold for decades to come in Hong Kong and the mainland China. It is also popular in Taiwan, Singapore and is becoming more common in the real estate markets in London, Sydney, Toronto and New York City.

In general, information asymmetry represents a more serious issue in sales of uncompleted flats than sales of completed flats. Information asymmetry specific to sales of uncompleted flats may include the inaccurate size of the properties, mismatch of fittings and finishes, default in middle of construction (Leung, Hui and Seabrooke 2007).

First-hand residential properties

Residential property is defined under the *Ordinance* as any real property in the development or the phase constituting a separate unit used, or intended to be used, solely or principally for human habitation, excluding any premises used or intended to be used solely or principally as a hotel or guesthouse as defined by section 2(1) of the *Hotel and Guesthouse Accommodation Ordinance* (Cap 349).[27] Section 6(3) further points out that a residential property under the *Ordinance* includes, where the context permits, a residential property to be constructed. Overall, the *Ordinance* applies to residential properties sold in both completed and uncompleted development.

According to section 10, the development has to be situated in Hong Kong. As a matter of fact, first-hand residential properties located overseas attract the interests of local investors too: every so often there are road shows held by local real estate agents to promote sales of first-hand residential properties in the UK, Canada, the USA, Malaysia, Singapore, Australia, New Zealand, etc. The sales practices are not subject to the regulation of the *Ordinance* even though the promotion takes place in Hong Kong. By the same token, the *Ordinance* does not apply to promotional activities taken place in Hong Kong or promotional materials circulated in Hong Kong for first-hand residential properties located in mainland China.

A few exceptions for developments situated in Hong Kong are recognized to exclude the application of the *Ordinance*: the first one is where the development is a completed development and at least 95 per cent of the number of the residential properties in the development have been held under a tenancy (other than a government lease) for a continuous period of at least 36 months or for several periods that in the aggregate equal at least 36 months since the issue of occupation permit (or the issue of a certificate of compliance or consent to assign in case of a specified New Territories development).[28]

Probably unexpected to the public and the vendor itself, transactions of a couple of flats in 2014 in a 20-year-old development named *Full Art Court* firstly completed in 1998 triggered the very first prosecution act after the commencement of the *Ordinance* by the Department of Justice upon the reference of SRPA in January 2016 (Mingpao 2016). The development consists of 35 residential units of around 200 sq. ft. Eight units were sold before the commencement of the *Ordinance*. The remaining 27 units remained unsold and unleased until 2014, where the vendor sold some of the units in a very low profile manner (HKET 2016; AD 2016a; Mingpao 2016). The *Ordinance* was in full effect then and is therefore applicable to the sale of the units in the development, as exception is given only to completed development where 95 per cent of the number of residential properties were held under a tenancy for a continuous period of at least 36 months. The vendor did not realize that the sale was subject to the regulation of the *Ordinance* and did not prepare sales brochure and price lists in the way requested by the *Ordinance*. The verdict was handed down on 3 August 2016 in the Kwun Tong District Magistrate, where the judge held that the vendor had violated 19 offences of the *Ordinance* in selling the residential units in *Full Art Court* and was liable for a fine of HK$720,000 (AD 2016b).[29]

Conclusion

This book will discuss regulation on information asymmetry for better consumer protection in the context of sale of first-hand residential properties in Hong Kong. It is the very first book that provides a comprehensive analysis on the effectiveness of Hong Kong's leading transparency-oriented regulatory regime based on the *Residential Properties (First-hand Sales) Ordinance*. Major rules of the *Ordinance* are individually analysed and assessed of its effectiveness in their operation since the commencement of the *Ordinance* in 2013. Meanwhile, the discussion will offer key insights and practical solutions for exploring and addressing information asymmetry and property misdescription issues in the real estate market in Hong Kong.

It is almost impossible to thoroughly explain the rationale behind the making of every major rule in the *Ordinance* without tracing the emergence and development of these rules in the time of the Consent Scheme (since 1969). It is equally difficult to comprehend the significance of the new regulatory framework centred on the *Ordinance* without looking at its evolution over the past 60 years along with the rapid development of Hong Kong's first-hand real estate market.

This brings us to Kowloon in 1954, discussed in the following chapter.

Notes

1   www.heritage.org/index/country/hongkong
2   It should be added here that enhancing transparency does not always require the compromise of business freedom. Many believe that transparency is a prerequisite of a free and efficient market. The smooth operation of the *Ordinance* after its commencement in 2013 may be a good example of how regulator-facilitated transparency could substantially improve the efficiency of real estate markets.
3   www.investopedia.com/terms/t/transparency.asp
4   www.nobelprize.org/nobel_prizes/economic-sciences/laureates/1996/
5   www.nobelprize.org/nobel_prizes/economic-sciences/laureates/2001/press.html
6   *Residential Properties (First-hand Sales) Ordinance*, A2291.
7   Regulation 2, Part 1, The Consumer Protection from Unfair Trading Regulations 2008.
8   Section 2(3), the UK Consumer Rights Act (CRA) 2015. For a more detailed analysis on the implication of the latest UK legislation in the construction industry, see Philip Britton, *Adjudication and the 'Residential Occupier Exception': Time for a Rethink?*, the revised edition of the joint first prize entry in the Hudson Prize Essay Competition 2014, the Society of Construction Law, May 2015.
9   Regulation 2 and 3, Part 1, The Consumer Protection from Unfair Trading Regulations 2008.
10 A 'skyscraper' is defined by Emporis as a multi-story building whose architectural height is at least 100 metres. www.emporis.com/building/standard/75/skyscraper. © Emporis, March, 2016.
11 A 'high-rise building' is defined by Emporis as a structure whose architectural height is between 35 and 100 metres. A structure is automatically listed as a high-rise when it has a minimum of 12 floors. www.emporis.com/building/standard/3/high-rise-building © Emporis, March 2016.
12 Hong Kong has 1,294 skyscrapers according to Emporis: www.emporis.com/statistics/most-skyscrapers. © Emporis, March 2016.
13 http://en.wikipedia.org/wiki/Hong_Kong.
14 Apart from these three, a number of apartments in some public rental estates (公屋) were sold to tenants in the 1980s under the Flat-for-Sale Scheme by the Hong Kong Housing Society and under the Tenants Purchase Scheme by Hong Kong Housing Authority from early 1998 to the end of 2006. Plus, the Hong Kong Housing Society also built 13 estates of around a total 12,000 units for sale under the Sandwich Class Housing Scheme to lower-middle or middle-income residents. Those units are tradable only after the alienation restriction period and therefore constitute a tiny minority in the market.
15 http://en.wikipedia.org/wiki/Mei_Foo_Sun_Chuen
16 For example, the development *Uptown* in Hung Shiu Kiu consists of 734 flats, including 37 independent houses.
17 An example: the *Seasons Monarch* in Kam Tin.
18 Schedule to *Buildings Ordinance (Application to the New Territories) Ordinance*, (Cap 121).
19 Section 5, Part 1, *Residential Properties (First-hand Sales) Ordinance*, A2309.

20 For the definition of a green form applicant and a white form applicant, see www. housingauthority.gov.hk/en/residential/shos/surplushosflats/definition/0,,,00.html
21 Hong Kong Housing Authority: *Eligibility for Purchasing a Flat in the HOS Secondary Market*, www.housingauthority.gov.hk/en/residential/hossecondarymarket/eligibility2/ 0,,,00.html
22 A premium must be paid by owners to the Housing Authority for removal of the alienation restrictions before the flat can be let, sold or assigned in the open market: see Schedule to the *Housing Ordinance* (Cap 283).
23 Doctor of Laws *honoris causa, the University of Hong Kong, 2005.*
24 Section 4(1), Part 1, *Residential Properties (First-hand Sales) Ordinance*, A2305-2307. Similarly, a phase of a development is a completed phase of the development if an occupation permit has been issued in respect of every building in the phase; and it will be an uncompleted phase of the development if it is not a completed phase of the development.
25 Ibid., section 4(2), A2307.
26 'A presale is a sale of commercial housing prior to the completion of construction upon the payment of deposit or the contract price by the purchaser to the developer under an agreement to deliver the property on a specified date. The birth place of presale is Hong Kong. Presale has been widely adopted by developers ever since it was introduced to the mainland (since the 1990s), which has dominated the market of commercial housing in China.' See Tang Lie Ying, *A Study on Mortgage-related Issues in Sale of Commercial Residential Properties*, Law Press (China), 2008, page 41. '所謂商品房預售，是指房地產開發企業將正在建設尚未竣工的商品房預先出售給買受人，由買受人支付定金或者商品房價款，雙方約定在未來確定的日期，由預售方交付建成的房屋給買受人的法律行為。'商品住房預售，源於香港。自賣   '樓花'飄入內地之後，風行各地，商品房預售已成為與商品房現售並存的房屋銷售的兩種方式之一，並且，已經在商品房銷售中佔據主導地位。'唐烈英，《商品住房買賣貸款按揭法律問題研究》，法律出版社，2008，第41頁。
27 Section 6, *The Residential Properties (First-hand Sales) Ordinance*, A2309-2311.
28 Ibid., Section 10(3)(4).
29 Case No.: KTS21568-572、595-608/15.

References

AC (2002) Small House Grants in the New Territories, Audit Commission Hong Kong, para. 2.4, 15 October 2002, p.3.
AD (2016a) '富雅閣律師：違規屬不幸', 3 June 2016, *Apple Daily*, http://hk.apple. nextmedia.com/financeestate/art/20160603/19638840
AD (2016b) '同珍富雅閣違規罪名成立 罰款72萬', 3 August 2016, *Apple Daily*, http:// hk.apple.nextmedia.com/realtime/finance/20160803/55447446
Britton, P (2015) Adjudication and the 'Residential Occupier Exception': Time for a Rethink?, the revised edition of the joint first prize entry in the Hudson Prize Essay Competition 2014, the Society of Construction Law, www.scl.org.uk
CC (1991) A Study on the Disclosure of Information to Prospective Purchasers of Uncompleted Unit, October 1991, Consumer Council, Hong Kong.
CC (2014) Study on the Sales of First-hand Residential Properties, p. 1, 11 November 2014, Consumer Council, www.consumer.org.hk/ws_en/competition_issues/reports/ 20141111.html.
Chan, H.S., Chan, Y.K., Cheng, W.S., and Sze, K.W. (2015) Regulating the Sale of First-hand Residential Properties in Hong Kong: a Study of Policy and Administrative Dynamics, Capstone project report submitted in partial fulfilment of the requirements of

the Master of Public Administration, Department of Politics and Public Administration, The University of Hong Kong, pp. 46–48.

Chau K.W., Wong, S.K. and Yiu, C.Y. (2003) Price Discovery Function of Forward Contracts in The Real Estate Market: An Empirical Test, *Journal of Financial Management of Property and Construction*, 8(3), pp.129–137.

Churchwell, C. (2003) Corporate Transparency Improves for Foreign Firms in US Markets, Harvard Business School Working Knowledge Series, http://hbswk.edu/item/3489.html, 26 May.

Circus, P. (2011) *Promotional Marketing Law: A Practical Guide*, 6th Edition, Bloomsbury Professional, p. 1.

Fan, C.S. (2005) The Consent Scheme in Hong Kong: Its Evolution and Evaluation – Home Purchaser Behaviour in Housing Society's Property Transactions Before and After the Asian Financial Crisis, Ph.D Thesis, Department of Real Estate and Construction, Faculty of Architecture, the University of Hong Kong, September 2005, pp. 6–71.

Goo, S. H. (2010) Regulation of Sale of Off-the-plan Property, *The Conveyancer and Property Lawyer*, Issue 2, 2010, pp. 129–131.

Granados, N, Gupta, A. and Kauffman, R. (2005) Transparency Strategy in Internet-Based Selling, *Advances in the Economics of Information Systems*, pp. 80–112.

Hagel III, J. and Brown, J.B. (2014) How to Deepen Customer Loyalty: Be Transparent, *Fortunate Magazine*, 2 April 2014.

HKET (2016) 富雅閣涉違規賣樓 表證成立, 3 June 2016, *Hong Kong Economics Times.*

HKHA (2015) Housing in Figures 2015, Hong Kong Housing Authority 2015.

Lai, R.N., Wang, K. and Zhou, Y. (2004) Sale before Completion of Development: Pricing and Strategy, *Real Estate Economics*, 32(2), pp. 329–357.

LC (2006) Background Brief on Processing of Small House Applications and Review of Small House Policy, CB(1)986/05-06(01), *Legislative Council*, 28 February 2006. For definitions of 'indigenous villager', 'recognised village' and 'small house grant', see www.landsd.gov.hk/en/legco/house.htm

LC (2011) Private Housing Land Supply, Following is a question by the Hon Albert Chan Wai-yip and a written reply by the Secretary for Development Mrs Carrie Lam in the Legislative Council today, Legislative Council, 9 March 2011.

LC (2013) Background brief on 'Residential Properties (First-hand Sales) Ordinance and the Sales of First-hand Residential Properties Authority' prepared by the Legislative Council Secretariat, 2 July 2013, LC Paper No. CB(1)1391/12-13(03), Panel on Housing, Legislative Council. www.legco.gov.hk/yr12-13/english/panels/hg/papers/hg0702cb1-1391-3-e.pdf

Lee, A. and Goo, S. H. (2008) The Sale and Purchase of Uncompleted Flats in Hong Kong, The International Conference *The Judicial Reform of Macau in the Context of Globalization*, the Faculty of Law, the University of Macau, p. 3.

Leung, B., Hui, E. and Seabrooke, B. (2007) Asymmetric Information in the Hong Kong Forward Property Market, *International Journal of Strategic Property Management*, November 2007, pp.92.

Lin, D (2012) The New Rules for Sales of Uncompleted Flats, *Law Lectures for Practitioners 2010*, Cheng, ML., Jen, J & Young, JYK (Eds.), *Hong Kong Law Journal Ltd* & Faculty of Law, the University of Hong Kong.

Lindholm, A.L., Gibler, K.M. and Levainen, K.I. (2006) Modeling the Value-adding Attributes of Real Estate to the Wealth Maximization of the Firms, *Journal of Real Estate Research*, 28(4), pp. 445–475.

LRC (1995) Reports on Descriptions of Flats on Sale, The Law Reform Commission of Hong Kong April 1995, p. 5.

Merry, M. (2008) Protection of Purchasers of Uncompleted Residential Flats – The Hong Kong Experience, *HKU-NUS-SMU Symposium Paper*, Singapore, November 2008.

Merry, M. (2011a) Lessons of the Illegal Structures Controversy, *Law Lectures for Practitioners* 2011.

Merry, M. (2011b) Land in New Territories, *Land Law III Lecture No. 7*, The University of Hong Kong, 18 November 2011, p. 7.

Miller, T. and Kim, A.B. (2016) 2016 Index of Economic Freedom, *The Heritage Foundation*, 2006.

Mingpao (2016) 銷監局首控發展商　富雅閣涉19宗罪, 30 January, 2016, http://news.mingpao.com/pns/dailynews/web_tc/article/20160130/s00004/1454089575168

Schnackenberg, A. (2009) Measuring Transparency: Towards a Greater Understanding of Systemic Transparency and Accountability, Department of Organizational Behavior Weatherhead School of Management Case Western Reserve University, 2 September 2009.

Schwarcz, D. (2014) Transparently Opaque: Understanding the Lack of Transparency in Insurance Consumer Protection, *61 UCLA L.* REV.394 (2014).

Starke, G. (2016) What's in a Name: Transparency, *Innoq blog*, web log post, 18 May 2016, www.innoq.com/en/blog/whats-in-a-name-transparency/

Stiglitz, J.E. (2001) Information and the Change in the Paradigm in Economics, *Prize Lecture,* 8 December 2001.

SRPA (2013) Vision, Mission and Values, The Sales of First-hand Residential Properties Authorities, 2013, www.srpa.gov.hk/en/vision-n-mission.html

Tang, L.Y. (2008) A Study on Mortgage-Related Issues in Sale of Commercial Residential Properties, *Law Press (China)*, 2008, p. 41.

THB (2011) Public Consultation on the Proposed Legislation to Regulate the Sale of First-hand Residential Properties, The Transport and Housing Bureau, November 2011, para. 9, p. 4.

Tsang, D. (2011) From Strength to Strength, *Policy Address 2011-12*, 24 October 2011, pp. 22–25.

2 The way to legislation

Introduction

Before the commencement of the *Residential Properties (First-hand Sales) Ordinance* (the *Ordinance*) in 2013, the sale of first-hand uncompleted residential properties in Hong Kong was mainly regulated under two Schemes: the Consent Scheme administered by the Lands Department and the Non-Consent Scheme administrated by the Law Society of Hong Kong.

The contractual basis for the operation of the Consent Scheme is a clause on restriction on alienation (see Chapter 1) inserted by the government in the land grant. The Consent Scheme applies wherever a development is being erected on a parcel of land subject to a restriction on alienation prior to compliance with all the conditions in the land grant governing the land and the registered land owner wants to sell any units in the development before it is complete; besides first-hand sales of residential properties in a development standing on newly granted government leases, the Consent Scheme applies to sales of residential properties where an *exclusion order* made under *the Landlord and Tenant (Consolidation) Ordinance* (Cap 7) contains clauses prohibiting owners from entering into agreements for the sale of uncompleted units without the prior consent of the Director of Lands (Lands D 2016).

Where there are no lease conditions requiring the consent of the Director of Lands to initiate the sale, for example developments on plots of land purchased from previous government leases, the practice of presale is administrated by the Law Society of Hong Kong under the *Non-Consent Scheme*.[1] The Non-Consent Scheme does not operate directly on developers; instead it imposes professional obligations to the solicitors acting for developers to comply with Rule 5C of the *Solicitors (Practice) Rules and other Practice Directions*, which includes the adoption of a standard form of agreement for sale and purchase mirroring the one used in the Consent Scheme. The Lands Department (2016) revised the standard form of the agreement for sale and purchase for the Consent Scheme in June 2016 after the enactment of the *Contracts (Rights of Third Parties) Ordinance* (Cap 623).

Under the Consent Scheme, a developer cannot sell first-hand residential properties in advance of the completion of the development unless it obtains the consent of the Director of Lands (Lands D 1999a). The consent is granted based on the developer's commitment to comply a variety of conditions set out in a number of Circular Memoranda issued by the Legal Advisory and Conveyancing Office (LACO, known as the Land Office before 1993).[2] The consent granted by the Director of Lands is confined to the entering of preliminary agreements for sale and purchase (PASP) and agreements for sale and purchase (ASP) only; developers need to apply for 'consent to assign' when the development is completed.

As far as the sale of private properties is concerned, the implementation of the Consent Scheme is complemented by the self-regulation of the Real Estate Developers Association of Hong Kong (REDA). Established in the year 1965 under the chairmanship of Dr Henry Fok,[3] REDA's members include all the major developers in Hong Kong. Before 2013, REDA used to issue, from time to time, guidelines on Sales Descriptions of Uncompleted Residential Properties for the reference of its members. These guidelines were voluntary measures applied to member developers, which developers without REDA membership are encouraged to follow (Lands D 1999b). For quite a long time the guidelines were published only on the website of the Estate Agents Authority for public viewing,[4] as REDA did not establish its own website until September 2011.[5] It has been observed that REDA's regulation had clear advantages of flexibility in rule making, expertise and sensitivity to regulatory cost, yet the weakness of this form of industrial self-regulation was that it had little public or governmental involvement, and if there is close connection or friendly relation between REDA and its member developers it may not necessarily be impartial (Goo 2010).

The Consent Scheme and the Non-Consent Scheme remain operative upon the commencement of the *Ordinance* in 2013, but measures and rules regarding the design and contents of sales brochures, price lists, advertisements and show flats have been replaced by the *Ordinance*.[6]

What happened to the operation of the Consent Scheme that eventually gave rise to the enactment of the *Ordinance* in 2013 to take over some of its major responsibilities? An account of the development of the first-hand real estate market in Hong Kong is helpful for an understanding of the historical background against which this piece of legislation stepped into the regulatory regime.

1961–1991: The early development of the Consent Scheme

The emergence of pre-sale

Back in the 1940s, private residential properties were only affordable by the wealthy class of the society. To the general public, the market was basically inaccessible due to the large amount of money needed to be advanced immediately to the vendor by the purchaser upon the signing of the contract. The status quo was about to change with the invention of a revolutionary payment method said to be introduced first by Dr Henry Fok Ying Tung in the 1950s. Legend had it that Dr Fok started to discuss the idea of soliciting purchasers and selling residential properties in instalments prior to the construction of the development somewhere between 1953 and 1954 (Leng 2005). In promoting the residential units within the building that his company was about to construct on Kowloon Marine Lot No. 39, Dr Fok came up with a revolutionary method of payment under which purchasers would pay a portion of the overall price as deposits prior to the construction of the building, then pay off the balance in instalments throughout the construction period. The great flexibility provided by the payment method made the apartments suddenly affordable to a much larger class of citizens. At the same time, money collected from the advanced payment could be used in the construction of the development. The idea was experimented in the sale of a residential building on the Public Square Street in Yau Ma Tei.[7]

The sale was believed to be the first off-plan sale, in Hong Kong but also in the world; it set up the precedent of sale of first-hand real estate property in Hong Kong that adopted a pay-by-instalment payment method (Leng 2005). The trial turned out to be a massive success in every aspect. The response to the sale was overwhelming. Within days all the units were sold out, despite the fact that the building was still under construction. The innovation soon led to an expansive development of the business within one year, Dr Fok's company erected more than one hundred buildings equating to a total of over six hundred floors on the Public Square Street, and sold flats totalling approximately 500,000 square feet. And perhaps it was on account of this innovation that Dr Fok grew into a legendary figure so overwhelming, that people in Hong Kong, Macau and the Mainland have never since ceased to write and read about his life. The story of how Dr Fok invented off-plan sales (or in Chinese, 賣樓花) is still being heard of today. As Malcolm Merry (2008) accounted:

> [B]y the 1950s… entrepreneurs offered the public the chance to purchase flats which were only at the planning stage. They took deposits and periodic payments towards the price which they used to buy the land and construct the building. Lawyers devised a means by which flats could be owned. Purchasers had the benefit of paying for their flats over time (banks would not lend to ordinary people for property purchase then), at a price free of future fluctuations and which might be discounted.

The successful experience in Yau Ma Tei served as a catalyst that resulted in a surging residential real estate market. The payment method was soon adopted by other developers and a wave of construction took place in the city. The local real estate market was vitalized by the cash flowing from citizens from all walks of the society who could not have afforded residential properties but for Dr Fok's innovation.[8] Probably beyond Dr Fok's expectation, his little experiment on the sale of *uncompleted* flats initiated the transformation of Hong Kong from a fishing village in the 1850s to the world's most expensive property market. Later, when a market-oriented economy was resumed (starting from 1979) in mainland China under Deng Xiaoping's administration, the 'Hong Kong Mode', i.e., the practice of sale-prior-to-completion, soon gained its popularity in mainland China after the economy took off in the early 1990s (Tang 2008).

The beginning of the Consent Scheme

From the outset, presales as novel economic activities were in general unregulated by the government (Fan 2005).[9] But there was very high degree of risk that was inherent in the practice of pre-sale. This could include the risk of non-delivery or delayed delivery; the risk of fraud or insolvency of the developer or its building contractors; the risk of competing interests if the developer mortgaged the land to raise funds for other business (Merry 2008). Just a few years after the historic breakthrough in Yau Ma Tei, questionable practices associated with presales emerged. The year 1961 saw the first incident where one developer, the Peony House West Block Limited, got into a serious financial crisis before completing the development. In the end, the company was not able to continue the building before it went into liquidation. A total of 299 purchasers had to pay a further 30 per cent of the original purchase price just to get the building completed (Fan 2005). This incident was the first ever event in the history of sales of uncompleted flats that signalled the necessity for governmental regulation. The then British Hong Kong government started to discuss whether presales should be prohibited by law.

Eventually, the government gave up the idea of banning presales; instead, they saw from the Peony House West Block Limited incident the need to monitor the practice. As Merry (2008) recalled, in terms of the form of regulation, the British Hong Kong government opted for using administrative means over legislation and self-regulation. The initial form of government control was to insert a restrictive clause on alienation of land prior to the consent of the government in the Conditions of Lands Grant. This was the underlying principle of the Consent Scheme first introduced on 20 December 1961. The government required that a 'letter of consent' be issued by the Land Officer before any presales could take place. The issue of the 'Letter of Consent' was primarily concerned with the financial undertaking of developers to complete the property and was dependent on the proportion of money invested in the land purchase and construction by the time of application.

Merry (2008) described the essence of the Consent Scheme as follows:

> The non-statutory regime of control operates through the medium of a restrictive covenant in the government grant and the need of the developer for consent from the Lands Department (the government land authority) to relaxation of that covenant to the extent of entering into agreements for the advanced sale of units in the proposed development and for assigning those units once they have been finished.

The year 1964 marked the first reform of the Consent Scheme. The Land Office Circular Memorandum No. 19 inserted certain standard clauses into the agreement for sale and purchase; it also introduced two standard forms of 'statutory declaration' for developers and their solicitors. The developer had to declare the financial ability and the method of financing with an audited financial statement or a balance sheet which suggested that the net asset of the developer exceeded the cost of the development. The solicitor had to declare that the lease concerned had to have at least ten years to run from the estimated date of building completion and in the case the lease had less than ten years to run, a renewal agreement had been ascertained; the building plans had been approved by the Buildings Department; the property was free from encumbrances, and the required terms were included in the agreement for sale and purchase (RGD 1964).

The reform was not well received by developers. Non-compliance of the new requirements occurred in sales by a number of developers. According to Fan (2005), the reasons included the belief that the new system imposed too many liabilities on developers and their solicitors; developers were unwilling to bear the liabilities; and practically it was impossible for them to disclose all details at the time of submission. The requirement on statutory declaration was implemented on a discounted basis against developers in the sales of uncompleted flats for quite a long time after 1965.

In 1979, statutory declarations were reintroduced to the Consent Scheme, together with the adoption of a standard agreement for sale and purchase. But from that time onwards the requirement of statutory declaration only applies to solicitors.

Today, the function of the statutory declaration by solicitors in specified form includes verification of facts and exhibition of documents from the architect's certificate, the agreement for sale and purchase and the deed of mutual covenants. The declaration needs to be registered at the Land Registry prior to the start of the presale. In addition, the solicitor needs to declare that the developer has complied with the requirements in relevant LACO Circular Memoranda (LSHK 2004). The last part of the statutory declaration, i.e., the compliance of relevant LACO Circular Memoranda, was first added in February 1991 with the issue of the Land Office Circular Memorandum No. 101 (RGD 1991). The significance of the declaration is to fortify compliance with the Consent Scheme through the reputation and professional status of the solicitor, which, once approved, would have to be registered at the Land Registry prior to the making of the first sale (Merry 2008).

1991–2012: The new direction

The emergence of a new focus

As observed by Sarah Nield (1990), before the Land Office Circular Memorandum No. 101 came into effect, the only objective of the Consent Scheme was to ensure that developers were financially able to complete the developments; this resulted from the two types of inherent risks posed to off-plan purchasers: the buildings may never be completed; or if completed, the conditions of the flats may differ from what purchasers originally expected. Indeed, the operation of the Consent Scheme before 1991 primarily concerned the financial capacity of the developers. In other words, consent to presale would be granted to a developer if the government was satisfied with the financial status of the developer to complete the construction of the respective development. Beyond that, no particular consideration seemed to be given on the manner developers described the properties in the sales literature.

The deficiency of the Consent Scheme caught the attention of the Consumer Council as early as 1977, which in 1989 became a major concern to the Council. The Council made a number of recommendations in its Report entitled 'A Study on the Disclosure of Information to Prospective Purchasers of Uncompleted Unit' (CC 1991). The recommendations, most accepted by the government, formed a brand new department of regulations in the Consent Scheme with the issue of Land Office Circular Memorandum No. 101 in 1991. The issue of this memorandum was undoubtedly a milestone for the Consent Scheme, for it is the first memorandum in the history of the Scheme to demand mandatory disclosure of information about the property for sale. It provided a list of items, the information of which had to be included in the sales brochure and price lists, such as location plan, layout plan drawn to scale, salient points of government lease, detailed plan of a typical floor, schedule of flat size, fittings and finishes, anticipated completion date of the building, salient points of the deed of mutual covenant, miscellaneous payments upon delivery of unit, names of contractors and other authorized persons, price of individual units, purchaser procedure, payment terms, responsibility for legal fees, instalment payment methods and interest rates in case of a restricted choice of mortgage, number of units available for sale. RGD (1991) entitled 'minimum information to be provided to prospective purchasers of uncompleted units', the lists represented the embryonic form of the regulatory regime.

From February 1991, solicitors needed to declare that developers had complied with the requirements in the Circular Memorandum No. 101; developers needed to attach copies of sales brochures to the Lands Office when applying for the consent to presale. Fan (2005) remarked that, although the Land Office Circular Memorandum No. 101 was subsequently amended by LACO Circular Memoranda Nos. 4, 40, 40A, 40C and 54, the basic principles and standards remained intact. The issue of Land Office Circular Memorandum No. 101 introduced a completely new perspective into the Consent Scheme, i.e., consumer protection. For the first time it directed the development of the Scheme to regulate disclosure of information of the residential properties. This new direction has become the theme of rounds of improvements of the Consent Scheme in the past two decades and the golden thread throughout the evolution of the regulatory regime.

The 1995 Report on Description of Flats on Sale

Soon after the issue of Land Office Circular Memorandum No. 101, the Law Reform Commission established a sub-committee under the chairmanship of Mr Derek Roebuck in November 1992 to consider appropriate measures to tackle misleading information and particulars in the sales literature. The study for the sub-committee revolved around the question of 'should the law governing the protection of prospective purchasers and purchasers of uncompleted residential property in relation to inadequate or misleading sales information or particulars be changed and, if so, in what way?', a term of reference decided by the then Acting Attorney General and the then Acting Chief Justice (LRC 1995). The 'Report on Description of Flats on Sale' was published after a period of deliberation lasting 29 months and public consultation in 1995. The Report gave recommendations on measurement of floor area, fittings and finishes, location and layout plans, date of completion, charges levied on transfer of title to sub-purchasers, financing arrangements, preliminary agreement for sale and purchase, right of inspection prior to completion of transaction and defect liability period, deed of mutual covenant, conditions of the land lease, prices and number of units for sale and internal sale, miscellaneous information, availability of sales brochure, and enforcement.

These ground-breaking works provided for a workable framework to develop a much more comprehensive regulatory system both in the context of and beyond the Consent Scheme, which, 18 years after the publication of the Report, became reality in April 2013. It should be highlighted that in Chapter 15 of the Report, the Law Reform Commission had considered three possible means to enforce the measures for protection of purchasers of uncompleted units, viz., self-regulation, administrative measures and legislation; the Commission offered the view that legislation was the most effective way to bring about the intended results and ensure adherence to a uniform set of standards (LRC 1995).

Although eventually the Report did not lead to a proposal of legislation in the 1990s, its significance for the later development of the regulatory system can never be overstated. Its influence started to become apparent in the later development of the Scheme from the beginning of the millennia.

LACO Circular Memorandum No. 40

In May 1999, the Lands Department consolidated all the prevailing rules and instructions in relation to sale of uncompleted flats in private residential developments in LACO Circular Memorandum No. 40. The Memorandum possesses all the details on the operation of the Scheme from documents to be submitted with each application, to financial requirements, bank undertaking, development progress, application procedure, statutory declaration, lease approval, and most important, the consent terms. It made a distinction between private sale and public sale; the latter was subject to tighter governmental control on mandatory disclosure of information and conduct of sale (Lands D 1999).[10] Although subsequently a number of provisions in the memorandum (including the private-public-sale distinction) had been varied or abolished, this memorandum remained as the principal memorandum that retained a comprehensive view of the Consent Scheme before the *Ordinance*.

Sales Descriptions of Uncompleted Residential Properties Bill

The recommendations by the Law Reform Commission had inspired the draft of a Sales Descriptions of Uncompleted Residential Properties Bill in April, 2000.

Public consultation for the Bill was sought by the government, but sadly the Sales Descriptions of Uncompleted Residential Properties Bill did not make its way to legislative reading when the consultation period ended in July 2000. Lee and Goo (2008) believed that, apart from developers' lobbying, capital gains by the purchasers from the properties also contributed to the persistence of the status quo.

While the attempt to regulate off-plan sales by legislation was met with frustration, a new memorandum was issued in December 2001 to further the government's efforts to regulate information disclosure and sales description. LACO Circular Memorandum No. 40C (Lands D 2001) required that developers issue sales brochures containing accurate information on the location plan, the layout plan, salient points of government lease, detailed plan of a typical floor, schedule of flat size, fittings and finishes, anticipated completion date of the building, salient points of the deed of mutual covenant, carpark, date of printing of sales brochures, names of contractors and other authorized persons, maintenance of slopes, preliminary deposit, and a prominent statement on the forfeiture of the deposit upon cancellation. This represented another round of substantial development of the regulatory system, and the Consent Scheme has taken a more structured form since then.

Review of the Consent Scheme in 2004

The operation of the Consent Scheme was smooth and almost incident-free until 2003. Between 1998 and May 2003, the Lands Department approved about 243 consents for presales of uncompleted flats; 241 of them went out with timely delivery of flats (LC 2004). Nonetheless, the two failed projects by one small developer led to a comprehensive review of the Consent Scheme in 2004.

In 2003, the construction of two presale developments in Tuen Mun was affected by the financial problems of the developer, Gold Face Holdings Limited: first, the development named *Aegean* failed to complete as scheduled and then the construction of *Villa Pinada* was suspended until both were taken up by the receiver company appointed by the mortgagee bank. The common law rule on priority suggested purchasers of the uncompleted flat would lose priority to the mortgagee bank (who held a security over the lot under the building mortgage over the property) even if they had paid off the entire purchase price (LC 2004). This was remedied by a new measure introduced by LACO Circular Memorandum No. 54, which inserted into the building mortgage an irrevocable undertaking by the mortgagee bank to the developer to unconditionally discharge any unit and release it from the security if the full contract price has been paid by a purchaser (Lands D 2004).[11]

After 2004, the focus for an effective administration by the Consent Scheme has shifted from checks and balances on the developer's financial resources to information disclosure and sales descriptions of the property for sale.

Rapid development since 2010

In 2006, the government signalled the necessity of regulation by legislation after some developers' repeated non-compliance with REDA's guidelines. Moreover, dubious sales practices occurred on a remarkable frequency from 2006 to 2009 (Chan et al 2015). As summarized by this 2015 study, questionable practices in a number of sales had inspired the making of new rules into the regulatory regime, which include (i) the sale of *Arch* in 2005, where the vendor disclosed misleading information on transaction price in bundle sales (see discussion in Chapter 12); (ii) the sale of *Apex* in 2006 where a development located in the industrial area in Kwai Chung, New Territories, advertised its location as in Kowloon and exaggerated its proximity to the MTR station (see discussion in Chapter 6); (iii) the sale of *Lake Silver* in 2009, where illustrations in the sales brochure on the environment of the property deliberately ignored unfavourable details (see discussion in Chapter 6); (iv) the sale of *39 Conduit Road* in 2009, which introduced an unprecedented approach in skipping unlucky numbers in floor numbering and where a bundle sale gave rise to another record high price release, followed by a number of transactions were cancelled after the signing of the agreement for sale and purchase (to be discussed in Chapters 7 and 12).

All of these dramas led to a radical development of the Consent Scheme in 2010. In April of that year, high government officials unveiled proposals for new rules aiming to *enhance transparency* in first-hand property transactions.[12] On 1 June, REDA issued guidelines to implement the new rules introduced by the Transport and Housing Bureau with immediate effect.[13] On 2 June, LACO published LACO Circular Memorandum No. 62, which not only incorporated the new measures in the latest REDA guidelines, but also consolidated rules scattered throughout previous issues of REDA guidelines into the Consent Scheme.[14] In addition, new issues such as disclosure of information on prefabricated external walls were introduced to the Scheme.[15] On 10 August, two additional measures regarding disclosure of information were enclosed in a new issue of REDA guidelines. On 1 September, the Lands Department revised Annex I to the LACO Circular Memorandum No. 62 and issued LACO Circular Memorandum No. 63.

Celebrated improvements were brought in, including the abolition of the distinction between private sales and public sales, construction of unmodified show flats, compulsory disclosure of district name, area of non-structural prefabricated walls, and information on related party transactions, bulk sales and collapsed transactions. It has introduced a better balance in information supply in the developer-led market, pointing to the emergence of a more consumer-conscious regulatory regime (Lin 2012).

To reflect the changes, a standard agreement for sale and purchase was enclosed in LACO Circular Memorandum No. 63, which was further revised by LACO Circular Memorandum No. 66 in November 2011.[16] Annex I to the *Memorandum* was further revised in March 2012 by LACO Circular Memorandum No. 68, where a new requirement on the exhibition of cross-section plan of building was added to address the controversy in the *Oceanaire* in which one feature unit located on the ground level is described by the sales brochure as situated on the podium floor.

But even this governmental-industrial multi-pronged regulation system was a stepping stone to a more advanced regulatory regime. It turned out that LACO Circular Memorandum No. 68 was the last memorandum issued under the Consent Scheme on measures to enhance transparency for sale of residential units in uncompleted private developments.

2012–2013: From Consent Scheme to legislation

Report on Regulation of Sale of First-hand Residential Properties by Legislation

In October 2012, merely four months after the issue of LACO Circular Memorandum No. 62, the then Chief Executive Donald Tsang set up a Steering Committee to discuss the prospects and specific issues on regulating sales of first-hand residential properties by legislation. The four-month interval suggested that the effectiveness of the new measures encompassed by LACO Circular Memorandum No. 62 was hardly tested before the discussion to review and reform it for an advanced regulatory system started.

In the course of 11 months with a total of 20 meetings held on a bi-weekly basis, the Steering Committee had reviewed the operation of existing regulations and recommended appropriate measures to be taken in the proposed legislation. Transparency, fairness and greater consumer protection were the key considerations in the deliberation of the Steering Committee. Mr D.W. Pescod, the Chairman of the Steering Committee, handed the 'Report on Regulation of Sale of First-hand Residential Properties by Legislation' *(the Report* or *the Steering Committee's Report* hereafter)* to Miss Eva Cheng Yu-wah, the Secretary of Transport Housing in October 2011. The Report provided the foundation for the first draft of the *Residential Properties (First-hand Sales) Bill* by the Lands Department in November 2011.

In regards to the scope of the legislative framework, the Committee considered that the proposed legislation should apply to sales of both uncompleted first-hand residential properties and completed first-hand residential properties, including projects developed under old lease conditions, within the Consent Scheme and the non-Consent Scheme, and those outside the two schemes. The majority of the Committee members were under the impression that there were no major differences between sales of uncompleted and completed first-hand residential properties; it would be artificial and not defensible to draw a line between the two in terms of legislative control.[17]

According to the Committee, sales brochures, price lists, advertisements, show flats, disclosure of transaction information, sales arrangements, and conveyancing procedures were key features to be regulated. For information to be contained in the sales brochure, the Committee reviewed the requirements in LACO Circular Memorandum No. 62 and added the items of internal dimension of units, scale of the location plan, thickness of floor slab, an aerial photo of the development, and information on gross floor area concessions and energy efficiency of buildings.[18] No amendment was made to the definition of saleable area but the Committee recommended that information on gross floor area per flat and unit price based on gross floor area should not be quoted in the sales brochure, price lists or any advertisements.[19] The Committee demanded a greater number of units than required by the Consent Scheme be disclosed in the first and subsequent price lists;[20] and that information be disclosed on special payment terms including all kinds of gifts, advantages and bonuses in connection with the flat sale, as well as any price adjustment factors affecting the actual price of the flat.[21] It was of the opinion that certain controls should be set up over all forms of advertisements and developers should be made the source of the information (SC 2011).[22]

The most revolutionary recommendation by the Committee was to criminalize misrepresentation and dissemination of false or misleading information to induce a person to buy a specified property.[23] In terms of enforcement mechanism and penalties, the Committee was of the view that a new and dedicated enforcement agency be established to supervise sales of first-hand residential properties and monitor compliance with the requirements set out in the legislation.[24] In addition, the Committee proposed the establishment of an online centralized property information platform archiving market information regarding first-hand private residential properties in Hong Kong for public viewing and inspection (SC 2011).[25]

The Enactment of the Residential Properties (First-hand Sales) Ordinance

Approximately one month after receiving the Steering Committee's Report, the Lands Department completed the first draft of the *Residential Properties (First-hand Sales) Bill* (hereafter the *draft Bill*, or *the Bill put up for public consultation*) in November 2011.[26] Public opinion on the *draft Bill* was sought for a period of three months from November 2011 to January 2012. 959 submissions were made to the Transport and Housing Bureau by way of email, facsimile or post or via the designated e-forum, among which was REDA's 35-page submission on the *draft Bill*.[27] In February 2012, the Transport and Housing Bureau published a report to summarize respondents' views and the Administration's responses on the salient provisions in the *draft Bill*, claiming widespread support from the public to the proposed legislation (THB 2012).[28]

The Transport and Housing Bureau introduced the *Residential Properties (First-hand Sales) Bill* (hereafter the *Bill*) to the Legislative Council on 16 March 2012. Then in a House Committee meeting held on 23 March 2012, Members of the House Committee agreed to form a Bills Committee to study the *Bill*. The Bills Committee had held 20 meetings in total for the study of the *Bill* under the chairmanship of Hon Chan Kam-lam (LC 2012).

During the reading of the *Bill*, the Bills Committee has considered presentations from 21 organizations and individuals. Among them, the Law Society of Hong Kong submitted two reports to the Legislative Council on the *Bill* on 23 April and 6 June, raising issues including the definition of 'vendor', exemptions for professionals such as architects and solicitors, definitions of saleable area, price lists, etc. REDA also invited opinions from Lord Pannick, Tristan Jones and Wilson Leung on some provisions in the *Bill* and submitted their *Joint Opinion* (dated on 19 April, 2012) to the Legislative Council on 20 April. The *Joint Opinion* discussed the constitutionality of several requirements of the draft legislation, i.e., the prevention of provision information related to gross floor area and the requirement to include minimum number of units in the price list. Despite the force of arguments enclosed in the *Joint Opinion*, no change was eventually made to the relevant provisions of the *Bill*. Later, in a press release, REDA (2012) expressed the view that the *Bill* was flawed in some aspects and might have been rushed through into legislation without due consideration of the views of all stakeholders.

Some legislators regarded the reading of the *Bill* was, in general, rushed with inadequate consultation and debate; some believed that the government could have allocated a longer period to digest and provide timely feedback against the received comments from all stakeholders; some suggested that the time to gather expert comment was very limited. According to Legislator Ms Audrey Eu, some of the views from the Law Society were not addressed before no amendment could be made to the *Bill* in the reading process. She commented that the *Bill* did have deficiencies or omissions but it takes time for the deficiencies or omissions to be rectified (Chan et al. 2015).

Overall, the entire legislative process consisted of three stages spanning over 22 months: the deliberation by the Steering Committee from October 2010 to October 2011; the draft of the *Bill* and public consultation from November 2011 to January 2012; and the third stage: the reading and the deliberation by the Bills Committee from March 2012 to June 2012.

On 29 June 2012, the *Bill* passed through the Legislative Council after the third reading and the *Residential Properties (First-hand Sales) Ordinance* was published in the *Gazette* on 6 July 2012 (LC 2013).

The *Ordinance* gives statutory definitions to residential property, development, completed development, uncompleted development, a phase of a development, multi-unit building, deed of mutual covenant, floor area, saleable area, sales brochure, price list, register of transactions, associate corporation, subsidiary and holding company, modified show flats and unmodified show flats. It extends the definition of *vendor* in the draft *Bill* to include 'the person engaged by the owner of the residential property to co-ordinate and supervise the process of design, planning, constructing, fitting out, completing and marketing the development or phase'.[29]

The major parts of the *Ordinance* (Parts 2 and 3) set out mandatory requirements for sales brochure, price lists, show flats, advertisement and sales arrangements. The *Ordinance* states the standard of provision of information in sales brochures to be accurate in every material aspect at the date on which it is printed.[30]

The *Ordinance* integrates rules on disclosure of transaction information from previous LACO Circular Memoranda and REDA guidelines: it refines the template for register of transactions, prescribes the timeline information concerning different stages of the sale must be entered into the register of transactions, and sets out a forfeiture at 5 per cent of the purchase price with a lead time of five working days after the date on which the person enters into the preliminary agreement for sale and purchase.[31] A clear meaning of 'reservation' is given as to mean *an expression of intent to purchase*. The *Ordinance* adopts the time of issuance of price list as the cut-off date after which general reservation is allowed; it adds one requirement that reservation of a particular unit is not allowed even after the issuance of price list.[32]

The *Ordinance* clarifies the confusion left by the draft *Bill* on the nature of the agreement of sale and purchase between a company or a statutory corporation and its associate company or holding company to the effect that an agreement of sale and purchase of such type is to be disregarded in determining whether an agreement of sale and purchase has been entered into in respect of a residential property.[33] This is to prevent developers from circumventing the legislation by decanting a development under two or more agreements for sale and purchase to related companies which can then sell the residential properties as second-hand properties (THB 2012).[34]

Following the Steering Committee's suggestion, the *Ordinance* criminalizes *misrepresentation* and *dissemination of false or misleading information*; in addition, it creates a new offence on *containing false or misleading information in advertisement*. Penalties include fine and imprisonment; the maximum penalty can be up to HK$ 5 million with imprisonment of up to seven years.[35]

The commencement of the Ordinance

The *Ordinance* came into full operation on 29 April 2013. To ensure the implementation of the *Ordinance*, the Sales of First-hand Residential Properties Authority (SRPA) was set up according to section 86(1) of the *Ordinance* within the Transport and Housing Bureau of the Government of Hong Kong Special Administrative Region. According to the Authority, the objectives of the *Ordinance* are to create a clear, fair, balanced, practical and efficient mechanism to regulate the sales of first-hand residential properties, and to protect the interest of residential property purchasers through enhancing transparency and making contravention of the mandatory requirements criminal offences (SRPA 2013a).

The SRPA is considered as highly autonomous in performing its duties, which, compared to REDA, is not easily affected by external forces or the pressure given by the public or relevant stakeholders (Chan et al. 2015).

The Sales of First-hand Residential Properties Electronic Platform (SRPE) is established under section 89 of the *Ordinance*. The vendors of individual first-hand residential developments, the sales of which are subject to the *Ordinance*, must make available and update on the Platform all the sales brochures, price lists, and registers of transactions for the reference of the Authority as well as the public.[36]

It should be highlighted that it is not the duty of the Authority to ensure that the sales brochures, price lists and registers of transactions provided by developers have complied with the requirements of the *Ordinance* before they are made available. That remains the responsibilities of the developers. However, the Authority is under the statutory duty to conduct the compliance check upon receiving the sales brochures and price lists submitted by the developers. Still, the power to adjudicate whether the vendor has breached the requirements of the *Ordinance* is not vested in the Authority, but essentially in the Judiciary. In other words, the role of the Authority is one of oversight. As such, the Authority does not possess the power to impose stoppage of a sale or monetary penalty in cases of possible breach of the requirements of the *Ordinance* (SRPA 2013b). If the Authority has spotted questionable sale practices, it can ask the vendor for examination, revision or explanation and, at the same time, consider referring the case to the Department of Justice for consideration of prosecution.

Apart from administering and supervising compliance with the provisions of the *Ordinance* and maintaining SRPE, the SRPA is also tasked with administrative duties of public education on matters relating to the sales of first-hand residential properties; providing the trade with practice guidelines and handling complaints (SRPA 2013c).

The Authority's undertaking of public education on matters relating to the sales of first-hand residential properties is a major progress of the new regulatory regime and complements the *Ordinance*'s efforts to create transparency in the real estate market. In the past three years, when a questionable practice was spotted in their examination and investigation, the Authority would usually issue a reminder to purchasers and prospective purchasers shortly. In their own words, 'if the nature of the possible breaches is a serious one, and that the case in question may bring substantial loss to the prospective purchasers, for the sake of consumer protection, the SRPA will, without prejudice to the legal proceedings, disclose the cases of possible breaches as soon as possible so that prospective purchasers could act cautiously' (SRPA 2013b). This sheds light on the consumer protection function of the SRPA: firstly, the Authority is equipped with a thorough understanding of the *Ordinance* and the Consent Scheme, thus their assessment is highly persuasive; secondly, its examination of sales brochures and price lists, as well as investigation of sales practices, take place at or around the same time of the sale; their timely reminder, therefore, may effectively draw the attention of would-be purchasers to the issues.

In addition, the Authority also handles complaints from the public including prospective purchasers in the sales of first-hand residential properties. If a purchaser is aggrieved by the sales practice of the developer, she can make a complaint to the SRPA (2013d). For example, in the sale of one residential unit in the *Full Art Court* in 2014, the vendor did not provide to the purchaser any formal sales brochure or price list as required by the *Ordinance*; later, when the agreement for sale and purchase was cancelled (for reasons relating to payment), the purchaser filed a complaint to the Authority (Standard 2016).[37]

In a nutshell, the role the SRPA plays in protection the interests of purchasers and prospective purchasers in sales of first-hand residential properties can hardly be over-stated. In this regard, it is critical to expand the public's awareness of the function and powers of the Authority. The Consumer Council's survey in

2014 revealed that only 40 per cent of the respondents had heard about the SRPA (CC 2014).

At the same time, it must be highlighted that after the enactment of the *Ordinance* and the establishment of SRPA, the Consumer Council continues to play a critical role in the collective efforts to ensure the implementation of the *Ordinance* after 2013. In addition to processing complaints from purchasers of first-hand residential properties, the Council can hear cases on a broader setting: complaints weren't restricted to the *Ordinance*-related issues or issues related to sales of first-hand residential properties alone: for example, unfair commercial practices arising from sales of commercial properties, sales of second-hand residential properties in Hong Kong and promotional activities on sales of overseas first-hand residential properties in Hong Kong, as long as the aggrieved parties were acting as a consumer in the dealings.

More significantly, the Council has been carrying out independent studies on the effectiveness of the *Ordinance* and its implementation in protecting consumer in the first-hand residential market sector since the enactment of the new legislation. In 2014 the Council conducted a comprehensive review of the implementation of the *Ordinance* since 2013 'as an indication of its ongoing commitment to making the marketplace a safer environment for consumers'. A number of recommendations were given, based on 17 filed works to sales of first-hand residential properties in 2014. The Study raised concerns on questionable practices observed in these first-hand sales after the enactment of the *Ordinance*, especially in the area of distribution of advertisement, sales arrangement and conduct of estate agents. Overall, the Council applauded the Administration for bringing the legislation into being and considered the introduction of the *Ordinance* a key milestone in the market for first-hand sales of residential properties. The Study also sheds lights on the operation of the Authority in fulfilling its duties under the *Ordinance* (CC 2014).

All in all, collective efforts have been made in the new regulatory regime by both the SRPA and the Consumer Council to enhance consumer protection in the residential market.

Conclusion

For anyone who is interested in how innovated commercial practices have stimulated the continuous development of a regulatory regime, Hong Kong offers a most persuasive example with the evolution of its regulatory regime over sales of first-hand residential properties. The many rounds of development within and beyond the Consent Scheme since its introduction in 1961 were triggered by various practices which were either unfair, untrue, unconscionable or misleading. The administrative Scheme kept evolving to address novel challenges for a market of higher transparency while maintaining certain balance of interests among all the stakeholders. The continuous efforts culminated in the enactment of the *Ordinance* in 2012.

The discussion in the next chapters of this book will demonstrate the fact that, just like the regulatory system itself, every major requirement of the *Ordinance* has its own evolutionary process. For example, it took years of participative discussions by the government, the Legislative Council, the Consumer Council, developers, and professional associations of surveyors, architects and lawyers to reach a statutory definition of the *saleable area*.

This brings us to the discussion of the next chapter.

Notes

1 For a plain description, see Joyce Ng, 'Consent scheme sets rules for developers', *South China Morning Post*, 18 January 2011.
2 Section 2, Legal Advisory and Conveyancing Office Circular Memorandum No. 40 (hereinafter LACO Circular Memorandum No. 40); see also section 11.1.1, Part I in Annex to *LACO Circular Memorandum No. 40*, 28 May 1999.
3 Doctor of Social Sciences honoris causa by the University of Hong Kong in its 149th Congregation in 1995.
4 Estate Agents Authority (EAA), *Guidelines issued by The Real Estate Developers Association of Hong Kong (REDA)*, www.eaa.org.hk/en-us/Consumer-Corner/Guidelines-issued-by-REDA.
5 The Real Estate Developers Association of Hong Kong (REDA), www.reda.hk.
6 Discussion on other conditions Vendors must fulfil to obtain the consent of the Director of Lands to enter into the agreement of sale and purchase would be outside the scope of this book.
7 For details of the land of this historic sale, see Dr Fan Chi Sun, *The Consent Scheme in Hong Kong Its Evolution and Evaluation – Home Purchaser Behaviour in Housing Society's Property Transactions Before and After the Asian Financial Crisis*, pp. 6–9.
8 The story was recorded in Chinese Literature for example; see Chapter 12, *The Biography of Fok Ying Tung* by Leng Xia, China Xiju Publication House.
9 Dr Fan Chi Sun was of the view that the method of disposal may, in case of grant of Crown Lease with conditions, have had breached the conditions of lease grant; an example is in the Conditions of Exchange of a residential/commercial site, Inland Lot No. 7185 granted in 1954, the Special Condition (1) states: 'The lessee, his executors, administrators and permitted assigns shall not assign, mortgage, charge, underlet or part with the possession of or otherwise dispose of the new lot in question or any part thereof or any interest therein nor enter into any agreement so to do unless and until he has expended upon the erection of buildings on the new lot the sum required in clause 6(a) of the General Conditions and has in all other respects observed and complied with the General and Special Conditions to the satisfaction of the Director of Public Works and the Land Officer. Every assignment, mortgage, charge, sub-letting or other alienation of the said new lot or any part thereof shall be registered at the Land Office.' See Dr Fan Chi Sun, The Consent Scheme in Hong Kong Its Evolution and Evaluation – Home Purchaser Behaviour in Housing Society's Property Transactions Before and After the Asian Financial Crisis, pp. 8–9.
10 Section 11, *LACO Circular Memorandum No. 40*, 28 May 1999, pp. 10–18. Requirements on disclosure of information in public sale were extended to govern private sales in December, 2011: paragraph I(a), *LACO Circular Memorandum No. 40C*, 10 December 2001, p. 1.
11 'A mortgagee bank holding a security over the lot under a building mortgage ("BM") will now be required to include an irrevocable undertaking in the BM to the developer to unconditionally discharge any unit and release it from the security upon completion of the sale and purchase (the terms of which have been approved by the mortgagee

bank), where the entire proceeds of that sale have been paid into a stakeholder account to be opened with the mortgagee bank and operated in the manner described in Paragraph 2 in this Section II.' Paragraph 1.1, section II, *LACO Circular Memorandum No. 54*, 8 July 2004, p. 16.

12 Among whom are the Financial Secretary John Tsang Chun-wah and the Secretary for Transport and Housing Eva Cheng. See Paggie Leung, Olga Wong and Fanny W. Y. Fung, 'More ideas to make flat sales less murky; Ministers propose developers clean up their act', *South China Morning Post*, 22 April 2010.

13 Also known as Nine Measures and Twelve Requirements, or '九招十二式' in Chinese.

14 Among which are the guidelines issued on 10 October 2008; 30 June 2009; 7 October 2009; 23 November 2009; 27 November 2009; and 27 April 2010. The only measure of the June REDA Guidelines that was not included in LACO Circular Memorandum No. 62 was in section 2: the rule on en-bloc sale based on an aggregate amount of considerations.

15 Which is not talked about by REDA guidelines; see B 2(a)(i) in Revised Annex I to LACO Circular Memorandum No. 62 in *LACO Circular Memorandum No.63*.

16 A similar standard agreement for sale and purchase is in Schedule 5 to the *Residential Properties (First-hand Sales) Ordinance*.

17 Paragraph 3.7, Chapter 3, Report of the Steering Committee on Regulation of Sale of First-hand Residential Properties by Legislation, October 2011, p. 9.

18 Ibid., pp. 13–20.

19 Ibid., paragraph 6.5 to paragraph 6.7, p. 26.

20 Ibid., paragraph 5.10 and paragraph 5.12, p. 23.

21 Ibid., paragraph 6.9 and paragraph 6.11(e), pp. 27–28.

22 Ibid., paragraph 8.8, p. 39.

23 Ibid., paragraph 12.5, p. 61.

24 Ibid., paragraph 15.7, p.74.

25 Ibid., paragraph 16.6, p.77.

26 The draft Residential Properties (First-hand Sales) Bill was in the Annex to the consultation paper entitled 'Public Consultation on the Proposed Legislation to Regulate the Sale of First-hand Residential Properties' published by the Transport and Housing Bureau in November 2011.

27 Paragraph 4, Report on Public Consultation on the Proposed Legislation to Regulate the Sale of First-Hand Residential Properties, Transport and Housing Bureau, March 2012, p. 2.

28 Ibid., paragraph 5.

29 Section 7, Part 1, *Residential Properties (First-hand Sales) Ordinance*, A2311–A2313.

30 Ibid., section 22 (2), Part 2 – Division 2, A2345.

31 Ibid., section 52 and section 53, Part 2 - Division 7, A2399–A2401.

32 Ibid., section 34, A2367.

33 Ibid., section 11(1) and (2), A2319–A2321.

34 As raised by the Consumer Council in their submission to the Draft Bill. See Paragraph 24, Report on Public Consultation on the Proposed Legislation to Regulate the Sale of First-Hand Residential Properties, Transport and Housing Bureau, March 2012, p. 7.

35 Sections 70, 75, 76, and 78, *Residential Properties (First-hand Sales) Ordinance*, A2429–A2450.

36 The Sales of First-hand Residential Properties Electronic Platform: www.srpe.gov.hk/opip/default.htm.

37 Case No.: KTS21568–572、595–599、600–608/15.

References

CC (1991) A Study on the Disclosure of Information to Prospective Purchasers of Uncompleted Unit, October 1991, Consumer Council, Hong Kong.

CC (2014) Study on the Sales of First-hand Residential Properties, pp. 9–12, 11 November 2014, Consumer Council, www.consumer.org.hk/ws_en/competition_issues/reports/20141111.html.

Chan, H.S., Chan, Y.K., Cheng, W.S., and Sze, K.W. (2015) Regulating the Sale of First-hand Residential Properties in Hong Kong: a Study of Policy and Administrative Dynamics, Capstone project report submitted in partial fulfilment of the requirements of the Master of Public Administration, Department of Politics and Public Administration, The University of Hong Kong, pp. 61–68, pp. 86–90, p. 100.

Fan, C.S. (2005) The Consent Scheme in Hong Kong: Its Evolution and Evaluation – Home Purchaser Behaviour in Housing Society's Property Transactions Before and After the Asian Financial Crisis, Ph.D Thesis, Department of Real Estate and Construction, Faculty of Architecture, the University of Hong Kong, September 2005, pp. 6–71.

Goo, S. H. (2010) Regulation of Sale of Off-the-plan Property, *The Conveyancer and Property Lawyer*, Issue 2, 2010, pp. 130–132.

HB (2000) Sales Descriptions of Uncompleted Residential Properties Bill, Housing Bureau, 2000.

Lands D (1993) Legal Advisory and Conveyancing Office Circular Memorandum No. 4, Lands Department Consent Scheme, Legal Advisory and Conveyancing Office, Lands Department, 9 September 1993.

Lands D (1999a) Legal Advisory and Conveyancing Office Circular Memorandum No. 40, Lands Department Consent Scheme, Legal Advisory and Conveyancing Office, Lands Department, 28 May 1999.

Lands D (1999b) Legal Advisory and Conveyancing Office Circular Memorandum No. 40A, Lands Department Consent Scheme, Legal Advisory and Conveyancing Office, Lands Department, 21 July 1999.

Lands D (2001) Legal Advisory and Conveyancing Office Circular Memorandum No. 40C, Lands Department Consent Scheme, Legal Advisory and Conveyancing Office, Lands Department, 10 December 2001.

Lands D (2004) Legal Advisory and Conveyancing Office Circular Memorandum No. 54, Lands Department Consent Scheme, Legal Advisory and Conveyancing Office, Lands Department, 8 July 2004.

Lands D (2010) Legal Advisory and Conveyancing Office Circular Memorandum No. 63, Lands Department Consent Scheme, Legal Advisory and Conveyancing Office, Lands Department, 1 September 2010.

Lands D (2012) Legal Advisory and Conveyancing Office Circular Memorandum No. 68, Lands Department Consent Scheme, Legal Advisory and Conveyancing Office, Lands Department, 22 March 2012.

Lands D (2016) Legal Advisory and Conveyancing Office Circular Memorandum No. 72C, Lands Department Consent Scheme, Legal Advisory and Conveyancing Office, Lands Department, 28 June 2016.

LC (2004) System for Pre-sale of Residential Properties: Review of the Consent Scheme, 2 February 2004, *LC Paper No. CB(1)859/03-04(1)*, Panel on Planning, Lands and Works and Panel on Housing, Legislative Council.

LC (2012) Bills Committee on Residential Properties (First-hand Sales) Bill, Paper for the House Committee, 15 June 2012, LC Paper No. CB(1) 2192/11-12, Legislative Council. www.legco.gov.hk/yr11-12/english/hc/papers/hc0608cb1-2192-e.pdf

LC (2013) Background brief on 'Residential Properties (First-hand Sales) Ordinance and the Sales of First-hand Residential Properties Authority' prepared by the Legislative Council Secretariat, 2 July 2013, LC Paper No. CB(1)1391/12-13(03), Panel on Housing, Legislative Council. www.legco.gov.hk/yr12-13/english/panels/hg/papers/hg0702cb1-1391-3-e.pdf

Lee, A. and Goo, S. H. (2008) The Sale and Purchase of Uncompleted Flats in Hong Kong, The International Conference *The Judicial Reform of Macau in the Context of Globalization*, the Faculty of Law, the University of Macau, p. 3.

Leng, X (2005) *The Biography of Fok Ying Tung*, China Xiju Publication House, Chapter 12.

Lin, D (2012) The New Rules for Sales of Uncompleted Flats, Law Lectures for Practitioners 2010, Cheng, ML., Jen, J. and Young, J.Y.K. (Eds.), Hong Kong Law Journal & Faculty of Law, the University of Hong Kong, pp. 78–118.

LRC (1995) Report on Description of Flats on Sale, the Law Reform Commission of Hong Kong, April 1995.

LSHK (2004) Consent letter from the Lands Department to the Solicitors of the developers, Chinese Conveyancing Reference Material, Law Society of Hong Kong, 15 November 2004, www.fjt2.net/gate/gb/www.hklawsoc.org.hk/pub_c/publications/04-578.asp

Merry, M. (2008) Protection of Purchasers of Uncompleted Residential Flats – The Hong Kong Experience, *HKU-NUS-SMU Symposium Paper*, Singapore, November 2008.

Nield, S. (1990) The Sale of Uncompleted Buildings, *Law Lectures for Practitioners 1990*, pp. 285–318.

REDA (2012) Residential Properties (First-hand Sales) Bill, *Press Release*, 30 May 2012, http://reda.hk/2012/05/30/residential-properties-first-hand-sales-bill/.

RGD (1964) Land Office Circular Memorandum No. 19, Land Office, the former Registrar General's Department, 1964.

RGD (1991) Land Office Circular Memorandum No. 101, Land Office, the former Registrar General's Department, 21 February 1991.

SC (2011) Report of the Steering Committee on Regulation of Sale of First-hand Residential Properties by Legislation, The Steering Committee on Regulation of the Sale of First-hand Residential Properties by Legislation, October 2011.

SCMP (2010) More Ideas to Make Flat Sales Less Murky; Ministers Propose Developers Clean up Their Act, *South China Morning Post*, 22 April 2010, Hong Kong.

SCMP (2011) Consent scheme sets rules for developers, *South China Morning Post*, 18 January 2011, Hong Kong.

SRPA (2013a) Welcome Message, the Sales of First-hand Residential Properties Authority, www.srpa.gov.hk/en/welcomemsg.html.

SRPA (2013b) SRPA's Response on Sales Brochures and Ordinance, *Press Releases*, the Sales of First-hand Residential Properties Authority, April 26 2013, www.info.gov.hk/gia/general/201304/26/P201304260683.htm.

SRPA (2013c) Role and Function, the Sales of First-hand Residential Properties Authority, www.srpa.gov.hk/en/role-n-function.html

SRPA (2013d) Enquiries and Complaints, the Sales of First-hand Residential Properties Authority, www.srpa.gov.hk/en/complaint-enquiry.html

Standard (2016) Sales team failed to follow property rules, court told, *the Standard*, 3 June 2016 www.thestandard.com.hk/section-news.php?id=170123

Tang, L.Y. (2008) A Study on Mortgage-Related Issues in Sale of Commercial Residential Properties, *Law Press (China)*, 2008, p. 41.

THB (2012) Report on Public Consultation on the Proposed Legislation to Regulate the Sale of First-Hand Residential Properties, Transport and Housing Bureau, March 2012.

3   Saleable area[1]

Introduction

In dealing with a claim on misrepresentation of floor area in the sale of a residential unit, Gerald Godfrey made the following comments with regard to the internal area of a flat:

> [T]he area of a flat like this is not the only matter which affects its value and that matters such as the flat's state of decoration, its outlook (harbour or mountain view) and its height (upper or lower floor) are all of material importance. But that is not to say that the area is of no material importance. On the contrary. The market takes considerable note of what is the going rate per sq. ft. in placing an approximate price on a property.[2]

The above observation highlights a number of key elements that affect a residential property's market price, i.e., the area of a flat, the state of decoration (see Chapter 5), the view (see Chapter 6) and the height of the apartment (see Chapter 7). All these factors have a direct impact on the value of the residential property, yet as a matter of perception the internal flat area appears to be the one factor that is most closely associated to the property value. This is because, while decoration, inner structure, location, view, height and floor number, together with a few other factors such as the age of the development (to be discussed in Chapter 8), will jointly determine the *average price* of the property, i.e., price per square-foot, ultimately, it is the size of the flat that will determine the *overall price* of the flat on sale.

As it is by the space of exclusive possession that a residential unit is made into a home for the property owner, no information can be more critical to a prospective purchaser of uncompleted flats than that about the area of her exclusive possession.

Construction and surveying glossaries offer a wide range of terms for internal floor area of a residential unit. For example, *net internal area* and *gross internal area* (RICS 2007), *built-up area*, *covered area*, or *saleable area* and *gross floor area* by the Consent Scheme.

Back to 1997, miscalculation of saleable area in *Verbena Heights*, a sale of residential units by the Housing Society, once caused public outcry. The method of calculation on saleable area adopted by the Housing Society for that project included the thickness of external walls. The structural walls of *Verbena Height* were not built strictly vertical throughout all floors; instead, they were in a step form which result in different thickness on different floor levels. The original figures of the saleable areas as enclosed in the sales brochure did not reflect the area difference on a floor-by-floor basis. As a result, some purchasers believed the saleable area of their units was miscalculated and demanded recession of the contracts. The Housing Society ended up providing a lease of three years to the purchaser-turned-tenants, who opted for recession over the human fault made by the Project Architect in the course of the saleable area calculation (as in their own words) (LC 1997).

In *Citilite Properties Ltd v Innovative Development Co Ltd*, the saleable area quoted by the vendor was only close to the gross floor area of the property: while the agreement listed the saleable area of the property as 7,864 sq. ft., the actual saleable area of the property was only 6,596.50 sq. ft.; its gross floor area (ascertained in accordance with the Building (Planning) Regulations reg. 23(3)(a) on certain assumptions relating to the exercise of the discretion vested in the Building Authority) was 7,959.30 sq. ft. In the end, the purchaser was awarded damages according to the difference between the warranted saleable area of 7,864 sq. ft. less the actual saleable area of 6,596.5 sq. ft. times a unit rate of $6,170 per sq. ft.

When developers calculated the saleable area on their own terms, disputes of this kind arose. The constituents of saleable area of residential properties had been severely debated over the decades. It wasn't until 2008 that a standardized definition of saleable area was incorporated into the Consent Scheme. Still, calculation of saleable area remained the central issue in the draft of the *Bill* and public consultation in 2012. In the end, the *Ordinance* settled the matter by offering a refined statutory definition of saleable area in section 8.

Towards a standardized definition

For decades, residential properties were purchased and sold in Hong Kong without a standardized method of measurement on saleable area. Areas of yards, terraces, gardens all used to be included in the calculation of saleable area under the Consent Scheme. Media questioned how it should be a legitimate practice for developers to have the discretion to include common areas and external facilities such as parking spaces and gardens into the saleable area (SCMP 2007). Nonetheless, some had argued that Hong Kong had adopted a unified measurement on saleable area for decades by referring to a concept of *sale floor area* used by the Rating and Valuation Department (CPPCL 2006). The *sale floor area* was defined as the floor area exclusively allocated to the unit including balconies and verandahs but excluding bay windows, yards, gardens, terraces, flat roofs, carports and common areas such as stairs, lift shafts, pipe ducts, lobbies and communal toilets. It is measured from the outside of the exterior enclosing walls of the unit and the middle of the party walls between two units (RVD 2013).[3] The Rating and

Valuation Department has adopted the definition since the 1970s to measure all the completed units in Hong Kong for rating purposes, but the definition has never become popular in the residential property market, partially because of the Department's reluctance to make the data freely available to the public.

The call for a unified calculation measurement of saleable area was not addressed until the 1990s, where 'in June 1993, the then Buildings and Land Department, in conjunction with the Law Society of Hong Kong, completed a review of the definition of saleable area for use in ASP's (*author – agreement for sale and purchase*) approved form under the Consent Scheme in future' (Lands D 1993).

The ever first definition of the saleable area under the Consent Scheme was provided as follows:

'Saleable area' means:

(i)   in relation to a unit enclosed by walls, the floor area of such unit (which shall include the floor area of any balconies and verandahs), measured from the exterior of the enclosing walls of such unit except where such enclosing walls separate two adjoining units in which case the measurement shall be taken from the middle of those walls, and shall include the internal partitions and columns within such unit; but shall exclude the common parts outside the enclosing walls of such unit provided that if any of the enclosing walls abut onto a common area, then the whole thickness of the enclosing walls which so abut shall be included;

(ii) in relation to any cockloft, the floor area of such cockloft measured from the interior of the enclosing walls of such cockloft;

(iii) in relation to any bay window which does not extend to the floor level of a unit, the area of such bay window measured from the exterior of the enclosing walls or glass windows of such bay window and from the point where the bay window meets the wall dropping to the floor level of a unit but excluding the thickness of such wall;

(iv) in relation to any carparking space, the area of such carparking space (the dimensions of which are more particularly set out in Schedule 3) measured from the interior of its demarcating lines or enclosing walls, as the case may be;

(v)   in relation to any yard, terrace, garden, flat roof or roof, the area of such yard, terrace, garden, flat roof or roof measured from the interior of their boundary lines, and where the boundary consists of a wall, then it shall be measured from the interior of such wall; Where the Property consists of any of the above-mentioned items, the saleable area of each of such items shall be specified and described separately in Schedule 3.

The definition was welcomed by the Hong Kong Law Reform Commission in its 'Report on Description of Flats on Sale' in April 1995, who recommended that the definition be made law by the Legislative Council (LRC 1995). The Commission considered that the definition 'represents the actual floor space that purchasers can enjoy exclusively'.[4] This, as the later disputes over the definition had proven, was a rather cursory and hurried view. The recommendation by the Law Reform Commission was not accepted by the Legislative Council then.

In March 1999, the Hong Kong Institute of Surveyors issued a 'Code of Measuring Practice' with a similar definition (HKIS 1999). The *Code* had been voluntarily followed by developers.

In early 2007, this issue finally made its appearance in the agenda of the Legislative Council. In the summer of the same year, a second panel discussion on this issue took place in the Council, where lawmakers urged REDA to request its members to highlight the information of saleable area in sales brochures (LC 2007). One year later, on 17 June 2008, a third panel discussion was held in the Council and the debate was centred on the constituents of saleable area. It was after this panel discussion that REDA made 'a major concession' 'by agreeing to exclude bay windows and air-conditioner plants when calculating the saleable area of new flats' (SCMP 2008).

Following the consensus reached in the last panel discussion, the Hong Kong Institute of Surveyors issued a '*Supplement to the Code of Measuring Practice*' on 18 August 2008. It stated that the saleable area shall include balcony and other similar features such as veranda and utility platform but it shall not include the area of *ancillary accommodation* which included cockloft, stairhood, bay window, yard, terrace, garden, flat roof, roof, plant room, air-conditioner platform, and lift lobby (HKIS 2008).

Then, via the issue of LACO Circular Memorandum No.60 in October 2008, a standardized definition of saleable area became part of the Consent Scheme.[5] The saleable area was defined as follows under the Consent Scheme:

> 'Saleable Area' means the floor area of a unit enclosed by walls (inclusive of the floor area of any balconies, utility platforms and verandahs but exclusive of the Other Areas), which area (including any balcony, utility platform or verandah enclosed by walls) shall be measured from the exterior of the enclosing walls of such unit, balconies, utility platforms or verandahs (as the case may be) except where such enclosing walls separate two adjoining units, balconies, utility platforms or verandahs (as the case may be), in which case the measurement shall be taken from the middle of those walls, and shall include the internal partitions and columns within such unit, balconies, utility platforms or verandahs (as the case may be); but shall exclude the common parts outside the enclosing walls of such unit, balconies, utility platforms or verandahs (as the case may be), and for balconies, utility platforms or verandahs, shall exclude the whole thickness of the enclosing walls or boundary which abut onto the unit Provided That if any of the enclosing walls abut onto a common area, then the whole thickness of the enclosing walls which so abut shall be included. Where a balcony, utility platform or verandah is not enclosed by a solid wall, the floor area of such balcony, utility platform

or verandah shall be measured from the external boundary of the said balcony, utility platform or verandah.

Thus under the Consent Scheme, the saleable area of a given residential unit refers to the floor area of a unit enclosed by walls measured from the exterior of the enclosing walls with exclusion of parts identified as 'other areas' plus the area of balconies,[6] utility platforms and verandahs[7] (if any). The *other areas* included the areas of cockloft, bay window, car parking space, yard, terrace, garden, flat roof, roof and air conditioning plant room:

'Other Areas' means: (i) the area of any cockloft which shall be measured from the interior of the enclosing walls and shall include the internal partitions and columns within such cockloft; (ii) the area of any bay window which shall be measured from the exterior of the enclosing walls or glass windows of such bay window and from the point where the bay window meets the wall dropping to the floor level of a unit excluding the thickness of such wall; (iii) the area of any carparking space which shall be measured to the centre of its demarcating lines or the interior face of its enclosing walls, as the case may be; and (iv) the area of any yard, terrace, garden, flat roof, roof and air-conditioning plant room which shall be measured from the interior of their boundary lines, and where boundary consists of a wall, then it shall be measured from the interior of such wall.

The above definition was not substantially challenged in the deliberation of the Steering Committee in 2011. When the *Residential Properties (First-hand Sales) Bill* was published in the Gazette in March 2012, minor amendments were made to the definition. Firstly, the *Bill* explicitly stated that saleable area includes the area of the internal partitions and columns within the residential property. Secondly, it also made clear, for the first time, that saleable area excludes the area of any common part outside the enclosing walls of the residential property. As the saleable area is measured from the exterior walls, the *Bill* set out that in the case that two adjoining residential properties separated by one wall, the measurement is to be taken from the middle of the wall.

The definition was not further amended upon the enactment of the *Ordinance* in July 2012 and becomes the statutory definition of saleable area for Hong Kong in April 2013. As section 8(1) of the *Ordinance* provides:

Saleable area, in relation to a residential property –

(a) means the floor area of the residential property;
(b) includes the floor are of every one of the following to the extent that it forms part of the residential property –
    (i) a balcony;

(ii) a utility platform;

(iii) a verandah; and

(c) excludes the area of every one of the items specified in Part 1 of Schedule 2 to the extent that it forms part of the residential property.

Section 8(2) states that the floor area shall be measured from the exterior of the enclosing walls of the residential property; it shall include the area of any internal partitions and columns within the residential property. Section 8(3) states that the area of a balcony, utility platform or verandah is to be measured from the exterior of the enclosing walls. Then Part 1 of Schedule 2 gives a list of specified items includes: (1) an air-condition plant room; (2) a bay window; (3) a cockloft; (4) a flat roof; (5) a garden; (6) a parking space; (7) a roof; (8) a stairhood; (9) a terrace; and (10) a yard.[8] The list essentially includes the constituents of what was used to be collectively addressed as *other areas* under the Consent Scheme.

To summarize, saleable area, or '實用面積' in Chinese, will include the areas of following parts measured from the exterior of the enclosing walls: (i) the floor area of a residential unit measured including the area of internal partitions and columns; (ii) the area of balcony, utility platform or verandahs, if any.[9]

In practice, developers will list the area information of the excluded items under the heading of *area of other specified items* next to the information of saleable area in the sales brochure. For illustration, the excerpt information from the sales brochure of *Mount Nicholson Phase I* (a pre-sale of residential houses in the Mid-Level in 2016) in Table 3.1 provides a typical example of presentation of floor area information after the commencement of the *Ordinance*. The developer has listed the information on *saleable area* and *area of other specified items* of the property next to each other, thus with cross-reference a prospective purchaser can easily identify the area of different parts of the residential property. The developer has highlighted, in the note below the table in the sales brochure, that the area of balcony, utility platform and verandah (in case of availability) has been calculated into the saleable area; in addition, the area of balcony, utility platform and verandah has been separately calculated and listed following the information of the saleable area.

The question then is: does the statutory definition of saleable area convey to the purchaser the clear picture of the internal floor area of the property on sale? What is the rationale for the inclusion of balcony and utility platform as well as for the exclusion of certain items such as bay window? Will this cause confusion? The analysis below starts with the parts the areas are included in the calculation then proceeds to those the areas of which are excluded from the calculation.

Table 3.1 Area of Residential Properties in the Phase in the Sales Brochures of Mount Nicholson Phase I, page 69.

AREA OF RESIDENTIAL PROPERTIES IN THE PHASE
期數中的住宅物業的面積

Description of Residential Property 物業的描述 House No. 洋房編號	Saleable Area (including balcony; utility platform and verandah (if any)) sq. metre (sq. ft.) 實用面積 (包括露台，工作平台及陽台(如有)) 平方米 (平方呎)	Area of other specified items (Not included in the Saleable Area) 其他指明項目的面積 (不計算入實用面積) sq. metre (sq. ft.) 平方米 (平方呎)									
		Air-Conditioning Plant Room 空調機房	Bay Window 窗台	Cockloft 閣樓	Flat Roof 平台	Garden 花園	Parking Space 停車位	Roof 天台	Stairhood 梯屋	Terrace 前庭	Yard 庭院
House 15 洋房 15	805.879 (8,674) Balcony 露台: 4.991 (54) Utility Platform工作平台: –	3.992 (43)	–	–	18.441 (198)	404.342 (4,352)	122.478 (1,318)	109.455 (1,178)	–	–	197.397 (2,125)
House 16 洋房 16	741.214 (7,978) Balcony 露台: 4.950 (53) Utility Platform工作平台: –	4.482 (48)	–	–	17.137 (184)	479.632 (5,163)	141.198 (1,520)	91.243 (982)	–	–	118.999 (1,281)
House 17 洋房 17	741.693 (7,984) Balcony 露台: 4.950 (53) Utility Platform工作平台: –	4.485 (48)	–	–	17.225 (185)	445.943 (4,800)	157.709 (1,698)	92.211 (993)	–	–	115.564 (1,244)
House 18 洋房 18	747.854 (8,050) Balcony 露台: 4.950 (53) Utility Platform工作平台: –	4.226 (45)	–	–	17.419 (187)	338.459 (4,181)	161.037 (1,733)	92.211 (993)	–	–	150.645 (1,622)
House 19 洋房 19	741.438 (7,981) Balcony 露台: 4.950 (53) Utility Platform工作平台: –	4.400 (47)	–	–	15.405 (166)	294.123 (3,166)	143.425 (1,544)	89.930 (968)	–	–	96.163 (1,035)
House 20 洋房 20	751.885 (8,093) Balcony 露台: 4.950 (53) Utility Platform工作平台: –	3.922 (42)	–	–	15.075 (162)	268.364 (2,889)	130.725 (1,407)	91.840 (989)	–	–	105.100 (1,131)

Table 3.1 continued

1. The saleable area is calculated in accordance with Section 8 of the Residential Properties (First-hand Sales) Ordinance.
2. The floor areas of balcony, utility platform and verandah, if any, are calculated in accordance with Section 8 of the Residential Properties (First-hand Sales) Ordinance.
3. The areas of other specified items (not included in the saleable area) are calculated in accordance with Part 2 of Schedule 2 to the Residential Properties (First-hand Sales) Ordinance.

Notes: The areas in square metres have been converted to square feet based on a conversion rate of 1 square metre = 10.764 square feet and rounded off to the nearest integer.

The area of the Parking Space specified in the section "Area of Residential Properties in the Phase" in this sales brochure includes the area of the entire carport of the House (as indicated in the section "Floor Plans of Parking Spaces in the Phase" in this sales brochure). For the area inside the carport which is designated under the land grant for the parking purpose, please refer to the area of parking space under the section "Floor Plans of Parking Spaces in the Phase" in this sales brochure.

1. 實用面積是按《一手住宅物業銷售條例》第8條計算得出的。
2. 露台、工作平台及陽台 (如有) 之樓面面積是按《一手住宅物業銷售 條例》 第8條計算得出的。
3. 其他指明項目的面積 (不計算入實用面積) 是按《一手住宅物業銷售 條例》附表2 第2 部計算得出的。

備註: 以平方呎列出的面積以1平方米＝10．764平方呎換算, 並以四捨 五入至整數。

本售樓說明書「期數中的住宅物業的面積」一節所列停車位之 面積包括相關洋房之車房 (車房於本售樓說明書「期數中的停車位」 一節有所標示) 之全部面積。批地文件指明車房內 用作停放車輛的地方之面積, 請參閱本售樓說明書「期數中的 停車位的樓面平面圖」一節之車位面積。

Enclosed walls, balconies and green features

An issue which people often do not comprehend fully is that, according to the statutory definition of saleable area, the floor area is *measured from the exterior of the enclosing walls*. In other words, the saleable area as quoted by developers covers the area of enclosing walls. In case two adjoining residential properties shared one enclosing wall, section 8(4) of the *Ordinance* provides that the measurement is to be taken from the middle of the wall. Technically speaking, saving the function of separating two residential units, the space occupied by the enclosing walls is not a usable part of the property, therefore it may be contrary to common sense to term it as *saleable*. Also it is very controversial to regard the space taken up by the enclosing wall as part of the internal space of an apartment. Unless they have a professional background in relevant fields, a purchaser is unlikely to perceive such space as part of the saleable area of the residential area, especially if she tries to interpret the concept based on common sense or ties the concept of saleable area to internal floor area or exclusive possession. Thus it is desirable to request developers include the complete definition of saleable area, i.e., section 8 and Part 1 of Schedule 2 of the *Ordinance*, in both Chinese and English in the sales brochure and price list. Provision for sales brochure is contained in section 11(3) in Part 1 of Schedule 1 to the *Ordinance* and provision for price list section 31(3)(b).

Similarly, a balcony is less useful, and is therefore less desired, than indoor space, except perhaps where the balcony affords a tremendous view.[10] Empirical research shows that in general a balcony has a positive effect on the value of a property irrespective of the quality of the view; but it also has negative effects on property prices by causing air and noise pollution; balconies located on the low stories of the buildings will cause additional security concerns (Chau, Wong and Yiu 2003).

Under such circumstances it seems to be logical for developers in Hong Kong to avoid excessive design of enclosing walls and balconies in order to make the properties on sale more appealing to purchasers. Sadly, the opposite turns out to be true. Developers hardly stop building residential developments with balconies and unnecessarily thick enclosing walls. It was revealed in January 2010 that 'the thickness of prefabricated external walls had nearly doubled from between 12.5cm and 18cm from 2003 to 2006, to an average of 30cm in the years after 2006', and as a result, 'Property purchasers could be paying more than HK$100,000 for exterior walls they do not need' (SCMP 2010a).

The reason might be multi-fold. The fact that the first-hand residential real estate market in Hong Kong is always a seller's market is definitely relevant. As the demand for first-hand residential properties far exceeds the supply, there is not really much bargaining power vested in purchasers to oppose the tendency.

A more fundamental reason may be the cost difference between building ordinary rooms on the one hand and enclosing walls and balconies on the other. In 2001 and 2002, the Lands Department, Buildings Department and the Planning Department jointly introduced a *Green and Innovative Building Scheme*. The

Scheme provides incentives for the incorporation of the following *environmentally friendly features*: balconies, wider common corridors and lift lobbies, communal sky gardens, communal podium gardens, acoustic fins, sunshades and reflectors, wing walls, wind catchers and funnels, non-structural prefabricated external walls, utility platforms, mail delivery rooms with mailboxes, noise barriers, and communal sky gardens for non-residential buildings. Subject to certain capping criteria differed from feature to feature, the area of these features will be exempted from the calculation of the gross floor area and site coverage (BD, Lands D and PD 2011a, 2011b).[11]

The purpose of the Scheme is to encourage the construction of green, energy-efficient features in new buildings. The areas of the listed features are exempted from the calculation of total gross floor areas of the building, viz., developers need not allocate to a share of the total building area (which is usually subject to the allowed maximum building area in the Land Grant) for the construction of green features. In other words, the area of green features is to be granted to developers at nil premium.

At the same time, the Scheme does not stipulate that developers should in turn give out the areas of the green features to purchasers for free or at a discounted price, perhaps taking into consideration the construction costs, which account to less than 50 per cent of the sale price per sq. ft. For example, the construction cost for a balcony was estimated to be HK$3,643 per sq. ft., a utility platform HK$1,543 per sq. ft. in 2009; in 2014, the approximate building costs for high-rise non-luxury private housing estate was between HK$16,700 and HK$18,300 per sq. m., i.e., between HK$1,552 and HK$1,700 per sq. ft.; for luxury private housing estate, the average costs are above HK$19,400 per sq. m. or above HK$1,802 per sq. ft. (SCMP 2009). Still, at the end of the day, they are sold at the same price as any other part of the property, which is priced after calculating the cost of construction and the land premium. As such, building green features represents a very lucrative business for developers.

Among the listed features are three items, the area of which, according to the statutory definition, is calculated into the saleable area: *balconies, utility platforms* and *prefabricated walls*. In consequence of this, developers are allowed to build balconies, utility platforms and walls at nil land premium while selling them to purchasers at the same price as any other internal floor area which are granted at the full premium. For example, in the sale of the *Orchard*, the developer paid a land premium of HK$2.37 million for an extra area of 5,089 square metres in floor space for green features, which later might have been sold at HK$366 million in total based on the average price of $6,700 per sq. ft.; in the sale of *Arch*, HK$9.7 million was paid for extra space measuring 3,067 square metres for the eco-friendly facilities worth of HK$339 million valued by the end of the sale; in the sale of *Metro Harbourview*, HK$10 million land premium for 4,896 square metres for green features which was worth HK$226.5 million; and in the sale of *Grand Promenade* the developer paid zero premium for green features areas but might have generated HK$783 million out of the extra 12,143 square metres of ecological facilities (SCMP 2009). The media uttered the view that perhaps the low cost is the driving incentive other than being green and innovative (SCMP 2010b).

Yet, as the definition of saleable area includes the area of balconies, utility platforms and prefabricated walls, the Scheme operates harmoniously under the new regulatory framework based on the *Ordinance*: developers can even boost the saleable area of a residential unit through inclusion of green features.

From the perspective of purchasers, however, balconies, utility platforms and walls are not of the same degree of usability compared to an enclosed room. Price being equal, a purchaser will almost certainly prefer a larger room to a smaller room with a balcony. This is especially the case if we take into consideration the average flat size and the average bedroom size in Hong Kong. The little extra area occupied by the balcony could have been a substantial improvement to the confined indoor area. The building of balconies under such circumstances is not in the general interests of purchasers.

From the perspective of developers, building green features not only helps the vendor to embrace the requirement of sustainable development but also increases the floor area it can build and sell for any given project. Eventually it is more profitable to build a small bedroom with a large balcony than to build a large bedroom with a small balcony, or without a balcony. Now imagine no such Scheme were ever implemented and developers had to build balconies over the floor area granted at full premium. It is unlikely that developers would still choose the design of balcony over internal floor area. In this sense, the Scheme has encouraged a design tendency that prioritises the benefits of developers over the actual need of property users.

In this regard, the Scheme needs immediate revision if not permanent suspension. Eventually, balconies, utility platforms and prefabricated walls should be taken off the list of green features.

Meanwhile, a reduced capping percentage of green features with regard to the total development floor area should be welcomed. In January 2011, the Buildings Department set out *10 per cent* overall cap of the total gross floor area of the development for amenities and green features (BD 2014a). The requirement came into effect from 1 April 2011.

In addition to the general 10 per cent capping percentage, the government has revised the maximum area to be exempted per residential unit of the three saleable-area-related green features in 2006 and 2011 respectively (BD, Lands D and PD 2011a, 2011b). According to the latest standard, for balconies, the summation of areas to be exempted per residential unit used to be 2m² or 4 per cent of the Usable Floor Space of the unit (whichever is the greater), subject to a maximum of 5 m².[12] It has been reduced to 1m² or 2.5 per cent of the Usable Floor Space of the unit (whichever is the greater), subject to a maximum of 3m² in 2011.[13] Plus, no more than 50 per cent of the area of the balcony is to be exempted from the calculation of GFA/Site Coverage calculations.[14] Similarly, no more than 50 per cent of the area of the utility platform is to be exempted,[15] and the maximum area to be exempted per residential unit has been reduced from 1.5m²[16] to 0.75m² in 2011.[17]

The case of non-structural prefabricated external walls is more complicated. In 2006, the maximum thickness of the wall to be exempted is 300mm[18]; it was reduced to 150mm in 2011.[19] However, the rule was later revised to further allow decorative finishes or stone panels of 7.5cm, which means 'a flat purchaser could still get a 22cm-thick, unusable wall within the saleable area of the flat' (SCMP 2011).

Although the total bonus area of non-structural walls developers shall be awarded for one development is capped, no limitation is set out for an individual residential unit. In one development, the area of non-structural prefabricated external walls per residential unit ranges from 0.405m² to 5.349m².[20]

With regard to disclosure of information on gross floor area concessions, the Consent Scheme started to require developers to disclose in the sales brochure the range of thickness of the non-structural prefabricated external walls of each block and *the total area* of the non-structural prefabricated external walls of each unit from June 2010 (Lands D 2010).[21] Under the *Ordinance*, whether the development has any non-structural prefabricated external walls or curtain walls must be disclosed in the sales brochure, together with the range of thickness and total area of these features.[22]

But the *Ordinance* does not explicitly request such information to be listed *immediately* below the information of saleable area, i.e., in the same manner the area information of balconies and utility platforms is presented, i.e., under section 31(2)(d) in price lists. There is no reason why the area of enclosing walls shall not be highlighted for the purchaser's reference. To better inform the purchaser, the *Ordinance* should have required developers to list the total area of non-structural walls in price lists and indicate conspicuously that their area, too, forms part of the saleable area.[23]

Alternatively, the statutory definition of saleable area shall be amended by excluding the area of balconies, utility platforms and enclosing walls from the calculation. This will make the saleable area much more reflective to overall enclosed indoor area of a residential property.

Areas excluded from saleable area

The definition of saleable area is formed by stipulating what is included in and what is excluded from the calculation. The items excluded from calculation are termed as *other areas* under the Consent Scheme. They used to be part of saleable area (Lands D 1993 & 1999). In 2001, the Lands Department required that 'The areas of any cockloft, bay window, car-parking space, yard, terrace, garden, flat roof, roof and any other area as may be permitted by LACO to be included in the saleable area should be specified separately' (Lands D 2001).[24] Then, in October 2008, the area of these features was excluded from the calculation of the saleable area (Lands D 2008).[25]

Cockloft, yard, terrace, garden, flat roof, and roof

For Hong Kong, residential units with a cockloft, a yard, a terrace, a garden or a roof are of minority in the local real estate markets. Usually they are featured units sitting on the top floors of a multi-storey building, or on the ground floors, or independent houses.[26] In general, these architectural structures greatly enhance the value of the property and such added value of course has always been adequately reflected in the selling price.

The exclusion of these items in the calculation of saleable area will give a clear picture of the indoor floor area of the property on sale, but at the same time it will also cause confusion as to the ownership of these areas: are they part of the property on sale or not? Save in the case of flat roof where the deed of mutual covenant designates that the roof is a common area of the building, in most cases if a residential property is sold with a cockloft, yard, terrace, garden, or flat roof, the area of the cockloft, yard, terrace, garden, roof or flat roof is indeed part of the property on sale, i.e., the owner will have exclusive possession of these areas against the rest of the world. Anyone but the owner will commit trespassing by stepping onto the part of the property without the consent of the owner.

In the example of House 20, Phase 1 of *Mount Nicholson*, the property on sale is an independent house with a yard, a garden which contains a swimming pool, a roof and a flat roof. In this case the yard, the garden and the roof all form an organic part of the estate and an inalienable part of the property over which the registered owner of the property shall claim full ownership.

The saleable area of the property calculated according to the statutory definition, i.e., 8,093 sq. ft. including 53 sq. ft. of balcony. At the same time, the area of the yard is 1,131 sq. ft., the garden 2,889 sq. ft., the roof 989 sq. ft. and the flat roof 162 sq. ft. It seems for cases like this, i.e., independent houses with big yards and/ or gardens, the saleable area may cease to be a reflective indicator for the actual area of the property on sale.

And citing the property price per sq. ft. based on saleable area in such cases is more like a mathematic exercise other than to provide meaningful statistics for the reference of the public. In this regard the absence of a statutory definition of gross floor area further complicates the case. Without a statutory definition on gross floor area, any citation of price per sq. ft. based on gross floor area is not possible, and therefore such price cannot be quoted for the cross-reference of the purchasers.

Thus an understanding that the *saleable area* does not equal the total area of the property on sale is critical. There are other areas which are equally *saleable* – as in the natural meaning of the word – yet not being calculated into the saleable area according to the statutory definition.

Car parking space

Car parking space may or may not be sold together with the residential unit under one contract.

It is a common practice for independent houses to have a built-in parking space in the basement, and it would be impossible to sell the independent house without selling the parking space. Even for the sale of residential properties in high-rise buildings, from time to time, parking space is given for free in a 'special offer' or 'promotion'. In these cases, the sale of the property and the sale of the parking space is governed by one agreement for sale and purchase.

When a car-parking space is sold with a residential unit under one contract, the value of the car-parking space will be added into the contract sum; the area of the parking space however is calculated into the *other areas* not the *saleable area*. As such, the unit rate based on saleable area of a residential unit which is sold with a car-parking space under one contract will be higher than a similar unit that is sold without. In this case, the unit rate per sq. ft. based on the saleable area of the property, if disclosed, will generate a *confirmation bias* in a prospective purchaser which might give her an impression that other units (which are sold without the bundle of parking space) have a higher cost-value ratio. In order not to mislead purchasers, the *Ordinance* requests the disclosure of such detail first in the price list issued by the developers, then in the Area Schedule in the sales brochure, and last in the Register for Transactions.[27]

The default situation in the sale of first-hand residential properties, though, is that the parking space is sold individually. Then, a separate agreement for sale and purchase will be executed in terms of the sale of parking space. And when this sale starts, the parking space may also be under construction. As such, the same set issues regarding disclosure of information for sale of residential properties would arise in the sale of parking space too: purchasers need to be informed by the developer on the area, dimension, location of the parking space, etc. The sale of the parking space in these cases is regulated by the Consent Scheme. Developers must issue sales brochure stating a list of information required to be included by the Lands Department (Lands D 2016).

In either case, if there is parking space in the development, the sales brochure for the development must disclose the information and set out the floor plans of parking spaces. The floor plan must show the location of the parking spaces, the number of the parking spaces and the dimensions and area of each of the parking space.[28]

Bay window

The term 'bay window' may refer to two completely different architectural structures for Hong Kong on the one hand and the rest of the world on the other. In England, for example, bay windows are often three-sided with one larger front window built parallel to the inside walls and two supporting sides angled towards the room. In many cases the bay structure runs from the ceiling to the floor. Such structure enhances the view and adds more light and space to the room.

Bay windows in Hong Kong's residential developments bear a different structure. Most are two-sided and L-shaped; if three-sided, the two slanted side windows are vertical to the front window. Most remarkably, all the bay windows in Hong Kong start several feet above from the floor slab and have a base that is significantly higher than the floor level.

The proliferation of bay windows in residential developments does not claim its popularity from the society. Like green features, bay windows have been favoured by developers for a very simple reason: they are granted by the government at nil premium. Since March 1980, the area of projecting windows has been exempted from the gross floor area calculations, provided it meets certain criteria.

The most critical condition is that the base of the window, unfortunately, has to be not less than 500mm above the finished floor level (BD 2014b).[29] The provision is responsible for a portion of internal floor room that is more or less of an embarrassing status for the property user. Being elevated to a level of at least 500mm above the ground, the bay window area cannot be used to accommodate furniture nor can it be converted into a desk in any decent sense (as there is no empty space beneath). Developers would often turn the area into a couch by the window in show flats; but for the majority of apartments in Hong Kong's high-rise buildings, a couch by the window is certainly not a likely option for most property users.

Under the current regulation, the area allowed for bay windows is nothing short of substantial. One bay window can be built for each room within the residential property, i.e., one for the living room, one for the dining room and one for every bedroom, provided the total area of the projecting window does not exceed 50 per cent of the total area of the external wall of the room where the projecting window is located (BD 2014b).[30] If the bay window is permitted to be replaced by internal floor area, it will release much space for the tiny rooms in a typical Hong Kong apartment.

Although the area of the bay window is excluded from the calculation of saleable area, it does not mean that the purchasers are getting them for free. In fact, the purchasers are paying the same price for the bay window and the internal floor area. In a 2010 site visit to a newly completed development in Ma On Shan, the Radio Television Hong Kong (2010) revealed the following facts. In a flat of three bedrooms, the bay window in the master bedroom is of 15.93 sq. ft. (80.5 inches × 28.5 inches), taking up 30 per cent of the internal floor area; the two bay windows in the two smaller bedrooms are 12.27 sq. ft. each or 27 per cent of the room area. Adding the areas of the three bay windows together and multiplying the total area (40.47 sq. ft.) by the unit rate per saleable area (HK$9,953), they revealed the price paid for the bay windows was about HK$ 403, 096. 'If the areas were not occupied by a bay window but were part of the room, it can have accommodated a wardrobe and a desk, enabling the rest of the room large enough to put up a bed,' said Lawrence Poon, the preceding President of the Hong Kong Institute of Surveyors.[31]

Waste of indoor area aside, the structure serves no good purpose in enhancing the outlook of the development or creating a sustainable built environment. Bay windows catch more sunlight and enable higher heat transfer into the room than a window flat to the wall. It is certainly a good thing that bay windows allow more light and heat to flow into the buildings in the British Isles; being placed in Hong

Kong, they just overheat flats in the city's high-rising buildings.[32] While the government is spending tremendous efforts on a sustainable built environment, the efforts are being reversed by the excessive use of air-conditioning to cool down the flats.

In 2008, the Urban Redevelopment Authority of the Singapore government rescinded, exempting the areas of bay windows from the gross floor area, claiming that the practice led to unintended and undesirable consequences (URA 2009). The same unintended and undesirable consequences have occurred in Hong Kong too, which requires a thorough revision of the policy to exempt areas for projected windows. It is one thing to exclude the area of bay window from calculation of the saleable area, it is another to deter developers from building bay windows. One compromised yet acceptable solution would be to cancel the condition that the base of the bay window has to start 500 mm above the finished floor level. In this way, developers will still enjoy some extra area for construction, and the purchasers will get a larger room.

Conclusion

Few will dispute the importance of accurate information on internal floor area in the sale of residential properties. For the *Ordinance*, an accurate, easy-to-understand definition of saleable area reflective of the internal floor area is of paramount importance in fulfilling the legislative purpose to enhance the transparency. The Steering Committee and the Legislative Council had the opportunity to give a new definition in drafting the legislation, yet they were justifiably reluctant to deviate from the established method of calculation by the Consent Scheme. In the end the statutory definition of saleable area seems to repeat the way of thinking under the Consent Scheme, representing the compromise made by developers in accommodating the growing awareness of the general public in information disclosure. Nonetheless, the Consume Council's 2014 survey suggested that an overriding majority of respondents (i.e., 87.9 per cent) agreed such standardization could facilitate prospective purchasers to compare the prices and sizes between different properties (CC 2014).

With regard to the new statutory definition, some tried to explain it in simple terms that saleable area 'only includes the area of the unit and any balcony, utility platform or verandah' (THB 2011). The statement represents a common understanding of the definition by the general public. Still, further attention must be drawn to the fact that for a precise measurement of the saleable area as defined in section 8, the area of the unit should exclude the areas of bay windows and other nine items listed in Part 1 of Schedule 2 to the *Ordinance*. In many cases, purchasers will perceive the saleable area of a residential unit as including the areas of the bay windows but excluding the areas of enclosing walls. But the statutory definition indicates just the contrary.

More difficult than assuming a reasonable purchaser will easily grasp the constituents accurately is giving a clear and precise summary of the definition. The attempt to acquire a closer understanding of the concept by referring to some other commonly-adopted methods of measurement may appear futile too. The saleable area as defined represents an area larger than carpet area, as it is measured from the *exterior of the enclosing walls* and covers the areas of balconies and utility platforms. The closest concept may be *built-up area* of a flat, yet the saleable area excludes the area of the bay windows. By the same token, the saleable area is not equal to the area of the owner's exclusive possession.

A major deficiency of the statutory definition is that the saleable area as defined only represents part of the entire area of the property that is being sold to the purchaser. The word 'saleable' seems to imply that the area excluded from the saleable area is *non-saleable*. It is true that the areas of bay windows, cocklofts, flat roofs, gardens are all excluded from the calculation of saleable area; but the exclusion from calculation in the saleable area does not render these parts free of charge. They still form an organic part of the residential unit as well as of the transaction and being paid by the purchaser. In this regard the abandonment of the concept of gross floor area does not serve the purpose of enhancing transparency, if not to the contrary (to be discussed in Chapter 4). The SRPA should educate the public that the parts constituting the saleable area under section 8 of the *Ordinance* is, still, just one part of property on sale.

Thus a more genuine pro-consumer approach would require a thorough review of the *Green and Innovative Building Scheme* and the regulation that exempts the area of projecting windows from the site coverage and grass floor area, i.e. *Projections in relation to Site Coverage and Plot Ratio Building (Planning) Regulations 20 & 21.*

Four traits should stand out as defining characteristics of the internal space of a residential flat: it must be *usable* (excluding the area of enclosing walls), *enclosed* (excluding the area of balconies, terrace, garden, roof, yard, utility platform, and air conditioning plant form), *grounded* (excluding projecting window base starting above floor slab) and *of the exclusive possession of the residents*. Should opportunity of revision and amendment of the *Ordinance* arise, the following adjustments could be made to the existing definition: it should exclude the areas of enclosing walls; exclude the areas of balconies, utilities platforms and prefabricated walls; and it should include the areas of the bay window, if any. The new definition would be better termed as *usable area* in English with the Chinese translation '實用面積'. The proposed definition essentially represents the carpet area of a unit, and would match a layman's perception of what the indoor area of the unit means.

Another advantage of indicating internal space of a flat with the proposed measurement of *usable area* is the clear demonstration on the area difference between identical flats located on different floor levels, for the internal space is slightly larger for those on upper floors due to the reduction of thickness of structural walls.[33] Such difference is not properly reflected under the current definition.

Notes

1 This chapter was previously published by Devin Lin in the *Construction Law Journal* © Thomson Reuters (Professional) UK Limited: D., Lin, On Saleable Area (2013) *Construction Law Journal*, Issue 4 at 284. Part of this chapter was presented in the *Modern Study in Property Law 2012* at the University of Southampton, England, in March 2012.

2 Per Gerald Godfrey J *(as he then was): Cheng Kwok Fai v Mok Yiu Wah Peter,* [1990] 2 HKLR 440.

3 The Rating and Valuation Department, Property Review 2013, para. 5.1, p.68. Note the Department changed the definition and adopted the statutory definition of the saleablea area after the commencement of the *Ordinance.* See Property Review 2016, para 5.1, p. 68.

4 'We therefore take the view that this definition should be recognized in legislation as the standardized method to describe floor area in all sales literature of uncompleted buildings.' Paragraph 1.21–1.24, *Report on Description of Flats on Sale (Topic 32),* Hong Kong Law Reform Commission, April 1995, pp. 15–16.

5 For a historic review on the evolution on the definition of saleable area, see Malcolm Merry, *Protection of Purchasers of Uncompleted Residential Flats – The Hong Kong Experience,* HKU-NUS-SMU Symposium Paper, Singapore, November 2008, p. 10.

6 A balcony is defined as 'any structure projecting from any wall of any building to carry a floor or roof load either cantilevered or supported by brackets' in Regulation 2(1) of Building (Planning) Regulations, Cap 123F.

7 A verandah is defined as 'any structure projecting from any wall of any building and supported by piers or columns' in Regulation 2(1) of Building (Planning) Regulations, Cap 123F.

8 Ibid, Part 1 in Schedule 2, A2553. The list takes off 'other facilities for the residential property' which were originally included in the draft *Bill* put up for public consultation.

9 Section 8(1), Part 1, *Residential Properties (First-hand Sales) Ordinance,* A2313.

10 Balconies and verandahs in Hong Kong can be either covered or uncovered. A covered balcony provides more privacy and inner space to the user of the flat than an uncovered one. The information whether the balcony is a covered or uncovered one was proposed to be disclosed in the sales brochure. See 1(e) in the Table to Section 20, Schedule 1, Part 2, *Proposed Legislation: Residential Properties (First-hand Sales) Bill,* page 91, Annex A to the *Public Consultation on the Proposed Legislation to Regulate the Sale of First-hand Residential Properties,* the Housing and Transport Bureau, November 2011.

11 Section 4, *Joint Practice Note No. 1: Green and Innovative Buildings,* Lands Department, Buildings Department and the Planning Department, February 2001, revised in January 2011; section 2, the *Joint Practice Note No. 2: Second Package of Incentives to Promote Green and Innovative Buildings,* Lands Department, Buildings Department and the Planning Department, February 2002, revised in January 2011.

12 Section 1(a)(vi) in Appendix A to *Joint Practice Note No. 1: Green and Innovative Buildings,* February 2001, revised in January 2011.

13 Section 1(a)(xi) in Appendix A to *Joint Practice Note No. 1: Green and Innovative Buildings,* February 2001, revised in January 2011.

14 Ibid, Section 1(a)(x) in Appendix A.

15 Section 1(b)(ii) in Appendix A to *Joint Practice Note No. 2: Second Package of Incentives to Promote Green and Innovative Buildings,* February 2002, revised in January 2011.

16 Ibid.

17 Ibid., Section 1(b)(iii) in Appendix A, revised in January 2011.

18 Ibid., Section 1(a)(ii) in Appendix A, revised in January 2011.

19 Ibid.

20 For example, in *Hermitage*, the area of non-structural prefabricated external walls per residential unit is between 0.405 m² to 5.349 m². See section 2 of the sales brochure of *Hermitage*.
21 B2(a)(i) in Annex I to *LACO Circular Memorandum No.62* in *LACO Circular Memorandum No.63*; now B2(a)(i) in Annex to *LACO Circular Memorandum No.68*. For the regulation regarding curtain walls, see (ii). This requirement was not contained in previous REDA Guidelines.
22 Section 4, Schedule 1 – Part 1.
23 Some developers do put a remark in the relevant section in the sales brochure; for an example, please refer to section 2 of the sales brochure of the *Hermitage*.
24 Paragraph 6, Appendix XII, *LACO Circular Memorandum No.40C*, 10 December 2001.
25 Paragraph 3(i)(ii), *LACO Circular Memorandum No. 60*, 10 October 2008.
26 Depending on where and who built them, cocklofts built on New Territories Exempted Houses are generally considered as unauthorized building works.
27 For price list, see the suggested New Template for Price List at Annex F to the *Report of the Steering Committee on Regulation of Sale of First-hand Residential Properties by Legislation*, October 2011; for area schedule in the sales brochure, see the suggested New Template for Area Schedule at Annex G; for Register for Agreement for Sale and Purchase, see section 59(1)(b), A2409–A2411.
28 Section 19(2)(l), Part 2 – Division 2, section 12, Part 1 of Schedule 1 at A2521, *Residential Properties (First-hand Sales) Ordinance*.
29 Paragraph 5(e), *Projections in relation to site coverage and plot ratio Building (Planning) Regulations 20 & 21*, Buildings Department, March 1980; revised in September 2014.
30 Ibid, paragraph 5(a), (b) and (c).
31 http://rthk9.rthk.hk/rthk/news/expressnews/news.htm?expressnews&20100722&55&685318
32 See the blog *Bay windows: Begone!* at http://www.batgung.com/hong-kong-bay-window.
33 Remark 3, Annex F to the *Report of the Steering Committee on Regulation of Sale of First-hand Residential Properties by Legislation*, October 2011.

References

BD (2014a) Building Design to Foster a Quality and Sustainable Built Environment, Buildings Department, 2014.
BD (2014b) Projections in Relation to Site Coverage and Plot Ratio Building (Planning) Regulations 20 & 21, Buildings Department, 2014.
BD, Lands D and PD (2011a) Joint Practice Note No. 1: Green and Innovative Buildings, Buildings Department, Lands Department and the Planning Department, first issued on February 2001and revised on January 2011.
BD, Lands D and PD (2011b) Joint Practice Note No. 2: Second Package of Incentives to Promote Green and Innovative Buildings, Buildings Department, Lands Department and the Planning Department, first issued on February 2002 and revised on January 2011.
CC (2014) Study on the Sales of First-hand Residential Properties, pp. 12, 11 November 2014, Consumer Council, www.consumer.org.hk/ws_en/competition_issues/reports/20141111.html.
Chau, K.W., Wong, S. K. and Yiu, C.Y. (2003) The Value of the Provision of a Balcony in Apartments in Hong Kong, *Property Management,* vol. 22, no. 3, pp. 250–64.

CPPCL (2006) Consultation Document by the Hong Kong Chamber of Professional Property Consultants Limited to the Chairman and Members of the Housing Committee of the Legislative Council, The Hong Kong Chamber of Professional Property Consultants Limited, 18 October 2006 .

LRC (1995) Report on Description of Flats on Sale, the Law Reform Commission of Hong Kong, April 1995.

HKIS (1999) The Code of Measuring Practice, Hong Kong Institute of Surveyors, March 1999, www.hkis.org.hk

HKIS (2008) The Supplement to the Code of Measuring Practice, Hong Kong Institute of Surveyors, August 2008, www.hkis.org.hk

Lands D (1993) Legal Advisory and Conveyancing Office Circular Memorandum No.1, Lands Department Consent Scheme, Legal Advisory and Conveyancing Office, Lands Department, 23 June 1993.

Lands D (1999) Legal Advisory and Conveyancing Office Circular Memorandum No. 40, Lands Department Consent Scheme, Legal Advisory and Conveyancing Office, Lands Department, 28 May 1999.

Lands D (2001) Legal Advisory and Conveyancing Office Circular Memorandum No. 40C, Lands Department Consent Scheme, Legal Advisory and Conveyancing Office, Lands Department, 10 December 2001.

Lands D (2008) Legal Advisory and Conveyancing Office Circular Memorandum No.60, Lands Department Consent Scheme, Legal Advisory and Conveyancing Office, Lands Department, 10 October 2008.

Lands D (2010) Legal Advisory and Conveyancing Office Circular Memorandum No. 62, Lands Department Consent Scheme, Legal Advisory and Conveyancing Office, Lands Department, 2 June 2010.

Lands D (2012) Legal Advisory and Conveyancing Office Circular Memorandum No. 68, Lands Department Consent Scheme, Legal Advisory and Conveyancing Office, Lands Department, 22 March 2012.

Lands D (2016) Legal Advisory and Conveyancing Office Circular Memorandum No. 72C, Lands Department Consent Scheme, Legal Advisory and Conveyancing Office, Lands Department, 28 June 2016.

LC (2007) Disclosure of Saleable Area in Sales Descriptions for Residential Properties, July 2007, *LC Paper No.CB(1)2084/06-07(02)*, Panel on Housing, Legislative Council.

LC (1997) Follow-up on the Miscalculation of Saleable Area at Verbena Heights Reply to the Questions raised by Hon Frederick Fung Kin Kee: 1997, Panel on Housing, Legislative Council, 14 November 1997, www.legco.gov.hk/yr97-98/english/panels/hg/papers/hg17116b.htm.

Lin, D. (2014) Defending Gross Floor Area, *Construction Law Journal*, no. 2, pp. 94–103.

RICS (2007) Code of Measuring Practice, A Guide for Property Professionals, RICS Guidance Note, 6th Edition, The Royal Institution of Chartered Surveyors

RTHK (2010) 新樓盤窗台愈建愈大 買家付數十萬購窗台 Radio Television Hong Kong, 22 July 2010, http://rthk.hk/rthk/news/expressnews/news.htm?expressnews&20100722&55&685318

RVD (2013) *Property Review 2013*, The Rating and Valuation Department.

RVD (2016) *Property Review 2016*, The Rating and Valuation Department.

SC (2011) Report of the Steering Committee on Regulation of Sale of First-hand Residential Properties by Legislation, The Steering Committee, October 2011.

SCMP (2007) What Exactly Are You Buying? It depends on who does the sums, *South China Morning Post*, June 2007, Hong Kong.

SCMP (2008) Major Concession over Calculation of Saleable Area of Flats, *South China Morning Post*, 18 June 2008, Hong Kong.

SCMP (2009) Green Policy Shift May Hit Purchasers, *South China Morning Post*, 30 June 2009, Hong Kong.

SCMP (2010a) Thick Walls May be Padding Purchasers' Costs, *South China Morning Post*, 25 January 2010, Hong Kong.

SCMP (2010b) Review Required on Green Features, *South China Morning Post*, 30 June 2010, Hong Kong.

SCMP (2011) Developers Allowed Grace Period on New Floor Area Rules, *South China Morning Post*, 1 February 2011, Hong Kong.

THB (2011) Public Consultation on the Proposed Legislation to Regulate the Sale of First-hand residential Properties, Transport and Housing Bureau, November 2011.

URA (2009) Circular to Professional Institutes, Circular No: URA/PB/2008/17-DCD, Urban Redevelopment Authority, Singapore Government Singapore, January 2009.

The Vendor of Hermitage (2010) Sales Brochure, 2010.

The Vendor of Mount Nicholson Phrase I (2016) Sales Brochure, 2016, www.mountnicholson.com.hk/brochure

4   Gross floor area[1]

Introduction

Before the commencement of the *Residential Properties (First-hand Sales) Ordinance* (the *Ordinance*) in April 2013, developers used to provide three quotations on the floor area of a new residential flat: the *saleable area*, the *unit covered area* and the *gross floor area*. As discussed in Chapter 3, certain parts were excluded from the calculation of the saleable area: cockloft, bay window, car parking space, yard, terrace, garden, flat roof, roof and air conditioning plant room. The excluded parts were collectively termed as *other areas* under the Consent Scheme. Together, the saleable area and other areas formed the *unit covered area* of a flat.[2] The *gross floor area* (GFA) of a unit was calculated by adding the unit covered area with an apportioned share of common area under the Consent Scheme.[3] Accordingly, two unit rates were provided, one calculated on the basis of the saleable area, another of the gross floor area.

Three quotations on floor area, two quotations on unit rate, a gang of concepts. Still, sale after sale, purchasers seem to have the same unsatisfactory perception upon delivery of the new apartment: *the flat shrinks*. The media remarks that 'Pick up a brochure for any new residential building and it will list the gross floor area of the apartments within. Go to the building itself, though, the floor area of a flat will be less than stated – sometimes by as much as 30 per cent' (SMP 2009a). The critique vividly catches the shared impression on the issue of *shrinkage* for commercial residential properties in Hong Kong. Some regarded the provision of quotation on the gross floor area of the flat was misleading because the quotation would convey the impression that the flat was larger yet the unit rate was lower. Some tried to describe the phenomenon by referring to an *efficiency ratio*, i.e., saleable area/gross floor area ratio. According to *South China Morning Post*, the ratio continues to drop from as high as 90 per cent in the 1980s, to around 80 per cent in the 1990s, then to about 70–75 per cent in the past 10 years (SMP 2009b). Notably two factors may contribute to this phenomenon – the exclusion of cockloft, bay window, car parking space, yard, terrace, garden, flat roof, roof from the calculation of the saleable area in 2008; and the trend to build clubhouse and recreational facilities within the development since the late 1990s.

To tackle the issue of *shrinkage*, the central question revolves around the measurement of gross floor area. Two directions emerged in the discussion before the enactment of the *Ordinance*: one, to standardize gross floor area; two, to abandon the concept completely. Much reluctance of defining gross floor area was seen in the Steering Committee's report (SC 2011); a similar view was expressed in the consultation paper by the Transport and Housing Bureau. The Steering Committee (2011) proposed to abandon gross floor area information per flat and the unit price based on gross floor area. But neither the report nor the consultation paper made it clear that gross floor area as an indicator of floor area should be avoided all together. In the end, the new regulatory system decided to disallow any quotation based on gross floor area in the sales literature. Will this bold move help create a market of higher transparency? Why was the Steering Committee reluctant to provide a statutory gross floor area along with the one on saleable area? In exploring the possibility of a workable statutory definition of gross floor area for the real estate market, this chapter compares the function of the real estate market without a quotation of unit rate based on gross floor area after the commencement of the *Ordinance* with the one before the *Ordinance*, i.e., when the provision of gross floor area and unit rate based on gross floor area was once legitimate.

Common area

When a purchaser of first-hand residential property becomes the owner of the property, she will have the exclusive possession of certain parts of the development; at the same time, she will join the other property owners of the development and become a co-owner of the other parts of the development, i.e., communal and ancillary facilities. This co-ownership of these facilities is represented by a share of the overall common area assigned to each residential unit in the development.

Therefore the Consent Scheme formulated the gross floor area of a residential unit by adding to the *unit covered area* a portion of common area. The unit covered area consists of the saleable area and *other areas*. Now under the *Ordinance*, with the provision of the a statutory definition on saleable area in section 8 and a complete list of specified items representing *other areas* enclosed in Part 1 of Schedule 2, the unit covered area of a residential property can be assured without difficulty. Then, defining gross floor area of a residential unit under such circumstances would be feasible *if* common area can also be defined.

The calculation of saleable area – as under the *Ordinance* now and before 2013 under the Consent Scheme – is still confined to a definite scope. In this respect, the calculation of common area represents a much more liberal practice. Under the Consent Scheme communal facilities such as lift lobbies, lift shafts, electrical meter rooms, refuse room and clubhouse used to be counted into the common area.[4] To the Steering Committee (2011), the common area shall include the areas of lift lobbies, lift shafts, electrical meter rooms, refuse room, clubhouse area, staircase, and transformer rooms. In practice, different developers had developed their own methods of measurement; even the same developer may apply different standards in different projects. Table 4.1 lists items that have been counted into the common area in three 2009 sales of residential properties all by one developer.

The above list is not representative, least exhaustive. Two developers included the space of *security systems* into the common area.[5] In one sale, the developer declared that common area included 'any areas not for exclusive use'.[6] Largely, the standard of measurement remained at the discretion of developers.

As such, will the requirement of information disclosure apply to common area too, i.e., should the information on how much of what is calculated be disclosed to purchasers? The Administration's response exhibited a surprisingly relaxed attitude towards full disclosure. The Steering Committee (2011) suggested that 'developers should only be required to provide area information on those communal facilities that are of interest to ordinary flat purchasers'. The Lands Department insist that disclosure is mandatory 'only if the relevant area information could be verified'.[7] The reason for partial disclosure, according to the Steering Committee, is that there are numerous types of communal facilities.

It is probably true that the types of communal facilities for residential developments in general may be numerous. But *for every individual development* the number of communal facilities is absolutely ascertainable. The flat owners are co-owners of the common areas and therefore they are entitled to know exactly what makes up the common area of the property. Higher transparency can only be achieved if full disclosure of all the communal and ancillary facilities is requested to be disclosed under the *Ordinance*, yet the new legislation only requests the disclosure of a few significant. Among the many facilities offered in a development which can claim a membership in the common area club, the *Ordinance* stipulates that the area information of *clubhouse, communal garden* or *play area for resident's use* needs to be set out in the sales brochure.[8]

Further, since the *gross floor area* consists of the *unit covered area* and the *common area*, and the former is already ascertainable under the *Ordinance*, the question then is: can common area be defined? As suggested by the government,

Table 4.1 *Common Area Constituents in the Latitude, the Aria and Yoho Mid-Town*

	Latitude	Aria	YOHO Mid-Town
Lift Lobbies / Sharfts	√	√	√
Lift Machines Rm	√	√	√
Staircase	√		
Pump Rm	√	√	√
Entrance Lobbies	√	√	√
Caretakers Offices	√	√	√
Refuse Room	√	√	√
F.S. Rm	√	√	√
E&M Rm	√	√	√
E&M Plant Rm	√	√	√
Owner's Committee Office	√	√	√
Clubhouse	√		√
Swimming Pool	√	√	
Jacuzzi		√	

the difficulty lies in the wide scope of different types of communal and ancillary facilities that an exhaustive list for presentation purpose is impossible. But that should not be the end of the story.

As communal facilities have infinite combinations from one development to another, common area cannot be defined by total enumeration, but it can be substantially quantified by listing the most popular ones. Equally practicable, common area can be defined by excluding non-common-area facilities from the overall area of the building. Both approaches are adopted by the *Building Management Ordinance* (Cap 344) in defining *common parts*. Under the *Building Management Ordinance*, the common parts could mean *the whole of a building, except such parts as have been specified or designated in an instrument registered in the Land Registry as being for the exclusive use, occupation or enjoyment of an owner*. Alternatively, it gives a list of facilities in Schedule 1 which together consist of the common parts of the development. The list includes the following facilities:

1   External walls and load bearing walls, foundations, columns, beams and other structural supports.
2   Walls enclosing passageways, corridors and staircases.
3   The roofs, chimneys, gables, gutters, lightning conductors, satellite dishes and ancillary equipment, aerials and aerial cables.
4   Parapet walls, fences and boundary walls.
5   Vents serving two or more flats.
6   Water tanks, reservoirs, pumps, wells, sewers, sewage treatment plants, drains, soil pipes, waste pipes, channels, water-courses, gutters, ducts, downpipes, cables, conduits, refuse chutes, hoppers and refuse container chambers.
7   Cellars, toilets, water closets, wash houses, bathhouses, kitchens and caretakers' flats.
8   Passageways, corridors, staircases, landings, light wells, staircase window frames and glazing, hatchways, roofways and outlets to the roofs and doors and gates giving access thereto.
9   Lifts, escalators, lift shafts and machinery and apparatus used in connection therewith and the housing thereof.
10 Lighting apparatus, air conditioning apparatus, central heating apparatus, fire fighting equipment and installations intended for the use and benefit of all of the owners generally and any room or chamber in which such apparatus, equipment or installation is fitted or installed.
11 Fixtures situated in a flat which are used in connection with the enjoyment of any other flat or other portion of the building.
12 Lawns, gardens and playgrounds and any other recreational areas.
13 Swimming pools, tennis courts, basketball courts, squash courts and premises containing or housing any other sporting or recreational facilities.
14 Clubhouses, gymnasiums, sauna rooms and premises containing health or leisure facilities.

15   Slopes, gradients and retaining walls including sea walls (if any) comprising or forming part of any land which is in common ownership with the building.

A practical statutory definition of common area can be premised on the second approach adopted by the *Building Management Ordinance* (or hereafter *'BMO'*). The list in the First Schedule to the BMO includes the most ordinary communal and ancillary facilities of an estate; therefore the chance that an estate has common parts other than those specified in the list is rare; and in exceptional cases where one or more unlisted facilities are present, the areas of the facilities are unlikely to be considerable.

If this advice can be adopted in the further revision of the *Ordinance*, it will help create a more transparent market in the first-hand residential property sector. As the incident on the status of lobby to fireman's lift in a 2015 sale (to be discussed below) suggested, the absence of a clear definition on common area sometimes will give developers leeway to include certain not-that-exclusive area in the saleable area of the property, which should be recognized as common area had there been a standard definition.

The Building (Planning) Regulations 41A, 41B and 41C require that every building in Hong Kong shall be provided with an adequate number of access staircases, fireman's lifts and/or firefighting and rescue stairways. The construction of the staircases, lifts and stairways allows firemen safe and unobstructed access to various floors of the building in the event of fire (BD 2015). The requirement applies to high-rise residential buildings too. It is not disputable that the staircases, lifts and stairways form part of the common area of the residential building. Still uncertainty will arise in terms of the status of the lobby to a fireman's lift. The lobby must be separated by walls and doors and without any obstruction and lockable door, to a protected exit.[9] In 2015, SRPA found vendors of three sales of first-hand residential properties had included the lobby to the fireman's elevator to form part of a first-hand residential property for sale to purchasers (SRPA 2015a, 2015b). The phenomenon raised two questions. Firstly, should the vendor be requested to disclose the status of the lobby in the sales brochure under section 20(1) of the *Ordinance*? The answer should be in affirmative in observation of the requirement enclosed in section 20(1) of the *Ordinance*. Secondly, does the lobby to the fireman's lift, too, constitute part of the common area? The Buildings Department gave an affirmative answer in its 2015 version of the *Code of Practice for Fire Safety in Buildings 2011*, which states that 'Such lobby should be designed as a common area and an integral part of the fireman's lift so that it could not be readily incorporated as part of any adjacent unit(s) of accommodation' (BD 2015).

Method of calculation

Two approaches of calculation

Once the overall common area of the estate is ascertained according to the approach suggested above, a share can be assigned to each flat. The ratio should be the calculated by dividing the total number of undivided shares of the development with the number of undivided shares assigned to each residential unit. Thus, one way to standardize gross floor area would be *standardizing the common area.*

Yet it has to be noted that under the current regulatory regime adding the unit covered area and a share of common area does not get the end result of gross floor area: this is because certain areas were excluded from calculation of gross floor area under the Green and Innovative Building Scheme. Before the Scheme, *gross floor area, construction area*, and *built-up area* were used interchangeably; all were termed as '建築面積' in Chinese. With the operation of the Scheme, *gross floor area* of a building partakes of a different meaning as the areas of green features, e.g., balconies, wider common corridors and lift lobbies, communal sky gardens, communal podium gardens, acoustic fins, sunshades and reflectors, wing walls, wind catchers and funnels, non-structural prefabricated external walls, utility platforms, mail delivery rooms with mailboxes, noise barriers, and communal sky gardens for non-residential buildings, are exempted from being calculated into the gross floor area (but are still included in the built-up area).

It seems rather unfair to include the areas of such green features into the calculation of saleable area yet, at the same time, exclude the areas from the calculation of gross floor area. In this way a high efficiency ratio will be created, or the comparison of the saleable area and the gross floor area may convey the impression of efficiency to the prospective purchaser. This situation can only be remedied by permanent suspension of the application of the Green and Innovative Building Scheme in residential properties. Accordingly, for the proposed standardized definition of gross floor area, the areas of green features should not be deducted from the calculation.

But still, that is not the only solution. A standardized definition of gross floor area independent of the calculation of common area not only exists in Hong Kong law but also was recommended to be applied to off-plan sales by the Law Reform Commission some 22 years ago. In its 'Report on Description of Flats on Sale', the Law Reform Commission (1995) recommended that, subject to one modification, the regulations 23(3) of the *Building (Planning) Regulations* (Cap 123F) shall be adopted as the standard definition of the gross floor area. Regulation 23(3)(a) provides: 'the gross floor area of a building shall be the area contained within the external walls of building measured at each floor level (including any floor below the level of the ground), together with the area of each balcony in the building, which shall be calculated from the overall dimensions of the balcony (including the thickness of the sides thereof), and the thickness of the external walls of the building.' To sum up, it consists of the three parts: '(i) the area contained within the external walls of building measured at each floor level; (ii) the area of each balcony calculated from the overall dimensions; and (iii) the thickness of the external walls of the building.'

The regulation allows deduction of areas at the discretion of the Building Authority, which includes any floor space that the Authority is satisfied is constructed or intended to be used solely for parking motor vehicles, loading or unloading of motor vehicles, or for refuse storage chambers, refuse storage and material recovery chambers, material recovery chambers, refuse storage and material recovery rooms, refuse chutes, refuse hopper rooms and other types of facilities provided to facilitate the separation of refuse to the satisfaction of the Building Authority, or for access facilities for telecommunications and broadcasting services, or occupied solely by machinery or equipment for any lift, air-conditioning or heating system or any similar service. The Law Reform Commission recommended taking away the discretion. Subject to this modification, the Commission considered the definition as clear and unambiguous as to leave no room for misunderstanding of the calculation of gross floor area. The fact it matches the gross floor area shown on the approved building plans is yet another advantage (LRC 1995).

Disclosure of information on concession on gross floor area

The definition of the gross floor area as enclosed in regulation 23(3)(a) of the *Building (Planning) Regulations* is referred to in the *Ordinance*. Developers must disclose information in application for concession on gross floor area of a building in the sales brochure if they have received concession on gross floor area of the building from the government and the calculation of the gross floor area of the building is modified from the method prescribed in regulation 23(3)(a) of the *Building (Planning) Regulations*.[10]

There are circumstances under which the Building Authority will endorse the application from the developers on concession on gross floor area of a building. If a part of the lot (adjoining street) where the building is erected is dedicated to the public for the purpose of passage or a street-abutting part of the lot is acquired by the government for the purpose of street widening, the Building Authority will give permission for a relaxed method of calculation of the plot ratio and gross floor area of the building.[11] The Authority may exercise the discretion under regulation 23(3)(b) disregarding any floor area that is constructed or intended to be used solely for parking, loading and unloading, refuse and material collection, and access facilities for telecommunication and broadcasting services. The third circumstance is the general exercise of the power invested by section 42(1) of *the Buildings Ordinance* by the Building Authority in permitting modification of regulation 23(3)(a) where any special circumstance renders it desirable for the Authority to do so. This refers to the *Green and Innovative Building Scheme*, under which the construction of environmentally friendly features are encouraged by way of exemption from calculation of gross floor area and site coverage (BD, Lands D and PD 2011).[12]

In any of the three cases (in particular the last scenario), developers must set out in the sales brochure: (i) the information on those areas in relation to which the power is exercised or the permission is given; (ii) the environmental assessment of the building; and (iii) information on the estimated energy performance or consumption for the common parts of the development.[13]

Necessity of a statutory definition

The question then is: is standardization of gross floor area necessary? The other side of the question is: is it feasible and if yes, is it constructive to serve the purpose of enhancing transparency by abandoning information on gross floor area in the sales literature?

The *Ordinance* has made a rather bold move which is quite revolutionary in nature for real estate market to ban the information on gross floor area in the sales literature. For sales brochure, section 20(2) states that sales brochure shall not set out any information on the size or unit price of any residential property in the development otherwise than by reference to the saleable area of that property. For price list, section 31(3)(a) states that a price list for the development must set out the saleable area under subsection (2)(b), the floor area under subsection (2)(d) and the area under subsection (2)(e). Section 31(9) states that a price list for the development must not set out any information in relation to a specified residential property in the development other than the information required by this section. The practical significance of section 31 is that no vendors shall provide information on the price based on gross floor area. Furthermore, for advertisement, section 71(4) provides that an advertisement must not give information on the size or unit price of any specified residential property other than by reference to the saleable area of that property.

This arrangement, being one of the most revolutionary measures brought to the regulatory system by the *Ordinance*, has had a mixed impact on the real estate market. On the one hand, purchasers' attention will be directed solely to the saleable area and therefore will not be misled into believing that the flat represents a larger space than what is quoted as the floor area. On the other, the missing of the information on gross floor area may also cause inconvenience for the purchasers themselves. Subject to the earlier discussion on a standardized definition on gross floor area in this chapter, information on gross floor area should be restored into the sales literature for the following reasons.

Firstly, despite not having a popularly accepted standardized definition, gross floor area has been cited for decades in the local real estate market. This sort of information has been historically provided and local purchasers are quite familiar with the quotation (Pannick, Jones and Leung 2012). As a concept it is so well accepted by the public and deeply embedded in the local practice that it is extremely difficult to uproot entirely.

The *Ordinance* attempts to ban information on gross floor area in the first-hand market; but it cannot, at the same time, restrict the prevalent practice of quoting gross floor area in the second-hand market. To abandon in the first-hand market the use of *the* concept of measurement in the second-hand market would split the market and can confuse the purchaser who is considering buying properties either first-hand or second-hand. Four years after the commencement of the *Ordinance*, quoting gross floor area and price information based on the gross floor area is still a popular practice in the sale of second-hand residential properties.

REDA raised the concern that not allowing developers to cite gross floor area in the first-hand market is discriminatory against owners of first-hand properties. According to REDA, the requirement rendered owners of first-hand residential properties not be on an even playing field with an investor who purchases flats from those owners and then resells the flats as second-hand (REDA 2012).

Secondly, just because the information on common area and gross floor area is not enclosed in the sales brochure and price list does not mean they are not being sold to the purchasers. In this regard, the arrangement deprives of the purchasers' right to know the gross floor area of the flat and, probably contrary to its purpose of enhancing transparency, actually creates information asymmetry. The wording of section 20(2) suggests that the *Ordinance* itself recognizes that the information on gross floor area is of the sort that is known to the vendor but is not known to the general public.

Gross floor area indicates all the areas paid by the purchasers in the deal. Such information is undoubtedly of the interest of the purchaser and therefore should be disclosed in the sales brochure and the agreement for sale and purchase. Ultimately, purchasers become co-owners of the whole estate including the common parts. They are also required under the Deed of Mutual Covenant to share the management fees of the common area (more discussion in Chapter 9). Although these parts are of less value to the property owner compared to the parts of her exclusive possession, it is undeniable that these parts still have value. A most recent quantitative research (Chau and Wong 2012) confirms that the value of common area is at 10 per cent of the internal floor area.[14] Thus REDA is correct to point out that information relating to gross floor area provides more details to potential purchasers with respect to the actual basis of calculating the purchase price of the residential properties. To include information on gross floor area in the price list and sales brochure gives purchasers a better idea of the nature and extent of the common areas serving exclusively the residential part of the development, which may impact on their use and enjoyment and the amount of management fees which they will have to bear (REDA 2012). In his interview with the *South China Morning Post* in an award-winning report (SMP 2009a), Chau also expressed a supportive view: 'If the common areas are sold to purchasers at the same price as a unit's internal area, it would be more reasonable for developers to disclose the composition and distribution of all common areas included in the gross floor area.'[15]

Thirdly, disallowing information on gross floor area in sales brochure and advertisement could potentially give rise to a constitutional challenge to the *Ordinance*. As pointed out by Lord Pannick QC, Tristan Jones, and Wilson Leung in their Joint Opinion (the 'Opinion') on the Bill, to restrict the use of information on gross floor area in the sales literature potentially infringes *the right to freedom of expression* under Article 27 of the Basic Law and Article 16 of the Bill of Rights. Article 16(3) of the Bill of Rights states any restriction on the freedom of expression shall only be such as provided by law and are necessary for respect or reputations of others or for the protection of national security or of public order or of public health or morals (*a legitimate aim*). The Opinion regarded the aim to not allow the use of gross floor area is to avoid confusion among purchasers and the aim cannot be justified as a legitimate aim. The reason according to the Opinion is that the courts should give a generous interpretation to its constitutional guarantee and therefore interpret Article 16(3) narrowly (Pannick, Jones and Leung 2012).

Regardless of how courts will interpret the right under Article 16(2), the fact that information on gross floor area is useful for the purchasers' reference alone is vital to reconcile the aim of not avoiding confusion among purchasers and the means of avoiding information on gross floor area in the sales literature.

Even if the judge is of the opinion the aim is legitimate, to justify the infringement, the government as the decision maker must give cogent reasons.[16] The reasons given by the government can be simply summarized as: (i) it is impossible to work out a definition of gross floor area in the foreseeable future; and (ii) the inconsistency among vendors regarding items in the constituents of apportioned share of common areas in their calculation of gross floor area render purchasers unable to carry out an apple-to-apple comparison of the size, price and 'efficiency ratio' of flats (THB 2012).

As discussed earlier, the inconsistency exists only because there is no definition of gross floor area. Given the availability of statutory definitions of gross floor area and common area, it is unlikely that the court will support the contention. Even if the court accepted that a workable definition of *GFA per flat* is impossible for the time being, the court would not see it as a cogent reason for an infringement of a vested constitutional right.

Further, the restriction hardly survives the proportionality test, i.e., that 'the means used to impair the right must be no more than is necessary to accomplish the legitimate purpose in question'.[17] As long as there is *one* possibility (not to mention existing statutory provisions) to standardize common area and gross floor area, the legitimate purpose in question, i.e., 'to provide information about flat size and flat price per sq. ft./metre in a clear, accurate and consistent manner' – in the words of the Transport and Housing Bureau and the Department of Justice – can be achieved without the need for infringing the right to freedom of expression. In other words, information on gross floor area itself is not misleading; it is the inconsistent ways gross floor area is calculated that makes the information misleading. The court may have tremendous difficulty in understanding why the government, instead of focusing on a standard way to calculate common area and gross floor area, run after developers trying to eliminate some well-established traditions in the business.

The government, citing *Kwok Hay Kwong v Medical Council of Hong Kong*[18] and *Chan Hei Ling Helen v Medical Council of Hong Kong*,[19] raised the point that less justification is required to restrict freedom of speech in advertisement where commercial gain is involved. First of all, the line of *Medical Council* cases is of little assistance to justify prohibition of information on gross floor area in sales brochure and price lists; even for advertisements, a neutral indicator and widely-accepted concept on floor area is unlikely to be considered as a commercial text itself. It is therefore more practical for the government to resort to the line of *Medical Council* cases to justify prohibition of more elaborate texts in advertisements.

Finally, the only way to effectively prevent new flats from 'shrinking' will be to impose an efficiency ratio, a minimum *usable area/gross floor area* ratio that a flat needs to meet. The ratio is implausible unless the definitions of both the usable area and the gross floor area are standardized. That being reached, a ratio no less than 80 per cent is proposed to be prescribed in the legislation to deter shrinkage of flats; exemption should be granted upon application in individual cases, e.g., sale of independent houses or featured apartments with swimming pool, garden or roof.

The advantage of dual pricing

The next question is, if gross floor area is defined and allowed, then should the unit rate of a flat be calculated on the gross floor area basis?

In 2009, when the then Chief Executive Donald Tsang Yam Kuen announced the measure to calculate the unit rate from both the gross floor area and the saleable area, the dual-pricing system was considered as revolutionary. For decades, the local real estate market has been using the *unit rate per sq. ft. calculated from the gross floor area.* As the undefined gross floor area represents an area much larger than the internal floor area of an owner's exclusive possession, it was argued that the quotation was misleading, 'because this creates the impression they are bigger and the price per sq. ft. lower than in reality' (SMP 2009c). So in November 2009, a new measure was introduced to the sales of uncompleted flats: in addition to the price per sq. ft. calculated from the *gross floor area*, the price list should provide the price per sq. ft. calculated from the *saleable area* (REDA 2009).[20] The information should be listed in a separate column entitled the 'Unit Rate of Saleable Area' in the standard Template for Price List (Lands D 2010; see Table 4.2).[21]

A standard Template for Area Schedule must be presented in the sales brochure (see Table 4.3).

The area schedule lists the saleable area, the unit covered area and the gross floor area of a unit respectively. The area of balcony and utility platform are highlighted in separate brackets within the column of the saleable area. For items in the *other areas* category, the area of bay window and air-conditioning plant room are prominently listed in two separate columns with other items in the category to be listed in a third column. The apportioned share of common area should also be separately listed.[22]

Both the Template for Price List as well as the one for Area Schedule in the Sales Brochure had been revised by the Steering Committee in 2011, when new templates were suggested: the price list is shown in Table 4.4.[23] The Area Schedule is shown in Table 4.5.[24]

The difference between the two versions is that information on unit covered area and gross floor area were no longer listed in the suggested new template.

Research on the Consent Scheme expressed the view that with a standard definition on the saleable area and the requirement for developers to calculate the price per sq. ft. with reference to saleable area, the pressure for a standardized

Table 4.2 Template for Price List, Appendix to Annex II in LACO Circular Memorandum No.62, 2 June 2010.

Template for Price List

樓盤名稱 Name of Development, 期數(如有) Phase (if any), 地區 Location

座數 Tower	樓層 Floor	單位 Unit	實用面積 (包括露台及工作平台) (平方呎) Saleable Area (including balcony and utility platform) (sq.ft.)	實用面積呎價 (元,每平方呎) Unit Rate of Saleable Area ($ per sq.ft.)	另 窗台 Bay window	冷氣機房 Airconditioning plant room	單位有蓋面積 (平方呎) Unit Covered Area (sq.ft.)	單位所分攤的公用地方面積 (平方呎) Apportioned Share of Common Area (sq.ft.)	其他面積 (平方呎) 其他如天台、平台、花園、閣樓、天井、大陽台、停車位等(須分別列出) Other Areas (sq.ft.) Other items such as roof, flat roof, garden, cockloft, yard, terrace, car parking space (must be listed separately)	冷氣機平台 (平方呎) Airconditioning platform (sq.ft.)	建築面積 (平方呎) Gross Floor Area (sq.ft.)	建築面積呎價 (元,每平方呎) Unit Rate of Gross Floor Area ($ per sq.ft.)	訂價 (元) Price ($)
5	1	A	581 (露台 : 22) (工作平台 : 16)		12	12	605	153			758		
		B											
		C											
		D											
		E											
	2	A	581 (露台 : 22) (工作平台 : 16)		12	12	605	153			758		
		B											
		C											
		D											
		E											

Table 4.3 Template for Area Schedule, Appendix III(A) in LACO Circular Memorandum No.62, 2 June 2010.

Template for Area Schedule in Sales Brochure

樓盤名稱 Name of Development, 期數(如有) Phase (if any), 地區 Location

座數 Tower	樓層 Floor	單位 Unit	實用面積 (包括露台及工作平台) (平方呎) Saleable Area (including balcony and utility platform) (sq.ft.)	窗台 Bay window	另 冷氣機房 Airconditioning plant room	單位有蓋面積 (平方呎) Unit Covered Area (sq.ft.)	單位所分攤的公用地方面積 (平方呎) Apportioned Share of Common Area (sq.ft.)	建築面積 (平方呎) Gross Floor Area (sq.ft.)	其他面積 (平方呎) (其他如天台、平台、花園、閣樓、天井、大陽台、停車位等須分別列出) Other Areas (sq.ft.) (Other items such as roof, flat roof, garden, cockloft, yard, terrace, car parking space (must be listed separately)	冷氣機平台 (平方呎) Air-conditioning platform (sq.ft.)
5	1	A	581 (露台:22) (工作平台:16)	12	12	605	153	758		
		B								
		C								
		D								
		E								
	2	A	581 (露台:22) (工作平台:16)	12	12	605	153	758		
		B								
		C								
		D								
		E								

Table 4.4 Suggested New Template for Price List, Annex F to Report of the Steering Committee on Regulation of Sale of First-hand Residential Properties by Legislation, October 2011.

Suggested New Template for Price List

樓盤名稱 Name of Development, 期數(如有) Phase (if any), 地區 Location, 第[x]張價單 Price List #[x]

座樓 Tower	樓層 Floor	單位 Unit	實用面積 (包括露台及工作平台)(平方呎) Saleable Area (including balcony and utility platform) (sq. ft.)	訂價 (元) Price ($)	實用面積 呎價 (元, 每平方呎) Unit Rate of Saleable Area ($ per sq. ft.)	屬該單位的其他面積 (不計算入實用面積) Other Areas of the Unit (Not included in the Saleable Area)		
						窗台 (平方呎) Bay window sq. ft.	冷氣機房/冷氣機平台 (平方呎) Air-conditioning plant room/ Air-conditioning platform (sq. ft.)	其他面積 (平方呎) (如有其他屬該單位的下述設施:-天台、平台、梯屋、花園、閣樓、天井、陽台及停車場 必須分別列出) Other Areas (sq. ft.) (If the unit includes the following facilities: roof, flat roof, stairhood, garden, cockloft, yard, terrace and carparking space, they must be listed out separately.)
5	30	A	581 (Balcony: 22) (Utility Platform: 16)	6,400,000	11,015	12	Air-conditioning Platform: 12	Roof: 200
		B						
		C						
		D						
	29	A	581 (Balcony: 22) (Utility Platform: 16)	6,200,000	10,671	12	Air-conditioning Platform: 12	–
		B						
		C						
		D						

(Figures shown in the template are for illustration only)

Table 4.5 Suggested New Template for Area Schedule in Sales Brochure, Annex H to *Report of the Steering Committee on Regulation of Sale of First-hand Residential Properties by Legislation*, October 2011.

Suggested New Template for Area Schedule in Sales Brochure

樓盤名稱 Name of Development, 期數(如有) Phase (if any), 地區 Location

座樓 Tower	樓層 Floor	單位 Unit	實用面積 (包括露台及工作平台) (平方呎) Saleable Area (including balcony and utility platform) (sq. ft.)	窗台 (平方呎) Bay window sq. ft.)	冷氣機房/冷氣機平台 (平方呎) Air-conditioning plant room/ Air-conditioning platform (sq. ft.)	其他面積 (平方呎) (如有其他屬該單位的下述設施:- 天台、平台、梯屋、閣樓、天井、陽台及停車場，必須分別列出) Other Areas of the Unit (Not included in the Saleable Area) (If the unit includes the following facilities: roof, flat roof, stairhood, garden, cockloft, yard, terrace and carparking space, they must be listed out separately.)
5	30	A	581 (Balcony: 22) (Utility Platform: 16)	12	Air-conditioning Platform: 12	Roof: 200
		B				
		C				
		D				
	29	A	581 (Balcony: 22) (Utility Platform: 16)	12	Air-conditioning Platform: 12	—
		B				
		C				
		D				

(Figures shown in the template are for illustration only)

definition of gross floor area might have eased (Goo 2010). This is true in the sense that, provided that the definition of saleable area is impeccable in indicating the internal floor area, the purchaser can draw from the information a genuine perception on the size of the property. The discussion in the previous chapter, however, suggests that the statutory definition of the saleable area under the *Ordinance* is, still, not flawless in performing the role. At the same time, the purchaser does have a right to know what else she is paying for if the floor area is not the only thing she is paying for.

In light of the necessity to standardize gross floor area and to replace the statutory definition of saleable area with a new definition of useable area, it is highly debatable why information about common area and gross floor area should not be listed back into the Area Schedule and the Price List in order to better inform the purchasers how much more is included into the sale. Otherwise, there is no way to restrain developers from adding more items into the calculation of common area and gross floor area. Moreover, the dual-pricing system that highlights the gap between the unit rate of gross floor area and the one of saleable area closely represents the efficiency ratio (the usable area/gross floor area ratio) of a flat: the larger the gap between the two quotations, the lower the efficiency ratio of the property.

Conclusion

In its reading of the draft *Bill* in the Legislative Council, the Bills Committee expressed the view that the Administration should work out a standardized definition of GFA for a property (LC 2012). As illustrated above, both gross floor area per flat and unit rate based on gross floor area are critical indicators for vendors and purchasers; and purchasers are best informed when the two indicators are provided together. The issue is not provision of information on gross floor area but the lack of a standardized definition of gross floor area.

Technically speaking it is possible to define gross floor area per flat based on one of the three calculation methods suggested earlier in this chapter. The technique problem of ascertaining the common area of a development can indeed be overcome by resorting to a representative list or refining the statutory definition of common part under 23(3)(a) of the Building (Planning) Regulations.

To conclude, transparency cannot be achieved by eliminating a vital indicator of floor area from the sales literature (in the risk of violating an invested constitutional right). Rather, to achieve transparency and more importantly to deter developers from building 'shrinking flats', the legislation should provide statutory definitions for both saleable area and gross floor area, and, most ideally, a minimum efficient ratio that every new residential unit must meet.

Notes

1 This chapter was previously published by the author in the *Construction Law Journal* © Thomson Reuters (Professional) UK Limited: Devin Lin (2014) Defending Gross Floor

Area, *Construction Law Journal*, no. 2, pp. 94–103. The article was presented in the Conference Modern Study in Property Law 2012 at the University of Southampton in March 2012.

2 Appendix III (A) and (B) in Annex to *LACO Circular Memorandum No.68*; Remark 2, Appendix in Annex II to *LACO Circular Memorandum No.62.*

3 Ibid.; Remark 3, Appendix in Annex II to *LACO Circular Memorandum No. 62.*

4 Appendix III (A) and (B) in Annex to *LACO Circular Memorandum No. 68*. www.landsd.gov.hk/en/legco/lcm.htm.

5 The sale of *One Pacific Height*; the sale of *Emerald Twenty Eight.*

6 See the sales brochure of *Beacon Lodge.*

7 'Taking into account the fact that there are numerous types of communal facilities, the vendor is only required to provide area information in respect of those communal facilities that are of interest to ordinary flat purchasers and where the relevant area information could be verified…', Public Consultation on the Proposed Legislation to Regulate the Sale of First-hand residential Properties, paragraph 20, page 8, the Housing and Transport Bureau, November 2011.

8 Section 20(1), Part 2 of Schedule 1, *Residential Properties (First-hand Sales) Ordinance*, A2533. The communal garden or play area for residents' use can located either on the roof, or on a floor between the roof and the lowest residential floor of a building or below the lowest residential floor of a building. See also Annex I, *Report of the Steering Committee on Regulation of Sale of First-hand Residential Properties by Legislation*, October 2011.

9 Clause D11.1 provides that 'Each point of discharge from a fireman's lift to the floor served, except at the fire service access point in Subsection D7, should be through a lobby having a floor area of not less than 2.25m² and a minimum dimension of 1.5m. The lobby should be separated from that floor by walls and doors having an FRR of not less than that required for the elements of construction in that floor, subject to a maximum of 120 minutes and complying with the requirements in Table C2'; see ibid.; D11.4.

10 Section 21, Part 2 – Division 2, *Residential Properties (First-hand Sales) Ordinance*, A2341.

11 Regulation 22(1) and (2) of the *Building (Planning) Regulations* (*Cap 123 sub. leg. F*).

12 *Joint Practice Note No. 2: Second Package of Incentives to Promote Green and Innovative Buildings*, February 2002, revised in January 2011.

13 Section 29, Part 3 of Schedule 1, *Residential Properties (First-hand Sales) Ordinance,* A2547.

14 'when the gross floor area is broken down into internal and communal areas, we found that the implicit price of internal area (elasticity = 0.969) is almost ten times that of communal area (elasticity = 0.110). A higher value is therefore attached to exclusively-owned space.' See Chau, K.W. and Wong, Siu Kei, *Externalities of Urban Renewal: A Real Option Perspective, Journal of Real Estate Finance and Economics* (forthcoming), 2012. Ibid., paragraph 31(a) on page 9 and paragraph 40(a) on page 12.

15 Olga Wong and Joyce Ng, Grand illusions, *Sunday Morning Post*, 27 September 2009. Olga Wong and Joyce Ng won the gold award for the best feature story in the Consumer Rights Reporting Awards 2010 with the entry. See Adrian Wan, Post reporters scoop consumer rights awards, *Sunday Morning Post*, 13 June 2010.

16 *Dr Kwong Kwok Hay v Medical Council of Hong Kong* [2008] 3 HKLRD 524, per Ma CJHC, paragraph 23(2).

17 Paragraph 36, *Leung Kwok Hung v HKSAR* (2005) 8 HKCFAR 229, pp. 253I.

18 [2008] 3 HKLRD 524.

19 Case No. CACV403/2006.

20 See REDA Guidelines issued on 23 November 2009.

21 See Appendix in Annex II to *LACO Circular Memorandum No. 62.*

22 Appendix III (A) and (B) in Annex to *LACO Circular Memorandum No. 68*; Appendix in Annex II to *LACO Circular Memorandum No. 62*.
23 Annex F to *Report of the Steering Committee on Regulation of Sale of First-hand Residential Properties by Legislation*, October 2011.
24 Annex H to *Report of the Steering Committee on Regulation of Sale of First-hand Residential Properties by Legislation*, October 2011.

References

BD (2015) Code of Practice for Fire Safety in Buildings 2011, Buildings Department, October 2015, www.bd.gov.hk/english/documents/code/e_fs2011.htm.

BD, Lands D and PD (2011) Joint Practice Note No. 2: Second Package of Incentives to Promote Green and Innovative Buildings, Buildings Department, Lands Department and the Planning Department.

Chau, K.W. and Wong, S. K. (2012) Externalities of Urban Renewal: A Real Option Perspective, *Journal of Real Estate Finance and Economics*.

Goo, S. H. (2010) Regulation of Sale of Off-the-plan Property, *The Conveyancer and Property Lawyer*, no. 2, pp. 138–139.

HTB (2011) Public Consultation on the Proposed Legislation to Regulate the Sale of First-hand Residential Properties, The Housing and Transport Bureau, November 2011.

Lands D (2010) Legal Advisory and Conveyancing Office Circular Memorandum No. 62, Lands Department Consent Scheme, Legal Advisory and Conveyancing Office, Lands Department, 2 June 2010.

Lands D (2012) Legal Advisory and Conveyancing Office Circular Memorandum No. 68, Lands Department Consent Scheme, Legal Advisory and Conveyancing Office, Lands Department, 22 March 2012.

LC (2012) Bills Committee on Residential Properties (First-hand Sales) Bill, Paper for the House Committee, 15 June 2012, LC Paper No. CB(1) 2192/11–12, pp. 8–10, the Legislative Council, Hong Kong. www.legco.gov.hk/yr11-12/english/hc/papers/hc0608cb1-2192-e.pdf

Lin, D. (2013) On Saleable Area, *Construction Law Journal*, no. 4, pp. 284–94.

LRC (1995) Report on Description of Flats on Sale, the Law Reform Commission of Hong Kong, April 1995.

Pannick QC, L., Jones, T. and Leung, W. (2012) Residential Properties (First-hand Sales) Bill-Joint Opinion, April 2012.

REDA (2009) REDA Guidelines for Sales Descriptions of Uncompleted Residential Properties, Real Estate Developers Association of Hong Kong, 23 November 2009.

REDA (2012) Submission of the Real Estate Developers Association of Hong Kong to the Transport and Housing Bureau Consultation Paper on the Proposed Legislation to Regulate the Sale of First-Hand Residential Properties, The Real Estate Developers Association of Hong Kong, pp. 7–12.

SC (2011) Report of the Steering Committee on Regulation of Sale of First-hand Residential Properties by Legislation, The Steering Committee on Regulation of the Sale of First-hand Residential Properties by Legislation, October 2011.

The Vendor of Aria (2009) Sales Brochure.

The Vendor of Beacon Lodge (2008) Sales Brochure.

The Vendor of Emerald Twenty Eight (2009) Sales Brochure.

The Vendor of Latitude (2009) Sales Brochure.

The Vendor of One Pacific Height (2008) Sales Brochure.

The Vendor of Yoho Mid-Town (2009) Sales Brochure.

THB (2012) Administration's Response to Issues Raised by Members at the Bills Committee Meeting held on 22 May 2012, (CB1) 2066/11–12(02) Transport and Housing Bureau, May 2012.

SMP (2009a) Grand Illusions; What You See Is Not Always What You Get When It Comes to Buying a New Apartment in Hong Kong, *Sunday Morning Post*, 27 September 2009.

SMP (2009b) Hong Kong's Incredible Shrinking Flats Revealed, S*unday Morning Post*, 27 September 2009.

SMP (2009c) Purchasers Entitled to Know True Size of Flats They Buy, Editorial, *Sunday Morning Post*, 27 September 2009.

SMP (2010) Post Reporters Scoop Consumer Rights Awards, *Sunday Morning Post*, 13 June 2010.

SRPA (2015a) SRPA Advises Prospective Purchasers on Lobby to Fireman's Lift, Press Releases, the Sales of First-hand Residential Properties Authority, October 23, 2015 www.info.gov.hk/gia/general/201510/23/P201510230356.htm

SRPA (2015b) SRPA's Response to Media Enquiries on Lobby to Fireman's Lift, Press Releases, the Sales of First-hand Residential Properties Authority, October 23, 2015 www.info.gov.hk/gia/general/201510/23/P201510230759.htm

5 Internal structure, fittings and finishes

Introduction

Apart from the size of the apartment, prospective purchasers may be keen to understand the internal partitions of the apartment on sale: i.e., how many rooms does an apartment have, can two small rooms be combined into a larger room (or in some cases can a large room be divided into small rooms), whether the apartment is sold with decoration, what kind of appliances and sanitary wares are installed in the kitchen and bathrooms etc. This brings the discussion to the description and presentation on what is *inside* a residential unit on sale.

The main sources of information to assist a purchaser in envisaging the flat in regards to its dimensions, height and internal partitions are show flats, the floor plan and information enclosed in the section entitled 'Fittings, finishes and appliances' in the sales brochure.

In architectural terms, a *floor plan* is a to-scale diagram demonstrating the relationships between apartments and communal facilities on a floor as well as rooms, spaces and other physical features within the apartment. The Law Reform Commission illustrated the critical role the floor plan plays in the decision-making process of a purchaser as follows: '[t]he floor plan is the predominant, if not the only, means by which the purchaser can make a rational decision in choosing a flat from among hundreds of units in an uncompleted building project or in making a choice between different building projects' (LRC 1995). This point of view is proved as true in a 2014 sale of an uncompleted flat, where the floor plan is the very document that reveals the nature of two rooms in a couple of units as store rooms which were addressed as bedroom and master bedroom by the vendor in some other parts of the sales brochure (SRPA 2014a).

The Law Reform Commission (1995) listed in its report a number of common complaints in relation to the floor plan. Some floor plans did not include dimensions or internal partitions of the individual units; some only included overall external dimensions of a unit; some stated the dimensions of the building site only; and some floor plans were not drawn to scale (LRC 1995). From October 2008, REDA required its member developers to include floor plans of typical and non-typical floors in the sales brochure; although floors with similar layout and external dimensions are allowed to be represented in one floor plan (REDA 2008). In recent years, with more effective measures being introduced to the regulatory regime, such practices gradually disappeared in the sales brochure, at least in sales under the Consent Scheme. In 2011, however, a misrepresentation on a floor plan occurred in a presale of first-hand residential properties under the Non-Consent Scheme: in the sale of the *Icon*, the materials printed by the estate agents had neglected some green features, i.e., balconies and utility platforms, in the floor plan (The Standard 2011).

With the commencement of the *Residential Properties (First-hand Sales) Ordinance* (the *Ordinance*), sales of first-hand properties, either under the Consent Scheme or the Non-Consent Scheme, will be subject to the same statutory requirement. The *Ordinance* requires that floor plans be set out in the sales brochure[1] and be drawn to a scale of at least 1:200.[2]

After the floor plan, the show flat set up by developers for the sale is another main source for information on major physical aspects of the residential units. A show flat is a property unit, or a structure resembling a property unit, that depicts the residential property for viewing by prospective purchasers or by the general public.[3]

Regulating the presentation inside the show flats was a major topic that called for the development of the regulatory regime in 2010 (Lands D 2010a, 2010b; REDA 2010). Being the most attractive sales presentation, the show flat makes the biggest visual impact on prospective purchasers and has the greatest potential to mislead them regarding the size, internal structure and fittings/finishes of the residential unit.

Physical dimensions

Enclosing walls

Whether the external dimensions or the internal dimensions of a flat should be disclosed in the floor plan was pondered upon in the 1990s. The Law Reform Commission (1994) suggested that floor plans in sales brochures should contain information on the external dimensions of individual units together with the critical width and length of internal compartments. The suggestion was turned down by the Law Reform Commission itself due to practicality concerns, for a plan illustrating both the internal and external dimensions of flats would 'result in too detailed a plan' (LRC 1995). Then, under the Consent Scheme, plans of typical and non-typical floors should be showing 'all principal external dimensions of the residential units and the external dimensions of individual compartments in each residential unit' only (Lands D 2012).

Finally the *Ordinance* takes one step further, requiring floor plans to state both *external* dimensions and *internal* dimensions of each residential property in accordance with the approved building plans for the development.[4] The floor plan is accompanied with a note informing prospective purchasers that 'the internal areas of the residential units on the upper floors will generally be slightly larger than the lower floors due to the reducing thickness of the structural walls on the upper floors'.[5]

For show flats, the general rule under the Consent Scheme was that the show flat must be identical to the size and dimensions as specified in the relevant building plans approved by the Building Authority and the sales brochure.[6] The floor plan must be displayed in a prominent location in the show flats.[7] In addition, the developer must deposit with REDA for record purposes: 'a certificate signed by the authorized person certifying that the external parameters of the show flats are identical to those of the actual unit(s)' (Lands D 2010a).[8]

The *Ordinance* requires that a plan that shows the dimensions of the show flat and its internal partitions be displayed in the show flat 'in such a manner that the plan is reasonably visible to any person entering the show flat'.[9] It seems that the certificate signed by the authorized person is no longer insisted upon by the *Ordinance*. The legislation should have preserved the rule in LACO Circular Memorandum No. 62 by engaging the endorsement of the authorized person on the floor plan, with perhaps one amendment that upon the commencement of the legislation the certificate should be deposited with the respective authority established under section 86, i.e., the Sales of First-hand Residential Properties Authority (SRPA).

As most sales offices are located in commercial buildings, e.g., shopping malls, the general rule is subject to one exception where the enclosing walls/boundary walls may give way to passageways due to fire-safety requirements. If enclosing walls cannot be erected for compliance with fire-safety requirements, the Consent Scheme required that 'a solid line should also be provided on the floor showing conspicuously the exact position and the identical thickness/width of the respective non-structural internal walls/partitions', with a notice of conspicuous size displayed in a prominent location of the show flats stating the fact that passageways are not part of the actual units (Lands D 2010a).

The exceptional scenario is further specified in the *Ordinance*: regulation 41(1) of the Building (Planning) Regulations provides 'every building shall be provided with such means of escape in case of emergency as may be required by the intended use of the building', thus if a passageway or a door is provided through an enclosing or boundary wall of a show flat as a means of escape, the vendor must provide a solid line on the floor showing the position and thickness of the enclosing or boundary wall and a notice stating that there is no such passageway or door in the residential property must be displayed reasonably visible to any person entering the show flat.[10] The new standard, i.e., 'reasonably visible to any person entering the show flat', indicates a high degree of objectivity, whereas the old standard under the Consent Scheme, i.e., 'of conspicuous size', is more subjective.

Entrance door

Before June 2010, most show flats did not have entrance doors. The viewers may easily mistake the open space connecting the show flats to the rest of the sales centre as part of the show flats. LACO Circular Memorandum No.62 provided that all show flats must display the main entrance doors (Lands D 2010a). The

Ordinance does not explicitly stipulate that the main entrance door should be displayed, but it states that the vendor must provide *doors* in the show flats in the same way as they will be provided in the residential property as depicted in the sales brochure for the development.[11]

Bay windows, A/C plant room, balcony and utility platform

For the floor plan, the external dimensions of the property should, of course, include the dimensions of balconies, utilities platforms and air-conditioning plant rooms. This seems to be an inherent requirement that the *Ordinance* does not even mention the dimensions of balconies, utilities platforms and air-conditioning plant rooms when addressing the drawing of the floor plan in section 10 of Part 1 of Schedule 1. The need of inclusion becomes apparent with a cross reference to the requirement for a show flat, where the *Ordinance* stipulates that the plan the vendor must display in the show flat must show the dimensions of the internal partitions, and any bay windows, air-conditioning plant rooms, balconies, utility platforms and verandahs.[12] An incident that occurred in the sale of the *Icon* (in which the floor plan failed to illustrate green features of the residential units) suggests that these requirements should be extended to marketing materials produced and provided by estate agents.

According to section 39(2) of the *Ordinance*, developers must include balconies, utility platforms or verandahs in the show flats with boundary walls/parapets.[13] Section 39 alone is silent on whether vendors should provide show flats air-conditioning plant rooms. The answer given by LACO Circular Memorandum No. 62 is in the affirmative; yet it also prescribed that developers ought not to include in the show flat any air-conditioning plant room which is located outside the units in the show flats (Lands D 2010a). The *Residential Properties (First-hand Sales) Bill* (hereafter the *Bill*) enclosed in the Consultation Paper by the Transportation and Housing Bureau (2011) required that for both modified and unmodified show flats, the dimensions of balconies, utility platforms, verandahs and air-conditioning plant forms must be the same as specified in both the sales brochure and the approved building plans for the development.[14] Back to the *Ordinance*, the question should still be answered in the affirmative, i.e., that air-conditioning plant rooms must be provided in show flats, as section 36 and section 37 provide that any bay windows, air-conditioning plant rooms, balconies, utility platforms and verandahs in unmodified show flat and modified show flat must be the same as those in the residential property as depicted in the sales brochure for the development.

Ceiling

The external/internal dimensions determine the size and two-dimensional layout of a residential property, but a third dimension must be added to appreciate the complete picture of the internal space of a unit. The floor height of a property is an essential element to the enjoyment of the property by the owner. The height may also play a critical part in the assessment of the property value for commercial properties, e.g., shops in particular. Misrepresentation on the height of the property was not common for sale of residential properties, but in one presale of commercial properties which took place in the not too remote past, the floor height of the pre-sold shop in *Wanchai Plaza* must have been inaccurately dealt with in the sales literature; otherwise it would be very difficult to understand why a couple of investors had purchased shops which cannot even accommodate a person of moderate height upon delivery.

This example illustrates the significance of floor height of properties, but according to media reports, in presales, the measurements and information on floor height are often ignored by the flat purchasers (SCMP 2007).

Among all the kinds of residential properties sold in Hong Kong, only the New Territories Exempted Houses are under statutory control in regard to the height of each storey.[15]

There are two principal ways to calculate the floor height of a residential unit: the *floor-to-floor height* and the *floor-to-ceiling height*. The difference between the two is that floor-to-floor height includes the thickness of the floor slabs, whereas the floor-to-ceiling height indicates the height of the space between the floor and the ceiling. The floor-to-ceiling height is termed as the *projected height* (or in Chinese, '預計高度') of a unit, i.e., the height of the residential property as calculated by deducting the thickness of the floor slab of the residential property from the floor-to-floor height of the residential property.[16]

The floor plan must state, in accordance with the approved building plans for the development, the floor-to-floor height of the residential units and the thickness of the floor slabs (excluding plaster) of each residential property.[17] But it does not need to state the floor-to-ceiling height, or the projected height. Some would-be purchasers may mistake the floor-to-floor height as the floor-to-ceiling height. It would seem, unless one has a relevant background in building, construction or conveyancing, few would take into consideration the thickness of the floor slabs. The Consumer Council also suggests the floor-to-ceiling height to be provided in the sales brochure, especially for a property with different internal floor heights. In this case, prospective purchasers will find it difficult to ascertain from the sales brochure what the actual head room will be (CC 2014). Thus the concept of projected height, viz., the floor-to-ceiling height, is the most suitable indicator of the floor height in the sale literature. It is therefore recommended to be clearly stated in the floor plan.

Show flats, both unmodified and modified, must construct a ceiling in such a way that the floor-to-ceiling height of the show flat does not exceed that specified in sales brochures and approved building plans (Lands D 2010a).[18] The *Ordinance* strictly prohibits the floor-to-ceiling height of the show flat exceeding that of the real unit; but it allows the floor-to-ceiling height of the show flat to be less than the corresponding projected height of the residential property. In such circumstance the vendor must display in the show flat a notice stating the difference between those heights.[19]

Fixed windows

Fixed windows are installed to minimise the noise impact on the residential properties; they may not have the same function as ordinary windows: i.e., in some cases fixed windows are never meant to be opened. Plus, the installation of fixed windows may indicate a high level of noise near the development. In 2014 the Authority advised prospective purchasers to be aware of the functions and implications of fixed windows by referring the information enclosed in the section entitled 'relevant information' in the sales brochures (SRPA 2014b).

Internal partitions

One of the main functions of a floor plan and a show flat is to present the internal structure of a flat, the number of rooms and the general layout of each compartment (living room, bed rooms, kitchen, bathroom(s) etc.) The *Ordinance* requires that the floor plan set out the information on the external dimensions of individual compartments in each residential unit[20] as well as the thickness of the internal partitions of each residential property.[21]

Depending on the number of family members and other circumstances, some purchaser may prefer a flat of three small bedrooms, while others enjoy two bigger rooms. Prospective purchasers of flats with multiple rooms may want to figure out whether the partition walls between the two small bedrooms can be removed. Similarly, some may prefer an open kitchen to an enclosed kitchen. In the sale of *Icon*, one purchaser described her flat bought at HK$9.7 million as resembling a 'rubbish dump' after discovering the promised open kitchen was replaced by a tiny room (The Standard 2011).

Imagine a purchaser who bought a unit of three rooms with the intention to convert the two small rooms into a big room was told that the partition wall between the small rooms cannot be removed. In such circumstance to argue that the purchaser is not getting what she has bargained for under the contract may be making a far-fetched statement, but practically speaking she could not enjoy the flat up to her expectations. Such expectations could indeed be created by the modified show flats in the first place – if an irremovable structural wall was not accurately presented in the show flat. Those grey areas, i.e., where the law of contract can barely provide any remedies for the purchasers, call for statutory protection. The Law Reform Commission (1995) has long recommended that floor plan clearly mark the *load bearing walls* of the unit.[22] It is critical that the floor plan differentiates load bearing walls and non-load-bearing walls. The *Ordinance* should have demanded disclosure of such information and accurate presentation in the floor plan.

For show flats, double standards are applied to unmodified and modified show flats. The internal partitions in the unmodified show flats must be the same as depicted in the sales brochure.[23] For modified flats, the *Ordinance* does not prohibit developers from removing partitions walls or doors if such exercise does not involve the structure of the building.[24] In these cases, the vendor need mark a solid line on the floor of the show flat showing the position and thickness of the partition; at the same time, they need to display in the show flat a plan with the details of the layout, orientation and thickness of all the internal partitions.[25] Such plan should, again, be reasonably visible for everyone entering the show flat.

Types of rooms

In the sale of *Double Cove Starview Prime in Double Cove Phase 3*, for Flats A and H on certain floors in one block of the development, the vendor had, on another occasion in the sales brochure, indicated the two rooms as the bedroom and master bedroom respectively. However, there was no window installed for the room addressed as the bedroom and only a fixed window which was not openable in the room addressed as the master bedroom (SRPA 2014a). As such, both rooms were not originally intended to be used as bedrooms. Such facts are clearly demonstrated in the floor plan with dark solid line enclosing the external dimension of store room 1 and store room 2.

For the better information of purchasers, the *Ordinance* may require the vendor to further highlight the types of windows for each room in the floor plan: i.e., window, fixed window (which is not openable) or no window.

Exposed pipes

A description of exposed pipes in sales brochures was first recommended by the Law Reform Commission (1995). The draft *Bill* enclosed in the Consultation Paper (THB 2011) suggested that the floor plan should specify the location of fittings/features affecting the enjoyment of a residential unit including the exposed pipes. But this requirement did not appear in the final draft of the *Bill* and therefore did not make its way to the *Ordinance*.

The existence of exposed pipes should be demonstrated, at least in unmodified show flats. If there are technical problems to showcase pipes in the show flat, a feasible way is to require developers to mark the parts which are affected by exposed pipes in the unmodified show flat and display a notice stating the fact.

Furniture

The practice of drawing a furnished room in the sales brochure caught the attention of the Law Reform Commission in 1995. 'There have been instances of the so-called 'Shrunk Flat'. The drawing in the sales brochure in such cases showed that the bedroom could accommodate a double bed, a side table and a wardrobe. In reality, however, the bedroom was found to be about 3 square metres only which was insufficient to fit a normal double bed' (LRC 1995). Sixteen years later, the Steering Committee felt the same need to regulate drawing of furniture shown on floor plans. In their words, 'a double-bed is shown in the floor plan of the bedroom but in reality, the size of the bedroom is actually not big enough to accommodate a double-bed.' The Committee recommends 'for floor plans

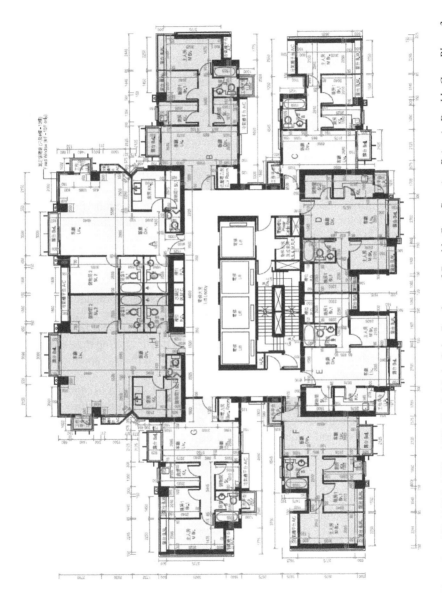

Figure 5.1 Floor Plan, 8/F-11/F & 16/F – 19/F, Block 25, the Sales Brochure of *Double Cove Starview Prime in Double Cove Phase 3*

Reproduced by kind permission of Henderson Land Development Company Limited and Dennis Lau & Ng Chun Man Architects & Engineers (HK) Ltd.

provided in the developers' website, any furniture shown must be drawn to scale with dimensions, and the scale of the floor plans should be specified' (SC 2011).

The issue was not highlighted when the *Bill* was introduced to the Legislative Council; but it was timely added to the *Ordinance* during the reading of the *Bill*. The *Ordinance* prescribes that if developers draw furniture on the floor plan, they must show the dimensions of the furniture.[26] With the information on dimensions of the furniture, mindful purchasers may get a clear picture on whether or not the size of the furniture has been deliberately cut down to exaggerate the flat size. Then it is a matter of degree on the mindfulness of the purchasers in paying attention to the information.

The only concern left would be whether the information on the size of the furniture could, in case such information suggests that the dimensions of the furniture drawn on the floor plan are unusual, effectively counter-balance the visual effect of a rather spacious room in the floor plan, given there is no general standard for pieces of furniture such as a couch or a dining table; even for furniture with a common standard, a double-bed, for example, varies from a standard, a Queen size to a King size.

A parallel phenomenon exists in show flats. Over the years, developers were seen to display shallow furniture in the show flats (SCMP 2009). The display of smaller-than-usual furniture is not explicitly prohibited by the *Ordinance*, but according to section 42 of the new legislation, the vendor must not restrict any person who views the show flat from taking measurements of the show flat. Thus purchasers can tell whether any furniture displayed in show flats is smaller-than-usual.

In some modified show flats some developers tried to convert the bay window into a desk, where they placed a slightly larger stone/wood countertop on the surface of the bay window. Books and sometimes a laptop were nicely placed on the countertop, and a chair was placed nearby to create the image of a working platform for the owner. With one or two inches' extended margin from the surface of the bay window, the stone/wood countertop blocks the solid wall underneath it. A viewer who does not pay attention to the space under the countertop may have believed it is a normal desk, i.e., empty space beneath the countertop. This practice is obviously misleading and should be disallowed in the construction of modified show flats.

Fittings, finishes and appliances

Nowadays in Hong Kong the sale of first-hand residential properties seldom concern the sale of raw apartments, i.e., apartments with almost no fittings and finishes. The default position is the majority, if not all, of the apartments in a development will be sold with basic fittings and finishes, i.e., tiles on the floor and oil paint on the wall, and a fully furnished kitchen with new appliances and bathrooms where sanitary items are installed.

In general, the developers will undertake the basic interior fitting out works for individual units and the common area of the development. The costs of the fitting-out works and the appliances form part of the contract price, yet sometimes they are said to be *gifts* from developers.

Being an intrinsic element to an optimal living environment for residents, the quality and design of fittings and finishes set the taste level of the development and spell the integrity of the developers. Empirical research suggested the connection between a developers' reputation, the housing quality and the transaction prices (Chau, Wong and Yiu 2007). Beyond that, purchasers may place great reliance on the descriptions in the sales brochure or refer to items displayed in show flats. The provision of accurate information in this area is critical for the reference of purchasers in sales of properties by private and public developers.

When the flats were handed to the owners of *Marina Habitat*, the Housing Society received a large number of complaints about the tiles in the kitchens and bathrooms. Both the sales brochure and the agreement for sale and purchase read 'high quality glazed ceramic tiles up to the ceiling'; the show flats also displayed the tiles from floor level to the ceiling; but in actual flats a part of the walls was not covered by the tiles. In the end, the Housing Society reimbursed the owners of the development for the difference (Fan 2005).

Description in the sales brochure

B17 in the Annex to the LACO Circular Memorandum No. 68 provided a recommended list in Appendix V on the items the *material* or *type*, or both of which should be specified in the sales brochure. Then in the *Ordinance* the list emerges as a more detailed table of two columns divided into four categories, i.e., exterior finishes, interior finishes, interior fittings and miscellaneous, enclosed in section 22, Part 2 of Schedule 1, which includes the following items: external wall, window, bay window, planter, verandah or balcony, drying facilities for clothing; lobby, internal wall and ceiling, internal floor, bathroom, kitchen; doors, bedroom, telephone, aerials, electrical installations, gas supply, washing machine connection point, water supply; lifts, letter box, refuse collection, water meter, electricity meter and gas meter, security facilities and appliances (Lands D 2010a, 2010b).[27]

The list is meant to be exhaustive, yet some must-haves are missing. One example is the *air-conditioner* suggested by the Law Reform Commission (LRC 1995). At the same time, for some developments, all the items listed in the Table are not present in all the units. How should the Table reflect such facts? This requires a detailed examination on the wording of section 22(1), Part 2 of Schedule 1.

The subsection states: *the sales brochure must, in relation to each item in the development specified in column 1 of the following table, set out the description specified opposite to it in column 2 of the table.* The first question is if one item is completely not applicable to the entire development, should the item still be included in the table? The answer must be yes. The subsection states that the sales brochure must set out a description in column 2 for each item specified in column

1, and no statement is made to the fact that any item specified in column 1 can be taken off from column 1 in case of inapplicability. Therefore, in the sale of *Wings IIIA*, a development with no bay windows, the developer has put the word 'Nil' in Column 2 opposite to the term Bay Window in Column 1.

A more complicated question arises when the item is available only in some of the units of the development. It should not be disputable that the vendor should include the item in the table, but does the subsection require the vendor to indicate the availability or – perhaps more properly put – the unavailability of the item? For example, in the development of *Wings IIIA*, town gas supply pipes were installed in a number of units but not all of the units. The sales brochure had only highlighted the units that were installed with the gas supply pipes in Column 2 opposite to Gas Supply in Column 1. This triggered the issue of a reminder by the SRPA, which stated the fact that gas supply pipes are not installed in the kitchens of some of the residential properties in the development (SRPA 2014c). In cases of such, it is the units *without* the installation of the gas pipes that most urgently call for the attention of the purchasers. The law could set out a more detailed requirement to guide vendors to list the units without the installation of a specified item in Column 2.

After availability, Column 2 needs to describe either the *type*, or the *material*, or both of the specified items. In cases of the bathroom and kitchen, the description should include whether the wall finishes run up to the ceiling. In cases of electrical installations and water supply, it needs to make clear whether the conduits or water pipes are concealed or exposed; and whether hot water is available.

In cases of lifts and appliances, the vendor must disclose the *brand name* and *model number*; in addition, the vendor must undertake that if the lifts or appliances of the specified brand name or model number are not installed in the development, products of comparable quality will be installed.[28] The requirement bears further clarification. At first glance it seems to provide additional protection to the purchasers in case of unavailability of the specified items. However, the subsection, i.e., section 22(2), Part 2 of Schedule 1, does not prohibit developers from using alternatives for lifts and appliances at all. The only requirement is that the alternatives must be of *comparable quality*. It does not stipulate that the alternatives can only be used if the specified lifts or appliances are not available. It therefore may open the backdoor for alternative materials. And whether the alternative is of 'comparable quality' may be completely subject to the assessment of the vendor. As such, the subsection may introduce uncertainty to the sale. It should perhaps be better drafted that the installation of alternatives must be proposed by the vendor and endorsed by the SRPA in case of genuine unavailability of the respective items specified in the sales brochure and the agreement for sale and purchase.

Other than lifts and appliances, developers are not required by the *Ordinance* to identify other attributes of the products, e.g. *brand names*, *country of origin*, or *classification*. Statements such as 'marble/granite to exposed surface' or 'wooden basin cabinet with natural stone countertop and sanitary fittings' could be good examples that comply with section 22, Part 2 of Schedule 1. However, the first statement does not prescribe the qualification of the marble/granite; and a purchaser cannot get much information from the second statement on the manufacturers of the cabinet or the colour of the stone counter top. In other words, the degree of disclosure permitted by the *Ordinance* may still leave prospective purchasers under-informed. This is especially true for sanitary wares and fittings. Overall, the *Ordinance* should have required more detailed specifications of fittings and finishes to be disclosed in the sales brochure.

At the same time, it seems that, subject to the general provision on misrepresentation and dissemination of false or misleading information as well as the requirement to set out the brand name and model number of appliances installed in the development, the new legislation does not prohibit the use of vague descriptions such as 'high class', 'of internationally known manufacturers', 'high quality', 'imported' and 'deluxe', which in the opinion of the Law Reform Commission should be avoided in the sales literature (LRC 1995).[29]

Display in the show flats

The display of fittings, finishes and appliances in the show flats is equally problematic. It was no secret that developers used to impress potential purchasers with fittings and finishes of higher quality and more luxurious brands in the show flats than those as prescribed in the contract.

LACO Circular Memorandum No. 62 demanded that fittings and finishes presented in the show flats ought to be identical to those specified in the agreement for sale and purchase and in the sales brochure.[30] It however allowed alternative fittings and finishes to be used in show flats provided they are *of comparable quality*. If so, a notice of conspicuous size had to be displayed in a prominent location (Lands D 2010a).[31] This may leave room for exaggeration and misrepresentation, for it was always up to the developer to decide whether the substitutes are of comparable quality to those specified in the agreement for sale and purchase. The Law Reform Commission (1995) suggested that 'the Authorized Person of the development project certifies that in his professional opinion the substitute materials are of comparable quality and standard to the intended materials.' Now under the *Ordinance*, mandatory provisions are required to be contained in the agreement for sale and purchase to the effect that if the vendor is prevented by force majeure or other reason beyond its control from obtaining such fittings, finishes and appliances, other fittings, finishes and appliances certified by the Authorized Peron to be of comparable quality may be substituted.[32]

The *Ordinance* provides in section 36(1)(e) that for unmodified flats, the fittings, finishes and appliances in the show flats must be the same as those in the residential property as depicted in the sales brochure; but it goes on to suggest that section 36 (1)(e) is satisfied, even if the fitting, finish or appliance in the show flat is different from what is depicted in the sales brochure for the development, provided that the vendor displays in the show flat a notice stating that the difference and the quality of the fitting, finish or appliance displayed in the show flat is *comparable to the quality of* that in the residential property.[33] Here the *Ordinance* may have taken a step back from the direction of enhancing transparency by allowing the presentation of alternative fittings, finishes and appliances in unmodified show flats, albeit of comparable quality.

Divergence of an even higher degree is granted to modified show flats, which can, as the *Ordinance* so stipulates, bring in fittings, finishes and appliances that will not be included in the residential property. The *Ordinance* requires developers to display a notice in the modified show flats setting out those to be included in the real flats and those not to be included.[34] The installation of appliances in modified show flats which will not be installed in the real flats is not constructive either for prospective purchasers to create a clear picture of the actual fittings, finishes and appliances to be installed in the real flat. The use of these equivalents risk causing confusion among purchasers.

This is to be contrasted with *The Consumer Protection from Unfair Trading Regulations 2008*, which prohibits the practice of 'promoting a product similar to a product made by a particular manufacturer in such a manner as deliberately to mislead the consumer into believing that the product is made by that same manufacturer when it is not'. If a trader, in this case, the vendor, engages in the practice, the person is guilty of an offence.[35]

It is therefore highly advised that alternative fittings and finishes should be strictly prohibited in both unmodified and modified show flats. It can hardly be justified that alternatives are used in the show flats simply because the items specified in the sales brochure are out of stock. The very fact that the item is out of stock even for show flats gives rise to the question about the vendor's capacity to source and install such items in all of the units.

Beyond that, the vendor should be allowed to enjoy a comparatively high degree of freedom in creating the modified show flats. Introducing alternative fittings and finishes (other than appliances) that can be installed yet are not provided in the real flats into the modified show flats will not be misleading provided they are well indicated as excluded items for real flats in the list. In addition, in case of uncertainty, cross-references can be conveniently made to the unmodified pairing flats.

Conclusion

The *Ordinance* has accepted and refined the major requirements regarding information disclosure on fittings and finishes under the Consent Scheme. For some regulations, the *Ordinance* has extended the requirement by the Consent Scheme even further, i.e., to replace the standard 'of conspicuous size displayed in a prominent location' by 'reasonably visible to any person entering the show flat' for any important notices, documents and plans to be displayed in the show flats. When it comes to the presentation on the items that require such notice, however, the *Ordinance* seems to exhibit a rather relaxed approach in regulating its presentation in the show flats, for example, allowing alternative fittings, finishes and appliances in both unmodified and modified show flats (albeit with notice of conspicuous size to be displayed nearby).

Overall, in the first four years since its commencement, the new legislation has appeared to be effective in enhancing the transparency in requesting information disclosure on internal partitions, fittings, finishes and appliances by implementing respective statutory requirements.

Notes

1 Section 19(2)(j), Part 2 – Division 2, A2335; Section 10, Part 1 of Schedule 1, A2517-A2519, *Residential Properties (First-hand Sales) Ordinance*. See also Section 10(1)(j), Division 2, Part 2, *Proposed Legislation: Residential Properties (First-hand Sales) Bill*, p. 14, Annex A to the *Public Consultation on the Proposed Legislation to Regulate the Sale of First-hand residential Properties*, the Housing and Transport Bureau, November 2011.
2 The scale must be marked on the plans. See ibid, section 10(2)(a), Part 1 of Schedule 1, A2517.
3 Ibid., section 12, Part 2–Division 1, A2327.
4 Ibid., section 10(2)(d)(i) and (ii), Part 1 of Schedule 1, A2517. See also section 10(2)(b) (i) and (ii), Schedule 1, Part 1, *Proposed Legislation: Residential Properties (First-hand Sales) Bill*, p. 84, Annex A to the *Public Consultation on the Proposed Legislation to Regulate the Sale of First-hand residential Properties*, the Housing and Transport Bureau, November 2011.
5 Ibid., section 10(2)(e), A2519.
6 Section 2 in Annex III to *LACO Circular Memorandum No. 62*.
7 Ibid., section 3.
8 Ibid., section 11.
9 Ibid., Section 39(3) and (6), Part 2 – Division 4, A2379. See also Section 36(4)(b), Division 4, Part 2.
10 Ibid., Section 39(4). See also section 36(4), Division 4, Part 2.
11 Ibid., Section 40(2), A2381. See also section 37(2) and section 38(2).
12 Ibid., section 39(3)(b), A2379. See also section 36(3).
13 Ibid., section 39(2), A2379. See also section 36(2).
14 This requirement applies to both unmodified show flats and modified show flats. For unmodified show flats, see section 23(1)(b); for modified show flats, see section 24(b), Division 4, Part 2, *Proposed Legislation: Residential Properties (First-hand Sales) Bill*, page 31, Annex A to the *Public Consultation on the Proposed Legislation to Regulate the Sale of First-hand residential Properties*, the Housing and Transport Bureau, November 2011.
15 Schedule to Cap 121, *Buildings Ordinance (Application to the New Territories) Ordinance*.
16 Section 12, Part 2 – Division 1, *Residential Properties (First-hand Sales) Ordinance*, A2327.
17 Ibid., section 10(2)(c), Part 1 of Schedule 1, A2517.
18 Ibid., section 36(1)(c) and 37(1)(c), Part 2 – Division 4, A2373-A2375. See also section 7 in Annex III to *LACO Circular Memorandum No.62*.
19 Ibid., section 39(5), Part 2 – Division 4, at A2379.
20 Ibid., section 10(2)(d)(iv), Part 1 of Schedule 1, A2519.
21 Ibid., section 10(2)(d)(iii), Part 1 of Schedule 1, A2519.
22 Paragraph 2.15 in the *Report on Description of Flats on Sale*, the Law Reform Commission of Hong Kong, April 1995, p. 25. The suggestion is not reflected in the *Ordinance*.
23 Section 39(3)(b) and 40(2), Part 2 – Division 4, *Residential Properties (First-hand Sales) Ordinance*, A2381. See also Section 27(2), Part 2, Division 4, *Proposed Legislation: Residential Properties (First-hand Sales) Bill*, p. 31, Annex A to the *Public*

Consultation on the Proposed Legislation to Regulate the Sale of First-hand Residential Properties, the Housing and Transport Bureau, November 2011.

24 Ibid., section 41(3), A2381. See also section 28(3), p. 31. Section 41(3) of the Buildings Ordinance provides that building works other than drainage works, ground investigation in the scheduled areas, site formation works or minor works in any building, if they do not involve the structure of the building, are exempt from the following requirements in the Buildings Ordinance: appointment and duties of authorized person, registered structural engineer or registered geotechnical engineer (sections 4); appointment and duties of registered contractors (section 9); appointment and duties of prescribed registered contractors and minor works (Section 9AA); approval and consent required for commencement of building works (section 14(1)); Occupation of new building (section 21).

25 See ibid., section 41(4), at A2381. See also section 38(4)(6).

26 Ibid., section 10(2)(b), Part 1 of Schedule 1, A2517.

27 Ibid., section 22, Part 2 of Schedule 1, A2535-A2541. See also Section 20, Schedule 1, Part 2, *Proposed Legislation: Residential Properties (First-hand Sales) Bill*, p. 91, Annex A to the *Public Consultation on the Proposed Legislation to Regulate the Sale of First-hand Residential Properties*, the Housing and Transport Bureau, November 2011. See also B16 and Appendix V in the Revised Annex I to *LACO Circular Memorandum No. 62 in LACO Circular Memorandum No. 63*.

28 Ibid., Section 22(2), Part 2 of Schedule 1, A2535.

29 As observed by the Law Reform Commission, see paragraph 3.4 in the Report on Description of Flats on Sale, the Law Reform Commission of Hong Kong, April 1995.

30 Section 9 in Annex III to *LACO Circular Memorandum No.62*. The list is in Appendix V in the Revised Annex I to *LACO Circular Memorandum No. 62 in LACO Circular Memorandum No. 63* and will be prescribed in Schedule 6 in agreement for sale and purchase, see the standard form of agreement for sale and purchase in *LACO Circular Memorandum No. 63*.

31 Section 9 in Annex III to LACO Circular Memorandum No. 62.

32 See Clause 31 in Schedule 5, A2603 or Clause 28 in Schedule 6, A2649, *Residential Properties (First-hand Sales) Ordinance*.

33 Ibid., section 36(1)(2), Part 2 – Division 4, A2371-A2373. See also section 23(1)(3), Division 4, Part 2, *Proposed Legislation: Residential Properties (First-hand Sales) Bill*, p. 28, Annex A to the *Public Consultation on the Proposed Legislation to Regulate the Sale of First-hand Residential Properties*, the Housing and Transport Bureau, November 2011.

34 Ibid., section 41(5), Part 2 – Division 4, A2383.

35 Regulation 2, regulation 8, paragraph 12 of Schedule 1, *The Consumer Protection from Unfair Trading Regulations 2008*.

References

CC (2014) Study on the Sales of First-hand Residential Properties, p. 69, Consumer Council, 11 November 2014, www.consumer.org.hk/ws_en/competition_issues/reports/20141111.html.

Chau, K. W., Wong, S. K. and Yiu, C. Y. E. (2007) Housing Quality in the Forward Contracts Market, *Journal of Real Estate Finance and Economics*, Vol. 34, No. 3.

Fan, C. S. (2005) The Consent Scheme in Hong Kong: Its Evolution and Evaluation–Home Purchaser Behaviour in Housing Society's Property Transactions Before and After the Asian Financial Crisis, Ph.D Thesis, Department of Real Estate and Construction, Faculty of Architecture, University of Hong Kong, September 2005, pp. 270–273.

Lands D (2010a) Legal Advisory and Conveyancing Office Circular Memorandum No. 62, Lands Department Consent Scheme, Legal Advisory and Conveyancing Office, Lands Department, 2 June 2010.

Lands D (2010b) Legal Advisory and Conveyancing Office Circular Memorandum No. 63, Lands Department Consent Scheme, Legal Advisory and Conveyancing Office, Lands Department, 1 September 2010.

Lands D (2012) Legal Advisory and Conveyancing Office Circular Memorandum No. 68, Lands Department Consent Scheme, Legal Advisory and Conveyancing Office, Lands Department, 22 March 2012.

LRC (1994) *Consultative Document by the Sub-Committee on Description of Flats on Sale – Local Uncompleted Residential Properties*, The Law Reform Commission of Hong Kong, April 1994, p. 11.

LRC (1995) *Report on Description of Flats on Sale*, The Law Reform Commission of Hong Kong, April 1995, pp.17–30.

REDA (2008) Guidelines for Sales Descriptions of Uncompleted Residential Properties, The Real Estate Developers Association of Hong Kong, 10 October 2008, p. 2.

REDA (2010) Guidelines for Sales Descriptions of Uncompleted Residential Properties, The Real Estate Developers Association of Hong Kong, 1 June 2010, pp. 1–2.

SC (2011) *Report of the Steering Committee on Regulation of Sale of First-hand Residential Properties by Legislation*, The Steering Committee on the Regulation of the Sale of First-hand Residential Properties by Legislation, October 2011, p. 48.

SCMP (2007) What exactly are you buying? It depends on who does the sums, *South China Morning Post*, 5 June 2007.

SCMP (2009) See-through walls but no transparency in show flats, *South China Morning Post*, 7 December 2009.

SRPA (2014a) SRPA advises prospective purchasers of Double Cove Starview Prime to ascertain the usage of the rooms in the flats they intend to purchase, The Sales of First-hand Residential Properties Authority, *Press releases*, 25 September 2014.

SRPA (2014b) SRPA advises prospective purchasers of first-hand Residential properties on fixed windows, *Press releases*, 27 March 2014, www.info.gov.hk/gia/general/201403/27/P201403270583.htm.

SRPA (2014c) SRPA advises prospective purchasers of The Wings IIIA to ascertain whether there is gas supply in kitchens of residential properties they wish to purchase, The Sales of First-hand Residential Properties Authority, *press releases*, 27 August 2014.

THB (2011) Residential Properties (First-hand Sales) Bill, Annex A to the Public Consultation on the Proposed Legislation to Regulate the Sale of First-hand Residential Properties, the Transportation and Housing Bureau, November 2011, pp. 14–91.

The Standard (2011) $10m flat sale row sparks heat over legal loopholes, 17 January 2011.

The Vendor of Double Cove Starview (2013) Floor plans of Residential properties in the phase, the Sales Brochure of Double Cove Starview Prime in Double Cove Phase 3, Sales Brochure.

The Vendor of Wings IIIA (2014) Information on common facilities in the development, 2014, pp. AXFFD01-AXFFD08.

6   Location

Introduction

'There are three things that matter in property: location, location, location.' Lord Harold Samuel's wise words are pursued as the golden rule for real estate investors all over the world (Safire 2009). In an open, fluid and transparent market, nothing matters more than location for the determination of the value of land: Hong Kong is of no exception. In the residential market, a 200 per cent or even much higher gap separates prestigious locations such as the Mid-Level, Peak, Stanley, Ho Man Tin from the rest of the city.

For every major sale of first-hand residential properties in town, the location of the development is always the focal point for prospective purchasers. When promoting new residential properties, developers will take great care and effort to illustrate the many positive aspects of the location of the property, e.g., natural environment, educational, commercial and leisure facilities nearby, traffic network, major government construction projects in the district, etc. In an encouraging atmosphere for commerce creativity, sometimes developers may have gone a little bit too far and end up over-glamorizing the location of the development. The marketing materials, and even the logo or property name, may involve misleading statements. This chapter scrutinizes the strength of relevant regulations in the *Residential Properties (First-hand Sales) Ordinance* (the *Ordinance*) and the Consent Scheme that purport to ensure full and frank disclosure of information on location and environmental features in the sales literature. To begin, it is helpful to summarize the key geographic and environmental factors that may affect the property value.

Location, prominent environmental features and property value

Hong Kong, Kowloon and the New Territories

The Hong Kong Special Administrative Region (HKSAR) has three parts: the Hong Kong Island (or Hong Kong), Kowloon and the New Territories. Residential properties located on the Hong Kong Island have the highest average price. With the rapid development in the New Territories since the 1980s, the average price for private domestic property in the New Territories is gradually edging towards the average price for Kowloon; still, it is around 30 per cent lower than the average price for properties on the Island side. The 2015 official statistic by the Rating and Valuation Department on the average price of private domestic properties (shown in Table 6.1) confirmed a remarkable price difference for properties located in Hong Kong, Kowloon, the New Territories and outlying islands (RVD 2016).

Although the most populated towns in the New Territories, i.e., Sha Tin, Yuen Long, Tai Po and Tsuen Wan, have an average price close to Hong Kong and Kowloon, apartments in Hong Kong and Kowloon of similar size, age, quality often record higher rates of price growth in a rising market than those in the New Territories and outlying islands (SCMP 2008).

Luxury housing areas

The private real estate market of Hong Kong is divided into a *prime* residential section and a *mass* residential section. Renowned luxury residential areas are distinguished by an average price per square foot multi-fold that of non-luxury sectors. The prime residential market is represented by some of the world's most distinguished residential areas: Mid-Level, Peak, Repulse Bay, Deep Water Bay, Stanley and Island South on the Island side, Kadoorie Hill, Kowloon Tong, Caldecott Road, West Kowloon, Beacon Hill and Ho Man Tin on the Kowloon peninsula side. Properties in these areas speak for fame, success, wealth and social status. Areas where high government officials, billionaires, elite and celebrities have resided for decades are believed to have excellent *fung shui* features. People who claim to have a profound understanding on *fung shui* believe that *fung shui* differs from area to area and every great area has its unique way to benefit its residents – something one just cannot attain elsewhere.

Mass Transit Railway network

Transport accessibility is another determining factor of property value in Hong Kong. The most significant element is the proximity to the Mass Transit Railway station (the MTR station). Hong Kong has developed a modern fast-speed railway network of ten lines for a total route length about 177 kilometres monopolistically run by the Mass Transit Railway Corporation Limited (after the merging of the MTR and Kowloon-Canton Railway in December 2007); the network (which is still developing) has 91 stations and ten main commuter lines after the running of the extension of the new South Island Line from Admiralty to the Southern District on 28 December 2016, covering the city's most populated areas from Central Business District to the peripheral of the city.[1] Being one of the world's most efficient, reliable and safe public transportation networks, it accounts for 35 per cent of domestic public transport in the city with the daily ridership reaching about 4.9 million passenger trips.[2]

Table 6.1 Private Domestic – Average Prices by Class for the years 2014 and 2015, Table 13, Hong Kong Property Review 2016, Rating and Valuation Department

私人住宅・各類單位平均售價

Private domestic – average prices by class

每平方米售價/m²

類別 Class		A			B			C			D			E		
年 Year	月 Month	港島 Hong Kong	九龍 Kowloon	新界 New Territories	港島 Hong Kong	九龍 Kowloon	新界 New Territories	港島 Hong Kong	九龍 Kowloon	新界 New Territories	港島 Hong Kong	九龍 Kowloon	新界 New Territories	港島 Hong Kong	九龍 Kowloon	新界 New Territories
2014		128912	104403	91436	129629	108820	81476	153720	138586	89607	183962	160259	85479	249984	235620	73677
2015*		146437	117993	107754	147993	121000	94343	171756	148758	101374	198841	166913	96960	238707	206485	89054
2014	10	133211	113331	95800	132068	112477	84318	158242	147216	93354	198327	176208	83946	(250511)	(197228)	87626
	11	134900	112186	97153	137402	113685	85454	167636	143987	94218	195271	141968	82498	(286672)	(205896)	73839
	12	138166	112619	101034	138205	119118	88665	159238	145756	95058	184926	(190669)	88881	(253795)	(192621)	76417
2015	1	142185	116929	104719	140527	121402	91268	172497	140574	97361	187518	173207	94158	212108	-	90613
	2	147092	119297	106392	145126	121840	92028	169071	151768	94277	215879	154503	96912	(206375)	(310947)	72891
	3	148875	112545	104778	150289	119964	92482	166777	138633	102627	189581	(186081)	95913	(227406)	(285667)	(81938)
	4	146094	116134	105166	148475	119159	93346	170560	151631	100716	198755	(197965)	101506	(230305)	(175436)	97235
	5	147960	118409	109038	151728	124110	95574	176366	153818	103624	195155	172690	88912	(245471)	(113863)	103147
	6	147821	122337	113816	153461	125591	97813	179459	158861	105736	209342	177783	95726	215963	(171254)	131290
	7	151462	123736	114705	152175	128291	99534	170908	154191	107064	193054	158491	96277	261183	(220875)	72531
	8	150395	124574	112796	153073	124979	99686	181770	146704	105710	198771	(144226)	106307	(263819)	-	81271
	9	149928	120022	108030	150115	117509	93686	174574	166294	101746	(191916)	(172404)	100499	(301318)	(196863)	(88326)
	10	144388	114392	100668	146295	111165	91530	160319	157851	95326	(198759)	(159643)	101059	(231285)	(248255)	(82420)
	11*	141356	109026	101264	138396	112485	87356	167668	136341	97364	188504	152237	98603	(226361)	(193424)	(80351)
	12*	134703	108357	100437	136496	108183	88482	150043	127397	98222	207501	(145886)	91319	239001	(232564)	(82790)

*Provisional figures
( )indicates fewer than 20 transactions
–No transaction record received by this department

*臨時數字
( )表示少於二十宗交易
–本署沒有收到到成交個案

For Hong Kong railway transportation has unparalleled advantages over other traffic modes: high frequency schedules, speed, close to zero accident rate, high level of safety, sustainable operation barring weather conditions, and long running hours. The MTR Corporation's management is celebrated as world class. All these make the railway the most popular traffic mode in the region. In addition to the railway network, the Corporation also develops a shopping and entertainment network in its high-traffic stations where convenient facilities are provided, e.g. shops, banks, postal boxes, road transport connections.

Every day thousands of commuters take MTR trains to go to work in the Central Business District of Hong Kong, i.e., Central, Admiralty, Wan Chai, Causeway Bay and Tsim Sha Tsui; those metropolitan areas feature numerous office towers, commercial centres, hotels, amenity facilities and tourist attractions. No other public traffic mode connects the rest of the city to Central better than the MTR network in term of traffic capacity at rush hours. MTR is also chosen by those who work in industrial districts such as Kwun Tong, Kwai Hing and live in residential towns such as Mei Foo, Lai Chi Kok and Tseung Kwan O.

The proximity to a MTR station brings much convenience and efficiency to the residents of a development in their everyday life. Such privilege is transferred into economic value and expressed as price premium. The latest generation of new towns in the New Territories like Tsing Yi and Tung Chung would not have been developed within a decade into popular residential hubs for white-collars working in Central, if the Tung Chung line had not been completed in June 1998, connecting Lantau Island to Central within half an hour.[3] An empirical research conducted in 2006 confirms the positive and significant effect on the increment of property price in Tuen Mun brought by the west rail line from as soon as the announcement of the project (Liu 2006).[4] The property price in Yuen Long and Tuen Mun soared up when the west rail line extended from Nam Cheong Station to Hung Hom Station on 16 August 2009. The fact that after the extension it takes only 30 minutes from Yuen Long to Tsim Sha Tsui has served as a strong stimulating factor for an immediate growth of about 20 per cent for property price in Yuen Long. The price of *Pacifica*,[5] a large-scale residential development in Lai Chi Kok increased significantly in September 2010 after the completion of a pedestrian subway connecting the development to the Lai Chi Kok station, which saves the residents about three to five minutes in their commute from home to the train platform. It is not difficult to understand why developments atop MTR stations often accommodate the most expensive properties in the district. One example would be *Gateway* above the Tuen Mun MTR station.

School nets

Intense competition for the young to enter popular primary and secondary schools in Hong Kong produces another positive factor for the appreciation of value for properties: the proximity to desired education facilities.

Apart from a few primary schools (e.g. private primary school, District Subsidy private schools and private schools of the English Schools Foundation) that accept direct application, the admission to government primary schools or government-aided school is administrated under the Primary One Admission System. Under the scheme, the territory is divided into some 30 school networks; as a matter of principle, a seat will be offered to the applicant by one school of the school net where the applicant resides with her family (EB 2016). A similar admission scheme operates in secondary school admission, with some secondary schools giving priority to the graduates from their sister primary schools. Like other places in the world, Hong Kong has popular schools and schools that are not that popular. Among the 36 school nets, some are teemed with prominent schools while for some other nets, good choices are few. The top four school nets in Hong Kong are School Net No. 11 (Central, Sheung Wan, Sai Ying Pun, Shek Tong Tsui, Kennedy Town, The Peak), No. 12 (Wan Chai, Causeway Bay, Happy Valley, Tai Hang, Jardine's Lookout, Soo Kun Po, Shiu Fai Terrace, Tung Shan Terrace, Lai Tak Tsuen, Villa Monte Rose, Evergreen Villa), No. 34 (Ho Man Tin, To Kwa Wan, Ma Tau Kok, Kadoorie Hill, Waterloo Road Hill, Oi Man Estate, Ho Man Tin Estate, Valley Road Estate, Chun Man Court, Dragon View, Cascades, Kwun Hei Court, Ma Tau Wai Estate, Chun Seen Mei Chuen, Majestic Park, Parc Regal, Lok Man Sun Chuen, Hillville Terrace, Horse Place, Jubilant Place, Sky Tower, Grand Waterfront, Celestial Heights) and No. 41 (Kowloon City, Kowloon Tong, Beacon Hill Road, Broadcast Drive, Mei Tung Estate).

The location maps for each school net are provided on the website of the Education Bureau.[6] Parents are required to indicate on the application form the school net they reside and submit proof of address with the application form. The boundaries of every school net are clearly defined; applications from residents living just one street away from the included area by the boundaries will be considered *after* applications from those residing within the boundaries. For parents, the only way to maximize a chance for a place in a good school for their children would be buying or renting a property in a top school net. The rentals and property prices within these four school nets are remarkably higher than their neighbouring areas.

Views

Views can be another value-adding element. The high-rise and high density nature in the city's skyline leaves little expectation for the view outside the windows for apartments and offices in lower floors of most buildings. Flats with unobstructed river, sea, harbour, mountain or park views are rare properties, which are always distinctively priced in the first-hand and second-hand markets. Being a metropolitan city at sea, Hong Kong has many world-class beaches. Some purchasers are willing to pay a premium for properties with full or partial sea view; some, though, are willing only if the property enjoys a sea view (Yu, Han and Chai 2007). For properties in some prominent locations, the sea view or harbour view enriches the property to such a degree that the view, or the capacity of seeing the view from the apartment, can be said as being of the essence of the agreement for sale and purchase. For example, a defining quality for some apartments in East Tsim Sha Tsui will be the view over the Victoria Harbour. Apartments with a permanent, and ideally unobstructed, harbour view are of the greatest investment potential. Very rarely are those apartments put up for sale. The transaction, if it happens, usually attracts headlines in the local media. Another example would be the residential properties overseeing the Sha Tin racecourse.

At the same time, properties surrounded by view-blocking buildings and other impediments to visibility are valued less. Highways and main roads impending a property also have negative impact on property price. Plus, some unfavourable locations or undesirable views negatively affect the value of the property significantly. Empirical research conducted in 2005 confirmed that graveyard views bring significant penalty to property values in Hong Kong (Yeung 2005).

The value of an unobstructed view is perhaps best illustrated in *Yang Dandan v Hong Kong Resort Company Limited* (to be discussed below and in Chapter 14). When her originally unobstructed sea view started to be permanently blocked for the first time by a new adjacent development developed by the same developer, the owner of a duplex apartment on the top two floors of a residential development in the Discovery Bay was so annoyed that she first demanded the developer repurchase the property from her at the contractual price or pay her compensation for her loss of sea view; when such request was rejected by the developer, she brought a claim against the developer for the loss of the view and, after the Court of First Instance held in favour of the developer in October 2015, she appealed to the Court of Appeal in 2016.[7]

The apartments with sea or mountain views perhaps also indicate a better air quality to be enjoyed by their residents than those without such views. Recent research implies that clean air has been highly valued by not only residents but also investors, whereas a high level of air pollution has a negative impact on housing value (Chau et al. 2011).

Issues and solutions

A sales brochure or advertisement on sale of first-hand properties will inevitably touch on the location and environmental features of the property on sale. How should such information be featured in the sales brochure or advertisement? As a starting point, the *Ordinance* stipulates that every sales brochure needs to contain a statement that 'there may be changes to the development and the surrounding areas'.[8] It is followed by requirements on inclusion of postal address, district name, Location Plan and Outline Zoning Plan in the sales brochure.

Postal address

From October 2009 onwards, the postal address of the development is provided in the sales brochure (REDA 2009; Lands D 2010a). The requirement was extended to printed advertisements and promotional materials in June 2010 (REDA 2010; Lands D 2010b). According to the *Ordinance*, sales brochures must state the name of the street at which the development is situated and the street number as allocated by the Commissioner of Rating and Valuation.[9] This requirement also applies to price list.[10]

District name

In 1982 Hong Kong started to implement the District Administration Scheme and divided the region into several administrative districts. Later, the Kwai Tsing District was split off from the Tsuen Wan District in 1985 and in 1994 the Yau Tsim District and Mong Kok District merged to become the Yau Tsim Mong District. Now Hong Kong has four districts on Hong Kong Island (Central and Western, Wan Chai, Eastern, and Southern), five districts in Kowloon (Yau Tsim Mong, Sham Shui Po, Kowloon City, Wong Tai Sin, and Kwun Tong) and nine districts in the New Territories (Kwai Tsing, Tsuen Wan, Tuen Mun, Yuen Long, North, Tai Po, Sha Tin, Sai Kung and Islands).[11] Each district has its own district council.

The 18 districts differ greatly in area and population. The average area of the four districts on Hong Kong Island and five districts in Kowloon is 14.07 km². For the nine districts on Hong Kong Island and Kowloon, the district name can be indicative in terms of location, proximity and general conditions of environmental features. This is especially true for properties located in the following four districts: Eastern, 12.44 km²; Wan Chai, 9.83 km²; Yau Tsim Mong, 6.99 km²; and Kowloon City, 10.02 km², where one can roughly tell by the district name the property value, investment potential and traffic conditions. For the other five districts in Hong Kong and Kowloon, however, the provision of district name alone becomes less informative, as each district has its own prime and non-prime residential areas. For illustration, the Southern District has Stanley, Repulse Bay, and Deep Water Bay in the high end, Pok Fu Lam, Cyberport, Aberdeen and Ap Lei Chou in the middle, and Wah Fu and Wong Chuk Hang in the low end.

When it comes to the nine districts in the vast New Territories with an average area of 105.94 km² each, the district name alone is not suggestive as to the status of the development. Take Yuen Long district as an example: Yuen Long town is the most prosperous area; Tin Shui Wai on the other hand has the lowest average property price in the SAR; Hung Shui Kiu, a small town located in the midland of the Tuen Mun – Yuen Long Corridor, is the least developed urban area in the district yet it holds the most promise to investors whose eyes are on the potential benefits from the planned transport infrastructure: the Deep Bay Link, Route 10, the Hong Kong–Shenzhen Western Express Line, etc.; Kam Tin and Pat Heung are rural areas with hundreds of villages. Take Tuen Mun as another example; while most areas in this district are regarded as mediocre, the area along the Golden Coast in So Kwun Wat is one of the most prestigious locations for luxury properties in Hong Kong.

As such, probably a smaller geographic unit after the district is needed to accurately indicate the location of the property within the district. But to a territory as small as the HKSAR, what is the next geographic division following district? There is no lower level of administrative division under district. There are, however, *sub-districts* in a purely geographical sense that are divided by the Rating and Valuation Department (RVD 2016). Table 6.2 lists all the sub-districts within the 18 districts.

Table 6.2 Districts and Sub-districts of HKSAR

Area	District	Sub-Districts
Hong Kong	Central and Western	Kennedy Town, Shek Tong Tsui, Sai Ying Pun, Sheung Wan, Central, Admiralty, Mid-levels, Peak
	Wan Chai	Wan Chai, Causeway Bay, Happy Valley, Tai Hang, So Kon Po, Jardine's Lookout
	Eastern	Tin Hau, Braemar Hill, North Point, Quarry Bay, Sai Wan Ho, Shau Kei Wan, Chai Wan, Siu Sai Wan
	Southern	Pok Fu Lam, Aberdeen, Ap Lei Chau, Wong Chuk Hang, Shouson Hill, Repulse Bay, Chung Hom Kok, Stanley, Tai Tam, Shek O
Kowloon	Yau Tsim Mong	Tsim Sha Tsui, Yau Ma Tei, West Kowloon Reclamation, King's Park, Mong Kok, Tai Kok Tsui
	Sham Shui Po	Mei Foo, Lai Chi Kok, Cheung Sha Wan, Sham Shui Po, Shek Kip Mei, Yau Yat Tsuen, Tai Wo Ping, Stonecutters Island
	Kowloon City	Hung Hom, To Kwa Wan, Ma Tau Kok, Ma Tau Wai, Kai Tak, Kowloon City, Ho Man Tin, Kowloon Tong, Beacon Hill
	Wong Tai Sin	San Po Kong, Wong Tai Sin, Tung Tau, Wang Tau Hom, Lok Fu, Diamond Hill, Tsz Wan Shan, Ngau Chi Wan
	Kwun Tong	Ping Shek, Kowloon Bay, Ngau Tau Kok, Jordan Valley, Kwun Tong, Sau Mau Ping, Lam Tin, Yau Tong, Lei Yue Mun
New Territories	Kwai Tsing	Kwai Chung, Tsing Yi
	Tsuen Wan	Tsuen Wan, Lei Muk Shue, Ting Kau, Sham Tseng, Tsing Lung Tau, Ma Wan, Sunny Bay
	Tuen Mun	Tai Lam Chung, So Kwun Wat, Tuen Mun, Lam Tei
	Yuen Long	Hung Shui Kiu, Ha Tsuen, Lau Fau Shan, Tin Shui Wai, Yuen Long, San Tin, Lok Ma Chau, Kam Tin, Shek Kong, Pat Heung
	North	Fanling, Luen Wo Hui, Sheung Shui, Shek Wu Hui, Sha Tau Kok, Luk Keng, Wu Kau Tang
	Tai Po	Tai Po Market, Tai Po, Tai Po Kau, Tai Mei Tuk, Shuen Wan, Cheung Muk Tau, Kei Ling Ha
	Sha Tin	Tai Wai, Sha Tin, Fo Tan, Ma Liu Shui, Wu Kai Sha, Ma On Shan
	Sai Kung	Clear Water Bay, Sai Kung, Tai Mong Tsai, Tseung Kwan O, Hang Hau, Tiu Keng Leng, Ma Yau Tong
	Islands	Cheung Chau, Peng Chau, Lantau Island (including Tung Chung), Lamma Island

The significance of disclosure of sub-district is still not recognized by the *Ordinance*. According to the *Ordinance*, advertisements and promotional materials must state the district in which the development is situated, the name of the street and the street number allocated by the Commissioner of Rating and Valuation.[12]

The requirement is to tackle the issue of liberal association of the property with prestigious locations in Kowloon and Hong Kong Island. In 2006, the Broadcasting Authority considered the advertisement for the sale of *Apex* in Kwai Chung, New Territories was misleading for claiming the development was situated in Kowloon; the Broadcasting Authority was of the opinion that location was crucial in the appeal of a real property advertisement (LC 2006). In the sale of *Bel Air*, the developer of at Cyberport marketed the property as 'Bel Air on the Peak, Island South', trying to attain two upmarket associations in one description.[13] But *Bel Air* is neither on the Peak nor on the south side of the Island. Similarly, *Island Crest* located on the first street of Hong Kong Island was boldly claimed to be in the 'West Mid-Level of Hong Kong Island' in its 2010 advertisement.

In 2014, a development located in Hung Hom under the Approved Hung Hom Outline Zoning Plan named itself '*Homantin Hillside*'. Soon after the sale started, the Sales of First-hand Residential Properties Authority issued a reminder that the location of *Homantin Hillside* is, instead, in Hung Hom (SRPA 2014a). It is noteworthy that the *Ordinance* does not touch upon whether a developer should be allowed to name a property after a sub-district name in Hong Kong when the property is not situated in that sub-district, a question to which the answer seems obvious.

The provision of the sub-district name as part of the actual address in the sales brochure serves the purpose to clearly indicate the location of the property within a district. It is therefore recommended that the name of the sub-district be provided in the sales brochure and advertisements. The actual address of a property should be presented in the following formation: Property Name, Street Number, Street, Sub-District Name, District Name and Area. For example, *Uptown*, No. 600 Castle Peak Road – Hung Shui Kiu, Hung Shui Kiu, Yuen Long, New Territories.

Location plan of the development

The sales brochure must display the *location plan* of the Development and the relevant *outline zoning plan*. Both must be printed at least 16cm in length and 16cm in width with the font size of the related legends being at least 10 point Times New Roman typeface.[14]

The location plan needs to show the location of the development, the name of every street, and every communal facility and prominent environmental feature that is situated within 250 metres from the boundary of the development. The facilities and prominent environmental features include 'crematorium, columbarium, mortuary, slaughterhouse, bus depot, railway depot, ventilation shaft for the Mass Transit Railway, library, museum, barrack, cargo working area, petrol filling station, LPG filling stations, oil depots, aviation fuel depot, marine fuel depot, sewage treatment works and facilities, landfills (including ex-landfills), landfill gas flaring plants, power plant (including electricity sub-stations), pylon, correctional institution (including a prison), addiction treatment centre, helicopter landing pad, clinic, fire station, ambulance depot, funeral parlour, cemetery, judicial facilities (including a court and a magistracy), refuse collection point, hospital, market (including wet markets and wholesale markets), police station, public carpark (including a lorry park), public convenience; public transport terminal (including a rail station), public utility installation, religious institution (including Church, temple and Tsz Tong), school (including kindergartens, primary schools, secondary school and vocational training schools), social welfare facilities (including elderly centres and homes for mentally disabled), sports facilities (including a sports ground and a swimming pool) and public park'.[15]

Thus in the sale of *City Point* in 2014, shortly before the sale started, the Town Planning Board announced in the amended outline zoning plan a proposed public columbarium development at a site within 250 metres from the boundary of the development. Within a week of the announcement by the Town Planning Board, the SRPA requested the developer to revise the sales brochure and highlight the proposed columbarium development in the location plan and outline zoning plan (SRPA 2014b).

In August 2016, Principal Magistrate Ernest Lin Kam-Hung held the vendor of *Ocean One* guilty for failing to indicate the presence of public toilets and power plants within 250 metres of the development set in the sales brochure (SCMP 2016).[16]

Outside the 43 types of facilities specified in the *Ordinance*, Merry suggests that *scrapyards* and *squatter huts* that are commonly seen in the New Territories can be unfavourable features to some property purchasers (Merry 2008).

As observed by Merry, Hong Kong is a society where many believe in *fung shui* and will find that 'features associated with death or disease near where they live is undesirable'. It is questionable whether the *Ordinance*'s disclosure-within-250-metre requirement is justifiable. Local people's perception of 'nearness' is certainly not confined to a distance of 250 metres when it comes to undesirable features. A purchaser will not stop from thinking negatively of a unit if it is 500 metres or one kilometre away from an unsightly amenity. Estate agents working in areas such as Aberdeen understand perfectly the price difference between a unit with a cemetery view and one without, regardless of how far away the cemetery is. When the location plan stops at the 250-metre edge, potential purchasers may wonder what lies outside the box.

At the same time, this requirement may work against the interests of developers too, for many positive features may be located nearby yet just outside that 250-metre diameter. This was the case of *Hermitage*: the MTR exits near the development are all located within walking distance but nonetheless all outside the 250-metre diameter. In this extreme case, after marking the 250-metre diameter as requested, the developer should be allowed to extend the 250-metre diameter by perhaps a couple of hundred metres more to show the entrances of the MTR stations nearby. Therefore for the interests of both purchasers and vendors it would be most ideal if the Location Plan shows communal facilities and prominent environmental features within 1,000 metres from the boundary of the whole development.

Relevant outline zoning plan

In addition to the location plan, the sales brochure needs to state the address of the website on which a copy of the *outline zoning plan* is available.[17] The outline zoning plan (or here after "OZP") needs to show 'the existing and proposed uses of land within 500m from the whole development'.[18]

The question remains whether it is informative to a layman purchaser, if the sole requirement is to provide extracts from the outline zoning plan drawn by the Town Planning Board, in which each lot of neighbouring land is plainly marked with planning terminology.[19]

Merry (2008) proposes that developers should disclose information, in the form of a note or remarks put below the outline zoning plan, on *planning intentions for the vicinity*: the type and height of buildings to be erected later over the neighbouring land. Such information may be vital, especially for those who find the views around the development very attractive.

For example, as found by the Court of First Instance in *Yang Dandan v Hong Kong Resort Co Ltd*, in the sale of *Chianti* in 2008, the sales brochure contains a master plan where to the east of the development on sale 'there was a green patch of open land marked with this description in both English and Chinese: 'Mid-rise Residential Development Area Under Planning' and '籌劃中中座發展項目' (collectively 'Amalfi' s Description')'.[20] A couple of years later the 'mid-rise residential development', upon completion of construction, turned out to be tall enough to interrupt the sea view of a duplex dwelling on the top two floors of *Chianti*. Then in a 2009 sale of a development standing near the coastal line at Ma On Shan, the developer devoted a number of pages in the brochure to the lake, sea and mountain views surrounding the estate. But just 13 days after the sale was first launched, media reported that another high-density estate would be built right in front of the development for sale, which, upon completion, would block many of the views that were being advertised (SCMP 2009b). The Consumer Council observed that in one 2014 sale the developer, when highlighting the infrastructure under planning, did state that they were not giving any warranty and that the infrastructure was subject to the government's approval or control (CC 2014).

The inclusion of the outline zoning plan in the sales brochure has worked in the favour of the vendor when facing a claim on misrepresentation in *Yang Dandan v Hong Kong Resort Co Ltd*. In the case the developer used the words 'mid-rise residential development' to describe the adjacent development that was under planning at the time of the sale of *Chianti* in the sales brochure, which also includes another statement to describe *Chianti* as 'five blocks of waterfront high-rises'. In deciding whether there was actionable misrepresentation at common law, the Court of First Instance expressed the view that no reliance could be proved if the statement 'Mid-rise Residential Development Area Under Planning' is accompanied by other statements such as disclaimers suggesting such information is for reference only. Among all the statements the Court paid particular attention to the mentioning of the Outline Zoning Plan in the penultimate page of the Sales Brochure, the provision of the most updated Outline Zoning Plan at the date of the printing of the sales brochure for free inspection in the sales office by the vendor as well as the provision of the information to check the Outline Zoning Plan online. The Judge found that 'the OZP would show that the stipulated maximum building heights of both Chianti and Amalfi were indeed the same', thus with all the steps done by the vendor to direct the attention of purchaser to the OZP, the purchaser should not have relied on the statement that contains the description of the adjacent development as *mid-rise*.[21]

Aerial photo

The Steering Committee considered it desirable to require developers to provide an aerial photo showing the development site and its vicinity; the photo should be obtained from the Lands Department at a cost (SC 2011). The aerial photograph must be the latest one as at the date of the printing of the sales brochure taken by the Survey and Mapping Office of the Lands Department at a flying height below 7,000 feet. When the photo is printed in the sales brochure, it should be at least 16cm in length and 16cm in width; and must show the development and the surrounding area within 250m from the boundary of the development.[22] The *Ordinance* encourages developers to include previous aerial photographs of the development in the same section with the latest one for cross-reference.[23]

For similar reasons stated in the discussion of location plan and outline zoning plan, it is proposed that a second up-to-date aerial photo showing the surrounding areas of 1,500 metres be added to complement the one of 250 metres.

The requirement of providing an aerial photograph in the sales brochure should be attributed to the observation of David Webb in the sale of a luxury residential property in 2010. The site of *Larvotto* is along the eastern fringe of the Ap Lei Chau Island across the Aberdeen typhoon shelter. The sales campaign had made a salient selling point out of the sea view and its proximity to the sea. David traced the site of the land to its auction in 1995, where the land was originally granted for industrial use. When the developer came to the Town Planning Board with a plan for 1,290 units in towers up to 50 stories in March 2002, the Board rejected the application out of the concern on the noise from the boatyards which are only 30 metres away from the development. According to the Environmental Protection Department, the noise from the steel boat repairing activities in the boatyards exceeds the noise limit set out in the Hong Kong Planning Standards and Guidelines. On 25 July 2003, the Town Planning Board rejected another plan of 1,336 units in five blocks up to 38 stories on a three-storey podium for the same reason. The plan was not approved until the applicant had agreed to incorporate mitigation measures including non-openable windows in January 2004 (Webb 2010).

To illustrate the proximity of the estate and the boatyards, Webb found assistance in the satellite image over the lot (Figure 6.1).

With the reference to the satellite image it was much clearer that the boatyards and sawmills all constitute prominent environmental features in the vicinity of the development, which embrace almost the entire sea area that abuts the shore of the plot. The noise being one issue, the other would be the prospect of redevelopment, which will potentially block the view. In this case the advertisements of *Larvotto* would be misleading if it only featured the yachts floating in the sea in an artistic way without showcasing the boatyards.

Thus, the statutory requirement under the *Ordinance* to insert the latest aerial picture (as at the date on which the sales brochure is printed) serves its purpose of bringing forth transparency into the sales literature.

Figure 6.1 Satellite View of the Ap Lei Chau Praya Road on 7 January, 2007

One may still argue that an aerial photo, while being a more vivid graphic illustration, adds very little to the location plan and the outline zoning plan. Is there any better idea to inform purchasers of the environmental features?

How about a collection of photos with horizontal views of the development with its environs that is taken within a reasonable distance from different angles? If the making of such photo series could be made into a standardized exercise (with details of the permitted distance, angle, lighting, time, number of photos from different angles etc.) then these photos, once included into the sales brochure, will be very helpful in providing a clear, informative and unambiguous illustration on the environmental features of the property. They will introduce a more realistic and daily perspective to view the estate and its environment, with more details of any environmental features *talis quails*. Such graphic presentation will complement the aerial photo taken by the Lands Department and provide the viewers a fuller picture of the environment of the property. The *Ordinance* should have required, or at least encouraged, developers to provide in sales brochure, advertisements and project website up-to-date photos – ideally in a collection of six from different angles – with horizontal views of the construction site taken within 500 metres from the boundary of the development. And at the same time, it is highly advised that prospective purchasers visit the construction site for better information on the environmental features of the property.

Layout plan of the development

A layout plan pictures the buildings, facilities and open areas within a development. Like the Location Plan and the Outline Zoning Plan, the Layout Plan must be included in the sales brochure.[24] But unlike the location plan or the outline zoning plan, the layout plan is drawn by the vendor. Upon the commencement of the *Ordinance*, the drawing of the layout plan is subject to the general standard that *the information set out in the sales brochure must be accurate in every material respect*.[25] The layout plan must show the location and layouts of the buildings, the open areas, facilities, and the undeveloped land (with the intended use), within the boundary of the development. If there are uncompleted buildings or facilities in the development, the layout plan must state the estimated date of completion of these buildings or facilities.[26]

The layout plan should include the immediate neighbouring area of the development, perfectly areas within 50 metres from the boundary of the development. This will illustrate the relationship between the development and the abutting streets, pedestrian ways/bridges and neighbouring buildings.

Name and logo

Just as recently the development located in Hung Hom named itself as *Homantin Hillside* (Mingpao 2014), a couple of years ago, the sales literature of *Aria* adopted the phrase 'Kowloon Peak' to describe the location of the development.

Aria is a high-rise residential development of 723 units located on Fung Shing Street, Ngau Chi Wan, Kowloon. The presale started in November 2009. Its newspaper advertisement described the development as 'a residence of peerless luxury sited on a premium location on Kowloon Peak' (SCMP 2009). The English part of the logo consists of the estate name and the phrase 'Kowloon Peak' with a '|' in between. The estate was unitarily referred to in pure text format as 'Aria | KOWLOON PEAK' instead of 'Aria' in the sales brochure. Hardly anyone who saw the logo would not imagine the development as standing somewhere in the Kowloon Peak.

'Kowloon Peak' is the name of a 603 metre (1,978 ft.) tall mountain in the northeast part of Kowloon Peninsula also known as *Fei Ngo Shan*. The crest of the mountain is the boundary between Kwun Tong district and Sai Kung district. Map 6.1 shows the location of *Aria* vis-à-vis the Kowloon Peak; the location of the *Aria* is indicated by a yellow arrow.

The contour map below (Map 6.2) shows that the sea level of the development's location – 51, Fung Shing Street (marked by the yellow arrow) – is in fact lower than 200 metres.

In geographic terms, it can be best said that the estate is at the foot of the mountain 'Kowloon Peak'. The developer advertised the property as 'on Kowloon Peak' and, together with the design of the logo, seemed to equate the location of the property with Kowloon Peak. This can be misleading if readers take it to mean that the property stands on the peak of *Fei Ngo Shan*.

More essentially, the geographical proximity to the Kowloon Peak does not make the sub-district Ngau Chi Wan, in general, in the vicinity of the peak/ comfortable radius from East Kowloon. According to the administrative division of Hong Kong, Ngau Chi Wan belongs to the district of Wong Tai Sin. Most premium residential areas, i.e., Ho Man Tin, Kowloon Tong and Beacon Hill in Kowloon are situated in the Kowloon City district. Ngau Chi Wan was in the neighbouring district to these established luxury sites. Even the property itself can fairly be considered as a luxury project (in an overall consideration of construction cost, design, unit size, market price, and location), that does not make the area a luxury site or premium location *per se*. In such circumstances, if developers are not required to disclose the names of the district and sub-district, a simple reference to a more prestigious location nearby may confuse the purchasers to the exact location of the property.

Transportation and education network

In the sales brochure, there is a full-page coloured graphic titled 'Transportation Network', highlighting the MTR connection of the development to other parts of Hong Kong.

Being declared as another *simplified version*, the illustration contained eight existing territory-wide MTR lines and featured only 14 MTR stations. The Diamond Hill MTR station was chosen to represent *the* MTR station near the estate. But geographically speaking the closest MTR station to the development is, instead, Choi Hung. The Development is one station away from the Diamond

Map 6.1 The Satellite image of Hammer Hill, Nagu Chi Wan and Choi Hung of HKSAR by Mapcarta in July 2016

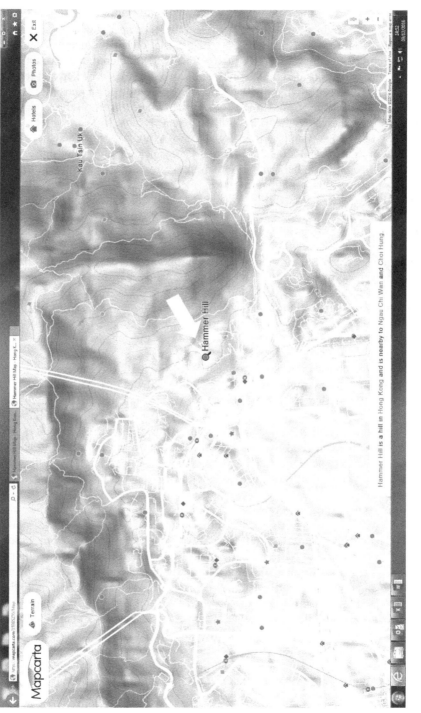

Map 6.2 The Contour Map of Hammer Hill, Nagu Chi Wan and Choi Hung of HKSAR by Mapcarta in July 2016

Hill station, not counting the distance from the estate to the Choi Hung station which requires minibus connection.[27] Why did the developer choose to showcase the Diamond Hill station instead of Choi Hung station? If the name 'Diamond Hill' accomplishing the campaign's luxury tone better is merely a guess, the fact that the former is considered as a middle-class residential area surrounded by modern private housing while the latter is dominated by public housing estates, may be a critical factor. Choi Hung is one of the remotest areas in the Wong Tai Sin district, bordering Kwun Tong and Sai Kung. Ngau Chi Wan, where Choi Hung MTR station is, stands at the very outset of Wong Tai Sin. The Choi Hung MTR station is named after the Choi Hung estate, which is a public housing estate. Diamond Hill, on the other hand, is much closer to Kowloon Tong and Prince Edward. Even in this case it is harmless to highlight the proximity with the Diamond Hill MTR station, the developer should have indicated Choi Hung MTR station too in the map.

Another prospect that only the Diamond Hill MTR can offer is the proposed Shatin to Central Link (the *SCL*). The Link is a planned strategic railway connection between Shatin, Southeast Kowloon and Hong Kong Island. In its preliminary design, Diamond Hill is an interchange station for SCL and the Kwun Tong line. The Link will connect Diamond Hill to Tai Wai in the north and Hung Hom in the south, then to Admiralty via a new Exhibition station (LC 2008). In March 2009, a couple of months before the sale, the 2008 preliminary design was confirmed by the report submitted to the legislative council (LC 2009) (Figure 6.2).

The design suggests that upon completion of the SCL, passengers can travel from Diamond Hill Station to Central via eight MTR stations: Kai Tak, To Kwa Wan, Ma Tau Wai, Ho Man Tin and Hong Hum on the Ma On Shan Line extension, or more precisely, the extended West Rail Line (West Rail Line will merge with Ma On Shan line upon the completion of extension); then Exhibition and Admiralty on the extended East Rail Line. For a trek from the Diamond Hill to Central, passengers need to change line twice: first at Hong Hum (from the West Rail Line to the East Rail Line), then at Admiralty (from the East Rail Line to the Island Line).

These details were not shown in the *Transportation Network* in the sales brochure. There the Link has been simplified to a line of three MTR stations only: Tai Wai, Diamond Hill and Central. The drawing bypassed the Hung Hom station, a major interchange station for West and East Rail Lines. The line was coloured differently (in orange) from all the other eight existing lines as if it were a separate MTR line and no interchange were required from Diamond Hill to Central. In this way, it may have misstated the design which indicates that the Link consists of two rail line extensions and ends at Admiralty. Besides, the commencement ofconstruction of SCL is scheduled in 2012. The project is estimated to be completed in 2020. Can the strategic position of Diamond Hill MTR station after 2020 be advertised in a 2009 sale? Regarding the estimated date of completion of SCL, the sales brochure simply stated that 'it is to be constructed soon'.

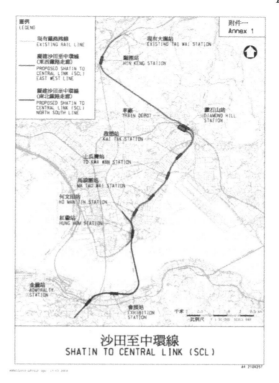

Figure 6.2 The Shatin to Central Link and MTR Kwun Tong Line Extension, Progress of the Shatin to Central Link, *Legislative Council Panel on Transport Subcommittee on Matters Relating to Railways*, CB(1)1137/08-09(05), Legislative Council, 31 March 2009

As shown in the *Transportation Network*, intermediate stations along the Shatin-Central-Link were deleted; the newly proposed Link was highlighted, yet no description was given on the date of commencement of construction or the estimated date of completion; stations of stronger connection with other parts of the city were chosen to pinpoint the location of the property. Although graphics are not allowed in the sales brochure after October 2009 (REDA 2009; Lands D 2012), a liberal illustration of the nearby MTR facilities may still appear in advertisements.

And some developers went even further. In one 2008 sale, the vendor mentioned an 'Aberdeen MTR station' on the South Island Line (West Section) three times in the sales brochure, among which was a map said to be resourced by the information on the website of MTR Corporation and a computer-generated photo of an Exit of the MTR Aberdeen Station.[28] By the time of the sale, the construction of Aberdeen MTR Station was contemplated but never officially decided. The Vendor seemed to advertise the prospect of the MTR station as a reality. Later the idea of the Aberdeen MTR station was eventually aborted when the MTR decided to end the South Island Line (West Section) at Kennedy Town.

Thus to ensure information accuracy, any illustration of the MTR network in advertisements must be accomplished with the most updated MTR System Map as displayed on the website of the MTR Corporation.[29] If a developer wishes to involve any ongoing MTR projects, e.g., the West Island Line, the Guangzhou–Shenzhen–Hong Kong Express Rail Link, Sha Tin to Central Link , Kwun Tong Line Extension and South Island Line (East), then the key information of the projects (i.e., date of commencement of construction; estimated date of completion) must be provided as stated in the relevant sections on the MTR website. The project websites must provide links to the relevant sections of the MTR website.

Progress was made in the presentation of the Shatin to Central Link by the Vendor of *Homantin Hillside* in the advertisement displayed on the website, where next to the graphic illustration on the Ho Man Tin MTR station, the Vendor clearly stated that for the proposed Shatin to Central Link, Tai Wai to Hung Hom Section is expected to start in 2019; Hung Hom to Admiralty Section is expected to start in 2021.[30] The SRPA (2014a) further reminded purchasers of the development that 'when Ho Man Tin Station, Hung Hom Station, Exhibition Station and Admiralty Station of the SCL come into operation, passengers boarding at Ho Man Tin Station and heading for Exhibition Station or Admiralty Station on Hong Kong Island will have to alight at Hung Hom Station for another railway line.'[31] The SPRA indeed can go one step further by requesting developers provide detailed information on the MTR station and the lines passing the station, *inter alia*, requirement of rail interchange to major destinations.

To highlight the connectivity of the location of the development, it has been very trendy for vendors to state in advertisements an estimated time from the property to the next MTR station or popular destinations: Central, Tsim Sha Tsui, the Airport or Lok Wu. The information is usually said to be provided by an *independent traffic consultant*. For example, in the 2016 sale of *Twin Regency*, the Vendor has included the assessment by an independent traffic consultant on the travelling time from the development to Yuen Long MTR Station, Long Ping MTR Station and the closed Bus Stop respectively. But what qualification a company must have in order to act as an independent traffic consultant is unclear. Therefore the assessment is questionable in its degree of authenticity. A similar opinion was expressed by the Consumer Council when it doubted whether the information could be viewed as reliable because travelling time would be affected by many factors (CC 2014).

To avoid misrepresentation and exaggeration, any statement with regards to the estimated time it takes from the development to a facility or a landmark location should be avoided in the sales literature.

Moreover, developers should be very cautious in making statements regarding the provision of shuttle buses or other transportation services in promoting the property. It was reported that some vendors advertised that it would arrange a route by ferry from the development to Central yet no application was made to the government by the time of the sale; and sometimes the Vendor did provide the shuttle bus service as promised but nonetheless the service was suspended for want of government approval (SCMP 2006).

Orientation, ingress/egress points for the development

Orientation is yet another critical variable for the enjoyment of the flat. Information about orientation is of significant interest to purchasers in Hong Kong, who, as observed by the Law Reform Commission, have special preference for units facing the south and end to avoid those facing west (LRC 1995). The *Ordinance* should have required that, in addition to the internal layout of all apartments and floors of the development, the floor plan provide information on the following aspects of a property: (i) the orientation of the development and apartments; (ii) the location of the ingress and egress points for the development; and (iii) the location of the residential tower in the development.

Views and surroundings

Merry (2008) observes that many show flats have installed display of photographic backdrops that 'may have only a tenuous connection with the views that will be given by the actual flats'. In other cases, while the view as shown on the photographic backdrops does feature the location of the development, the view is still hypothetical as it is in fact blocked by other buildings. In these cases, the display of photographic backdrops of splendid views is misleading and should be avoided.

In the sale of *Apex*, the advertisement featured the New York City skyline and the stunning Manhattan city with a model of *Apex* property tucked away in the bottom corner of the poster (SCMP 2006). The practice of inserting photos of places that are irrelevant to the property on sale in the advertisement is, up till today, generally allowed, yet with the enactment of the *Ordinance*, such practice, on a case-to-case basis may contravene the offence under section 70, i.e., publishing an advertisement containing information that is false or misleading in a material particular. Developers should avoid using photos the contents of which bear no relevance to the development on sale in the advertisement or sales brochure.

Lastly, some purchasers may not consider buying or living in apartments with views of cemeteries; at the same time, as discussed earlier, the view of a cemetery may introduce penalty in the price of the property when the purchaser wishes to resell the unit. The information is therefore worthy of disclosure in first-hand sales. In one 2014 sale, the SRPA advised purchasers of the fact that a grave is located north of Tower 3 and west of Tower 5 in the Phase of the Development (SRPA 2014c).

After that, developer should be allowed to make statements on the planning intention of the neighbouring land as to the best knowledge by the time of the sale, provided that the respective requirements by the *Ordinance* such as the provision of the Aerial Photo and the most updated outline zoning plan online and in the sales office are duly observed.

Location of the sales office

The possibility of misrepresentation on location is highly probably for sale of uncompleted flats, where the sale office may be miles away from the construction site. For example, in the sale of *Aria*, the sales office was suited in Tower 2 of the International Finance Centre in Central, Hong Kong, on the other side of the Victoria Harbour.

The sales office is the only place for a purchaser to view the show flats as well as mostly likely the place the preliminary agreement of sale and purchase is signed. Thus it is a must-go place for a purchaser. If the sales office is located near the property development site, then purchasers and would-be purchasers will get a first-hand view of the location on the location and environmental status of the properties on sale during their journey to the sales office. The Council found that in many sales, the sales offices located in shopping malls are actually far away from the actual property development sites and suggested that having the show flats located in the vicinity of development site would better facilitate prospective purchasers' convenience in visiting the site (CC 2014). In this way, much misrepresentation or misunderstanding on the location and environmental features of the properties could be avoided.

Conclusion

In Hong Kong and elsewhere, the value of first-hand residential properties is largely determined by the location. In the sale of completed flats, local purchasers can go to visit the development. In the sale of uncompleted flats, however, prospective purchasers who only visit the sales office may have to rely on the information about location and prominent environmental features provided by developers to make a decision. Even for sale of completed flats, purchasers may not possess accurate information as to the development potential of the area and therefore may pay great attention to any statement made by vendors in the sales literature with regard to the location of the property.

Compared to the practices in pre-2010 sales, the new measures implemented by the Consent Scheme after June 2010 and the *Ordinance* appear to be effective in preventing liberal, misleading and untrue statements of location in the sales brochure. Nonetheless, improvement can be made in the following aspects.

Firstly, developers should be requested to disclose the name of the sub-district of the development; vendors should not be allowed to name a property after a sub-district name if the property is not in that sub-district. Secondly, planning intentions for the vicinity must be accurately disclosed: if by the time of the sale a new building is approved to be constructed that will potential interrupt the views, such information should be included in the sales brochure. Thirdly, the presentation of the view of the property should be regulated to the extent that the view as presented must reflect the actual view of the residential property. Fourthly, in addition to the aerial photo, a collection of photos of the development with its environs taken from a horizontal perspective should be included in the sales brochure. Lastly, if a vendor makes reference to the MTR system in the sales brochure, it must highlight the closest MTR station to the development at the time of the sale. Vendors must also provide purchasers with detailed information if interchange is required from that MTR station to Central, Lo Wo, Airport and other popular destinations.

Notes

1 More details on the MTR system in Hong Kong and the latest development, see www.mtr.com.hk/en/customer/services/domestic_train_services.html and www.mtr.com.hk/en/customer/main/south_island_line.html
2 www.mtr.com.hk/eng/overview/profile_index.html
3 The train of Tung Chung line travels through the eight stations in 27 minutes along the route. http://en.wikipedia.org/wiki/Tung_Chung_Line
4 Liu Yat-ming, *External benefits and commuter rail development a case study of KCRC west rail and Tuen Mun*, dissertation submitted to the Faculty of Architecture in candidacy for the Degree of Bachelor of Science in Surveying, Department of Real Estate and Construction, the University of Hong Kong, April 2006, p.72, p.78. The research shows the West Rail Line (then the KCR West Rail) has brought the benefits of decreased transportation time, incurred land value and enhanced accessibility to Tuen Mun.
5 The development is located on 8 Shum Shing Road, Lai Chi Kok, Kowloon, completed in 2005.
6 www.edb.gov.hk/en/edu-system/primary-secondary/spa-systems/primary-1-admission/school-lists/index.html
7 For the judgment by the Court of First Instance: *Yang Dandan v Hong Kong Resort Co Ltd* [2015] HKEC 2050; the judgment of Court of Appeal: *Yang Dandan v Hong Kong Resort Co. Ltd* [2016] HKEC 1722.
8 Section 22 (3), Part 2 – Division 2, *Residential Properties (First-hand Sales) Ordinance*, A2343.
9 Ibid., section 1 (2), Part 1 of Schedule 1, A2491.
10 Ibid., section 31(1) (a), Part 2 - Division 3, A2359.
11 http://en.wikipedia.org/wiki/Districts_of_Hong_Kong
12 The district name requirement does not apply to sales brochures.
13 www.bel-air.com.hk/cyberport/jsp/location.html
14 Section 19 (2) (f) and (h), Part 2 – Division 2, A2335; section 6 and section 8, Part 1 of Schedule 1 A2509-A2515, *Residential Properties (First-hand Sales) Ordinance*.
15 Ibid., section 6 (3), Part 1 of Schedule 1, A2509-A2513.
16 Case No.: KTS8512-8517/2016.
17 Section 21 (1), Part 2 of Schedule 1, *Residential Properties (First-hand Sales) Ordinance*, A2533.
18 Ibid., Section 8 (2) (b), Part 1 of Schedule 1, A2515. See also B4 in the Revised Annex I to LACO Circular Memorandum No.62 in LACO Circular Memorandum No.63.
19 Such as GIC for Government, Institution or Community, R (A) for Residential (Group A) and CDA for Comprehensive Development Area. For one example, see section 4 of the sale brochure of the *Hermitage*, where the Approved South West Kowloon Outline Zoning Plan No. S/K20/24, Draft Mong Kok Outline Zoning Plan No.S/K3/27 and Approved Yau Ma Tei Outline Zoning Plan No. S/K2/20 are provided.
20 [2015] HKEC 2050.
21 Ibid., paragraph 20 and paragraph 47.
22 Section 7, Part 1 of Schedule 1, *Residential Properties (First-hand Sales) Ordinance*, A2513–A2515.
23 Ibid., section 30, Part 4 of Schedule, A2547–A2549.
24 Ibid., Section 19 (2) (i), Part 2 – Division 2, A2335; Section 9, Part 1 of Schedule 1, A2571.

25 Ibid., section 22 (2), Part 2 – Division 2, A2345.
26 Ibid., section 9 (2), Part 1 of Schedule 1, A2517.
27 Minibus 16S runs from *Choi Hung* MTR Station to *Aria*.
28 See the sales brochure of *Fadewater*.
29 www.mtr.com.hk/en/customer/services/system_map.html
30 www.homantinhillside.hk/en-us/location-and-greenery.php#d
31 www.info.gov.hk/gia/general/201411/20/P201411200802.htm

References

CC (2014) Study on the Sales of First-hand Residential Properties, pp. 69–78, Consumer Council, 11 November 2014, www.consumer.org.hk/ws_en/competition_issues/reports/20141111.html.

Chau, K. W., Wong S. K., Chan, A. T. and Lam, K. (2011) The Value of Clean Air in High Density Urban Areas, *High-Rise Building Living in Asian Cities,* 1st edn, (A. G. O. Yeh and B. Yuen ed.), Springer Verlag, pp. 113–128.

EB (2016) Primary One Admission for September 2016, Education Bureau, September 2016, www.edb.gov.hk/en/edu-system/primary-secondary/spa-systems/primary-1-admission/

Lands D (2010a) Legal Advisory and Conveyancing Office Circular Memorandum No. 62, Lands Department Consent Scheme, Legal Advisory and Conveyancing Office, Lands Department, 2 June 2010.

Lands D (2010b) Legal Advisory and Conveyancing Office Circular Memorandum No. 63, Lands Department Consent Scheme, Legal Advisory and Conveyancing Office, Lands Department, 1 September 2010.

Lands D (2012) Legal Advisory and Conveyancing Office Circular Memorandum No. 68, Lands Department Consent Scheme, Legal Advisory and Conveyancing Office, Lands Department, 22 March 2012.

LC (2006) ATV Fined for Contravention of Broadcasting Ordinance, CB(1)2078/05-06(01), Legislative Council, July 10 2006, p. 2.

LC (2008) Shatin to Central Link and MTR Kwun Tong Line Extension, *Legislative Council Brief*, THB(T)CR 10/1016/99, Legislative Council, 27 March 2008.

LC (2009) Progress of the Shatin to Central Link, *Legislative Council Panel on Transport Subcommittee on Matters Relating to Railways*, CB(1)1137/08-09(05), Legislative Council, 31 March 2009, www.mtr-shatincentrallink.hk/en/public-consultation/consultation-meeting.html.

Liu, Y. (2006) External benefits and commuter rail development a case study of KCRC west rail and Tuen Mun, dissertation submitted to the Faculty of Architecture in candidacy for the Degree of Bachelor of Science in Surveying, Department of Real Estate and Construction, the University of Hong Kong, April 2006, pp. 72–78.

LRC (1995) *Report on Descriptions of Flats on Sale*, The Law Reform Commission of Hong Kong, April 1995, p. 18.

Merry, M. (2008) *Protection of Purchasers of Uncompleted Residential Flats - The Hong Kong Experience*, HKU-NUS-SMU Symposium Paper, Singapore, November 2008, pp. 4–6.

Mingpao (2014) 'Homantin Hillside' to launch in October, name said to mislead purchasers, 8 August 2014.

REDA (2009) Guidelines for Sales Descriptions of Uncompleted Residential Properties, The Real Estate Developers Association of Hong Kong, 7 October 2009.

RVD (2016) Hong Kong Property Review 2016, The Rating and Valuation Department, 2016, www.rvd.gov.hk/en/publications/hkpr.html

Safire, W. (2009) Location, Location, Location, *New York Times,* 26 June 2009.

SCMP (2006) Market Farces, *South China Morning Post,* 11 September 2006.

SCMP (2008) HK Island shows solid price growth: overall increases strongest in past three years with Taikoo Shing rising 56 per cent, *South China Morning Post,* 5 March 2008.

SCMP (2009a) Cover advertisement, *South China Morning Post,* 17 October 2009.

SCMP (2009b) The pricey sea view that doesn't last for long, *South China Morning Post,* 8 June 2009.

SCMP (2016) Ground broken: Hong Kong property developer fined HK$200,000 for sales malpractice, *South China Morning Post,* 19 July 2016, Hong Kong. www.scmp.com/news/hong-kong/law-crime/article/1991764/ground-broken-hong-kong-property-developer-fined-hk200000

SC (2011) Report of the Steering Committee on Regulation of Sale of First-hand Residential Properties by Legislation, The Steering Committee on the Regulation of the Sale of First-hand Residential Properties by Legislation, October 2011, p. 15.

SRPA (2014a) SRPA advises prospective purchasers to note various issues on Homantin Hillside, *Press Releases,* The Sales of First-hand Residential Properties Authority, 20 November 2014, www.info.gov.hk/gia/general/201411/20/P201411200802.htm.

SRPA (2014b) SRPA advises prospective purchasers on proposed columbarium development near City Point, *Press Releases,* The Sales of First-hand Residential Properties Authority, 15 May 2014, www.info.gov.hk/gia/general/201405/15/P201405150750.htm

SRPA (2014c) SRPA Advises Prospective Purchasers on Access Roads within Boundary of Mont Vert for Public Access to Adjacent Private Land and Burial Grounds, the Sales of First-hand Residential Properties Authority, July 18, 2004, www.info.gov.hk/gia/general/201407/18/P201407180719.htm

The Vendor of Aria (2009) Location Plan, Sales Brochure, 2009.

The Vendor of Apex (2006) Advertisement, 2006.

The Vendor of City Point (2014) Sales Brochure, 2014.

The Vendor of Chianti (2008) Sales Brochure, 2008.

The Vendor of Fadewater (2008) Sales Brochure, 2008.

The Vendor of Inland Crest (2010) Advertisement, 2010.

The Vendor of Larvotto (2010) Project Website, 2008.

The Vendor of Lake Silver (2009) Sales Brochure, 2009.

The Vendor of Twin Regency (2016) Advertisement, 2016.

Webb, D. M. (2010) Larvotto – do you know the boatyard? *Webb-site.com,* 2010, https://webb-site.com/articles/larvotto.asp.

Yeung, J. (2005) The effect of Chinese culture on the implicit value of graveyard view in Hong Kong residential property market, Department of Real Estate and Construction, The University of Hong Kong, April 2005.

Yu, S. M., Han, S. S. and Chai, C. H. (2007) Modeling the Value of View in Real Estate Valuation: A3-D GIS Approach, Department of Real Estate, National University of Singapore, p. 12.

7 Floor number[1]

Introduction

As Malcolm Merry (2008) suggested, '[I]n crowded Hong Kong, landed property means principally flats in high-rise buildings'. As far as *location* is concerned, the concept entails another layer of meaning in Hong Kong's mega complex developments: in addition to the location of the estate, what matters to the purchaser is the location of the apartment within the development. This primarily concerns the floor level of the apartment.[2] The information about floor number is critical because dwellings situated on floors further away from the ground floor enjoy less noise and pollution and, usually, a better view. Any price list published by developers for sale of first-hand residential properties would suggest such a *premium by floor level*: every other element being equal (e.g., the same saleable area, internal partitions, design, orientation, residential tower, location, contractor, developer, time of release), an apartment sits on a higher floor (even one floor above) is *always* priced higher than the one below.[3] The information on the floor level of a flat, however, is principally misleading, if not completely deceptive, but only in the eyes of a foreigner. This is because developers, who are more willing to follow the local preference of certain numbers, usually omit 'unlucky' numbers such as 4, 14, 24, 34, 40, 41, 42, 43, 44, 45, 46, 47, 48, 49, 54 etc. in floor numbering. A new tendency is to deliberately introduce more numbers ending with 8 or 6 (e.g. 68 and 88) by skipping 'unlucky' and 'neutral' numbers.

This chapter deals with a unique phenomenon in Hong Kong: liberal floor numbering would not have been an issue if the following two realities did not co-exist in the city: firstly, Hong Kong transformed from a fishing village in the 1850s to a metropolitan city with an ever-growing concrete jungle of high-rise buildings; secondly, over the past four to five decades the local community has developed a deeply-entrenched belief in a numerology that overly glamorizes the number eight while demonizing the number four.

The practice of liberal floor numbering has brought much chaos to the local real estate market with a proper solution urgently required. It is not considered strange that many a skyscraper in Hong Kong has a fiftieth floor immediately above the thirty-ninth floor. The eightieth floor may sits on the sixty-second floor level above the ground level. Sometimes the lowest residential floor is numbered the fifth floor. In some cases the ground floor is either one or two floors above or below the ground level. With all this happening on a regular basis, one, in nowadays Hong Kong, cannot easily tell the exact floor level of a residential property by the floor number.

The issue is only loosely regulated by the Buildings Department via issuing Practice Notes for the reference of developers; there are no statutory powers vested with the Building Authority to reject a building plan based on floor numbering system. Theoretically speaking, under the current regulatory system, it is of the absolute discretion of developers to decide the fashion of numbering. The lack of effective control results in liberal practices that render floor numbers almost meaningless. This not only affects emergency services but also, as will be discussed later, sets the stage for misrepresentation. The enactment of the *Residential Properties (First-hand Sales) Ordinance* (the *Ordinance*) in 2012 represented one opportunity to regulate floor numbering by legislation, yet beyond requirements on disclosure of information about the number of floors of a residential development, the *Ordinance* does not prescribe how floors should be numbered in residential towers. Thus a revision to include a new rule or perhaps a new piece of legislation on floor numbering in all the residential, commercial and industrial buildings in the Special Administrative Region is necessary.

After a brief illustration on the culture and practices, this chapter sets out to discuss how floors should be numbered in high-rise buildings in Hong Kong. The focus is on the liberal number policy in newly built developments (first-hand properties), i.e. when properties are sold off-plan and the floor numbers are stated in sales brochures. There are two focal points in the proposed floor numbering system: one is the finding of the ground floor of a building, the other is the fashion of numbering floors above the ground floor. The discussion responds to a wide range of suggestions: the most conservative insists zero tolerance of omitting numbers while the most liberal argues for complete business freedom and an *inherent right* by the vendor in floor numbering. Essentially, three different approaches, two suggested by the government and one by the Judiciary, are compared in terms of *clarity* and *flexibility*. In reaching the conclusion of an optimal floor numbering system that best addresses the conflicts of common sense, logic and superstition, consideration is given to social, cultural, economic and administrative values.

Chinese numerology and the practice

In recent years, the Chinese community in Hong Kong has developed a popular numerology system where unique meanings, either positive or negative, are assigned to numbers based on their pronunciation in Cantonese. On the one hand, number eight '八' [pā:t] having the same sound as '發' (becoming rich) is considered as the super lucky number, capable of bringing wealth and prosperity to the associates. Second to it is number six '六' [lù:k] rhyming with '祿' (benefits). Along the same lines but with less popularity are the number two '二' [yih] having the same sound as '易' (easy) and the number three '三' [sā:m] as

'生' (life; good living). On the other hand, number four '四' [sēi], pronounced similarly to '死' (death), is seen as the most inauspicious number.

Similar phenomena are seen in other cosmopolitan cities in China such as Macau, Beijing, Shanghai, Chengdu, Chongqing, Tianjin, Guangzhou and Shenzhen. For cities in the Mainland, the meanings ascribed to individual numbers are based on their pronunciations in Mandarin. Therefore similarly to the culture in Hong Kong, the number four '四' [sì] which shares the same pronunciation – only differing in intonation – with the word death '死' [sǐ] is regarded as inauspicious; number eight '八' [bā] which rhymes with the word '发' [fā] (getting rich) is the most favoured single-digit number. The number five '五' is treated differently in the two cultures: in Cantonese the number is pronounced as [ŋ], sharing the same sound with the word '吾' (no, not), and is considered as neutral or less lucky; in Mandarin it is pronounced as [wǔ] which is close to the pronunciation of the word '我' [wǒ] (I, me, myself) and is in generally considered as a powerful and lucky number.

This little superstition would not have caused much controversy if Hong Kong were not the world's tallest, or the most vertical city (Emporis 2011; Cramer, Yankopolus and Group 2006).[4] No avoiding the fact that a convention has been firmly established in the local practices and fairly accepted by the public: for multi-storey buildings the digit 4 and any number that has one or more '4' in it, are omitted in floor numbering. This phenomenon can be compared to the dread of number 13 in the west. It has long been observed that 13 is skipped in floor and house numbering in countries like the US, UK and France by developers (Broderick 2002). Whereas the Western triskaidekaphobia only exhibits fear of the number 13, the local tetraphobia avoids the number 4 and any following numbers having the digit 4 – even there is no evidence suggesting that units sitting on these 'less lucky' floors are sold at a discount in the re-sale market (Chau, Ma and Ho 2000). It is worth mentioning that in commercial and residential properties number 13 is also avoided on a large scale in Hong Kong. In some cases numbers like '53' and '58' are also skipped for implying 'no life' and 'no prosperity'. Table 7.1 shows a few examples in recent residential developments.

On the other hand, empirical study suggests that units on lucky floors (floor number 8 or numbers that contain the number 8 as one of the digits – with the exception of 58) are sold with a premium; this is particularly the case during property booms (Chau, Ma and Ho 2000).

In October 2009, one developer pushed the boundary further. The developer of *39 Conduit Road* named the top two floors of a 46-storey building 68/F and 88/F, after omitting a total of 48 intermediate floor numbers in all (SCMP 2009a). The floor plan shows that 4, 13, 14, 24 and 34 are conventionally omitted, followed by a leapfrog from 39/F to 60/F for the upper section of featured units in the property. In all, 48 numbers in total were omitted only to enable the number 88 to be attached to the top floor of the building. This unprecedented approach has been criticized for being false and misleading. The public was bemused at the degree of freedom enjoyed by the developers in floor numbering.

Table 7.1 Omitted Floor or House Numbers in Recent Developments

Name of the Estate	Floor or House Numbers Omitted
One Pacific Heights	13, 14, 24, 34, 44
Dynasty	13, 14, 24, 34, 40, 41, 42, 43, 44, 45, 46, 47, 48, 49, 54, 64
Season's Monarch	4, 13, 14, 24, 34, 40-49, 54, 64, 74, 84, 94, 104, 114, 124,
(Season's Monarch is a	134, 140–149, 154, 164, 174, 184, 194, 204, 214, 224,
development of low rise	234, 240–249, 254, 264, 274, 284, 294
houses; the numbers listed	
are skipped in the numbering	
of houses).	
Hermitage	13, 14, 24, 34, 40–49, 53, 54, 58, 64, 74
Spectra	4, 13, 14, 24

Identifying the ground floor

To promote clarity in such circumstances, from 2010 onward, the Lands Department of the Hong Kong government requires that sales brochures issued by developers provide first, *the total number of storeys of each tower*; and second the *floor numbering* of the development, including any *omitted floor numbering* and refuge floors (Lands D 2010a, 2010b and 2012). The rule is drafted in such a brief way that it does not specify which floor is the starting floor for the purpose of calculation: is it the ground floor or the floor immediately above the ground floor? Under the traditional British numbering system, the starting point should be the floor immediately above the ground floor or above the upper ground floors; that is to say, the ground floor or any upper ground floors are excluded from the calculation of total number of storeys of a residential tower.[5] This requirement is missing in the *Residential Properties (First-hand Sales) Ordinance*.

A crucial aspect of a clear floor numbering system is to ascertain the ground floor of a building. A ground floor is usually understood as the floor that stands at or immediately above the ground on the level of the street adjacent to the building. The ground floor does not necessarily need to be the lowest floor of the building if there are floors in the building that are below the street level. If the way the ground floor is decided is subject to a common standard, there will be much clarity in floor numbering. The absence of a standard has given rise to misleading practices in the drawing of floor plans in the sales brochure to mislead the level of a floor vis-à-vis the street level of the adjacent pavement.

Balchita Ltd v Kam Yuck Investment Co Ltd & Anor tells the story of a presale of four shops on a 'ground floor' which was actually two levels below the street level.[6] In this case the floor plan did not employ conventional symbols suggesting level difference between the ground floor and the adjacent street; instead, dotted lines were used to represent the stairs linking the ground floor to the adjacent pavement. The purchaser thought the four shops were on the floor parallel to the street level and entered into the agreements with the vendor. The judge held that the dotted lines constituted misrepresentation.

In February 2012, when a seven-million-dollar featured unit in *Oceanaire* described by the sales brochure as on the 'podium floor' was completed, the purchaser found the dwelling was actually situated on the same level as the street adjacent to the building. The floor plan printed in the sales brochure suggested that the podium floor is immediately below a 'Floor 5' (The Standard 2012). The sales brochure was accused of misleading the purchaser into believing that the podium floor is higher than the ground floor by a graphic illustration linking the podium floor to the upper ground floor of the club house, a floor turns out, after completion, to be below the level of the ground floor of the street adjacent to the building. The accident happened just in time to pave the way for a new requirement to be included in the *Ordinance*, which requires that the sales brochure must set out a plan showing 'a cross-section of the building in relation to every street adjacent to the building' and 'the level of every such street in relation to a known datum and to the level of the lowest residential floor of the building'.[7]

But the legislation does not touch upon how the lowest residential floor of a building should be named, viz., should it be named as Ground Floor, or Podium Floor, or the First Floor. When the vendor of *Oceanaire* was asked about the legitimacy for the arrangement, the reply was that 'the floor plan is approved by the government'. Of course, the approval by the government does not justify the reasonableness of the arrangement. This calls upon the necessity of standardizing ground floor in Hong Kong.

The issue of identifying ground floor was considered in *Tai Tung On Enterprises Company Limited v Oriental Horse Company Limited*, where Recorder Edward Chan SC stated that the ground floor would be the floor at street level; if the building straddles over two or more streets at different levels, it may be necessary to resort to other information to find out which level is designated as the ground floor.[8] Following this rule, the floor immediately above the ground floor is numbered as the first floor; 'Podium Floor' (sometimes marked as P/F) should be avoided in floor numbering. Exception should be made if multiple floors immediately above the ground floor are used as car-parking space; in this case the floors designated for car-parking purpose shall be named as upper ground floors (viz., UG1, UG2, UG3 and etc.); the floor immediately above the highest upper ground floor should then be named as the first floor.

Three approaches of regulating floor numbering

After clearing up the controversy in finding the ground floor and the starting floor for the purpose of calculating the numbers of floor within a building, the following discussion turns to the central question of the paper: how floors above the ground floor (or the highest upper ground floor) should be numbered.

The Buildings Department of the Hong Kong Special Administrative Region Government states the basic principles of floor numbering in the 'Practice Note for Authorised Persons, Registered Structural Engineers and Registered Geotechnical Engineers'. In the most practical sense the Practice Notes are to provide guidelines for the reference of developers. The Building Authority is not vested with statutory powers under the *Buildings Ordinance* to reject building plans in case of liberal floor numbering.[9] If the Building Authority considers the plan of floor numbers inappropriate, it can only suggest the applicant make amendments (DB 2009).

Suffix approach

Shortly after the media reports on the controversial floor numbering in *39 Conduit Road*, the Buildings Department started to revise the *Practice Note* in late 2009. A stringent approach was suggested in December 2009: the omission of more than two floor numbers in a consecutive series was prohibited; and any omitted number has to be substituted with the floor number of the floor immediately below it with a suffix 'A' (and 'B' if two floor numbers in a consecutive series are skipped in the case of skipping 13/F and 14/F) (SCMP 2009b). Under this approach, the fourth floor will be marked as 3A; thirteenth floor as floor 12A and fourteenth as floor 12B; twenty-fourth Floor as Floor 23A etc.

Intermediate approach: omission of unlucky numbers

Later, compromise was made to the 'long-established local practice and customs' of skipping certain numbers: in the revised guidelines issued in May 2010, the Buildings Department relaxed the above proposed rules (SCMP 2010). An intermediate approach was enforced from 1 September 2010 onward. The approach insists that floor numbers are to be assigned in a logical and consecutive numerical series, yet omission is allowed of floor numbers 4, 13 and those ending with 4 *without replacement* (Buildings Department 2010). Under the regulation developers cannot omit numbers 40 to 49 (except floor 44) and other undesirable numbers like 53 and 58.

Zero tolerance approach to illogical and superstitious floor numbering

A third approach can be observed from the decision of *Tai Tung On Enterprises Company Limited v Oriental Horse Company Limited.* On 1 March 1994, a memorandum was signed whereby the original landowner agreed to sell the Defendant the first to twenty-fourth floors of 126 Caine Road which were then under construction. On 4 May, a formal agreement for sale and purchase was signed, where the property on sale was described as 'ALL THOSE FIRST FLOOR and its Flat Roof, SECOND, THIRD, FOURTH, FIFTH, SIXTH, SEVENTH, EIGHTH, NINTH, TENTH, ELEVENTH, TWELFTH, THIRTEENTH, FOURTEENTH, FIFTEENTH, SIXTEENTH, SEVENTEENTH, EIGHTEENTH, NINETEENTH, TWENTIETH, TWENTY-FIRST, TWENTY-SECOND, TWENTY-THIRD and TWENTY-FOURTH FLOOR and its ROOF THEREOF'. On 10 May, a Deed Poll (dated on 4/05/1994) was signed so as to effect the re-designation of floor numbers. At the same time, the Defendant began to sub-sell each floor of the property to other purchasers. In February, the Defendant issued a tentative price list in which the 24 floors were numbered from first to twenty-eighth without fourth, thirteenth, fourteenth and twenty-fourth floors. There was an express note that there was no 4/F, 13/F, 14/F & 24/F in the price list. In April, the Defendant offered to sell to Plaintiff the fifteenth floor. On 30 April, a binding provisional agreement for sale and purchase was signed by the Defendant and the Plaintiff; the description of the premises purchased was '15th floor of 126 Caine Road, Mid-levels, Hong Kong'. On 8 July, the agreement for sale and purchase was signed by the Plaintiff, 'all that 15th floor of the building which said floor for the purpose of identification only is shown and coloured pink on the Plan annexed hereto'; no plan however was annexed to the agreement at the time when it was executed by the Plaintiff. The Plaintiff had duly paid all the deposits and part payments due under the agreement. The agreement for sale and purchase was later signed by the Defendant on 10 June. On 15 October, the Plaintiff's solicitor asked the Defendant's solicitor to send a copy of the plan. After receiving the plan, the Plaintiff's solicitor discovered that the fifteenth floor of the building was numbered as eighteenth floor in the plan. The Plaintiff's solicitor tendered a draft assignment for the Defendant's solicitor for approval that the property should be described as 'EIGHTEENTH FLOOR', which was rejected by the Defendant's solicitor. The Plaintiff then sought to claim the refund of the amount of $1,623,196 paid on the ground that the Defendant was unable to assign the floor that the Plaintiff had contracted to purchase.

The core issue in this case was which floor was offered for sale. Recorder Edward Chan SC was of the view that 'the 15th floor as common English words must be understood as meaning the floor at the 15th level above the ground floor level of a building':

> [T]he words '15th floor' are plain in their meaning and there is no ambiguity in their meaning. There is also no latent ambiguity in the meaning of these words as the building constructed at the site is an ordinary building without any basement and without any level other than the one abutting Caine Road which could be said to be the ground floor. In these circumstances, I am of the view that it is not permissible to call in aid evidence on how the parties had come to conclude their agreement and it is not permissible to rely on matters set out in the price list which was alleged to have been shown to the Plaintiff when the agreement was being negotiated, even assuming that such price lists were in fact shown.

It seems that the ever present cultural phenomenon did not shed much light on the Judge's decision. Instead the reasoning is centred on common law principles and rules of interpretation. As a matter of basic principle, 'where the words of a written agreement have a clear and fixed meaning, not susceptible of explanation, extrinsic evidence is not admissible to show that the parties meant something different from what they have written.'[10] The approach shows zero tolerance of the local practice of skipping unlucky numbers in floor numbering. If priority is given to the unequivocal meaning of numbers, then a judge in Hong Kong may hold for a purchaser who finds her sixtieth floor flat on the fortieth level above the ground floor, for there is very little room to argue a number does not partake of a clear and fixed meaning as an indicator of sequence.

Legislating floor numbering: the correct approach

It is unfortunate that the *Residential Properties (First-hand Sales) Ordinance* does not provide a standard way of floor numbering in new residential buildings. Should floor numbering be a subject of legislation? If yes, which of the above three approaches should be adopted?

To regulate the way floors are numbered is indeed in line with the overall aim of the *Ordinance* to enhance transparency and eliminate information asymmetry in sales of first-hand properties. If numbers *can* be skipped, then the fashion must be prescribed by law. What Hong Kong needs here is a standard method of floor numbering that is logical, predictable and reliable. In fact the enormous efforts of Lands Department Consent Scheme and the *Ordinance* to demand disclosure of total number of storeys and omitted floor numbers would be unnecessary if there were such a standard.

Moreover, a clear floor numbering system endorsed by legislation can prevent disputes of what is being sold. Developers can sell and advertise properties appropriately while purchasers, especially those from overseas, can understand what they are undertaking to buy. If the status quo is not intervened by regulation, however, disputes over what is actually being sold are bound to arise. In extreme cases, a rogue vendor could take advantage of the messy situation to sell apartments on non-existing floors.

Then, which approach should be the standard for Hong Kong? Sixteen years on, is *Tai Tung On Enterprises Company Limited v Oriental Horse Company Limited* old-fashioned? Is it right for the government to allow developers to omit certain numbers without replacement? Should *the common Chinese practice of skipping 'unlucky' floor numbers'* – in the words of *Financial Times* (Lau 2010) – be regularized? If lucky numbers bring additional economic value to flats, can the law take one step further to allow creative numbering that assigns only lucky numbers to floors and houses?

Firstly, cultural influence should always be a consideration in law making. Hong Kong law has its tradition to give consideration to local circumstances. Here the special circumstance is the psychological attachment to special numbers that is present in the Chinese community (the predominant majority) in Hong Kong. An unlucky number associated with the property in many cases can affect people's perception of the property. As a starting point, the legislation should embrace, other than disregard, the local culture. Distinctive culture symbols are valuable assets to a community, a city and a region. Every culture has its own idols and taboos; they bring people together with a shared identity and belief. In this regard the local laws' reflection on the preference of eight and six over the dread of four could be a lively account of the local culture.

Secondly, the sturdily persisted preference has, already, transferred into economic values. From mobile phone numbers, car plates to floor numbers, discernment is habitually exercised to those rich in digit eight and digit six over those with four. Empirical research on the auction of car plates in Hong Kong shows that the number eight carries a significant premium with number four a significant discount; eight is associated with plates with significantly higher winning bids whereas the number four significantly lower; controlling for other factors, an ordinary four-digit plate with one extra eight on average was sold at 63.5 per cent higher whereas an ordinary four-digit plate with one extra four on average was sold at 11 per cent lower; the price difference goes to 94.8 per cent and 27.3 per cent for an ordinary three-digit plate (Ng, Chong and Du 2010). The benefits of omitting numbers such as four, 13 and those ending with four are apparent for developers: as there are no unlucky numbers in the entire building, units on each floor can sell at a good price. Developers are not the only ones that enjoy the benefits. The owners also benefit from the lucky numbering when they resell the flats. In property booms, a lucky floor number may itself give the vendor a premium (Chau, Ma and Ho 2000). To put it another way, these lucky floor numbers are not just numerical symbols but an inherent asset themselves. Essentially, the practice of liberal floor numbering does not do much harm to flat purchasers; it is a win–win situation for both developers and owners.

Under such circumstances, a strait-laced ideology that allows zero flexibility in floor numbering should be avoided. Otherwise, the law may itself be a 'curse' to those whose flats unfortunately sit on unlucky floors. When it comes to an issue that is able to mentally and emotionally affect a large number of people's perception on their properties in the region, it is wise to avoid a stringent approach.

Yet, if numbers can be skipped without replacement, what values do numbers have other than a mere symbol to distinguish one floor from another? In other words, why do we need numbers at all? Why don't we just name one floor 'prosperity', another floor 'money', another 'wealth', 'fortune', 'rich', '$', 'HKD', '£', '€', '¥', or whatever is desired? In some countries, such as England, people give names to houses and buildings; and it is not rare in Hong Kong to name buildings after a person (Merry 2011). Can we expand the tradition to give names to floors so as to substitute several undesirable numbers? (If yes, this might make the lives of firemen more difficult).

Numbers not only distinguish one floor to another but also speak the sequence of all the floors. As soon as the floor atop the third floor has been named as the fifth floor, the numeric meaning of that 'five' and of any following numbers is lost; because intrinsically and logically five comes after four which comes after three. That will be the only understanding of a reasonable person. To suggest anything otherwise will violate an order that has been established probably as early as numbers were perceived by human beings. After all, is it not misleading, confusing and contrary to common sense that a duplex on the top floor of a 46-storey building is literally on the 88th floor?

Conclusion

In a nutshell, regulating floor numbering in Hong Kong requires the art of making compromises between superstition and sanctity of numbers. If weighty consideration is given to the local triskaidekaphobia, equal consideration should be given to the sacred order of numbers. Allowing an overly liberal approach will lead to chaos and disorder yet disallowing any deviation from the numeric order would almost represent an arrogant ignorance of local values by the law. The approach endorsed by the proposed legislation must balance the two conflicting values.

The only approach that embraces both clarity and flexibility is the stringent approach suggested by the Buildings Department in 2009. As a general rule, floor numbers are to be assigned in a logical and consecutive numerical series; as an exception, numbers ending with four can be substituted with the floor number of the floor immediately below it with a suffix 'A'; and 12A and 12B for the thirteenth floor and fourteenth floor respectively. This should be complemented by another three rules. Firstly, the ground floor should be the floor at street level; if the building straddles over two or more streets at different levels, it may be necessary to resort to other information to find out which level is designated as the ground floor. Secondly, the floor immediately above the ground floor, or in exceptional cases above the highest upper ground floor shall be named as the first floor. Thirdly, the use of 'Podium Floor' or other words to the effect should be prohibited in floor numbering. Fourthly, the Building Authority shall be vested with statutory power to reject any building plan that breaches the regulations stated above. Together they shall constitute the major part of the proposed legislation on floor numbering in Hong Kong.

Notes

1 The article 'Legislating Floor Numbering in Hong Kong' upon which this chapter is based was first published by Devin Lin in the *International Construction Law Review* [2015] ICLR 173, https://i-law.com/ilaw/doc/view.htm?id=353094

2 A floor is defined as 'any structure forming the base of any storey and every joist, board, timber, brick, concrete or other substance connected with and forming part of such structure' in Regulation 2(1) of Building (Planning) Regulations, Cap 123F; a storey is defined as 'means the space between the upper surface of every floor and the upper surface of the floor next above it where such a floor exists and in the case of a top storey the space between the upper surface of that floor and the mean height of the ceiling or roof'.

3 A most recent example: in the sale of *Reach*, a Unit C on the nineteenth floor of Block 1 is priced at HK$ 6,726,000; one floor below, the Unit C on the eighteenth floor of the same Block is priced at HK$ 6,702,000; and the Unit C on the seventeenth floor of Block 1 is priced at HK$ 6,655,000; see the Pricelist published in May 2013 at www.hld.com/salesfile/PriceList/www.thereach.com.hk/PL_PT0046_01_201305211530.pdf. The sale of *Reach* is an off-plan sale of first-hand residential properties started before and continues after the commencement of the *Residential Properties (First-hand Sales) Ordinance* in April 2013.

4 According to *Emporis* (a worldwide information provider who runs the world's largest and most comprehensive database of skyscrapers and high-rise buildings), Hong Kong

outnumbers any other city in the world with about 1,352 skyscrapers and 6,606 high-rise buildings: www.emporis.com/statistics/most-skyscrapers. A *'skyscraper'* is a multi-story building whose architectural height is at least 100 meters': www.emporis.com/building/standard/75/skyscraper'A *'high-rise building'* is a structure whose architectural height is between 35 and 100 meters. A structure is automatically listed as a high-rise when it has a minimum of 12 floors: www.emporis.com/building/standard/3/high-rise-building © 2000–2016 Emporis GMBH. Hong Kong is dubbed as 'the World's Tallest City' in the Skyscraper Cities Ranking List, the Almanac of Architecture and Design 2006, edited by James P. Cramer and Jennifer Evans Yankopolus, Greenway Group.

5 The same understanding can be found in the sales brochure of *Hermitage*, in which a residential tower (taking Tower 1 as an example) starting with 8/F and ending with 81/F is primarily marked as a tower of 53 storeys, followed by a brick quoting the flooring numbering system and the omitted floor numbers; see section 1 of the sale brochure of the *Hermitage*.

6 [1983] 2 HKC 33.

7 Section 18, Part 2 of Schedule 1, *Residential Properties (First-hand Sales) Ordinance*, A2531.

8 [1996] HKCU 280 (HCMP003329/1994).

9 The specific considerations that enable the Building Authority to refuse to approve building plans are provided in section 16 of the Buildings Ordinance, which do not include the plan of floor numbers of a building.

10 Paragraph 12–104 of *Chitty on Contract* 27th edition; cited at pp. 8–9 in [1996] HKCU 280.

References

Broderick, P. (2002) *Bottom Line Conjures Up Realty's Fear Of 13, Realty Times,* 13 September 2002.

BD (2010) Standardization of Floor Numbering, *Practice Note*, Buildings Department, May 2010.

Chau, K.W., Ma, V.S.M. and Ho, D.C.W. (2000) The pricing of 'luckiness' in the apartment market, *Journal of Real Estate Literature*, vol. 9.1, pp. 31–40.

Cramer, J. P., Yankopolus, J. E. and Group, G. (2006) the Almanac of Architecture and Design, 2006.

DB (2009) Following is a question by the Hon James To Kun-sun and a reply by the Secretary for Development, Ms Carrie Lam, in the Legislative Council today, LCQ6, Floor Numbering of Buildings, Development Bureau, *Press Release*, 4 November 2009.

Lau, J. (2010) Hong Kong flat sale collapse knocks Henderson, *Financial Times,* 16 June 2010.

Lands D (2010a) Legal Advisory and Conveyancing Office Circular Memorandum No. 62, Lands Department Consent Scheme, Legal Advisory and Conveyancing Office, Lands Department, 2 June 2010.

Lands D (2010b) Legal Advisory and Conveyancing Office Circular Memorandum No.63, Lands Department Consent Scheme, Legal Advisory and Conveyancing Office, Lands Department, 1 September 2010.

Lands D (2012) Legal Advisory and Conveyancing Office Circular Memorandum No. 68, Lands Department Consent Scheme, Legal Advisory and Conveyancing Office, Lands Department, 22 March 2012.

SCMP (2009a) Unusual floor-numbering strategy a misleading gimmick, *South China Morning Post*, 19 October 2009.

SCMP (2009b) Draft Rules to Curb Skipping of Floor Numbers, *South China Morning Post*, 30 December 2009.

SCMP (2010) The number's up for developers who skip floors, *South China Morning Post*, 17 April 2010.

Merry, M. (2008) Protection of Purchasers of Uncompleted Residential Flats – The Hong Kong Experience, *HKU-NUS-SMU Symposium Paper*, Singapore, November 2008.

Merry, M. (2011) Do Naming Rights Run with Land? *Conveyancer and Property Lawyer*, vol. 75, pp. 233–240.

Ng, T., Chong, T. and Du, X. (2010) The Value of Superstitions, *Journal of Economic Psychology*, vol. 31(3), pp. 293–309.

The Standard (2012) Lowest Floor May Require More Details, the Standard, 1 March 2012.

The Vendor of 39 Conduit Road (2009) Floor Plan, Sales Brochure, 2010.

The Vendor of Hermitage (2010) Sales Brochure, 2010.

The Vendor of Reach (2013) Price List No.1, 3 July 2016, www.hld.com/salesfile/Price List/www.thereach.com.hk/PL_PT0046_01_201305211530.pdf.

8   Date of completion and lease term[1]

Introduction

After exploring various physical aspects of the residential unit, this chapter introduces a new dimension to the discussion: the time dimension of a residential unit in the Hong Kong Special Administrative Region (or *HKSAR*).

Our discussion on the time dimension in the context of sales of first-hand residential properties shall begin with the premise that time, in general, is of the essence in the conveyancing process of real estate properties. This requests performance must be carried out within the time limit specified by the agreement for sale and purchase. The arrangement is to promote certainty in transactions of land. Thus in one Hong Kong case where the contract suggested that time was of the essence in all respects and the buyer's solicitor was late by 10 minutes after the contractual completion time, Lord Hoffman held that the vendor was entitled to rescind the contract and forfeit the deposit, as 'in such circumstances a vendor should be able to know with reasonable certainty whether he may resell the land or not'.[2] The notion is so established in conveyancing practices in Hong Kong: as Merry (2008) observed, the provision is so common in Hong Kong that should it inadvertently be omitted the courts are prepared to imply it. However, a 2015 decision in *Many Gain Investment Ltd v Chan Fai Ho* by the Court of First Instance may suggest that absent an express provision in the sale and purchase agreement time may not be held as of essence under exceptional circumstances.[3]

It is therefore significant to point out first and foremost that for sales of first-hand residential properties in Hong Kong, the *Residential Properties (First-hand Sales) Ordinance* (the *Ordinance*) has provided in the standard agreement for sale and purchase that *time is in every aspect of the essence* of the agreement.[4]

The discussion then turns to two critical aspects relating to the time dimension of a first-hand residential unit, in particular of an uncompleted flat: the *date of completion* and the *lease term*.

As discussed in previous chapters, first-hand residential properties are usually sold off-plan in Hong Kong, viz., the sale starts before the completion of the construction of the development. While off-plan sales can benefit both the vendor and the purchasers in the early construction stages, it also raises the issue of incompletion or delayed completion (Merry 2008). And that is not the only risk.

All land in Hong Kong (except the land on which St. John's Cathedral stands) is leasehold; strictly speaking, purchasers do not own the property; instead, they are buying the right or perhaps better termed as certain interests to enjoy exclusive possession of the property for a period of time. The lease term runs from 50 years to 999 years in Hong Kong, yet there is no guarantee that the leases will continue to run after 30 June 2047. The Basic Law of the HKSAR prescribes only that 'One Country Two Systems' operates for 50 years from 1 July 1997. The political uncertainty surrounding the constitutional status of HKSAR after 2047 casts a shadow on the ownership of all the residential properties in the region in some 30 years' time.

Thus accurate information about the date of completion and the lease terms seems to be of paramount importance for a fair and transparent market. In ascertaining the lifespan of a first-hand residential property in Hong Kong starting from construction, this chapter examines how the Consent Scheme and the new legislation regulate disclosure of information about the time dimension of the residential property sold by developers.

Date of completion

The basic distinction between off-plan sale and a sale of completed flat lies in the certainty of date of delivery. A purchaser of an uncompleted flat wishes to know exactly when the construction will be completed and the flat will be ready for delivery. Decades after the emergence of off-plan sales in the 1960s, the date of completion was not required to be provided in sales brochures or price lists; the only place to find the information was the agreement for sale and purchase (Lands D 2011). As a result, purchasers could have been misled by developers and agents during pre-contract negotiations as to when the flat would be delivered to them. In August 2010 the Real Estate Developers Association of Hong Kong (REDA) required that the estimated date of completion should be provided in the *Register of Agreements for Sale and Purchase* (REDA 2010). Since the *Register* needs to be made available in the sales office and on the project website, prospective purchasers can get access to the information much earlier than before. Now under the *Ordinance*, section 71(2) requests the developer to state in the advertisement a date that is, to the best of the vendor's knowledge, the estimated material date for the development in the case of sale of any specified residential property in an uncompleted development or a completed development pending compliance.

Even so, the question remains whether such information is precise and therefore reliable. To understand the degree of precision, the following discussion will investigate the meanings of the word *completion* and the phrase *estimated date of completion*.

'Completion'

In an off-plan sale, the word *completion* refers to at least two significant events. Firstly, it could mean *the completion of the development*, and secondly, *the completion of the transaction.* To distinguish the two events, the Law Reform Commission (1995) used *construction completion* and *legal completion* respectively in its 1995 *Report on Description of Flats on Sale*. Legal completion, or the completion of the transaction, will be discussed in Chapter 12. The focus of this chapter revolves around *construction completion,* viz., the physical completion of the property: what is the standard against which a development can be fairly considered as having been completed, or completely constructed?

Neither the Consent Scheme nor the legislation provides a definition on construction completion. Under the Consent Scheme, Clause 4(1)(c) and (2) of the standard agreement for sale and purchase in *LACO Circular Memorandum No. 66,* if read together, prescribe that the vendor shall: (i) complete the Development in all respects in compliance with the conditions of the Government Grant, the building plans and the agreement for sale and purchase; and (ii) incorporate the fittings and finishes as set out in Schedule 6 into the property. For the *Ordinance,* clause 4(c) of the standard agreement for sale and purchase prescribes that the vendor shall complete the development or the phase of the development in all respects in compliance with the conditions either of the government Grant and/or the building plans (if any) on or before *the estimated material date* for the development or the phase of the development.[5]

'Material date'

The *Ordinance* has formulated a statutory definition on construction completion in the term *material date* (or in Chinese, '關鍵日期'). In relation to an uncompleted development or an uncompleted phase under the Consent Scheme, it refers to the date on which the conditions of the land grant are complied with in respect of the development or the phase of the development. In the case of NTEHs (New Territories Exemption Houses), it is the date on which the development is completed in all respects in compliance with the conditions subject to which the certificate of exemption is issued under the *Buildings Ordinance (application to the New Territories) Ordinance*; or in any other case the date on which the development or the phase of the development is completed in all respects in compliance with the approved building plans.[6] The *Ordinance* requires that the sales brochure set out the estimated material date of the development.[7] This was not required under the Consent Scheme.[8] Any advertisement to promote the sale of residential properties in an uncompleted development must state a date that is to the best of the vendor's knowledge *the estimated material date* for the development.[9]

In order to generate a better understanding by purchasers, it is critical to translate this *material date* into a layman's language. Many would mistake *the estimated material date* for the date of delivery of vacant possession. Simply put, completion (or in Chinese, '完工') does not equal to delivery (as in Chinese, '交樓'). There is no guarantee that the flat will be delivered to the purchaser on or before or even around the estimated material date. The reasons are as follows.

Firstly, the *estimated date of completion* under the Consent Scheme or the *estimated material date* in the *Ordinance* is subject to extension as may be reasonably granted by the Authorized Person. For example, in the sale of the Vendor of *Twin Regency* in 2016, a development with the material date estimated on 31 July 2017, the following statement is included in the sales brochure, advertisement and project website by the Developer: *'Material Date' means the date on which the conditions of the land grant are compiled with in respect of the Development. The estimated material date is subject to any extension of time that is permitted under the agreement for sale and purchase.*[10]

The conditions under which an Authorized Person can approve an extension of time for completion includes strike or lock-out of workmen; riots or civil commotion; force majeure or Act of God; fire or other accident beyond the Vendor's control; war; and inclement weather.[11] There is no ceiling on the number of extensions the Authorized Person can grant for one project; nor any maximum number of days per grant or per project.

Purchasers are only allowed to rescind the contract if the developer fails to complete the development by the date as extended by the last extension of time granted by the Authorized Person.[12] But they can challenge the decision of granting extension by the Authorized Person. In *Xchrx Kar Ho Development Co. Ltd v Fineable (Pacific) Ltd*, a case concerning an off-plan sale of residential properties under the Consent Scheme, a 113-day extension of date of completion was granted by the Authorized Person to the vendor developer right before the original completion date on 30 November 1997. The court found the extension reasonable and did not allow the dissatisfied purchasers to rescind the agreement for sale and purchase.[13]

In another case, purchasers were allowed to rescind the agreements for sale and purchase and recover their payments with interest. In *Yau Mai and Others v Mark Honour Ltd*, the Authorized Person issued five certificates to extend the completion deadline from 31 May 2000 to 27 August 2000 due to unexpected difficulties on the foundation works and inclement weather. After the developer failed to meet the extended deadline in August, the Authorized Person issued a sixth certificate to extend the deadline for a further 75 days on 11 September 2000. The development was only deemed to be complete upon the issue of the occupation permit on 20 October 2000. The judge supported the claims by the purchasers that the sixth extension was invalid and was not persuaded by the developer's view that it was the drastic drop of market prices that motivated the purchasers' claim.[14]

Secondly, the *estimated material date* in the *Ordinance* or the *estimated date of completion* under the Consent Scheme refers solely to *construction completion*. The mere completion of the construction, however, does not make the units assignable per se. Developers still need to apply, within 14 days after having completed the development, for the *consent of the Director of Lands to assign* and a *certificate of compliance*.[15] The administrative process may take months to complete (Merry 2008a). Developers are only in a position validly to assign the property after obtaining at least one of the two documents and they should notify purchasers in writing within one month after receiving the document.[16] In the case of the Non-Consent Scheme, developers need to apply for the occupation document within 14 days after completing the construction, and should notify the purchasers in writing within six months after the issue of the occupation document.[17] In the case of NTEHs, developers need to apply for a letter issued by the Director of Lands confirming that the Director of Lands has no objection to every building in the development being occupied.[18]

Thirdly, both the Consent Scheme and the *Ordinance* regard the issue of a certificate of compliance or the consent to assign as conclusive evidence that the Development has been completed or is deemed to be completed, as the case may be.[19] Then, in some cases, notwithstanding the construction is not actually completed by the estimated date, developers nonetheless claimed that they have completed the development by referring the estimated material date to the date of issue of certificate of compliance or the consent to assign.

The certificate of compliance is a document certifying that all positive obligations imposed under the land grant on the grantee of the land on which the development or phase is situated, and the grantee's successors and assignees, have been complied with to the satisfaction of the Director of Lands.[20] While there is almost no doubt that the construction is fully completed upon the issue of the certificate of compliance, the same cannot be said in the case of the consent of the Director of Lands to assign. The Lands Department has been seen to apply different standards in processing the applications in respect of the two documents. It seems that the Director of Lands will only issue the certificate of compliance when *all* the conditions have been complied with, but may grant the consent to assign if by the time of the application if the Director is satisfied that *most* conditions of grant have been complied with.[21] Thus developers can, by way of clause 13(a), discharge the duty under clause 4(c) as long as they obtain the consent to assign by or before the estimated material date, even if the construction work is overdue. As a result, 'purchasers may have to endure the disruption of continuing building work after they take up residence' (Merry 2008b). In one case, the consent to assign had been issued by the District Lands Officer of Yuen Long despite that 'some minor external finishing works, minor landscaping works and minor internal finishing works at the common area of the lot were acknowledged to be outstanding'.[22]

Notification to purchasers relating to estimated material date

In case none of the conditions (i.e., strike, lock-out of workmen, riots, force majeure or Act of God, fire, war, inclement weather, etc.) arise or the happening of the event does not in the opinion of the Authorized Person render it reasonable to grant any extension, purchasers are entitled, by notice in writing, to rescind the agreement for sale and purchase at liberty if developers fail to complete the development by the material date. If an extension of time is granted by the Authorized Person yet the developer fails to complete the development by the date as extended by the extension, purchasers are entitled to rescind the agreement for sale and purchase at liberty.[23] In either case, purchasers need to rescind the agreement within 28 days after the material date or the date as extended; otherwise they will be deemed to have elected to wait for completion.[24]

For those who wait for completion, they will have another chance to rescind the agreement if the development is not completed within a period of six months from the material date or the date as extended.[25] Where an opportunity is present, some purchasers may choose to rescind the agreement when the market is in a downward spiral, while many will elect to wait for completion when the market is on the upswing.

Apart from the estimated material date or the estimated date of completion, developers are supposed to complete the development by the *expiry date of the Building Covenant Period* (expiry date); if in the opinion of the Authorized Person that the development will not be completed by the expiry date, the developer shall promptly apply for and obtain such extension.[26] If it fails to apply and obtain the extension and fails to complete the development by the expiry date, purchasers may also be entitled to rescind the agreement, if by then the agreement for sale and purchase is not yet completed.[27]

Purchasers may not be aware of the occurrence of these defining events during the lengthy period towards completion and may therefore miss the chance to rescind the agreement. From July 2004 onward, the Lands Department required that developers notify purchasers in writing of any failure to apply for or obtain any necessary extension of the Building Covenant expiry date or to complete construction of the development before expiry of the Building Covenant; and of any failure to complete construction of the development by the contractual date for completion along with the reasons for any extension by the Authorized Person (Lands D 2004).

The same, however, cannot be inferred from case law. In a line of cases concerning one developer (a Tin Shui Wai Development Ltd) the central question was whether the agreement for sale and purchase implied the following obligations of the developer: (i) to inform the purchaser whether the development had been completed on or before the estimated date of completion within a reasonable time, or prior to the expiry of 28 days after such date, or prior to or at the time of the notice for the completion of the sale and purchase of the property; (ii) to provide timely information, material or evidence to the purchaser concerning the progress of the development to enable the purchaser to exercise its rights of rescission as aforesaid; and (iii) to answer purchasers' questions or requisitions concerning whether the development had in fact been completed.[28]

The court was of the view that developers were under none of the duties. In *Tin Shui Wai Development Ltd v Yiu Sun Hung & Woo Kwan Lee & Lo Solicitors (Third Party)*, the purchaser was told by both the developer and its solicitor that the development was almost ready to deliver. As a result, the purchaser did not exercise the right to rescind the agreement and the 28-day period expired. In the end, the developer did not obtain the consent to assign until six months later, during which there was a sharp downturn in the value of the property. Judge L. Chan struck out the pleading of the implied term on the ground that 'the term need only be implied or take effect when the development was about to be completed, it would be difficult to tell at what time or stage of the construction works that it should be implied or take effect.'[29]

Luckily, the court's difficulty to overcome the common law rule of implied contract is now remedied by the statutory and administrative requirements. In 2010, REDA required that: '[a]ny change to the estimated date of completion should be updated in the *Register* within five working days'.[30] Under the *Ordinance* developers should inform purchasers in writing within 14 days from the issue of an extension of time granted by the Authorized Person and furnish a copy of the certificate of extension;[31] or in case of application to extend the expiry date of the Building Covenant Period, notify purchasers in writing of such application and the terms of extension granted within 30 days after each event.[32] The *Ordinance* should in addition commit developers to the obligations of answering purchasers' questions or requisitions and informing purchasers whether the development had been completed on or before the material date, or prior to or at the time of the notice for the completion of the sale and purchase of the property.

Lease term

All the land in Hong Kong except that above St. John's Cathedral is leasehold. Before 1997, privately-owned land in Hong Kong had been held on Crown leases. For Hong Kong and Kowloon, leases of 999 years were granted by the British Hong Kong government from the 1840s to 1901; leases of 75 years were granted in the Island Peak, the South side of Hong Kong island and Kowloon from 1876 to 1899; leases of 150 years without a right of renewal were granted in the Peak in 1877; leases of 75 years with a single right of renewal for a 75-year period had been granted from 1899 till the 'Joint Declaration of the Government of the United Kingdom of Great Britain and Northern Ireland and the Government of the People's Republic of China on the Question of Hong Kong' (the *Joint Declaration*) came into effect on 27 May 1985; leases expiring on 30 June 2047 were granted during the pre-handover period from the effective date of the *Joint Declaration* to the handover in 1997 (Webb 2010). The *Joint Declaration* extended the term of all these Crown Leases expiring before mid-1997 to 30 June 2047 without payment of an additional premium;[33] while Article 120 of the Basic Law ensures those expiring after mid-1997 continue to run after 1 July 1997.[34] For the New Territories, leases of 75 years renewable for 24 years less three days were granted from 1898 to 1959; leases for 99 years from 1 July 1898 less the last three days were granted from 1959 onwards; in 1988, the term of all these New Territories leases were extended till 30 June 2047 without payment of any additional premium by Section 6 of the *New Territories Leases (Extension) Ordinance* (Cap 150) (Sihombing and Wilkinson 2011).

After the establishment of the Hong Kong Special Administrative Region, the SAR Government grants new Government leases by way of land sale or auction (Goo and Lee 2015). The grant of the lease is subject to the land grant conditions; the grantees will be deemed to hold the legal estate upon fulfilment of the conditions (Sihombing and Wilkinson 2011). All the new government leases by the SAR government have been granted for a fixed period of 50 years without a right of renewal; the only exception is the lease for the Hong Kong Disneyland, where a right of renewal for another 50 years is given. In today's time, the term of leases in Hong Kong ranges from 50 years, 75 years or 99 years to 999 years; exceptions are 21-year leases for petrol filling stations and 15 years for leases for recreational purposes (Lands D 2005).

By virtue of section 24 of the *Ordinance*, the sales brochure must state the date up to which the owner is liable for the government rent payable for the specified residential property.[35] But this alone is not enough.

Lease as a legal estate means a term of years absolute in land.[36] The constructive side of the leasehold system is that it brings the government huge revenues from upfront premiums out of land sales (and, much less significantly, from the ground rents), with which the government could invest in infrastructure, education and other enterprises. At the same time the leasehold system determines that owners of real properties in Hong Kong do not *own* the property. As explained by Zarathustra (2011): '[w]hen a real estate developer "buys" a piece of land from the government, it does not really "buy" the land. It only leases the land from the government for a given period of time. And if the developer builds 100 flats on that site and sells to 100 purchasers, each purchaser will be entitled to have one-hundredth of the right to use the land for a given period of time.'

Theoretically, the renewal of a lease can be assumed only if there is a renewal option in the lease agreement; when the lease term expires, the government has every right to resume the land and, in doing so, the buildings above it without compensation. Prior to the handover, there were instances where land was resumed by the British Hong Kong government upon the expiration of the land lease; in some cases a market premium equal to the value of the land was paid by the government. On 15 July 1997, the SAR government instituted a new land policy that principally allows automated renewal of non-renewable land leases for a term of 50 years without payment of additional premium (Lands D 2005).

The implementation of the land policy of extending non-renewable leases for a term of 50 years without payment of an additional premium puts the newly granted government leases in a similar position as those quasi-freehold leases, e.g., leases of 999 years or 75 years with a single right to renew for 75 years granted by the British Hong Kong Government before the Joint Declaration. With another 50 years to run after the expiry of the original lease, the additional premium becomes a distant issue. Empirical research (Chau et al., 2003) on how the market capitalizes on the length of a lease confirmed the market's almost indiscriminative evaluation on leases with different durations: the price differentials between quasi-freehold interests (999 years) and leasehold (50 years) range from just 1.23 per cent to 1.49 per cent.

All these, however, are subject to the uncertainty of the constitutional status of the HKSAR pending 30 June 2047, a date up to which the 'One Country, Two Systems' arrangement is guaranteed by the 1984 Joint Declaration.[37] Article 5 of the Basic Law stipulates that the capitalist system and way of life shall remain in Hong Kong unchanged for 50 years. The two authorities are completely silent on what is left after the elapse of the 50 years (Ghai 1999). As observed by Alice Lee (1998): '[t]here is no explicit hint, let alone formal guarantee, in the Basic Law or any other legislative instrument that the fifty-year term is to be extended or may be renewed.' The silence implies the transitory nature of the SAR under the principle of One Country Two Systems for a 50-year period: 'on the one hand, it is sufficiently long to boost the confidence of Hong Kong people and that of foreign investors in the SAR; on the other hand, it is reasonably short to allow the central government in Beijing to conduct a timely review of its policy regarding the region.' According to Johannes Chan (2002), the ultimate goal could be either 'to retain two equally thriving but different systems' or 'to assimilate Hong Kong into the mainland politically, legally, culturally and ideologically'. Robert Morris (2007), for example, was of the latter opinion, regarding the Basic Law as having an absolute lifespan of 50 years from 1997 to 2047.

Then, what title can the government pass to the tenants of the SAR land? As Lee explains: '[i]f the SAR was to cease to exist on 30 June 2047, any attempt to grant government leases for a term expiring after that date would be ineffective. It is a cardinal principle of property law that an owner cannot give a better title than that he himself holds' (Lee 1998).

From the legal point here and now, the ambiguity of the status of the HKSAR pending 2047 makes the grants of new government leases a speculative practice. As even the first batch of the new government leases will expire after 30 June 2047, what is the authority for the government to grant leases beyond 2047? In *Law Lectures for Practitioners 1998*, Lee has conducted extensive research on local, national and international laws as to the validity of the new government leases. Her analysis started with Article 7 of the Basic Law, which states that the land within the HKSAR shall be State property; this, in her opinion, determined that under no circumstances may the SAR government exercise any of the rights in a way inconsistent with the State ownership. She then noted that the unique wording of Article 123 suggests leases, either granted before or after the establishment of the HKSAR, if expiring after 1 July 1997, should be dealt with in accordance with *laws and policies formulated by the Region on its own*. Her further research into the relevant laws and policies formulated by the region (i.e., *the Hong Kong Reunification Ordinance*) only confirms that the relevant laws and policies are all subject to the Basic Law. Essentially, Lee concluded that: 'the Basic Law is the starting point as well as the destination'; but its constitutional nature determines that any guidelines for the management and alienation of SAR land provided by the Basic Law are vague and abstract (Lee 1998).

A similar view is expressed by Margaret Ng, who regards the capitalist system and way of life as geographically bound by the territorial limits of the HKSAR for 50 years under Article 5 of the Basic Law. Noticing the time and territorial limits of the HKSAR, Ng questions how it is possible for the SAR government to grant leases beyond 2047 (SCMP 2007).

Danny Gittings, however, offers a very different interpretation of Article 5. Gittings suggests that the structural arrangement of Article 5, viz., the separation of the first clause 'The socialist system and policies shall not be practised in the Hong Kong Special Administrative Region' and the second clause 'and the previous capitalist system and way of life shall remain unchanged for 50 years' by a comma, indicate that the 50-year specific time limitation does not apply to the guarantee for not practising the socialist system and policies in the region. He argues that Article 5 was never intended to provide for an automatic end to 'One Country, Two Systems' and the imposition of a socialist system in Hong Kong after 30 June 2047; the 50-year reference in the second clause was only the minimum period for the guarantee against making any fundamental changes to Hong Kong's capitalist system and way of life'. Gittings also makes the point that even in the most extreme scenario of Hong Kong being abolished as a separate entity after 2047, the rights granted under those leases need not necessarily disappear and that responsibility for any unexpired portion of those land leases would simply pass to the Central Government of People's Republic of China (Gittings 2011).

Since what will happen to the HKSAR beyond 2047 is still undecided and highly debatable until today, all the leases run with the risk of expiry on 30 June 2047 (instead of the original lease terms if beyond). As the year 2047 approaches, to some, the muddy situation means that people are buying fewer and fewer years of use of the properties (Zarathustra 2011). Under the circumstances, in addition to the government rent, the sales brochure should highlight the lease term of the lot of the development; and second, the *remaining years* (perfectly by the time of the estimated material time or by the time of the presale) before the lease expires. This represents the period the flat will remain in the exclusive possession of the owner if the HKSAR continues to exist after 2047; and lastly, the *remaining years* (either by the time of the estimated material time or by the time of the presale) before 30 June 2047.

Conclusion

With the implementation of the *Ordinance*, purchasers are well-informed on the estimated material date as well as the risk for the delay beyond the estimated material date. Given delay occurs every so often in construction, more efforts can be made for the better information of the purchasers by summarizing in the sales brochure the purchasers' rights under the agreement for sale and purchase in case of delay. Meanwhile, it is certainly in the interests of purchasers to know the estimated date of delivery of vacant possession besides the estimated material date.

It is also in the purchasers' interests to know the residual term of the lease and the condition of renewal. However, the uncertainty for the status of the HKSAR after 2047 renders it technically difficult for a definite answer to be included in the relevant sections in the sales brochure for the time being.

Notes

1 Part of the chapter's discussion on the Consent Scheme was included in the lecture manuscript entitled 'The New Rules for Sales of Uncompleted Flats' in the Book *Law Lectures for Practitioners 2010* by Hong Kong Law Journal Ltd & Faculty of Law, the University of Hong Kong.
2 Per Lord Hoffman, the *Union Eagle Ltd v Golden Achievement Ltd* [1997] A.C. 514.

3 *Many Gain Investment Ltd v Chan Fai Ho* [2015] HKEC 1553.
4 Clause 22, Part 1 of Schedule 5, *Residential Properties (First-hand Sales) Ordinance,* A2595; Clause 20, Part 1 of Schedule 6, A2643.
5 Ibid., Part 1 of Schedule 5, A2583.
6 Ibid., section 2, Part 1, A2297–A2299.
7 Ibid., section 1(5), Part 1 of Schedule 1, A2493.
8 There is no explicit requirement in *Annex to LACO Circular Memorandum No.68* that the sales brochure must include the information regarding the date of completion. Thus, according to *Appendix I of Annex to LACO Circular Memorandum No. 68*, if a developer wishes to include such information, it should be presented in the remaining parts of the sales brochure; that is to say, after the listed sections prescribed by Appendix I. Ironically, the *Notes to Purchasers of First-hand Residential Properties*, a document jointly published by the Estate Agents Authority and the Consumer Council which must be listed in the sales brochure by virtue of A13 in Annex to *LACO Circular Memorandum No.68*, does advise the purchasers to check the information on *expected completion date* in the sales brochure.
9 Section 71(2), Part 3, *Residential Properties (First-hand Sales) Ordinance*, A2431.
10 '「關鍵日期」指批地文件的條件就本發展項目而獲符合的日期。預計關鍵日期是受到買賣合約所允許的任何延期所規限的.' See the relevant webpage on the project website (updated on 7 November 2016) at www.twinregency.com.hk/en/
11 Inclement weather refers to rainfall in excess of 20 millimetres in a twenty-four hour period or a Black Rainstorm Warning Signal or the hoisting of Typhoon Signal No. 8 or above at any time between the hours of 8:00 a.m. and 5:00 p.m.; see ibid., clause 10, Part 1 of Schedule 5, A2589. See also clause 4(5)(a) in the standard form of Agreement for Sale and Purchase in *LACO Circular Memorandum No. 66*.
12 Ibid., clause 7, A2585-A2587. See also clause 4(4)(a) in the standard form of Agreement for Sale and Purchase in *LACO Circular Memorandum No. 66*.
13 HCA16759/1999.
14 [2004]3HKLRD653.
15 Clause 12, Part 1 of Schedule 5, *Residential Properties (First-hand Sales) Ordinance*, A2589. See also clause 4(6) in the standard form of Agreement for Sale and Purchase in *LACO Circular Memorandum No. 66*.
16 Ibid., Clause 14(a), Part 1 of Schedule 5, A2591. See also clause 5(1) in the standard form of the agreement for sale and purchase in *LACO Circular Memorandum No. 66*.
17 Ibid., clause 12 and clause 14(b), A2589–A2591.
18 Ibid., section 1(5)(c)(ii)(A), A2493–A2495.
19 Ibid., clause 13(a), Part 1 of Schedule 5, A2589-A2591. See also clause 4(7) in the standard form of the agreement for sale and purchase in *LACO Circular Memorandum No. 66*; Section (B) in the Annex to REDA Guidelines, 10 August, 2010. For sales under the Non-Consent Scheme, the issue of *Occupation Document* is conclusive evidence that the development is deemed to be completed; see clause 13(b), A2591; also, section 1(5)(c)(ii)(B) provides that *the development is deemed to be completed on the date on which an occupation permit for every building in the development is issued*; A2495.
20 Ibid., section 2(1), A2295.
21 For a judicial observation, see *Yau Chin Kwan and Yuen Suk Kuen v. Tin Shui Wai Development* Ltd, HCA 11520 of 1999.
22 *Tin Shui Wai Development Ltd v Yiu Sun Hung & Woo Kwan Lee & Lo Solicitors (Third Party)* [2005] HKEC 75, paragraph 5.
23 Clause 7, Part 1 of Schedule 5, *Residential Properties (First-hand Sales) Ordinance*, A2585–A2587. See also clause 4(4)(a) in the standard form of the agreement for sale and purchase in *LACO Circular Memorandum No. 66*.
24 Ibid., clause 8, A2587; if a purchaser elects to wait for completion, she will be paid, for the period from the material date or the date as extended by extension to the date of

completion, an interest at the rate of 2% per annum above the prime rate specified by The Hong Kong and Shanghai Banking Corporation Limited on all amounts paid under the agreement. See also clause 4(4)(b) in the standard form of the agreement for sale and purchase in *LACO Circular Memorandum No. 66.*

25 Ibid., clause 9, at A2587. See also clause 4(4)(c) in the standard form of the agreement for sale and purchase in *LACO Circular Memorandum No. 66.*

26 Ibid., clause 5, A2585. See also clause 4(2) in the standard form of the agreement for sale and purchase in *LACO Circular Memorandum No. 66.*

27 Ibid., clause 6, A2585. See also clause 4(3) in the standard form of the agreement for sale and purchase in *LACO Circular Memorandum No. 66.*

28 See *Yau Chin Kwan and Yuen Suk Kuen v. Tin Shui Wai Development Ltd.* HCA 11520 of 1999; *Yau Chin Kwan and Yuen Suk Kuen v. Tin Shui Wai Development Ltd.* CACV 3970 of 2001; *Tin Shui Wai Development Ltd v Yiu Sun Hung & Woo Kwan Lee & Lo Solicitors (Third Party)* [2005] HKEC 75; *Tin Shui Wai Development Ltd v Polykin Ltd* [2006] HKEC 806; *Liu Chung Fai & Anor v Tin Shui Wai Development Ltd & Anor,* [2007] HKCU 981.

29 Paragraph 30, [2005] HKEC 75: *Mr Yu has revised the plaintiff's position* in this case. He strenuously argued that *the Agreement could work without implying the term. I must agree with him that if the construction of the building had not even reached the requisite number of storeys, the defendant would have no difficulty in saying that completion had not taken place and therefore to rescind. In such circumstances, there was absolutely no need to imply the term and the Agreement could have worked without it. The imply term would only be useful and desirable when the development was about to be completed. But if the term need only be implied or take effect when the development was about to be completed, it would be difficult to tell at what time or stage of the construction works that it should be implied or take effect. It would also be difficult to formulate its content in order to time its application. This problem of formulation of when the term would bite rendered it incapable of clear expression.*

30 Section B, Annex to the REDA Guidelines on 10 August 2010.

31 Clause 11 of the standard agreement for sale and purchase, Part 1 of Schedule 5, A2589. See also clause 4(5)(b) in the standard form of agreement for sale and purchase in *LACO Circular Memorandum No. 66.*

32 Ibid., clause 5, A2585. See also clause 4(2) in the standard form of the agreement for sale and purchase in *LACO Circular Memorandum No. 66.*

33 'All leases of land granted by the British Hong Kong Government not containing a right of renewal that expire before 30 June 1997, except short term tenancies and leases for special purposes, may be extended if the lesses so wishes for a period expiring not later than 30 June 2047 without payment of an additional premium.' Paragraph 2, Annex III to the Joint Declaration of the Government of the United Kingdom of Great Britain and Northern Ireland and the Government of the People's Republic of China on the Question of Hong Kong, April 1984.

34 'All leases of land granted, decided upon or renewed before the establishment of the Hong Kong Special Administrative Region which extend beyond 30 June 1997, and all rights in relation to such leases, shall continue to be recognized and protected under the law of the Region.' Article 120, the Basic Law of the Hong Kong Special Administrative Region of the People's Republic of China.

35 Section 24, Part 2 of Schedule 1, *Residential Properties (First-hand Sales) Ordinance,* A2543.

36 Section 2, *Conveyancing and Property Ordinance* (Cap 219).

37 'The above-stated basic policies of the People's Republic of China regarding Hong Kong and the elaboration of them in Annex I to this Joint Declaration will be stipulated, in a Basic Law of the Hong Kong Special Administrative Region of the People's Republic of China, by the National People's Congress of the People's Republic of China, and they will remain unchanged for 50 years.' Section 3(12), *Joint Declaration*

of the Government of the United Kingdom of Great Britain and Northern Ireland and the Government of the People's Republic of China on the Question of Hong Kong.

References

Chan, J. (2002) Civil Liberties, Rule of Law and Human Rights: The Hong Kong Special Administrative Region in Its First Four Years, in S K Lau (ed.), *The First Tung Chee-Hwa Administration*, Chinese University Press, pp. 89–122.

Chau K.W., Wong, S.K. and Yiu, C.Y. (2003) Valuation of Lease Properties, *Department of Real Estate and Construction, Faculty of Architecture*, University of Hong Kong, p. 6.

Ghai, Y. (1999) *Hong Kong's New Constitutional Order: the Resumption of Chinese Sovereignty and the Basic Law*, Second Edition, Hong Kong University Press, 1999, p. 435.

Gittings, D. (2011) What Will Happen to Hong Kong After 2047, 42 *Cal. W. Int'l L. J.*, pp. 44–50.

Goo, S. H. and Lee, A. (2015) *Land Law in Hong Kong*, 4th Edition, LexisNexis Butterworths, Chapter 9.

Joint Declaration of the Government of the United Kingdom of Great Britain and Northern Ireland and the Government of the People's Republic of China on the Question of Hong Kong, April 1984. Para 2, Section 3(12).

Lands D (2004) Legal Advisory and Conveyancing Office Circular Memorandum No. 54, *Legal Advisory and Conveyancing Office*, 8 July 2004, p. 3.

Lands D (2005) Land Tenure System and Land Policy in Hong Kong, Lands Department, 28 November 2005. www.landsd.gov.hk/en/service/landpolicy.htm.

Lands D (2011) Legal Advisory and Conveyancing Office Circular Memorandum No. 66, *Legal Advisory and Conveyancing Office*, HKSAR, Lands Department, 11 November 2011.

Lands D (2012) Legal Advisory and Conveyancing Office Circular Memorandum No. 68, *Legal Advisory and Conveyancing Office*, LACO, HKSAR, Lands Department, 22 March 2012.

Lee, A. (1998) Leases beyond 2047, Law Lectures for Practitioners 1998, *Hong Kong Law Journal*, pp. 178–183.

Lin, D (2012) The New Rules for Sales of Uncompleted Flats, Law Lectures for Practitioners 2010, Cheng, ML., Jen, J & Young, J.Y.K. (Eds), Hong Kong Law Journal Ltd & Faculty of Law, the University of Hong Kong, pp. 78–118.

LRC (1995) Glossary of Terms in the Report on Description of Flats on Sale, The Law Reform Commission of Hong Kong, April 1995, pp. 14–16.

Merry, M. (2008) Protection of Purchasers of Uncompleted Residential Flats – The Hong Kong Experience, *HKU-NUS-SMU Symposium Paper*, November 2008.

Morris, R. (2007) Forcing the Dance: Interpreting the Hong Kong Basic Law Dialectically, in Hualing Fu, Lison Harris, and Simon N. M. Young (eds), *Interpreting Hong Kong's Basic Law: The Struggle for Coherence*, New York & Hampshire UK, pp. 97–111.

SCMP (2007) The Land We Stand On, *South China Morning Post*, 1 June 2007.

REDA (2010) Guidelines for Sales Descriptions of Uncompleted Residential Properties, The Real Estate Developers Association of Hong Kong, 10 August 2010.

Sihombing, J. and Wilkinson, M. (2011) *A Student's Guide to Hong Kong Conveyancing*, 6th Edition, LexisNexis Hong Kong, 2014, p. 88, pp. 92–95.

Webb, D. (2010) Hong Kong Land Lease Reform, Part 1, 7 October 2010. http://webb-site.com/articles/leases1.asp

Zarathustra (2011) Hong Kong Property: Actually, It's More Expensive Now Than 1997, *Also sprach Analyst,* 21 March 2011. www.alsosprachanalyst.com/real-estate/hong-kong-property-actually-its-more-expensive-now-than-1997.html

9 Deed of mutual covenant and land grant conditions

Introduction

A transaction of a residential property in an estate development is more than the assignment of interests in the residential unit. With the assignment of interests in land comes a bundle of obligations a purchaser has to shoulder for as long as she remains the owner of the property. As discussed in Chapter 4, upon the completion of the transaction, purchasers will eventually become co-owners of the real estate including the common area of the development. Merry (2008) explains the co-ownership in multi-unit building in this way:

> [T]he purchaser obtains a certain number of shares in the land along with the right to exclusive possession of the flat. The shares are notional and undivided, the flat though is real enough. All the purchasers become tenants-in-common of the land. This means, in legal theory, that they have unity of possession of the whole building and therefore are entitled to use every part of the building in common with their co-owners. Exclusive possession of a flat is achieved by covenants between all the owners contained in an agreement subject to which all assignments of flats by the developer are made.

Ownership aside, the management of the common area in a multi-unit development requires monetary contributions from every unit owner and the establishment of a responsible authority in the community to deal with all the matters in the management of the property. Theoretically speaking, a certain consensus must be reached through discussion by all of the owners. However, for first-hand residential properties, the identities of the future owners of the development cannot be ascertained at the early stage of the sale; and the identities of the purchasers may keep changing, for some will resell the property even before completion of the construction. Thus it is not practically possible for all of the owners to convene a meeting to discuss the relevant matters. Business efficacy requires that certain obligations be delegated to developers for the drafting of such agreements or by-laws, by which a purchaser will have to agree when entering into the preliminary agreement for sale and purchase with the vendor. The majority of these obligations are prescribed by an agreement entitled the *deed of mutual covenant* (or *DMC*), to which every unit owner of the development is a party. The contents of such an agreement is therefore of the interest of a prospective purchaser.

Being the co-owners of the building, every flat owner theoretically has the right to use and enjoy every part of the building (*a tenancy in common*). The deed of mutual covenant is an agreement among all the owners of the building that every owner, while sharing the ownership of common parts, will have exclusive use of their own flats. Accordingly, every unit owner shall contribute towards the management expenses in relation to the common parts in proportion to the management shares allocated to her unit (Goo and Lee 2015). Apart from being 'a means by which strangers could own flats and offices in tall buildings', the DMC contains covenants that set out the regulation framework of community matters in the development (Merry 2011). The *Residential Properties (First-hand Sales) Ordinance* (the *Ordinance*) describes the deed of mutual covenant as a legal document which defines the rights, interests and obligations of co-owners among themselves of the land and development.[1]

The sales brochure must provide a summary of the latest draft of every deed of mutual covenant in respect of the specified residential property as at the date on which the sales brochure is printed.[2] And, for the purpose of public inspection, the sales brochure must state that a copy of the latest draft of every DMC in respect of the specified residential property is available for inspection at the place at which the specified residential property is offered to be sold.[3] Developers and agents are required to inform the prospective purchasers of these obligations before the preliminary agreement for sale and purchase is signed.

At the same time, when a parcel of land is sold to the developer, the government may enclose conditions in the grant of the land (known as land grant conditions or LGC), which the grantee, i.e., developer, must observe or fulfil as long as it remains the lessee of the land. Some responsibilities in the land grant conditions have to be performed on a continuous basis while some other responsibilities will pass from developers to the property owners upon the completion of the transaction.

Merry (2008) observed that both the deed of mutual covenant and the land grant conditions may contain restrictions and conditions that can be 'prone to discourage purchasers who know about them' and 'influence their decision to buy' if disclosed. Common examples of land grant conditions are the maintaining of public facilities, open space or slopes around the development at the expense of owners. Such undertakings are originally derived from conditions of the government land grant which bind the vendor developer as government lessee, then pass to the purchasers as the developer's assignees and the new government lessees when the ownership of the unit changes.

Under the Consent Scheme and now the *Ordinance*, developers must disclose to purchasers the following salient points of the deed of mutual covenant in the sales brochure: (a) common parts; (b) the number of undivided shares assigned to each residential property; (c) terms of years for which the manager of the development is appointed; (d) the basis on which the management expenses are shared among the owners of the residential properties in the development; (e) the basis on which the management fee deposit is fixed; and (f) the area (if any) in the development retained by the owner for that owner's own use.[4] Salient points of land grant conditions that require disclosure include: (a) the lot number of the land on which the development is situated; (b) the term of years under the lease; (c) the user restrictions applicable to that land; (d) the facilities that are required to be constructed and provided for the government, or for public use or those to be managed, operated or maintained for public use at the expense of the owners of the residential properties in the development; (e) the grantee's obligations to lay, form or landscape any areas, or to construct or maintain structures or facilities, within or outside that land; and (f) the lease conditions that are onerous to a purchaser.[5]

Covenant related to pets keeping

One covenant that probably will deter some purchasers from considering buying an apartment would be the disallowance on keeping pets in the property. Although most private housing in Hong Kong does not have such regulation, the flats sold under the Home Ownership Scheme by the Hong Kong Housing Authority are usually sold with a covenant in the DMC that dogs are not allowed in the estates (SCMP 2010). In a 2010 District Court decision, a Clause 19 of Schedule 3 of the deed of mutual covenant ('Clause 19') reads 'No dogs, cats or pets or other animals or live poultry shall be kept or harboured in any Unit or any part thereof save and except with the prior written consent of the Manager'.[6] The plaintiffs were registered owners and occupiers of the flats who sought declaratory relief on the interpretation and enforcement of Clause 19 in the DMC. Deputy District Judge Roy Yu found that the right to exclusive possession guaranteed by the deed of mutual covenant was not absolute and the restrictive covenant did not conflict with the right to exclusive possession:

> [M]s. Chit's argument cannot be sustained as the right to exclusive possession as provided in the DMC is not an absolute right. Clause 4.1 provides that the right to possession is subject to the express covenants and provision in the DMC. And Clause 4.2 of the DMC provides that each owner for the time being of any unit is bound by the covenants, provisions and restrictions contained in Third Schedule of the DMC, which includes Clause 19. Accordingly, the Plaintiffs' right to 'exclusive' possession of their units is not an absolute right but is subject to the restriction of Clause 19. Accordingly, there is no conflict between these 2 clauses, but in any event the right to possession is subject to Clause 19 and the application for a declaration that Clause 19 overrides Clause 4.1 must fail.[7]

In contrast, in *Tsang Chi Ming v Broadway-Nassau Investments Limited & Anor*, the District Court held that a house rule to forbid raising of dogs was in conflict with the rights and privileges of the owners to enjoy their premises. In this case the building management company in Mei Foo Sun Chuen was empowered by the deed of mutual covenant to make House Rules for the management and upkeep of the Estate. In 1972 the company made rules to prohibit owners of the estates from keeping dogs and then was amended on 1 March 1993 as: 'Pets: No dogs, no matter how small, are to be brought or kept on the estate. Guide dogs for the blind people may, in certain circumstances, be allowed subject to prior approval of the Estate Management Office. Where permission is granted to the blind people under the above exception, the owner of the guide dog must exercise reasonable care to ensure no nuisance is caused to other residents.' After confirming the validity of the House Rule, the judge nonetheless found the House Rule was in conflict with Clause 1 of the deed of mutual covenant and the deed of mutual covenant should take preference:

> [I]n my Judgment keeping a pet in one's premises is within the right and privilege of the owner/occupant in enjoying his premises. By prohibiting the owners/occupants from keeping dogs in their flats, I find that Rule 3 does interfere with the owners'/occupiers' right to exclusive use occupation and enjoyment of their flats provided under Clause 1 of the DMC. The fact that some dogs may cause nuisance to other residents is no justification for adopting a broadbrush approach in disallowing all owners to keep dogs (however small). In particular, when taking into account Clause 9(1) DMC have already provided means/measures against possible nuisance that may be caused by dogs.[8]

The two cases are distinguishable on the ground that the former concerns a restrictive covenant in the DMC while the latter concerns a rule which was made pursuant to a covenant in the DMC. Beyond that, different policy considerations regarding public housing on the one hand and private housing on the other may also explain the divergence in the outcomes of the two cases.

For some estates, the deed of mutual covenant would principally prohibit keeping animals in flats but at the same time prescribe that the restriction would be relaxed if the manager has given permission. In *Lee Yin Hong v Serenade Cove (IO)*, the Court of Appeal recognized an implied duty by the incorporated owners to exercise their discretion reasonably and not to withhold their consent unreasonably, if consent from the incorporated owners were needed to keep pets in flats.[9]

In LACO Circular Memorandum No. 64, the Lands Department suggests that any house rules made by the manager shall not be inconsistent with or contravene the deed of mutual covenant, or land grant conditions (Lands D 2011). Thus the provision in the deed of mutual covenant is crucial for the later enjoyment of the flat by the owner. Accordingly, the *Ordinance* shall have designated any restrictive covenants on pet raising as a salient point in the deed of mutual covenant for the better information of would-be purchasers.

Responsibility to maintain slope

Apart from passive obligations, the deed of mutual covenant may also contain positive covenants, e.g., to share expenses and costs for construction and maintenance of infrastructure outside the building. Such responsibility may be derived from the land grant conditions. One example is to maintain the slope adjacent to the development.

In 2007 the Ombudsman's office published a report regarding the Housing Authority's inadequate disclosure to purchasers on slope maintenance responsibility in one sale of flats under the Home Ownership Scheme (or *HOS* hereinafter). In that case, an estate of two-phases was developed by the Housing Authority. The first phase was pre-sold one year before the Lands Department leased a slope to the Housing Authority as a works area on the condition that the lessee would be responsible for managing and maintaining that slope until further notice. Five months later the first phase was completed and a deed of mutual covenant was entered into which provided that: 'the responsibility for managing and maintaining all slopes in the estate shall be collectively borne by the owners of the estate.' After the second phase was completed and the Owners' Corporation was formed, the Lands Department refused to resume the slope. The Owners' Corporation took the claim to the Ombudsman that the Housing Authority had shifted the maintenance responsibility and the owners were not informed of such responsibility during the sale of the HOS flats.

As discussed by the Ombudsman's report, the responsibility for maintaining all slopes was disclosed by the Housing Authority to the purchasers in the following ways: (a) a reminder in the sales brochures of both Phases I and II to refer to the land lease and the DMC and where necessary, seek professional advice; (b) purchasers were shown the outline of the deed of mutual covenant when they selected their flats at the Home Ownership Centre and which indicated that owners would be responsible for maintaining 'all slopes' under the government lease; (c) purchasers were requested to sign a declaration that they understood their responsibility for managing and maintaining slopes as specified in the land lease and deed of mutual covenant; and (d) solicitors representing both the Housing Authority and the HOS flat purchasers had explained the salient points of the deed of mutual covenant to purchasers (Ombudsman 2007).

Still, in this case the Ombudsman showed much sympathy towards the flats owners in this case and seemed not entirely convinced that the Housing Authority had discharged its duty of information. With regard to the disclosure of the responsibility to maintain the slope in the sale of the first phase, the Ombudsman appeared to be dissatisfied with the Housing Authority from the fact that the Housing Authority, after the slope was leased and it decided to pass the slope maintenance responsibility to the future owners of the estate and did not notify the purchasers of the change of situation in a timely manner. In this regard, it seemed that the inclusion of the 'all slopes' clause in the deed of mutual covenant was not enough to settle the matter. For the sale of the second phase, the Ombudsman found the information given by the Housing Authority did not make clear the particular responsibility as to the slope and it was a serious issue for the sales brochure to omit this. Overall, the Ombudsman found that the responsibility to maintain the slope was a significant issue affecting the purchasers' interests; and the Housing Authority in the case, while focusing on the technicalities (stating the slope maintenance responsibility was in the DMC) failed to have made full and timely disclosure of all information to purchasers and was deficient in keeping purchasers clearly informed. The Ombudsman urged the Housing Authority to bear the responsibility of maintaining the slope until the Lands Department resumed it. It can be inferred that the Ombudsman was of the opinion that a mere provision in a deed of mutual covenant was insufficient to fulfil the obligations as Vendor in the sale. The information should have been made out more clearly and timeously.

From June 2010 onward, LACO Circular Memorandum No. 62 imposed a duty upon developers to inform prospective purchasers 'if the Land Grant Conditions require the owners to maintain at their expense any slopes within and/or outside the lot... each owner will be obliged to make contributions towards the costs of such work'. The Vendor must prepare a plan in the sales brochure showing the slopes and any retaining walls or other related structures already constructed or to be constructed within and/or outside the lot.[10]

Now under the *Ordinance*, if the land grant requires owners of the residential properties to maintain any slope at their own cost, the terms of the requirement must be stated in the sales brochure, together with a plan showing the slope and a statement that each of the owners is obliged to contribute towards the costs of the maintenance work. The requirements apply where the developer has undertaken to maintain the slope. If the deed of mutual covenant states that the manager of the development has the owners' authority to carry out the maintenance work, the sales brochure must state the authority.[11]

For sales of properties in Hong Kong, whenever the location plan indicates that the development is in a hilly area of the city, the purchasers should be aware of the possibility that the maintenance of slopes could be a relevant issue. In these cases the developers should spare no efforts in making full disclosure of the responsibility in the sales brochure. Thus in the sale of *Mount Nicholson Phase I*, a luxury development in the Mid-Levels, the sales brochure had prepared a section entitled 'Maintenance of Slopes'. In the section, the vendor stated that 'the land grant requires the owners of the residential properties in the Development to maintain any slope at their own cost'. It then states that: '[e]ach of the owners is obliged to contribute towards the costs of the maintenance work' before pointing out the manager of the development has the owners' authority to carry out the maintenance work under the deed of mutual covenant.[12]

Government, institutional or community facilities and public open space

In Hong Kong, land may be granted for both private and public purposes. In a land sale or land grant, any government bureaux or departments may propose the inclusion of public facilities to meet public needs; the developer may also propose such facilities in their planning applications to the Town Planning Board.

According to the Development Bureau, public facilities within private developments can broadly be categorized into four groups: (i) Government, Institution and Community (GIC) facilities such as community halls, elderly centres, kindergartens etc.; (ii) public open spaces (POS); (iii) pedestrian passage and vehicular access, e.g. walkways, footbridges and rights of way; and (iv) Public Transport Terminus.

Depending on the specific conditions in the land leases or deeds of dedication, most facilities are handed over to related government bureaux or departments upon completion; but some of them are required to be managed and maintained by the private developers or owners on an ongoing basis. The owners of estates in these cases are required first, to permit the public to lawfully use such facilities and not to allow the area to be obstructed and second, to manage and maintain such facilities to the satisfaction of the government (DB 2011). This means that the owners are under a duty to share the cost of maintenance, until the facilities are resumed by the government.

Take *Hermitage* as an example: the development contains a government-supported residential care home for the elderly as well as two covered footbridges and two pedestrian walkways that will later be open to the public, and accordingly the developer is under a duty to make it clear to the purchasers that 'the purchasers of the Units will have to meet a proportion of the expense of managing, operating and maintaining the items in the management charges apportioned to their Units'.[13] Under the Consent Scheme, the facilities should be marked in a different colour in the plans showing the location of the facilities.[14]

For a long time, this information may only be vaguely referred to in the agreement for sale and purchase. Before 2010, many purchasers became aware of these obligations not from the agreement for sale and purchase but from the bills sent by the building manager. Sometimes protests from co-owners of residential buildings took place against the burdens imposed by the land grant conditions. In November 2009, residents of a development at Diamond Hill protested about the HK$1.4 million the 1,600 flats owners have been paying on a yearly basis for a period of 10 years to maintain an escalator connecting the development with another building, which was claimed to be rarely used by the owners. Although obligations of such kind must have been clearly set out in the agreement for sale and purchase, many of the purchasers remained completely unaware of the obligations until they were asked to contribute to the cost (SCMP 2009).[15]

The maintenance of public facilities may not be the only burden to be shouldered by the owners. Another burden would be to manage public open space that is located in the development. The burden in many cases turns out to be a substantial one. For example, it was reported that the owners of *Metro Harbourview* have been paying HK$2 million a year to maintain a 9,800-square-metre public garden (SCMP 2008).

What's more, as sometimes developers may designate some common facilities within the development to be shared by the public for entertainment in return for some government concession and allowance in the development intensity under a *deed of dedication*, the question whether in these cases the deed of dedication should be included in the sales brochure would arise (Goo 2010).

After 2010, developers must, as required by the Consent Scheme, disclose information in the sales brochure on any government, institutional or community facilities, public open spaces and public facilities within the development to be constructed. Prominent statements should be included in the brochure if 'the public have the right to enter into and use the public open space and the public facilities freely and without payment of any nature'; or if 'the public open space and the public facilities are to be managed, operated and maintained at the expense of the owners and the owners will have to meet a proportion of the expense of managing, operating, and maintaining such public open space and public facilities in any management expenses apportioned to their units'. [16]

Then after 2013, the *Ordinance* requests that the sales brochure set out provisions of any land grant and deed of dedication or of any deed of mutual covenant in respect of the specified residential property that concern public facilities and open spaces; the sales brochure must contain a description of any facilities to be constructed and provided for the government or public use, or to be managed, operated or maintained for public use at the expense of the owners of the residential properties in the development coupled with a plan to show the location of those facilities and open spaces; the plan must highlight those facilities and open spaces by colour or shade in the same manner as in the land grant or the deed of dedication; and the sales brochure must mention that those facilities and open spaces are for public use and the general public has the right to use the facilities or open spaces in accordance with the land grant or the deed of dedication.[17] In addition, section 16 of Part 1, Schedule 1 of the *Ordinance* requires the developer to set out the provisions of the land grant and the deed of dedication, and of every deed of mutual covenant in respect of the specified residential property, that concern facilities that are required under the land grant to be constructed and provided for the government or for public use or to be managed, operated or maintained for public use at the expense of the owners of the residential properties in the development.

In 2014, the SRPA reminded the purchasers of *Mont Vert* that, according to special condition No. 30 of the land grant for the lot on which stands the development, purchasers may share the costs of constructing and maintaining within the lot unobstructed roads and footpaths leading to adjacent private land and burial grounds and letting the public pass on the said access roads and footpaths free of cost for the purposes of passage (SRPA 2014).

The *Ordinance* could have gone one step further to require developers, whenever practical, to list in the sales brochures the *exact or estimated approximate maintenance fees* per square foot, or the total amount that all the co-owners of the building will have to pay to discharge the obligations under the government land grant. As texts usually are less glaring than numbers, there is still good reason to suppose that many purchasers will be caught off guard when they are asked to pay for the maintenance fees of public facilities. Since the expenses are borne collectively by purchasers, prospective purchasers are entitled to know at least *roughly* how much they will need to pay on a monthly basis to discharge the burden.

A cross-reference to the established practice in the 1990s would suggest that to disclose the estimated fees allocated per unit or per square foot at the time of sale is feasible. The sales brochure used in the sale of *Pictorial Garden Phase 3* had provided information on the estimated management fees on a block-to-block basis. In 2012, the vendor of *High Point* also provided estimated management fees per unit in the sales brochure.

Conclusion

The significance of information to purchasers about positive obligations brought by land grant conditions or negative restrictions enclosed in a deed of mutual covenant before signing the preliminary agreement for sale and purchase is well recognized by the Consent Scheme and the *Ordinance*. With the implementation of the measures under the regulatory regime, purchasers are in general adequately informed of the contents of the deed of mutual covenant and land grant conditions.

The room for improvement would be to disclose the obligations in a more straightforward manner, i.e., *quantification*. Wherever an estimation is possible, vendors should be encouraged to present to prospective purchasers the estimated monthly costs in order to discharge the burden imposed by land grant conditions for a specified residential unit. However, as many a sale of first-hand residential properties in Hong Kong take place months before the completion of construction, when the sales brochures are prepared, it may not be easy for the vendor to estimate a cost which may be charged years afterwards. As such, it may already be good enough for the new legislation to require, in sections 15 and 16 in Part 1 of Schedule 1, that vendors set out summary of land grant and information on public facilities and public open spaces in the sales brochure.

Notes

1 Section 2(1), Part 1, *Residential Properties (First-hand Sales) Ordinance*, A2397. See also Clause 1(1)(h) in the standard form of agreement for sale and purchase in *LACO Circular Memorandum No. 66.*

2 Ibid., section 19 (2)(n), Part 2 – Division 2, A2337.

3 Ibid., section 21, Part 2 of Schedule 1, A2533–A2535.

4 Ibid., section 14(2), Part 1 of Schedule 1, *Residential Properties (First-hand Sales) Ordinance*, A2523; for the Consent Scheme, see B9 in Annex to the *Legal Advisory and Conveyancing Office Circular Memorandum No. 68.*

5 Ibid., section 15(2) and section 16(2), Part 1 of Schedule 1, *Residential Properties (First-hand Sales) Ordinance*, A2523; for the Consent Scheme, see B10 in Annex to the *Legal Advisory and Conveyancing Office Circular Memorandum No. 68.*

6 李延康 v 韻濤居業主法團, DCCJ004861 2008.

7 Ibid., para.26.

8 DCCJ 1704/2007, paragraph 67.

9 [2011] HKEC 1309. On the facts of that case the Court of Appeal held that the incorporated owners had acted reasonably to withhold the consent, taking into consideration of the noise and mess caused by the dogs.

10 B22 in Annex to *LACO Circular Memorandum No .68;* originally in B21 in the Revised Annex I to *LACO Circular Memorandum No.62* in *LACO Circular Memorandum No. 63.*

11 Section 27, Part 2 of Schedule 1, *Residential Properties (First-hand Sales) Ordinance*, A2543–A2545.

12 Sale Brochure of Mount Nicholson Phrase 1, pp. 238–239.
13 Section 11 of the sale brochure of *Hermitage.*
14 B11(c) in the Annex to *LACO Circular Memorandum No. 68.*
15 'Most purchasers were unaware of the terms when they decided to buy flats, leading some to feel they had been duped,' said Legislator Leung Yiu-chung. See Ng Yuk-hang, 'Developers should list maintenance fees in sales brochures: lawmaker', *South China Morning Post,* 16 November 2009.
16 Ibid., B10(d), B11(a) and (b). Similar rules can be found in section 16(2)(a)(b), (4), (5) and (6), Part 1 of Schedule 1, the *Residential Properties (First-hand Sales) Ordinance,* A2525–A2529.
17 Section 16, Part 1 of Schedule 1, *Residential Properties (First-hand Sales) Ordinance,* A2529.

References

DB (2011) Background Information on Provision of Public Facilities within Private Developments, *Development Bureau,* January 2011. www.landsd.gov.hk/en/legco/pfpd.htm

Goo, S. H. (2010) Regulation of Sale of Off-the-plan Property, *The Conveyancer and Property Lawyer,* Issue 2, 2010, p. 137.

Goo, S. H. and Lee, A. (2015) *Land Law in Hong Kong,* 4th Edition, LexisNexis Butterworths, Chapter 16.

Lands D (2010a) Legal Advisory and Conveyancing Office Circular Memorandum No. 62, *Legal Advisory and Conveyancing Office,* Lands Department, 2 June 2010.

Lands D (2010b) Legal Advisory and Conveyancing Office Circular Memorandum No. 63, Legal Advisory and Conveyancing Office, Lands Department, 1 September 2010.

Lands D (2011a) Legal Advisory and Conveyancing Office Circular Memorandum No. 66, Legal Advisory and Conveyancing Office, Lands Department, 11 November 2011.

Lands D (2011b) Legal Advisory and Conveyancing Office Circular Memorandum No. 64, Guideline 17, Legal Advisory and Conveyancing Office, Lands Department, 28 June 2011.

Lands D (2012) Legal Advisory and Conveyancing Office Circular Memorandum No. 68, Legal Advisory and Conveyancing Office, Lands Department, 22 March 2012.

Merry, M. (2008) Protection of Purchasers of Uncompleted Residential Flats – The Hong Kong Experience, *HKU-NUS-SMU Symposium Paper,* Singapore, November 2008.

Merry, M. (2011) Do Naming Rights Run with Land? *Conveyancer and Property Lawyer,* v. 75 n. 3, pp. 237–238.

Ombudsman (2007) *Issue No.1 of Reporting Year 2007-2008,* the Office of the Ombudsman, November. Para. 9–11, 13–16, 17–20.

SCMP (2008) Owner Buyout of Public Open Space Proposed, *South China Morning Post,* 1 June 2008.

SCMP (2009) Developers Should List Maintenance Fees in Sales Brochures: Lawmaker, *South China Morning Post,* 16 November 2009.

SCMP (2010) Hos Flat Owners Challenge Dog Ban, Private-housing Court Ruling could Pave Way, *South China Morning Post,* 15 March 2010.

SRPA (2014) SRPA Advises Prospective Purchasers on Access Roads within Boundary of Mont Vert for Public Access to Adjacent Private Land and Burial Grounds, the Sales of First-hand Residential Properties Authority, July 18 2004, www.info.gov.hk/gia/general/201407/18/P201407180719.htm

The Vendor of Mount Nicholson Phrase I (2016) Sales Brochure, pp. 238–239.

The Vendor of Hermitage (2010) Sales Brochure.
The Vendor of High Point (2012) Sales Brochure.

10 Price list[1]

Introduction

In previous chapters we have examined how the *Residential Properties (First-hand Sales) Ordinance* (the *Ordinance*) regulates disclosure of information on the physical dimension (i.e., floor area, internal structure, location, height) and on the contractual dimension (i.e., time of delivery, leasehold and mutual deed of covenants) of first-hand residential property. From this chapter onwards, the focus of the discussion will shift from the *residential property on sale* to the *sale*. Like information on the residential property, information on the sale is of great value to prospective purchasers. In this and the following two chapters we will explore a number of issues in the transaction of first-hand residential properties: information on price and the publication of price lists; sales arrangement (Chapter 11); the conveyancing procedure and the disclosure of transaction information (Chapter 12).

The price of the property is undoubtedly critical information. This chapter investigates the preparation and provision of price lists in first-hand sales: what kind of information needs to be included in the price lists and how should those lists be made available to the public. Is any pricing information that is known to the developer not known to the purchaser? If yes, will the implementation of the *Ordinance* help abolish or reduce the information asymmetry?

To start with, the price information of properties on sale is contained in price lists. And a sale of first-hand residential properties requests the publication of one or more price lists. The scale of a multi-unit development in Hong Kong ranges from a dozen flats, to a hundred or a thousand apartments. The high end of the sliding scale appears in mega developments under new government leases in Kowloon and New Territories (e.g., development atop Mass Transit Railway stations), which concerns a large piece of land and a condition of a minimum number of units to be built and offered. A development of such scale can sometimes contain over 1,000 units.[2] According to the *Ordinance*, a *development* can either be a building or a collection of buildings where the construction of those buildings can be regarded as one single real estate project by reason of the engineering, structural or architectural connection between the buildings.[3] A development of a number of buildings may be divided into two or more phases if developers need to obtain from the Building Authority consent in writing for the commencement of the building work of the phase and approval in writing in accordance with the regulations.[4]

Developers must, as requested by section 29, prepare a *price list*, a document setting out the price of each specified residential property in the development or in each phase.[5] In the sale of *Full Art Court* in 2014, the vendor, without recognizing the apartments of the development that were being offered for sale fell into the category of first-hand residential units, only prepared a handwritten price list (HKET 2016). On 3 August 2016, it was held that the vendor had committed an offence under the *Ordinance* by preparing a handwritten price list and nothing else (AD 2016a).[6]

Vendors are required to set out in the price list the name and location of the development and in respect of a specified residential property, the overall price of the property, a description of the residential property, the saleable area, and the price of the residential property per square foot of the saleable area and per square metre of the saleable area.[7] Developers do not have to price all the units in a development or a phase of a development in one list. They can issue a number of price lists to sell the units in batches. Most importantly, according to section 32(1) of the *Ordinance*, every price list must be issued at least *three days immediately before* the date on which the units included in the respective price list are put for sale by developers.[8] This leads to several questions: firstly, what is the legal effect of the issue of price list in first-hand sales? Secondly, can the lists be revised? Thirdly, how many price lists can be issued for one development (or a phase of one development)?

The nature of price lists

More than a century ago, the English court held in *Grainger v Gough* that price lists for circulating purpose did not amount to an offer.[9] This remains as the rule of thumb till today. Thus in the sale of first-hand residential properties, the price list, or any description on individual flats in the price list, is not an *offer* by the developer but *an invitation to treat*. If the description of each unit in the price list were an offer, the developer would be bound to sell the unit to anyone who accepted it. The fact that each unit is unique and can be sold only once by the vendor suggests that the law cannot make a developer in breach of contract to any other person that *agrees* to buy the property at the specified price. Meanwhile, vendors' dominion over their own properties supports the position that developers will have the *freedom not to deal* with a particular purchaser. That freedom cannot be protected if developers are bound to sell the property once it is included in the price list.

For sales of first-hand residential properties, the contract is formed at the time the preliminary agreement for sale and purchase is signed by the vendor and the purchaser; without signing the agreement, neither developers nor purchasers will be bound by merely expressing the interest to sell or to buy a unit on the price list.

As first-hand sales usually proceed in batches, should the law require a minimum number of units to be enclosed in each price list issued by the vendor? Early research suggested that for better protection of purchasers and a more efficient market, developers should be encouraged to provide a price list of all units available in a private sale at least three days before the sale (Goo 2010).

The legislation seems to take a less stringent view. Section 30 of the *Ordinance* stipulates that if there are 30 or fewer residential properties in the development the price list must set out the prices of all the specified residential properties in the development; if there are more than 30 but less than 100 residential properties in the development, each price list must include the prices of at least 30 specified residential properties (subject to the exception of a price list setting out the prices of all those specified units that have never been so set out or the exception that the prices of less than 30 specified residential properties in the development have never been set out in any price list); if the development contains 100 or more residential properties the first price list for the development must set out the prices of at least whichever is the greater: at least 20 per cent of the number of residential properties in the development or 50 specified residential properties (subject to the exception of a price list setting out the prices of all those specified units that have never been so set out or the exception that the prices of less than 50 specified residential properties in the development have never been set out in any price list for the development) and any subsequent price list must set out prices of at least 10 per cent of the number of residential properties in the development (subject to the exception of a price list setting out the prices of all those specified units that have never been so set out or the exception that the number of specified residential properties in the development the prices of which never been set out in any price list for the development is less than 10 per cent of the number of residential properties in the development).

In January 2012, REDA opposed the requirement of including a minimum number of flats in price lists, arguing the arrangement was to effectively force owners to sell the relevant number of flats so stipulated in the price lists, which in its opinion 'clearly amounts to an unlawful infringement of the owner's rights under Article 105 of the Basic Law' (REDA 2012). The argument can be disposed of easily by making reference to the nature of price list as *an invitation to treat*.

The fact is that despite the statutory requirement enclosed in section 30, the *Ordinance* does not require developers to sell a minimum number of flats in a development – developers are indeed free, under the legislation, to retain as many units as they wish. Essentially, price list being an invitation to treat means that developers are not bound to sell any properties included in the list. The legislation requires a minimum number of flats to be included in the price list *if* the developer wishes to sell some (or all) of the flats in the development. For the units included in the price list, the *Ordinance* is silent as to whether the vendor must sell all of them. It is hard to infer from the legislative intention such obligation. In other words, the common law principle remains operative with the commencement of the *Ordinance*: notwithstanding the requirements on issuance of price lists by the *Ordinance*, vendors are *not* required to offer for sale any of the properties included in the published price list (THB and DJ 2012). The *Ordinance* only insists that if the vendor intends to sell a unit, the vendor has to sell it according to the price as enclosed in the price list.

Information to be contained in price lists

The price list must present the overall price of a specified residential property as well as the price of the residential property per square foot of the saleable area and that price per square metre of the saleable area.[10] The price list must not set out any price information based on the gross floor area of the property.

At the same time, the price list must set out the terms of payment, the basis on which any discount on the price is available and any gift, or any financial advantage or benefit, to be made available in connection with the purchase of a specified residential property in the development.[11] Every so often a certain discount may be offered by the vendor to particular groups of purchasers (e.g., members of the vendor company's purchaser club) according to different conditions of sales. Usual financial advantages or benefits offered by a developer would be a concession in mortgage interest rate, a provision of a second-mortgage or stamp duty subsidy or rebate.

In most cases, not all residential units of a development are sold at a discount or at the same discount or with a provision of any financial advantage. Most likely a few units in the opening batch of the sale would proceed on these terms and end up with a lower price than the average price of the batch. The developers may wish to highlight arrangements on the discounts/financial advantages in the advertisement – which is fine – and then provide an average price, average price per square foot or per square metre, average discounted price, average discounted price per square foot or per square metre in the advertisement. The latter practice was regarded by the Authority as 'highly likely to amount to misrepresentation or dissemination of false or misleading information' in contravention of sections 76 and 78 of the *Ordinance* (SRPA 2014). This is because the same residential unit may be priced differently due to the applicability of the discounts varying from person to person. Thus the discounted price may not be the actual transaction price if the unit is sold to a purchaser who cannot enjoy the discounts. For the same reason, the average discounted price quoted based on the discounted price is also misleading. Citing a discounted price which may be realized under certain conditions in advertisement may mislead prospective purchasers as to the actual price of the property. The Authority advises that a *price range* should instead be provided by vendors for a better understanding of would-be purchasers.

In the sale of *Ocean One* in 2013, the vendor used words '10% off Discount' (or in Chinese, '九折發售') in the advertisement where the 10 per cent discount only applied to purchasers who opted for one particular set of terms of payment. It was held in November 2016 by the Kwun Tong Magistrate Court that such practice was misleading, as purchasers might be led to believe the 10 per cent off discount applies to all the units in the development; because of this, the vendor was held guilty for contravening relevant provisions on advertisement in the *Ordinance* (AD 2016b; OD 2016a).[12]

Similarly, in the sale of the phase *Graces* in the development *Providence Bay* in Tai Po, the advertisements contained wording '$14,563 per sq. ft. after discount for the first 50 units' (in Chinese, '首批50伙折實價$14,563'). On 24 November

2016, the Kwun Tong Magistrate Court held that the advertisement contained false or misleading information, for it did not explain the meaning of 'after discount', or the basis for the calculation of the advertised price, i.e., $14,563 per sq. ft., or any conditions to become eligible purchasers who can purchase the property at the discounted price (AD 2016c; OD 2016b).[13]

Revision

Meanwhile, price list as an invitation to treat also means that under common law developers are not bound to sell any properties at the price as specified in the list. If the sale is entirely subject to common law, developers could rule out any price included in the price list from as early as the time that the list is published. If this were the case, no sale could proceed with any certainty and efficiency. Thus as a general rule, the *Ordinance* stipulates that the vendor may sell a specified residential property *only* at the price of that property as set out in the relevant price list.[14] Therefore in cases of over-pricing or under-pricing, developers are not allowed to immediately offer a new price for the units included in the price list. This is clearly stated in the *Ordinance* that the price of a specified residential property in a development may only be set out in one price list for the development or for the phase of the development of which the residential property forms a part.[15] But, as discussed earlier, the *freedom not to deal* will always grant a developer the lawful right to refuse to offer any listed units for sale (although it is unlikely that any developer would be doing so in these days, as behaviour will attract headlines in the local media and generate negative perception of the developer by the public). All in all, the right to refuse to sell serves as a protective mechanism for developers in case of under-pricing; this is particularly the case for the *first* price list of a sale; vendors always get the chance to revise the price in the subsequent price lists.

If a listed unit is not put up for sale because of under-pricing or the original price turns to be too high to attract a purchaser, developers can revise the price only through issuing a *revision* to the original price list (a revised price list) according to section 29(4) of the *Ordinance*.[16] The revised list, like a new price list, must be made public three days before the units can be sold at the revised price (THB 2012). In other words, section 32(1) applies to a new list as well as any revised list. Under such arrangement, it remains the case that vendors still enjoy the freedom to revise the prices according to market response, but they cannot exercise the right immediately. A lead time of at least three days has to pass before the unit can be offered for sale again. Section 35(1)(b) further provides that after revision the unit can be sold only at the revised price.

The Consumer Council (2014) observed that in some 2014 sales the revised price lists were issued on the same day or next day following release of the initial price list. According to the Council, 'the practice of making frequent changes to price lists will not only be confusing to prospective purchasers but will also negate the attempts through legislation to prevent the speculation of price information to the detriment of consumers.' While the law should respect the vendor's freedom not to deal and adjust the price according to the market response, it is legitimate to prohibit any immediate revision of the price lists by clearly stating the lead time required for the issue of the revised price lists.

Can the price be revised after the unit is sold by the vendor to another person at the price mentioned in the price list? Principally no. Section 35(2), however, does allow revision of the price in the following situations: (a) as stipulated in Clause 23 of the agreement for sale and purchase in Schedule 5, in case of alternation, the purchaser price shall be adjusted in proportion to the variation of the measurements of the parts of the Property affected; (b) a change in the terms of payment as set out in the price list for the development under section 31(5)(a); and (c) the availability of any gift, or any financial advantage or benefit, as set out in the price list for the development under section 31(5)(c), in connection with the purchase of the residential property. Then section 59(4) of the *Ordinance* goes on to request vendors to enter the details and that date in the Register of Transactions (a key document on transaction prices that under section 60 of the *Ordinance* must be disclosed and updated on a daily basis as the sale proceeds; to be discussed in Chapter 12) within one working day after the price is revised. The SRPA (2013) has illustrated how such revision can be made in its *Guidelines on Register of Transactions*.[17]

Abolition of private sale and public sale in 2010

Compared to the trouble involved in revising the price of a *listed* unit, developers can always, legitimately and at ease, revise the prices for any units to be included in future price lists. It is truly at the advantage of developers to sell units in batches so the prices of the residential units to be released in further batches can be revised according to the market's response.

Since the issue of every price list represents one opportunity to revise the price, the fewer units that are included in one price list, the more times developers can revise the price and avoid the risk of irrational pricing. Developers have been seen to take advantage of the arrangement to such an extent that the sales arrangement for the entire project can be considered as unfair. As observed by the government, 'prospective purchasers will only have access to the prices of a small number of properties in a development at any particular point of time and can only make their decisions with very limited knowledge about the overall prices of the properties in the development' (THB and DJ 2012). This was particularly the case before June 2010 when there used to be a distinction between private sales and public sales.

In 1999, the Circular Memorandum No. 40 issued by the Legal Advisory and Conveyancing Office of the Lands Department (hereinafter *LACO*) officially recognized the practices of *public sale* and *private sale*, providing that uncompleted flats could be sold either in a public sale or a private sale. Although the later practice might have departed greatly from the original purpose, a private, or internal, sale was originally intended to be a genuine sale of flats at a discounted price confined to corporate purchasers and, after 2001, to employees or people who had a close connection with the developers. A public sale, on the other hand, was a sale by ballot open to the public. Separate rules used to apply to the two types of sales. For a private sale, a list of the prices of not less than 20 flats or 20 per cent of the total number of flats on offer at the first batch needed to be provided 24 hours before the sale (REDA 2006). For a public sale, the price list had to be provided 'not less than 7 working days before the commencement of registration for the ballot', but no minimum number of units was required to be included in the first price list (Lands D 1999). The distinction left vendors remarkable discretion in deciding how flats would be released. Under a framework with a blurred dividing line between a private sale and a public sale, developers could freely choose to base their selling strategies on the private sale mode or the public sale mode, taking advantage of either the late disclosure of price list (24 hours before sale in a private sale versus seven days in a public sale) or the minimum number of flats to be included in the first price list in a public sale (one in a public sale versus 20 in a private sale) (Lin 2012).[18]

This vendor-led selling mechanism made the sale sometimes unpredictable to ordinary purchasers. The degree of discretion a developer had under the arrangement was out of proportion even viewed against the legitimate need to adjust sales strategies in light of market response. The arrangement attracted much criticism from society (SCMP 2010a; CC 2010). After a detailed analysis on the problems under both modes, Goo (2010) suggested that 'such distinction between internal sale and public sale should no longer be maintained'.[19] In June 2010, the Lands Department abolished the practice by introducing one set of rules governing the deadline for the issue of the price list and the minimum number of units to be put up in the first price list.

Minimum number of units to be included in price lists

The rules on the minimum number of units to be included in the first price list were first enclosed in the REDA Guidelines on *Sales Descriptions of Uncompleted Residential Properties* issued on 1 June 2010; with slightly different formulae they appeared in *LACO Circular Memorandum No. 62* published on 2 June 2010 (Lands D 2010). REDA's version is more clearly summed up by dividing the developments into two categories according to the total number of units to be constructed:

a   for small-scale developments with less than 100 units in total, the minimum number of flats to be included in the first price list will be 30 units or 30% of the total number of units (whichever is the higher) put up for sale in each batch;

b   for large-scale developments with 100 units or more in total, the minimum number of flats to be included in the first price list will be 50 units or 50% of the total number of units (whichever is the higher) put up for sale in each batch.

(REDA 2010)

The rules had drawn many complaints after the announcement of REDA's version. The phrase 'in each batch' subtly inserted after 'the total number of units put up for sale' was seen as a 'severely watered-down interpretation of the administrators' intention to put up half the total number of flats available for sale' (SCMP 2010b).

While the rule prescribed the minimum number of units to be put up in the first price list 'in each batch', the minimum number of units to be enclosed 'in each batch' was still unregulated. Developers could increase the number of times of price revision by dividing the total units into more batches. Another issue was that the rules were completely silent as to how the subsequent price lists in that batch should be issued (SC 2011).

The Steering Committee established to draft the legislation made a bold suggestion in reforming the regulation, suggesting that the requirements be formulated on a prescribed percentage directly to the *total number* of residential units of a development or a phase of a development. They proposed a clear-cut solution free of any shadow cast by the 'sale by batch' arrangement. They divided the development (or a phase of development) into three categories according to the number of the units in the development. If the development has 30 units or less, then *all* units must be included in the first price list; if more than 30 units but less than 100 units, each price list must contain at least 30 units; if the developer has more than 100 units to sell, then the first price list, subject to a minimum number of 50 units, must include at least 20 per cent of the total number of units of a development or a phase of a development with each subsequent price list including at least 10 per cent of the total number of units of a development or a phase of a development (SC 2011).

The proposal was accepted by the government and eventually endorsed by the Legislative Council. For developments of 30 or fewer residential properties, section 30 of the *Ordinance* requires only one price list be issued and it must set out all the specified residential properties in the development.[20] For developments of more than 30 but less than 100 residential properties, each price list must set out the prices of at least 30 specified residential properties in the development.[21] The requirement is further explained in section 30(3) that the requirement is regarded as having been complied with if the prices of less than 30 specified residential properties in the development have never been set out; this exempts the developers from the requirement when it comes to the last price list of the sale.[22] The concern may be academic, for developments of less than 100 units are a tiny minority in off-plan sales in Hong Kong and when the number of units is less than 100, vendors may place very little expectation on price revision opportunities between batches.

Greater attention should be paid to the issue of price lists for developments of 100 or more residential properties. The first price list must set out at least 50 specified units or 20 per cent of the total number of the residential properties in the development if that outnumbers 50; this means that for a development of fewer than 250 units, the first price list must contain 50 flats. Subsequent price lists need to contain at least 10 per cent of the number of residential properties in the development; but a new subsection is added that the 10 per cent requirement will be regarded as having been complied with if the number of specified residential properties in the development the prices of which have never been set out in any price list for the development is less than 10 per cent of the number of residential properties in the development; this resolves the problem that the units of the last price list may not constitute 10 per cent of the total number of units in a development.[23]

The simplicity of the new arrangements brings transparency and predictability to the sale. But the constitutionality of such arrangement in relation to Article 6 and Article 105 of the Basic Law is open to doubt. Article 6 of the Basic Law provides that 'the HKSAR shall protect the right of private ownership of property in accordance with law'; and Article 105 protects the owner's right to disposal of property and right to compensation for lawful deprivation of their property. Even though the provision does not *force* developers to sell any properties of a development, some still question whether the requirement on publication of price lists with a minimum number of properties prior to the sale interferes with a vendor's right to dispose of property of its own as guaranteed under Article 105 of the Basic Law (Pannick, Jones and Leung 2012).

It is obvious that the requirement restricts, to a certain degree, the exercise of the right by developers, for under the new regulation developers cannot sell flats without publishing a price list with a minimum number of units at least three days in advance; and for those who wish to sell only a small portion of the properties in the development, they need to include units not intended for sale and assign hypothetical prices to them just to meet up the required minimum number of units in the price list. The question then is whether such restriction is justifiable.

The proportionality test formulated by the Court of Final Appeal in *Leung Kwok-hung & others v HKSAR* requires that the restriction must be *rationally connected* with one or more legitimate purposes and should be *no more than is necessary* to accomplish the purpose.[24] According to the government, the purpose for the introduction of the requirement is to 'ensure prospective purchasers to get a fuller picture of the prices of a considerable number of properties in a development through price lists' (THB & DJ 2012). There is little room to challenge the legitimacy of the purpose, but much effort is needed to prove that the measure prescribed in section 30 of the *Ordinance* is *rationally connected* with the purpose. According to Lord Pannick, Tristan Jones and Wilson Leung (2012), providing purchasers with hypothetical prices of properties that are not for sale does not serve the objective of giving consumers a fuller picture of prices. They argued that a price list would only give purchasers a fuller picture of prices if the properties on the list were in fact going to be offered for sale at the prices in the list. They however did not seek to illustrate why the requirement in section 30 is *not* connected to the purpose in sales where *all* the flats are intended for sale.

The requirement in section 30 serves the purpose of giving a fuller picture of prices in sales where most or all flats are intended for sale. Anything less cannot ensure the degree of certainty as does the arrangement. While it is not entirely wrong to argue that the arrangement will go against the purpose in cases in which only a small portion of residential properties are intended for sale by the vendor, such a scenario is rare in the first-hand sales of residential properties in Hong Kong.

Moreover, section 10(3) may apply to exclude the application of the *Ordinance* for the sale of the small portion of residential units in a completed development, i.e., where at least 95 per cent of the number of the residential properties in the development have been held under a tenancy (other than a government lease) for a continuous period of at least 36 months or for several periods that in the aggregate equal at least 36 months since the issue of occupation permit (or the issue of a certificate of compliance or consent to assign in case of a specified New Territories development).[25]

Date of issuance

Under the Consent Scheme, not less than three calendar days prior to the commencement of sale, price list(s) of the residential units to be offered for sale to the public must be made available (Lands D 2010). It was argued that a price list should preferably be made available to purchasers seven days before the sale (Goo 2010). After lengthy deliberation in the Bills Committee (LC 2012) and perhaps with the goodwill to balance the interests of the purchasers and developers, the *Ordinance* in the end adopts the position of the Consent Scheme and provides that during a period of at least *three days* before a date of the sale, the vendor must publish the relevant price list.[26] According to the Consumer Council's survey, nearly half of the respondents (i.e., 44.5 per cent) considered three days insufficient (CC 2014).

The three days' lead time is appropriate for *subsequent* price lists but not for the first one issued in a sale. The *first* price list should be ideally made at least *five* days before the commencement of the sale. The issue of the first price list usually sets the tone for the entire sale campaign and attracts large media coverage. Purchasers of the first batch bear the highest risk of irrational pricing, for they enter into the agreements with no reference to past transactions. The gap between the issue of the first price list and the commencement of sale forms a 'pre-sale cooling period'. Five days will be sufficient for prospective purchasers to make enquiries and inspections, discuss with professionals and deliberate a decision; a three-day gap may lead to a rush decision given the risk involved in purchase a flat in the first batch. To conclude, the sale should begin, at least *five* – if not seven – calendar days after the issuance of the first price list.

Conclusion

Regulation of the issuance of price lists in sales of residential properties constitutes a major part of the new legislation to tackle high pressure sales tactics and promote information disclosure and transaction transparency throughout the sale. The most glaring example is that the legislation has solved, with remarkable precision, the undecided problem of how to divide and release flats in batches in first-hand sales by prescribing the minimum number of flats to be included in the first and subsequent price lists. With the commencement of the *Ordinance* in April 2013, developers can no longer issue infinite number of price lists (with infinite number of flats in each issue) in one sale. Other progress includes the extension of collection of money to expression of intent as a way of reservation and the three-day statutory period for the issuance of a revised price list.

This part of the legislation clearly exhibits the tendency of prioritizing consumer protection over business freedom. Undoubtedly by imposing a number of measures to regulate the fashion in which price lists are issued, the legislation takes away, in many aspects, the discretion originally enjoyed by developers in conducting the sale. None of the restrictions falls short of the proportionality test laid down in *Leung Kwok-hung & others v HKSAR*. Beyond that, the legislation does not intervene with certain discretion enjoyed by developers the exercise of which is already subject to business ethics, for example, *the freedom not to deal*, an inherent right of property owners recognized by law.

Some provisions in this part of the legislation have attempted, at the same time, to balance the interests of other stakeholders in the sale as well. If solely speaking from the perspective of consumer protection, the legislation could have extended a little longer the period between the issuance of the first price list and the commencement of sale as well as the one between the issuance of the first price list and the legitimate time of making and accepting reservations.

Notes

1 Part of the chapter's discussion on the Consent Scheme was included in the lecture manuscript entitled 'The New Rules for Sales of Uncompleted Flats' in *Law Lectures for Practitioners* (2010) by Hong Kong Law Journal Ltd & Faculty of Law, the University of Hong Kong.
2 Examples of mega developments in recent years are *Yoho Mid-Town, Lake Silver* and *Heritage*.
3 Section 3(1), Part 1, *Residential Properties (First-hand Sales) Ordinance*, A2303.
4 As prescribed in section 14(1) of the *Buildings Ordinance* (Cap 123); see also ibid., section 3(3), A2305.
5 Section 2(1), Part 1, at A2301 and Section 29(1) and (2), Part 2 – Division 3, at A2353, *Residential Properties (First-hand Sales) Ordinance*.
6 Case No.: KTS21568–572、595–599、600–608/15.
7 Section 31(1) and (2), Part 2 – Division 3, *Residential Properties (First-hand Sales) Ordinance*, A2359–A2361.
8 Ibid, section 32(3), Part 2 – Division 3, A2365.
9 [1896] AC 325; the rule also applies to advertisements and display in shops; see *Partridge v Crittenden* [1968] 1 WLR 1204.
10 Section 31(2), Part 2 – Division 3, A2359, *Residential Properties (First-hand Sales) Ordinance*.
11 Section 31(5), Ibid.
12 Case No.: KTS8512–8517/2016.
13 Case No.: KTS15705–15719/2016.
14 Section 35(1)(a), Part 2 – Division 3, *Residential Properties (First-hand Sales) Ordinance*, A2369.
15 Ibid., section 29(3), Part 2 – Division 3, A2353.
16 See Paragraph 9 and 10, Guidelines on Register of Transactions, the Sales of First-hand Residential Properties Authority, 5 April 2013.
17 Section 29(4), Part 2–Division 3, *Residential Properties (First-hand Sales) Ordinance*, A2353.

18 Since December 2002, the ceiling of private sale percentage was abolished: *LACO Circular Memorandum NO.40D*, 3 December 2002; and in February 2001, private sales, previously confined to corporate purchasers, became open to natural persons: *LACO Circular Memorandum NO.40B*, 2 February 2001.
19 For a detailed analysis on situations under both modes, see Goo, S. H. (2010) Regulation of Sale of Off-the-plan Property, *The Conveyancer and Property Lawyer*, Issue 2, 2010, pp. 133–135.
20 Section 30, Part 2–Division 3, *Residential Properties (First-hand Sales) Ordinance*, A2353.
21 Ibid., section 30(2), A2353.
22 Suppose in a hypothetical sale of a development of 80 units, the first 30 units enclosed in the first price are sold out before a second price list of 30 units is issued and are sold out; then there will be about 20 units to be put on sale but in this case if the developer issues a price list of 20 units, it is in breach of the rule. But for the arrangement in section 30(3), developers would have no choice but to include all the units in one price list if the development has less than 60 units in all; otherwise they would breach the regulation in issuing a price list of less than 30 units.
23 Section 30(4), (5) and (6), *Residential Properties (First-hand Sales) Ordinance*, A2355–A2357.
24 (2005) 8 HKCFAR 229.
25 Section 10(3) and (4), *Residential Properties (First-hand Sales) Ordinance*.
26 Section 32(1),(2) and (3), Part 2–Division 3, *Residential Properties (First-hand Sales) Ordinance*, A2365; regarding the requirement of provision of price lists on the project website, see also REDA Guidelines on June 1, 2010, section 8. The developer is required to make a copy of a relevant price list available to the enforcement authority and provide an electronic copy of the relevant price list to the electronic database under section 89(1); see section 32(4)(b), A2365.

References

AD (2016a) 同珍富雅閣違規罪名成立　罰款72萬, 3 August 2016, *Apple Daily*, http://hk.apple.nextmedia.com/realtime/finance/20160803/55447446
AD (2016b) Ocean One廣告誤導罰36萬, *Apply Daily*, 11 November 2016.
AD (2016c) 海鑽開售前刊誤導性廣告 發展商遭罰款20萬, *Apply Daily*, 24 November 2016. http://hk.apple.nextmedia.com/realtime/news/20161124/55958817
CC (2010) Study on the Sale and Purchase of First-hand Private Residential Properties in Hong Kong - The Rights of Consumers to Reliable Property Market Information (Executive Summary), Consumer Council, 26 July 2010.
CC (2014) Study on the Sales of First-hand Residential Properties, p. 15, p. 62, Consumer Council, 11 November 2014, www.consumer.org.hk/ws_en/competition_issues/reports/20141111.html.
Goo, S. H. (2010) Regulation of Sale of Off-the-plan Property, *The Conveyancer and Property Lawyer*, Issue 2, 2010, p. 134.
HKET (2016) 富雅閣涉違規賣樓 表證成立, 3 June 2016, *Hong Kong Economics Times*
HTB (2011a) *Public Consultation on the Proposed Legislation to Regulate the Sale of First-hand Residential Properties*, The Housing and Transport Bureau, November 2011.
HTB (2011b) Residential Properties (First-hand Sales) Bill, Annex A, *The Public Consultation on the Proposed Legislation to Regulate the Sale of First-hand Residential Properties*, The Housing and Transport Bureau, November 2011.
Lands D (1999) Legal Advisory and Conveyancing Office Circular Memorandum No. 40, Lands Department Consent Scheme, Legal Advisory and Conveyancing Office, Lands Department, 28 May 1999.

Lands D (2001) Legal Advisory and Conveyancing Office Circular Memorandum No. 40B, Lands Department Consent Scheme, Legal Advisory and Conveyancing Office, Lands Department, 2 February 2001.

Lands D (2002) Legal Advisory and Conveyancing Office Circular Memorandum No. 40D, Lands Department Consent Scheme, Legal Advisory and Conveyancing Office, Lands Department, 3 December 2002.

Lands D (2010) Legal Advisory and Conveyancing Office Circular Memorandum No. 62, Lands Department Consent Scheme, Legal Advisory and Conveyancing Office, Lands Department, 2 June 2010.

LC (2012) Bills Committee on Residential Properties (First-hand Sales) Bill, Paper for the House Committee, 15 June 2012, LC Paper No. CB(1) 2192/11-12, Legislative Council. www.legco.gov.hk/yr11-12/english/hc/papers/hc0608cb1-2192-e.pdf

Lin, D (2012) The New Rules for Sales of Uncompleted Flats, Law Lectures for Practitioners 2010, Cheng, ML., Jen, J & Young, JYK (Eds.), Hong Kong Law Journal & Faculty of Law, the University of Hong Kong, pp. 78–118.

Lin, D (2013) Regulation of Sales Arrangements and Disclosure of Transaction Price in Off-Plan Sales in Hong Kong, *Australian Property Law Journal*, vol. 21, pp. 251–264.

OD (2016a) 麗新Ocean One違銷售條例判罰款, *Oriental Daily*, 11 November, 2016

OD (2016b) 售樓廣告誤導賣方罰20萬 官嘆小市民難置業, *Oriental Daily*, 24 November, 2016. http://hk.on.cc/hk/bkn/cnt/news/20161124/bkn-20161124121130293-1124_00822_001.html

Pannick, L., Jones, T. and Leung, W. (2012) Residential Properties (First-hand Sales) Bill -Joint Opinion, pp. 14–17, April 2012.

REDA (2006) Guidelines for Sales Descriptions of Uncompleted Residential Properties, The Real Estate Developers Association of Hong Kong, 25 August 2006.

REDA (2010) Guidelines for Sales Descriptions of Uncompleted Residential Properties, The Real Estate Developers Association of Hong Kong, 1 June 2010.

REDA (2012) Submission of the Real Estate Developers Association of Hong Kong to the Transport and Housing Bureau Consultation Paper on the Proposed Legislation to Regulate the Sale of First-Hand Residential Properties, the Real Estate Developers Association of Hong Kong, January 2012, p. 14.

SC (2011) *Report of the Steering Committee on Regulation of Sale of First-hand Residential Properties by Legislation*, The Steering Committee on the Regulation of the Sale of First-hand Residential Properties by Legislation, October 2011, pp. 23–59.

SCMP (2010a) When 'private sale' means anything except private, *South China Morning Post*, 19 July 2012.

SCMP (2010b) Developers try to get round control measures, *South China Morning Post*, 2 June 2010.

SCMP (2011) Steep fines to stop deposit ploy on flats, *South China Morning Post*, 11 October 2011.

SRPA (2013) Guidelines on Register of Transactions, the Sales of First-hand Residential Properties Authority, 5 April 2013. www.srpa.gov.hk/files/pdf/guidelines/Guidelines_on_Register_of_Transactions_Eng.pdf

SRPA (2014) SRPA's Response to Media Enquiries on Discounted Price or Any Types of Average Price, 10 January 2014, www.srpa.gov.hk/files/pdf/press/140111/press_140111_Eng.pdf

THB & DJ (2012) Administration's Response to Issues Raised by Members at the Bills Committee Meeting held on 22 May 2012, Transport and Housing Bureau, Department of Justice, CB(1) 2066/11-12(02), May 2012, pp. 2–5.

11 Sales arrangement

Introduction

That a price list must be made available at least three days immediately before the date of the sale – the statutory requirement enclosed in section 32(3) of the *Residential Properties (First-hand Sales) Ordinance* (the *Ordinance*) – has been highlighted in the discussion in the previous chapter. The question then is what action can (or can't) a vendor or an intended purchaser take in the three-day gap after a price list is made available? Section 34(1) of the *Ordinance* further provides: 'the vendor must not seek any general expression of intent from any other person on the specified residential properties in the development, and must reject such a general expression of intent, before the first day on which copies of any price list setting out the prices of those specified residential properties have been made available under section 32(3).' Just exactly what does this 'expression of intent' mean in a sale of first-hand residential properties? What if two or more purchasers are interested in purchasing one particular residential property the price of which is enclosed in the price list? This brings us to the discussion on sales arrangement in sales of first-hand residential properties.

In the broad sense, sales arrangement concerns how a sale of first-hand residential properties shall start and be carried out. This includes the following aspects: (a) information on the time, date and venue of the sales office; (b) information on the residential units on sale for a given transaction day; and (c) the price information on the units available for the sale. It also concerns the methods to determine the order of priority in case of two or more purchasers competing to buy one specified residential unit.

In general, sales arrangement is the most loosely regulated area of practice by the new legislation: besides section 34, this is mainly discussed in one other section of the *Ordinance*, i.e., section 47. The brevity of the section could indicate a legislative intention supporting a high degree of freedom in processing the sale by developers, e.g., how to accept reservations, arrange balloting procedures, register the selection of flats by the purchasers, etc. The statutory provision is further explained by the Guidelines on Sales Arrangements and Other Information issued by the SRPA (2013a). Plus, the Authority has set out best practices including employing a template to disclose information on sales arrangement for developers to follow (SRPA 2013b).

Even with these further efforts provided by the Authority, there is not too much regulation on sales arrangement, compared to the degree of interference by the legislation on other commercial practices in the first-hand sales. On one hand, in observation of the principle of business efficacy and a vendor's constitutional right to freedom of disposing of her property, it is reasonable not to prescribe rigid rules on how to sell new flats by statute: as every sale differs in terms of scale, market response, purchasers' desirability, promotion schemes and provision of financial facilities, agency engagement and so on, the vendor may need to adopt different measures in order to maintain the order of the sale. But, on the other hand, less regulation could give rise to the occurrence of misleading, unfair or even aggressive sales practices by a vendor or an agent in processing the purchaser's intention to buy a particular residential property. It seems that without much regulation by the *Ordinance*, sales arrangement remained a rather problematic area *after* the commencement of the *Ordinance* in April 2013. The 2014 Study on the implementation of the *Ordinance* by the Consumer Council (2014) discussed a number of questionable practices discovered in field visits of 17 sales of first-hand residential properties in June and July 2014.

Notification on the date of the sale

Section 47 of the *Ordinance* stipulates that three days immediately before a date of the sale the vendor must make available, both in hard copies and online, a document containing 'the date and time when, and the place where, the specified residential property will be offered to be sold; the number of specified residential properties in the development that will be offered to be sold; the method to be used to determine the order of priority in which each of the persons interested in buying any of those specified residential properties may select the residential property that the person wishes to purchase and the method to be used to determine the order of priority in case two or more persons are interested in purchasing a particular specified residential property.'

The wording '*immediately before*' in section 47(1) clearly suggests that the date of the sale itself is excluded from the counting of the three days. SRPA further points out that the three days includes all Saturdays, Sundays and Public Holidays (SRPA 2013a). Thus if a sale is arranged to start on a Sunday, information on sales arrangement must be made available at least on the preceding Thursday.

The SRPA recommends as a best practice for the vendor to send a copy of the document containing information on sales arrangements to the Authority on the first day on which the document is made available to the public (SRPA 2013b). According to an illustration given by the Authority, if a vendor wishes to sell a property on 4 January, she must make available a document containing such information on the sales arrangements for the reference of the public in hard copies and online by 1 January and send a soft copy to the Authority by 23:59 on 1 January.

The three-day-before-sale requirement sets out the *minimum* number, i.e., three days before the sale, as the cut-off day on which the vendor must make available the information on sales arrangement. A vendor can of course make available such information much earlier than three days immediately before the sale starts. The SRPA did not go further to suggest that it would be a best practice if the vendor could disclose such information earlier than three days as required by the statute to give prospective purchasers more time to consider. According to the 2014 Survey by the Consumer Council though, 46.9 per cent of respondents opined that three days was inadequate for consideration and preferred a longer disclosure period (CC 2014).

The discussion in Chapter 10 suggests that three days' lead time is appropriate for the issue of *subsequent* price lists in a sales campaign; the *first* price list should ideally be made *five* days before the start of the sale. Similarly, for the ever first sales arrangement of a sale of a batch of units in a new development, it would be more sensible if such information was disclosed at least *five* days before the commencement of the sale so the general public will know the location of the sales office and the information about the properties enclosed in the first batch. For the subsequent batches, three days' lead time is sufficiently long for intended purchasers to consider and, as to be discussed below, register their intention.

Lastly, a vendor is allowed to make changes to the sales arrangement after the document of the sales arrangement is made available and before the intended date of sale prescribed therein. The SRPA requests that the revised sales arrangement be made available on the designated website for inspection and in hard copies for the collection of the public. More crucially, the residential properties affected by the changes should only be sold or offered to be sold after the revised sales arrangements have been made available to the public for a period of at least three days (SRPA 2013b).

Register of intention

The document containing information about the details of sales arrangement is not the only thing that must be made available three days immediately before the sale. As discussed in Chapter 10, a similar requirement applies to the release of price lists: during a period of at least three days immediately before the sale, the vendor must make the relevant price list available.[1] The document of sales arrangement discloses the information about what properties are on sale and when and where to buy, while the price list informs prospective purchasers of the price of the properties. Section 47(4) further stipulates that during the three-day period the specified residential property must not be sold or offered to be sold before the date of sale. Under such circumstances, it is guaranteed that, after the vendor making available the price list and the document of the sales arrangement, a prospective purchaser will have at least three days to consider whether she will participate in the sale or not.

When to register

This is, however, not to say a purchaser can do nothing during the three-day period other than sitting at home and considering. Can an eager purchaser pay the developer some money prior to the sale in order to reserve a flat or, at least, to maximize her chance to be allocated a flat to buy? Under the Consent Scheme developers were not allowed to receive deposits before the first price list was announced. The Steering Committee took one step further in suggesting that developers may face a fine of up to HK$500,000 if they did so (SC 2011). There had been much debate in the Steering Committee's Report on a legitimate time at which developers should be allowed to accept money for the purpose of reservation of units. Two dates were suggested: *the date of the issuance of price list*, and *the date of the commencement of sale*. The first draft of the *Residential Properties (First-hand Sales) Bill* adopted the date of the issuance of price list but the Lands Department expressed that that date was chosen in the Draft Bill solely for presentation purpose and the government was open to public opinion as to which is a more appropriate time point to allow collection of money (HTB 2011a). Nonetheless, in the end, the *Ordinance* does choose *the date of the issuance of price list* as the cut-off date after which reservation is allowed.[2] This means that reservation can be made at most three days before the date of the commencement of the sale.

From the perspective of consumer protection, the more proper point after which developers can accept money for reservation seems to be *the commencement of sale* instead, i.e., the first day the property is offered to be sold. First, if developers are allowed to accept reservation immediately after the price list is made available, such behaviour will de facto initiate the sale: reservation as a technique may operate to the advantage of experienced purchasers, professional investors, speculators but not of ordinary purchasers.

Second, the information on reservation requests received after the issue of the price list, i.e., the number of registrations of intent submitted, is likely to send out a strong signal on the market's response to the property on sale. Since the details of the properties reserved are not required to be disclosed under the *Ordinance*, developers do not have to cite the exact number of registrants of intent as received. Atmosphere-building activities that purport to stimulate the market can take place during the time gap. False impressions could be easily created. Reservation after the commencement of sale (for units to be released in future batches), however, does not have such influence on creating the atmosphere: 'because once a sale begins, all transactions will have to be disclosed within 24 hours. It doesn't matter how many cheques you boast you have collected,' as observed by Mr Lawrence Poon, the preceding Chairman of General Practice Division of Hong Kong Institute of Surveyors (SCMP 2011).[3]

Overall, it is worth reconsidering whether it serves the purpose of enhancing transparency by allowing reservation on the *date of the issuance of price list*.

Expression of intent

On a related matter, the *Ordinance* not only prevents any collection of money before the vendor makes the relevant price list available, but prohibits other behaviours that may have similar effects. This is achieved by extending the act of collection of money to a broadly-defined concept of 'expression of intent'.

Under the *Ordinance* there are two types of expressions of intent: *general* expression of intent and *specific* expression of intent. A specific expression of intent is defined as an expression of intent to purchase a particular residential property among those specified residential properties or all of those specified residential properties on the basis that subject to an agreement being made, the expression does not bind the maker; a general expression of intent is made without being specific about any particular residential property.[4] The expression of intent includes but is not limited to a payment of money; an expression of intent can be accompanied without any payment of money. In this way, an oral expression of interest still can, depending on the circumstances of the case, amount to an expression of intent. As a general rule, the *Ordinance* prohibits developers from seeking or accepting any expressions of intent before the price list is made available. And after the price lists are published and made available in sales offices and the project website, developers cannot seek *specific* expression of intent, viz. to reserve a particular unit for a particular purchaser, until the sale starts.

A careful reading of the rule will reveal a twist in the wording: while most if not all cases of expressions of intent are made by prospective purchasers, the rule does not prevent purchasers and the public from *making* the expression of intent. It merely requires developers *not to seek* any expressions of intent (*a passive obligation*) and, in case such expressions are advanced to them, to *reject* any expressions of intent (*an active obligation*).[5] The *Ordinance* however does not define the word 'seek', which may require further interpretation by case law in the near future. In a seller's market the word should partake the plain meanings of both 'accept' and 'register'.

Expression of intention is usually not relevant if the sale proceeds on a first-come, first-served basis. But the seller's market status may imply that for any sale of first-hand residential properties, there are more purchasers than flats. As such, not every purchaser of intention can be allocated a flat. Therefore in many sales, a ballot arrangement has to be held to determine the order of priority. In order to participate in the ballot, a prospective purchaser needs to have her general expression of intention registered with the vendor.

Theoretically a prospective purchaser can of course make such an expression of intent earlier than the publication of the price list but such expression of intent must be rejected by the vendor prior to the issue of price list under section 34(1). All in all, the provision in section 34(1) suggests that a would-be purchaser can make a general expression of intent to the vendor as soon as the price list is made available, i.e., three days immediately before the sale. If the prospective purchaser wants to make a specific expression of intent, according to section 34(2), the vendor can accept such expression of the intent only on or after the first day the property is offered on sale.

In practice, though, making a general or specific expression of intent cannot be done purely orally or in writing, but has to be accomplished by supplying a copy of the purchaser's identity card and a cashier order in the sum stated in the sales arrangement by the vendor. The application is often submitted to the vendor by the real estate agents. If, in the end, the purchaser is not allocated the quota to purchase the property or, even with a quota but the purchaser nonetheless decides not to purchase the property, the cashier order will be returned to the registrant. It would be ideal if the new legislation provides a deadline for the return of the cashier order, e.g., within a week after the first date of the sale.

Information on the number of registrations of intent

As the registration of intent before the sale starts may indicate the market's response to the property, the information on the number of genuine registrations of intent by prospective purchasers is critical: over 70 per cent of respondents uttered the view that their assessment of the actual market demand and supply situations would be affected if there were claims of the vendor receiving a huge number of registrations of intent before the commencement of the sale (CC 2014). In this regard it is critical to ensure that the public extracts from such information a rational view on how the market responds to the sale. This cannot be achieved without a detailed examination on the way registration of intent is invited in every sale. To start, it is crucial to understand that the number of registrations of intent does not equal the exact number of purchasers who are demonstrating a strong will to buy or the number of flats that are demanded.

First, from sale to sale, a purchaser is allocated different quotas of submitting the registrations of intent and every registration may be entitled to buy a different number of units. In different sales, every purchaser may be allocated one or two or even three registrations of intent. Each registration must be submitted with one cashier order. In most cases, one registrant is entitled to submit a maximum two registrations of intent representing two balloting rights. As the registration of intent can be in individual or joint names, a couple, for example, can submit a total of three registrations of intent: one in the name of the wife, one in that of husband and one in their joint names.

At the same time, depending on the vendor of every sale, each registration may entitle the purchaser to purchase a different number of properties: for some, one, for some, two and for others, three. Moreover, in some sales, the developer will adopt a further correction process to revise the number of properties the registrant can buy in case of double registrations of intention submitted by a husband, a wife and in their joint names: in other words, under the arrangement the vendor allows the couple to submit multiple registrations of intention to increase their chance of being chosen, but does not allow the increase of the quota in case more than one registration from the couple is chosen.

Thus, as observed by the Consumer Council (2014), in some sales one purchaser could be entitled to buy two residential properties with one registration of intent whereas in other sales a married couple is allowed to submit six registrations of intention but at the end of the day they are allowed to purchase only one property in the development.

Secondly, in some cases, the estate agents seemed to vaguely indicate that the registration of intent with cashier order is a prerequisite to view the property. In 2006, it was reported that some vendors demanded a cashier order of HK$50,000 in order to see the price lists (SCMP 2006). An extreme case occurred during one fieldwork conducted by the Consumer Council in 2014, in which the fieldworkers were asked for and in the end actually provided a cashier order in an amount of HK$2,000,000 to the estate agent in order to obtain permission to view the particular property (CC 2014).

Thirdly, in some cases, purchasers were offered the extra cashier orders in the balloting draw in order to increase their chances. The Council's survey revealed that the tendency is rising, as 46.4 per cent of respondents who purchased first-hand properties in 2013–14 replied *yes* to the question concerning the offer of extra cashier orders by related sales persons compared with only 8.8 per cent before 2013 (CC 2014). This practice not only inflates the number of registrations of intent received but also undermines the fairness of the drawing procedure. Plus, as the Council noted, 'the extra cashier orders provided by sales persons might give an illusion of an active property environment to the public'. The practice should be prohibited by law or guidelines issued by the Authority under section 88 of the *Ordinance*.

While many registrations of intent were submitted by determined purchasers, some were submitted under the persuasion of the real estate agents to try their luck. The registrants in these cases may not care too much about the result and may give up the right to purchase a property eventually. As there is no penalty to opt against buying after registering the intent with the cashier order, the act of registration does not necessarily represent a serious intention of purchase. The water is further muddied when the estate agents and sales people acting for the developer submit registrations of intent on their own. Save where the agents and sales staff are at the same time genuine purchasers, the only purpose of doing so is to boost the figure of the registrations of intention received, to help generate an image of overwhelming response by the market.

'An inflated number of registrations of intention' became a big issue for the year 2014 in sale of first-hand residential properties in Hong Kong. According to the Consumer Council, in one sale in 2014, around 10,000 registrations of intent were reported to have been received by the vendor before the sale started; the number of units offered for sale on the first date of sale was 492 and the number of units sold on that date was 428. In another case, the reported number of registrations of intent in the press was 2,600, the number of units offered for sale on the first date of sale was 220 yet and the number of units actually sold on the first date of sale was 189 (CC 2014). In the last case, the number of flats actually sold consists of merely 7.2 per cent of the total number of registrations of intent received. Thus it is highly questionable how reliable the number of registrations of intent is to reflect the actual demand for the property.

In 2015 the SRPA issued a new Practice Note to require the vendor of first-hand residential properties to indicate the number of registrations of intent and/or cashier orders which are submitted by estate agents and/or salespersons for themselves when making public the total number of registrations of intent and/or cashier orders they have received in respect of a development or a phase of a development. The Practice Note further explains that if an individual estate agent licensee submits through the estate agency company she works for the registration(s) of intent in her name solely or together with other individual(s) and/or company (companies) jointly or in the name of a company of which the individual licensee is a shareholder and/or director, as registrant(s), she shall be regarded as submitting the registration of intent for herself. If a company licensee through itself submits the registration(s) of intent in its name solely or together with other individual(s) and/or company (companies) jointly or in the name of a company of which the company licensee is a shareholder and/or director, as registrant(s), the company is regarded as submitting registrations of intent for itself (SRPA 2015a).

At the same time, the Authority reminded the public that the registration of intent is 'a reference only, not as an indicator of the sales volume of a development/ phase'.

Information on the deadline to submit registration of intent

Section 34 of the *Ordinance* provides the earliest time in a sale when the vendor can accept expressions of intent from prospective purchasers; but the legislation does not stipulate the latest time before which a purchaser's registrations of intent can be accepted by the vendor. The latest time for submission seems to be at the discretion of the vendor, yet such information must be accurately disclosed otherwise a prospective purchaser may be pressed to submit the registration of intent based on a wrong understanding of an imminent deadline of submission. In the investigation conducted by the Consumer Council in 2014, in one sale the fieldworkers were told by an estate agent during their visit to the sales office that the deadline was in the evening of that day and in order not to miss the chance, the fieldworkers needed to register immediately; in fact the deadline for submission of the registration of intent was one day after that day (CC 2014).

Therefore the vendor should be requested to disclose in the document containing information about sales arrangement the deadline for submission of registration of intention and, if ballot drawing will be held, the date and time of the ballot drawing.

Selection of flats

Selection by balloting

The 2014 Report by the Consumer Council suggested that ballot drawing is becoming increasingly popular in sales of first-hand residential properties in Hong Kong. The mainstream is to have a one-off computer ballot drawing; yet in some sales multi-phases of ballot drawing will be held. Registrants may be invited to observe the ballot process and be notified of the ballot results. The Council has suggested that developers be requested to disclose the drawing result on the website designated for the project (CC 2014).

In some cases, the vendor requested the purchaser be personally present during the ballot drawing in order to be eligible for the drawing result. The vendor's presence is not essential for the drawing; such request will impose unnecessary burdens on the shoulders of the purchasers. The SRPA expresses the view that such arrangement is unreasonable and should be avoided (SRPA 2015b).

A more problematic issue arises after the result of the draw is announced. How much time should be given to an eligible purchaser to consider whether to buy a flat and, if she decides to buy, to select the flat. The Consumer Council's survey revealed that nearly half of the respondents who purchased a property before 2013 believed the time given to make a purchase decision is inadequate; the same conclusion was drawn by more than 40 per cent of respondents who purchased a property between 2013 and 2014 (CC 2014). In extreme cases, the purchasers were given 'minutes' to close the deal.

An issue of which people are often ignorant is that even after the balloting, a successful registrant has the right *not* to buy a unit. An eligible purchaser may decline to buy a unit in the development if the remaining units do not suit her needs or preferences. Such right of the purchaser should be respected by the vendor and the estate agents and protected by the law. However, the right may not be well exercised by the eligible purchaser if she was under pressure to make a decision within hours or even minutes after the result of the draw was announced. The Consumer Council encloses in its 2014 Report a case where real estate agents might have engaged in certain practices that could be regarded as aggressive in encouraging an eligible purchaser to make a decision after the draw:

> [W]hen the fieldworker was able to select the properties which were still available, the fieldworker was surrounded by at least 4 estate agents and pressurized to make a quick decision in minutes on the preferred choice of property, as many people were queuing up. Other estate agents nearby also persuaded the fieldworker to select a property first and re-consider the decision later. From knowing to deciding, the whole selection process only took a few minutes. To end, the field worker was under intense pressure for not purchasing.
>
> (CC 2014)

To respect the vendor's freedom in deciding how to sell the properties, the *Ordinance* does not provide a statutory lead time between the announcement of results and the selection of flats. For a vibrant property market in Hong Kong, it is indeed not advisable to set out a statutory lead time. The SRPA suggested in 2015 that vendors arrange the balloting session and the flat selection session on two separate days so registrants will have at least one night to think over the flat selection matter (SRPA 2015b). The flat selection shall include the matter of whether to buy or not, as well as the matter of which unit to buy.

But the vendor's freedom in deciding how to sell the properties must be balanced with the purchasers' need for some reasonable amount of time to consider whether to buy and what to buy after being allocated a quota. Purchasers who intend to buy should be given adequate time to select their flats after the ballot. Many who have participated in the ballot may not yet have had the opportunity to ponder upon selection of flats due to two factors. One, before the ballot it is uncertain whether they can buy a flat and two, it is also uncertain which flats are still available for them to select. The vendor should grant the purchaser some reasonable time to select the flat after the draw.

At the same time, business efficacy requires that the purchaser convey to the vendor her decision in a prompt manner so the rest of the sale can proceed accordingly. Still, the purchasers who participated in the draw are, in most cases, genuine purchasers who wish to buy a residential property in the development. By the time of the ballot, they are expected to have certain knowledge of the property (i.e., location and environment of the development, flat sizes and internal structure, fittings and finishes and so forth). What is unknown to them before the draw is whether and which units are available for them to select. Therefore once the result of the draw is announced and the remaining choices become clear, it should not take them too much time to select one or two residential properties according to their budgets and preferences.

Overall, *one calendar day* should be a reasonable time for purchasers after they have been officially notified by the vendor: after a written message sent by the vendor to the purchaser or her real estate agents. In other words, it would be reasonable for the developer to request the purchaser make a decision within 24 hours *after* she has been notified of the result from the draw. Developers can of course give the eligible purchasers more time to make a decision; but in any case, no less than 24 hours should be given. In a nutshell, the purchaser should have at least 24 hours to make a decision after notification of the result; yet best practice would suggest that developers give the eligible purchaser 48 hours after the notification of the result.

The vendor should arrange the time slots of the eligible purchasers according to the priority determined by the draw. If the purchaser, after being given 24 hours (or longer) to make a decision, did not attend the session to select the flat, she will lose priority over subsequent purchasers of the same batch.

Last but not least, the *Ordinance* does not interfere with the particulars in arranging the balloting. This also indicates the legislation's respect to the freedom enjoyed by the vendor in disposing of her properties. Indeed the vendor can be very creative in terms of how to pick the winners of the ballot. In a 2014 sale which involved sales of residential units in a number of buildings each containing eight units, the vendor announced the arrangement that priority would be given to group registrants of up to eight individuals/companies who entered into the draw as a group with the intention to purchase all the eight properties in one building. Non-Group Registrants did not enjoy any priority and would select units after Group Registrants. According to SRPA, such arrangement is acceptable under the *Ordinance*, since the vendor at the same time reminds the non-group registrant of the risk that no residential property may be available for sale after the selection of the group registrants (SRPA 2013c).

Selection on first-come, first-served basis

The Consumer Council's survey in 2014 suggested that before 2013, more than 50 per cent of sales of new flats proceeded on a first-come, first-served basis. For the years 2013 and 2014, this method still accounted for about one third of the sales (CC 2014).

The advantage of this method of sale is that it is transparent in its simplicity. But the arrangement is not free of problems. If a sale is premised on the first-come, first-served basis, eager purchasers may have to queue outside the sales office a day and a night before the date of the sale. Inconvenience aside, this may also cause disputes and chaos in the venue where the sale takes place. Because of this, the Authority has advised vendors to avoid using such methods from 2015 onwards (SRPA 2015a). Furthermore, the Consumer Council observed that one developer had inserted an additional selection process on top of first-come, first-served: in a 2014 sale, the vendor reserved a 'rotation' right to allocate properties to purchasers by a specific sequence consisting of seven estate agency companies (CC 2014).

Information on progress of the sale

While the sale proceeds, the units available for selection will decrease in number. Even for sales in which new units are released on a daily basis, the units available for selection will change at different hours of the day. For a prospective purchaser who visits the sales office after the sale started, what units are being offered for sale by the time she arrives at the sales office would be of her great interest. The purchaser may wish to know all the units that are still available for selection. The information about remaining flats, if not accurately disclosed, may affect the purchaser's consideration. For example, if the vendor's sales staff or the agents, for whatever reason, suggest only a portion of units available for selection to the prospective purchaser, then she may have to make a decision to buy an apartment she would otherwise not purchase had she been provided with a wider range of options. In the circumstance, a full and timely disclosure on the information on availability of specified residential properties for selection at sales office is much needed so that the prospective purchaser can make an informed decision. The survey conducted by the Consumer Council (2014) reveals that 'Units available for selection at the time of sale' was regarded by most respondents as at the top of the important items at the sales office (followed by 'sales brochures and price lists prepared by developers').

Meanwhile, the Consumer Council pointed out that, without the disclosure of the number of units still available for selection on the day of the sale, some estate agents may aggressively entice a prospective purchaser to submit a registration of intent by stating that 'most units are sold out and very few are left' (CC 2014). Under *The Consumer Protection from Unfair Trading Regulations 2008*, 'falsely stating that a product will only be available for a very limited time, or that it will only be available on particular terms for a very limited time, in order to elicit an immediate decision and deprive consumers of sufficient opportunity or time to make an informed choice' is a prohibited unfair commercial practice; a trader (which includes agents acting on behalf of the vendor) who engages in such practice is guilty of an offence.[6]

The *Ordinance* did not touch upon how such information shall be disclosed by the vendor. In April 2015 the SRPA issued a *Practice Note* to recommend as best practice that vendors make public at sales offices the information on the progress of sale on each and every date of sale, including showing which residential properties are offered for sale at the beginning of that date and updating which residential properties have been selected and which residential properties have been sold during that date (SRPA 2015c).

In the Practice Note, the SRPA designed a template to make available the information which needs to be displayed in a manner that it is reasonably visible to any person entering in the sales office and needs to be updated as soon as possible after the change in status has taken place. In the template the vendor needs first to state the date and the time when the information was last updated. Then the vendor needs to display, mainly, two kinds of information according to its latest status. First, the total number of residential properties in the development/ phase as well as the total number of residential properties in the development/ phase sold before that date; the total number of specified residential properties in the development/phase offered for sale on the date and the total number not offered for sale on that day. Second, the status of each of the residential properties offered for sale on that day must be indicated in a Matrix in the Template, or a 'consumption table' as the Authority later termed it in its press release (SRPA 2015b, 2015c).

The status of a specified residential property in the sale can take the following four forms: (i) the specified residential property is available for selection (which is requested to be shown as blank in the Matrix); (ii) the specified residential property has been selected by prospective purchaser but the preliminary agreement for sale and purchase has yet to be signed by the prospective purchaser; (iii) the specified residential property has been selected by prospective purchaser and the preliminary agreement for sale and purchase has been signed by the purchaser at an earlier time on that particular date of sale: the specified residential properties falling into this category is no longer available for selection by prospective purchasers on that day; and (iv) the specified residential property that is not offered for sale for that day: for this category, the Authority does not request, as part of the best practices, the vendor to disclose any relevant information for these properties; instead, the Authority only suggests the vendor shade the relevant part of the Matrix in case the presentation in the form of a matrix may inevitably show some of those residential properties which are not being offered for sale on a particular date of sale (SRPA 2015c).

The above best practice further enhances the transparency of the sale by preventing the vendor from selectively disclosing units offered on sale on that day; but it does not stipulate the maximum time a vendor can have between the signing of the preliminary agreement for sale and purchase and a respective update on the status in the Matrix. As best practices, non-compliance by the vendor will not be regarded as contravention of the *Ordinance* or a commission of an offence under the *Ordinance* per se (SPRA 2015c). Thus a vendor could still delay the update of the Matrix if she so wishes. A lot of excuses can be found for a vendor to delay the update by a couple of hours in a busy day of sale. At the same time, a preliminary agreement for sale and purchase can be signed shortly after a purchaser selects a unit. It would not be practical to request a vendor, in these cases, to update the Matrix twice during that short transitory period within minutes or hours of a transaction day, i.e., from status (ii) to status (iii). In fact, the amount of information to be presented by the Matrix is substantial and it could be overwhelming to request a timely update by manual in some mega sales. The Authority should suggest the vendor use a computer program to assist updating the Matrix as the sale proceeds: in this case the Matrix shall be displayed in an electronic screen in the sales offices.

Conclusion

As discussed at the beginning of this chapter, sales arrangement is arguably the least regulated part by the *Ordinance* among all commercial practices in first-hand sales of residential properties. With more degree of freedom granted to the vendor, more questionable practices had arisen in this area. This may explain why issues regarding sales arrangement were heavily featured in the Consumer Council's 2014 Study. The deficiency has been much compensated with the issue of a number of practice notes by the SRPA. The practice of the employment of the 'consumption table' in the sales office has indeed encouraged developers to go the extra mile after fulfilling the requirements under the *Ordinance* in order to enhance transparency and fairness in the sales (LC 2016).

The degree of enhanced regulation requires sensible consideration by the Authority to balance the necessary degree of discretion to be enjoyed by the vendor in order to arrange the sale and the degree of risk of occurrence of misleading or unconscionable practices with less regulation. The bottom line is to ensure the sale proceeds in a transparent and fair manner. It is anticipated that this part may be further enriched in the amendments of the *Ordinance*.

It is worth noting that this part of the legislation also concerns the acts and practices by sales persons or agents. In general, sales persons or agents are under the regulation of Estate Agents Authority which is a statutory body established under the *Estate Agents Ordinance*. In other words, the issue of cross regulation or double regulation may arise when it comes to unprofessional or misleading practices by sales agents in the sale of first-hand residential properties.

Notes

1 Section 32 (1)(3), Part 2–Division 3, *Residential Properties (First-hand Sales) Ordinance*, A2365.
2 Ibid., section 34(1)(2), Part 2–Division 3, A2367.
3 Joyce Ng and Ng Kang-chung, *Steep fines to stop deposit ploy on flats*, South China Morning Post, 11 October 2011. For a detailed analysis on the requirements of timely disclosure of transaction information by the *Residential Properties (First-hand Sales) Ordinance*, see Chapter 13 and Devin Lin, *Regulation of Sales Arrangements and Disclosure of Transaction Price in Off-Plan Sales in Hong Kong* (2013) *Australian Property Law Journal*, Volume 21, p. 251.
4 Section 34(4), Part 2–Division 3, *Residential Properties (First-hand Sales) Ordinance*, A2369.
5 Ibid.
6 Regulation 2, regulation 8, paragraph 7 of Schedule 1, *The Consumer Protection from Unfair Trading Regulations 2008.*

References

CC (2014) Study on the Sales of First-hand Residential Properties, p. 16, pp. 25–28, p. 37, pp. 41–47, pp. 84–87, Consumer Council, 11 November 2014, www.consumer.org.hk/ws_en/competition_issues/reports/20141111.html.
HTB (2011a) Public Consultation on the Proposed Legislation to Regulate the Sale of First-hand Residential Properties, The Housing and Transport Bureau, November 2011.
HTB (2011b) Residential Properties (First-hand Sales) Bill, Annex A, *The Public Consultation on the Proposed Legislation to Regulate the Sale of First-hand Residential Properties*, The Housing and Transport Bureau, November 2011.
LC (2016) The work of the Sales of First-hand Residential Properties Authority, Legislative Council Panel on Housing, CB(1)861/15-16(01), April 2016, p.8.
Lin, D. (2013) Regulation of Sales Arrangements and Disclosure of Transaction Price in Off-Plan Sales in Hong Kong, *Australian Property Law Journal*, vol. 21, pp. 251–264.
SC (2011) *Report of the Steering Committee on Regulation of Sale of First-hand Residential Properties by Legislation*, The Steering Committee on the Regulation of the Sale of First-hand Residential Properties by Legislation, October 2011, pp. 23–59.
SCMP (2006) Market Farces, *South China Morning Post*, 11 September 2006.
SCMP (2011) Steep fines to stop deposit ploy on flats, *South China Morning Post*, 11 October 2011.
SRPA (2013a) Guidelines on Sales Arrangements and Other Information, The Sales of First-hand Residential Properties Authority, 5 April 2013, pp. 2–3. www.srpa.gov.hk/files/pdf/guidelines/Guidelines_on_Sales_Arrangements_and_Other_Information_Eng.pdf
SRPA (2013b) Practice Notes on Sales Arrangements and Other Information, The Sales of First-hand Residential Properties Authority, 5 April 2013, pp. 2–3. www.srpa.gov.hk/

files/pdf/practice-notes/Practice_Notes_on_Sales_Arrangements_and_Other_
Information_Eng.pdf

SRPA (2013c) SRPA's Response to Media Enquiries, *Press releases,* The Sales of First-
hand Residential Properties Authority, 24 June 2013.

SRPA (2015a) SRPA Advises Vendors on How to Mention the Number of Registrations of
Intent Received by a Development, *Press Releases*, The Sales of First-hand Residential
Properties Authority, 20 August 2015, www.info.gov.hk/gia/general/201508/20/
P201508200363.htm

SRPA (2015b) SRPA Launches New Measures to Enhance Transparency of Sale of First-
hand Residential Properties, *Press releases,* The Sales of First-hand Residential
Properties Authority, 29 April 2015, www.info.gov.hk/gia/general/201504/29/
P201504290556.htm

SRPA (2015c) Practice Note on Making Public Information on the Availability of Specified
Residential Properties for Selection by Prospective Purchasers at Sales Office，The
Sales of First-hand Residential Properties Authority, 29 April 2015, www.srpa.gov.hk/
files/pdf/practice-notes/Practice_Notes_on_Flat_Availability_Eng.pdf

12 Transaction[1]

Introduction

This chapter discusses the disclosure of information on transactions in sales of first-hand residential properties: this essentially concerns the *transaction price* and *transaction volume* achieved in a given day of sale. Fischer Black (1986) has distinguished two types of trade in the market: one, *information trading* (i.e., trade on information where the traders are expected to profit) and two, *noise trading* (i.e., trade on imperfect observation or trade on the arbitrary element in expectations that leads to an arbitrary rate of inflation consistent with expectations). Black rightfully points out that in a market where 'there is so much noise around', traders may not know they are trading on noise; instead, they may think they are trading on information. In modern times, noise trading happens whenever the trader tries to follow the market trend without complete and timely access to the first-hand information on price or transaction volume. 'Noise' is made in all kinds of real estate sales.

In the vibrant real estate market in Hong Kong, new flats are usually released in batches in first-hand sales. Purchasers of subsequent batches were seen to have been misled by the information about transaction volume and prices in earlier batches disclosed by developers. Recent empirical research further indicates that there are more noise traders in the presale market due to lower transaction costs (Yiu, Wong and Chau 2009). In first-hand sales of residential properties, information about price and volume achieved in previous transactions is critical for subsequent purchasers to make a rational judgement. Frank, full and timely disclosure of past transaction information by developers brings purchasers closer to the value of the units based on demand and supply. However in practice, price was seen to be manipulated by developers through price lists provision, internal sales and selective information on transaction records (Merry 2008). Before 2009, developers were not required to release any transaction information; as such, buyers were under high risk of being misled by transaction prices selectively released by developers, which, in case of applicability, could also contain no detail about any gifts or incentives given by the developer to the purchasers (Goo 2010).

From 2010 onwards, the Hong Kong government introduced a number of measures to promote transparency in the first-hand market by the Legal Advisory and Conveyancing Office Circular Memoranda (hereinafter LACO Circular Memoranda) under the Lands Department Consent Scheme; which now form part of *the Residential Properties (First-hand Sales) Ordinance* (the *Ordinance*).

This chapter revolves around the question of how developers shall disclose past transaction records. To answer the question, the discussion begins with the signing of the preliminary agreement for sale and purchase. Then it investigates different types of transaction and the respective requirements on information disclosure imposed by the Lands Department Consent Scheme and the new legislation. The analysis will reveal the extent to which information about past transaction records is timely and accurately released to the public under the *Ordinance*.

The conveyancing procedure

Disposition of land by sale in Hong Kong involves five stages: pre-contract, contract, between contract and completion, completion and post-completion (Goo and Lee 2015). For presales, the usual practice is that 5 per cent of the price is paid upon signing of the *preliminary agreement for sale and purchase* (or PASP), followed by another 5 per cent upon signing of the *agreement for sale and purchase* (or ASP) within five working days; the agreement for sale and purchase is required to be registered at the Land Registry within one month from the date of the preliminary agreement for sale and purchase.[2] Before the commencement of the *Ordinance*, a third 5 per cent for individual purchasers or 10 per cent for corporate purchasers was payable within 60 days after the signing of the preliminary agreement for sale and purchase; the balance would not become due until the developer is in a position validly to assign the property, viz., the developer, upon completion of construction, has obtained the consent to assign or the certificate of compliance issued by the Director of Lands.[3] The assignment needs to be registered in the Land Registry within one month from the date of execution of the assignment.[4]

On 1 September 2010, the Lands Department inserted a term in the consent letter that a 10 per cent preliminary deposit must be paid on the execution of the preliminary agreement for sale and purchase, which means 10 per cent of the contract price is forfeited if the purchaser does not proceed to the signing of the agreement for sale and purchase (Lands D 2010b).[5] The amount of forfeiture is revised back to 5 per cent of the purchase price by the *Ordinance*.[6]

Preliminary agreement for sale and purchase

The transaction in Hong Kong starts with a provisional, or, a preliminary agreement for sale and purchase; many of them are drafted by solicitors or provided by estate agents. The first question is whether the preliminary agreement for sale and purchase signed in a presale is a binding contract for the sale of land or, in the words of Gerald Godfrey, a *mere agreement to agree*?[7] It is necessary to first look at the case law's response to the nature of PASP in general. Notwithstanding the wide use of these provisional agreements, there is no explicit prescription in Hong Kong law on the nature of such agreement. On the contrary, it has been held that it is a matter of construction whether a PASP constitutes a binding agreement for sale and purchase or otherwise, depending upon the intention of the parties as evidenced by the words used in the agreement.[8] Goo and Lee (2015) remark that when signed by the seller and the purchaser such agreement is usually binding as it indicates the parties' intention to be bound.

With regard to the nature of PASPs used in presales, the Law Society suggested that the preliminary agreement for sale and purchase signed for a sale of a flat under the Consent Scheme is *not* a binding agreement for the purchaser but is binding on the vendor; whereas the preliminary agreement for sale and purchase signed for a sale under the non-Consent Scheme is a binding agreement.[9] The only explanation to the divergence is that the Law Society so intended. Otherwise, it would be very difficult to explain that the nature of a provisional agreement changes from binding to non-binding when the sale of land is subjected to different administrative schemes.

The *Ordinance* provides a standard PASP for all the sales of first-hand residential properties in Schedule 4, Division 3. The standard preliminary agreement does not expressly suggest itself as a binding agreement or a non-binding agreement. In deciding whether a preliminary agreement binds the parties, Malcolm Merry (1993) expresses the following view:

> the fact that an agreement contemplates that it will lead to and be replaced by another agreement does not render it not binding, or indicate that its purpose is solely to set out the procedure leading to the making of a binding contract. All the basic terms were present, parties, property, price. Payment of price was elaborated upon. Most significantly, terms were inserted dealing with how each party could withdraw from the transaction: these terms would be futile unless the agreement was otherwise intended to be binding.

Despite being locally called a 'lum see' agreement (which means *temporary*), the PASP in off-plan sales, like any other provisional agreements used in the sale of second-hand properties, is a legally binding contract. Thus section 53 of the *Ordinance* states that 'if the purchaser executes the agreement for sale and purchaser within 5 working days after signing of the preliminary agreement for sale and purchase, the vendor must execute the agreement for sale and purchase within 8 working days'.[10] Meanwhile, Clause 7 in the standard PASP prescribes that 'if the purchaser fails to execute the agreement within 5 working days after the date on which the preliminary agreement is signed, the preliminary agreement is terminated; the deposit paid by the purchaser is forfeited to the vendor and the vendor does not have any further claim against the purchaser for the failure.'[11] In a word, after signing the PASP, developers cannot unilaterally choose not to proceed to sign the agreement for sale and purchase (or *ASP* hereafter); the purchaser, who is also bound by the PASP, can choose not to proceed only at the cost of the forfeiture.

Lead time and forfeiture

Under the Consent Scheme there is five working days' lead time between the signing of PASP and the ASP. How many days should be given to make the arrangement fair and genuine? At one extreme, David Webb (2009) suggests that a statutory cooling-off period of *five to ten business days* be set up for the sales of new apartments; and the purchaser, after sobering up, can come back to the vendor and get a full refund with no conditions. The idea of a cooling-off period is supported by the Consumer Council. The Steering Committee, however, considers such a cooling-off period is one-sided, which will encourage speculation and lead to light decisions. It suggests that the ASP should be signed within *six working days* after the signing of the PASP, i.e., the ASP must be signed by the purchaser within three working days after signing the preliminary agreement and by the vendor within a further three working days thereafter (SC 2011). Thus, the draft *Bill* shortened the proposed period to three days for the purchaser.[12] The *Ordinance* does not endorse the shortened lead period enclosed in the draft *Bill* by restoring to a lead time of five working days as under the Consent Scheme.[13]

A longer cooling-off period will stimulate speculations only if the forfeiture is nominal. Given the amount of money involved in every transaction and the current level of forfeiture (5 per cent of the purchase price), caution should be exercised before the PASP is signed, be it first-time purchasers, investors and speculators. The Steering Committee regards 5 per cent of the purchase price as appropriate. In his interview with the *South China Morning Post* in 2011, Ambrose Ho Pui-him, the vice-chairman of the Consumer Council, said the percentage of the forfeiture amount during the proposed cooling-off period should fall to below 5 per cent of the purchase price, citing the amount being 1.25 per cent of the purchase price in Singapore (SCMP 2011). The 2014 Survey by the Consumer Council suggested that 44.6 per cent of the respondents considered the 5 per cent forfeiture amount reasonable whereas roughly the same number of respondents (i.e., 45.1 per cent) were of the view that the cooling-off period of five working days would be inadequate for prospective purchasers to make a formal decision (CC 2014).

The length of the lead time and the amount of forfeiture should go hand in hand. The longer the lead time given to purchasers after signing the PASP, the more amount of forfeiture should be imposed; the shorter the lead time, the less the forfeiture. To balance the need of consumer protection and business efficacy, ideally the ASP should be signed within *seven* working days (excluding Saturdays, Sundays and public holidays) by the purchaser and *ten* days by the vendor after the signing of the PASP; *3 per cent* of the total purchase price should be forfeited if the purchaser does not proceed to sign the ASP.

Mandatory provisions for PASP and ASP

The *Ordinance* sets out mandatory provisions to be incorporated in both PASP and ASP. Section 54 provides that the owner must not enter into a preliminary agreement for sale and purchase in respect of the specified residential property with any person unless that preliminary agreement contains the provisions set out in Schedule 4. Section 55 provides that the owner must not enter into the agreement for sale and purchase with any person unless that agreement contains the provisions set out in Schedule 5 if the development or the phase of the development is an uncompleted development, or Schedule 6 if the development or the phase of the development is a completed development pending compliance, or Schedule 7 if the development or the phase of the development is a completed development but not a completed development pending compliance. Section 57 stipulates that the owner commits an offence if section 54 or 55(2) is contravened.

On 3 August 2016 in the Kwun Tong Magistrate Court, the vendor of *Full Art Court*, who in ignorance failed to observe the relevant requirements on mandatory provisions for ASP in the *Ordinance*, was convicted of the respective offence (HKET 2016; AD 2016).[14]

Disclosure of transaction information

Register of transactions

The disclosure of past transaction information used to be completely voluntary by developers. According to Rule 1 enclosed in REDA Guidelines issued on 1 June 2006, member developers were free to decide on whether or not to make public the results of their sales, but if they choose to publicize, any information provided must be as accurate as possible (REDA 2006).

One of the best-known regulations on disclosure of transaction information is the 'five-day disclosure rule', first implemented on 23 November 2009 by REDA that member developers should 'provide in their website and sales offices information on the ASPs within five working days after the signing of the PASPs'.[15] Ever since the announcement of the rule, it has been observed that most REDA developers do not wait for five days to release the transaction information; in fact, most transaction records are uploaded onto the project website within 24 hours after the signing of the PASP. Therefore nothing was new in the Steering Committee's 2011 proposal (SC 2011) that transaction record to be disclosed within 24 hours upon the signing of the PASP. The Steering Committee further suggested that the disclosure of the transaction in a *Register* would be an effective means to enhance market transparency – provided of course such timely disclosure is full and frank.

Several landmark sales in late 2009 and early 2010 illustrated that, despite the timely disclosure of past transaction records, developers could still mislead the market by selective information on *related party transactions, en-bloc sales* and what would be termed *aborted transactions*. LACO Circular Memorandum No. 62 paid close attention to these three types of transactions, and developers were required to highlight the nature of the transaction in the Register if it fell into one of the above categories. The Steering Committee's report recognized yet another type of questionable transaction arising from a sale in early 2011, i.e., a discounted sale within a sale, where a car-parking space was priced at HK$1 to a celebrity purchaser of a flat in the estate.

Nothing else can better showcase the advancement of the regulation on disclosure of transaction information than the evolution of the Register itself. The following template for 'Register for Agreements for Sale and Purchase' was enclosed in REDA Guidelines issued on 27 November 2009. It contained the information of the residential unit, the date of signing the ASP, the purchaser price and the date of cancellation (as shown in Table 12.1).

Two columns, one on related party transactions with members of the board of the developer and their immediate family members and another on cancellation of the ASP, were added into the Register by REDA Guidelines on 10 August 2010 (as shown in Table 12.2).[16]

Then in 2011, the new template (see Table 12.3) recommended by the Steering Committee, refreshingly titled as 'Register of Preliminary Agreements for Sale and Purchase (PASPs) and Agreements for Sale and Purchase (ASPs)', added information about the preliminary agreement for sale and purchase.

Columns (A), (B) and (G) represent new information that demand disclosure. Columns (A) and (B) concern information about aborted transactions with column (G) about discounted transactions.

The Steering Committee (2011) suggests that information regarding the signing of PASP, i.e. columns (A), (E), (F), (G) and (H), should be added to the Register within 24 hours after the signing of the relevant preliminary agreements for sale and purchase; information about ASP, i.e. column (C), should be entered into the Register within one working day after the signing of the relevant agreements for sale and purchase. Since the Register is accorded with so much information, it would be better if from left to right the columns be listed in the chronological order of the events: viz., columns (E), (F), (G) and (H) to be placed before columns (A), (B), (C) and (D).

The *Ordinance* brings forth further improvements to the template; the 'Register of Transactions' should contain nine columns: a description of the specified residential property; a description of the parking space that is sold together with the residential property under one single PASP or ASP; the date of any PASP; the date of any ASP; the price of any transaction; the details and date of any revision of that price under section 35(2); the terms of payment (including any discount on the price, any gift, or any financial advantage or benefit, made available in connection with the purchase); the date on which any ASP is terminated; whether the purchaser is or is not a related party to the vendor.[17]

The column 'terms of payment' should include details on 'any discount on the price, any gift, or any financial advantage or benefit, made available in connection with the purchase'; this aims to catch package sales of an apartment and a car-parking space, making the Register a comprehensive information platform to disclose different types of non-typical transactions occurring in a sale.

As an illustration of the Register after the implementation of the *Ordinance*, the following is page 10 of the Registration of Transactions in a 2016 sale of *Alassio* in the Mid-Levels (Table 12.4).

Table 12.1 Template for Register for Agreements for Sale and Purchase for Uncompleted Residential Units, REDA Guidelines on Sales Descriptions of Uncompleted Residential Properties, 27 November 2009

Template for Register of Agreements for Sale and Purchase for Residential Units
Name of Development, Phase No. (if any), Location
樓盤名稱、期數（如有）及地區

Register of Agreements for Sale and Purchase for Residential Units
住宅單位買賣合約記錄

Date of ASP 買賣合約日期	Residential Unit (with carparking space if any) 住宅單位（及車位，如有）			Purchase price of the Residential Unit 住宅單位售價	Date of cancellation (if applicable) 取消日期（如適用）
	Tower 座數	Floor 樓層	Unit 單位		

Note:
1. The above-mentioned Agreements for Sale and Purchase ("ASPs") are signed pursuant to the Preliminary Agreements for Sale and Purchase ("PASPs") entered into by the purchasers and the Developer.
   以上買賣合約是根據買賣雙方較早前所簽的臨時買賣合約訂立。
2. The register is listed in chronological order of the date of ASPs.
   以上買賣合約的記錄以日期排序。
3. The ASPs will be registered in the Land Registry within one calendar month from the date of the respective PASPs. The above information may be removed from this Report upon registration of the respective ASPs in the Land Registry.
   物業的買賣合約會於其臨時買賣合約日期的一個月內在土地註冊處登記。故以上資料在各自的買賣合約於土地註冊處登記後有可能會從此報告書內刪除。
4. This register is for information only. Accuracy of information on each entry shall be subject to the true copies of the respective ASPs, which will be registered in the Land Registry.
   以上買賣合約的記錄只供參考之用。本記錄內所有買賣合約的準確性以相關買賣合約的正本為準。相關買賣合約的正本將於土地註冊處登記。

Updated on: _____
更新日期：

Signed By: (Authorized Signature of the Developer)

Source: The Real Estate Developers Association of Hong Kong.

Table 12.2 Template for Register for Agreements for Sale and Purchase for Uncompleted Residential Units, Annex, REDA Guidelines on Sales Descriptions of Uncompleted Residential Properties, 10 August, 2010.

Template for Register of Agreements for Sale and Purchase for Uncompleted Residential Units

Name of Development, Phase No. (if any), Location
樓盤名稱、期數（如有）及地區

Register of Agreements for Sale and Purchase for Uncompleted Residential Units
未建成住宅單位買賣合約紀錄

Date of ASP 買賣合約日期	Residential Unit (with carparking space if any) 住宅單位（及車位，如有）			Transacted price 單位售價	The transaction involves members of the Board of the Developer or their immediate family member 與發展商的董事局成員或其直系親屬有關連的交易	Date of cancellation of ASP (if applicable) 買賣合約取消日期（如適用）
	Tower 座數	Floor 樓層	Unit 單位			
					√	

Source: The Real Estate Developers Association of Hong Kong.

Table 12.3 Template for Register of Preliminary Agreements for Sale and Purchase (PASPs) and Agreements for Sale and Purchase (ASPs), Annex J to the Report of the Steering Committee on Regulation of Sale of First-hand Residential Properties by Legislation, October 2011.

Template for Register of Preliminary Agreements for Sale and Purchase (PASPs) and Agreements for Sale and Purchase (ASPs)
公布臨時買賣合約及買賣合約的交易記錄標準範本

Name of Development, Phase No. (if any), Location
樓盤名稱、期數(如有)及地

(A) Register of PASPs/ASPs 住宅單位臨時買賣合約／買賣合約記錄
(Important Note: Please read with particular care those entries with only the date of the PASPs shown. They are transactions which have not yet proceeded to the ASP stage. For those transactions, the information shown is premised on PASPs and may be subject to change.)
(重要告示：閱讀那些只顯示臨時買賣合約日期的交易項目時請特別小心，因為有關交易並未簽署買賣合約，所顯示的交易資料是以臨時買賣合約為基礎，有關交易資料日後可能會出現變化。)

(A)	(B)	(C)	(D)	(E)			(F)	(G)	(H)
Date of PASP 臨時買賣合約簽署日期	The PASP has not proceeded further* 簽署臨時買賣合約後再未有進展*	Date of ASP 買賣合約簽署日期	Date of cancellation of ASP (if applicable) 取消買賣合約的日期 (如適用)	Residential Unit (if carparking space is included, please also provide details of the carparking space) 住宅單位 (如包括車位，請一併提供有關車位的資料)			Transacted Price@ 成交金額@	Payment Terms# 付款條款#	The transaction involves members of the Board of the Developer or their immediate family members; or senior staff members of the Developer 有關交易涉及發展商的董事局成員或其直系親屬或發展商的高級職員
				Tower 座數	Floor 樓層	Unit 單位			
∧	∧								√

*If the PASP does not proceed to ASP within six working days after the signing of the PASP, a "√" should be put in the column on the seventh working day after the signing of the PASP.
如在簽署臨時買賣合約後的六個工作天內未有簽署買賣合約，請在簽署臨時買賣合約後的第七個工作天在本欄加上"√"號。

Developers should indicate whether the unit is transacted at the list price, with special payment adjustment factors affecting the actual price of the Unit (such as promotional and preferential schemes) or if gifts (e.g. sale of carparking space at less than market value), advantages or bonuses, as well as any price adjustment factors affecting the actual price of the unit are offered in connection with the sale of the Unit. The payment terms should correspond with those listed on the price lists.
發展商須列明該單位是以訂價成交，或會否因購買該單位而該出出增品（例如以低於市價的車位），利益或獎賞，以及任何付款條款影響實際樓價的因素。有關的付款條款應與價單所列的相符。

@ The price list(s) can be found in the following website.
下述互聯網可連結到有關價單。

Table 12.4 Page 10 of the Registration of Transactions in the sale of Alassio

(A) 臨時買賣合約的日期 (日-月-年) Date of PASP (DD-MM-YYYY)	(B) 買賣合約的日期 (日-月-年) Date of ASP (DD-MM-YYYY)	(C) 終止買賣合約的日期 (日-月-年) Date of termination of ASP (if applicable) (DD-MM-YYYY)	(D) 住宅物業的描述 (如包括車位，請一併提供有關車位的資料) Description of Residential Property (if parking space is included, please also provide details of the parking space)			(E) 成交金額 Transaction Price	(F) 售價修改的細節及日期 (日-月-年) Details and date (DD-MM-YYYY) of any revision of price	(G) 支付條款 Terms of Payment	(H) 買方是賣方的有關連人士 The purchaser is a related party to the vendor
			大廈名稱 Block Name	樓層 Floor	單位 Unit 車位 (如有) Car-parking space (if any)				
13/04/2016	20/04/2016		殷然 ALASSIO	22	E	HK$35,027,000		價單第1號 – 建築期付款計劃(照訂價) Price List No. 1 – Stage Payment (List Price) 包含「特別優惠」條款 "Special Discount" included 包含「印花稅現金優惠」條款 "Stamp Duty Cash Benefit" included	
13/04/2016	20/04/2016		殷然 ALASSIO	23	E			價單第1號 – 建築期付款計劃(照訂價) Price List No. 1 – Stage Payment (List Price) 包含「特別優惠」條款 "Special Discount" included 包含「印花稅現金優惠」條款 "Stamp Duty Cash Benefit" included	
			殷然 ALASSIO	22	C	HK$14,545,000		價單第1號 - 建築期付款計劃(照訂價) Price List No. 1 – Stage Payment (List Price) 包含「特別優惠」條款 "Special Discount" included 包含「印花稅現金優惠」條款 "Stamp Duty Cash Benefit" included	

Within 24 hours after the signing of the PASP, the owner must enter in the Register of Transactions the following information: description of the specified residential property; description of the parking space that is sold together with the residential property under that preliminary agreement; the date of the PASP; the price of any transaction; the terms of payment; whether the purchaser is or is not a party related to the vendor.

If the deal proceeds further, then within one working day after the date on which an ASP is executed, the vendor must enter the date of the ASP in the Register. If the purchaser does not sign the ASP within five working days after the date on which the PASP is signed, the vendor must, on the sixth working day, indicate that fact.[18] The *Ordinance* does not prescribe the manner to indicate such information in the Register of Transactions. Had the fact occurred, the information could not be sufficiently disclosed if the vendor simply leaves the column 'the date of any agreement for sale and purchase' blank. Shortly before the enactment of the *Ordinance* in April 2013, the SRPA (2013) issued the *Guidelines on Register of Transactions* and, in the template of the Register of Transaction in the Annex, set out how to show the fact that the PASP has not proceeded further in the Register:

Similarly, within one working day after the date on which the agreement for sale and purchase is terminated, the vendor must indicate the fact and enter the date of termination in the Register of Transactions.[19]

The Register of Transactions should be made available from the first date of the sale at the place where the sale is to take place; its electronic copy should be uploaded and updated on the website for inspection from the first day of the sale till the date on which the first assignment of each specified residential property has been registered in the Land Registry.[20]

Transactions by related parties

The requirement to indicate 'whether the purchaser is or is not a related party to the vendor' is to prevent price manipulation through inside dealings. As Malcolm Merry (2008) observes:

[T]he technique favoured by developers and agents is to release the flats for sale in batches. The tone of asking prices is set by prior 'internal sales'. These are sales of certain flats, often the better ones, to parties connected with the developer, before launch of the flats for sale to the general public. The 'purchasers' are typically companies controlled by senior staff of the developer or the agents. The sales, although not at prices negotiated at arm's length, are genuine and the object of such purchasers is not to use the flat themselves, but rather to speculate for resale. This object is furthered, and their risk lessened, by later manipulation of supply of flats. In the meantime the estate agent is able to say, accurately if not entirely truthfully, to members of the public and the press when the flats go on general sale that a certain rate per square foot has already been achieved.

Table 12.5 Template of the Register of Transaction kept for the purpose of section 60 of the Residential Properties (First-hand Sales) Ordinance annexed to the Guidelines on Register of Transactions, SRPA 2013.

範本/Template

根據《一手住宅物業銷售條例》第 60 條所備存的成交記錄冊

Register of Transactions kept for the purpose of section 60 of the Residential Properties (First-hand Sales) Ordinance

(A) 臨時買賣合約的日期 (日-月-年) Date of PASP (DD-MM-YYYY)	(B) 買賣合約的日期 (日-月-年) Date of ASP (DD-MM-YYYY)	(C) 終止買賣合約的日期 (如適用) (日-月-年) Date of termination of ASP (if applicable) (DD-MM-YYYY)	(D)* 住宅物業的描述 (如包括車位，請一併提供有關車位的資料) Description of Residential Property (if parking space is included, please also provide details of the parking space)					(E) 成交金額 Transaction Price	(F) 售價修改的細節及日期 (日-月-年) Details and date (DD-MM-YYYY) of any revision of price	(G) 支付條款 Terms of Payment	(H) 買方是賣方的有關連人士 The purchaser is a related party to the vendor
			大廈名稱 Block Name	屋號 (House number)/屋名 (Name of the house)	樓層 Floor	單位 Unit	車位 (如有) Car-parking space (if any)				
2-10-2013	簽訂臨時買賣合約後再未有進展 The PASP has not proceeded further		2		10	A		$4,000,000			√
3-10-2013	8-10-2013		2		10	B	No. 13	$4,500,000	在 5-10-2013，基於法例第 35(2)(a)條所容許的原因，售價更改為$4,502,000 On 5-10-2013, the price adjusted to $4,502,000 due to the reason allowed under section 35(2)(a) of the Ordinance		
3-10-2013	8-10-2013			House No. 5				$8,500,000			

In very brief wording, REDA Guidelines issued on 1 June 2010 required developers to indicate any transactions 'which involve the members of the Board and their immediate family members in the Register'.[21]

In 2011 the Steering Committee's Report added 'senior staff members of the developer' to the category. According to Note (4) attached to the Template for Register of PASPs and ASPs in Annex J, 'members of the board' means *all executive directors, non-executive directors and independent non-executive directors*; 'immediate family members' means *parents, spouse, sons and daughters; 'senior staff member' means a person who, under the immediate authority of the board of directors, exercises managerial functions but does not include a receiver or manager of the property of the company or a special manager of the estate or business of the company appointed under section 216 of the Companies Ordinance (Cap 32)* (SC 2011).

In the case that the vendor is a corporation (i.e., a developer company), the *Ordinance* considers the following people a related party to the vendor: a director of that vendor or a parent, spouse or child of such a director; a manager of that vendor; a private company of which such a director, parent, spouse, child or manager is a director or shareholder; an associate corporation or holding company of that vendor; a director of such an associate corporation or holding company, or a parent, spouse or child of such a director; a manager of such an associate corporation or holding company. If the vendor is an individual, then a related party is a parent, spouse or child of that vendor or a private company of which such a parent, spouse or child is a director or shareholder. If the vendor is a partnership, then a related party includes a partner of that vendor, or a parent, spouse or child of such a partner or a private company of which such a partner, parent, spouse, child is a director or shareholder.[22]

Do the above categories cover all the personnel with close connections with the vendor? In March 2010, 39 flats of a luxury residential project in Tsim Sha Tsui were reported to have been sold by one developer to its business partners, including seven flats to its *managing director's son, cousin and uncle* by way of a VIP sale. The developer had published the transaction prices, but did not at the same time provide any details regarding the backgrounds of the purchasers. A member in the Legislative Council then questioned whether in doing so 'the developer is trying to benefit its friends and asking them to help create an impression that the property is very marketable' (SCMP 2010a).

The *Ordinance* does not recognise categories of people of close familial connections with the vendor such as uncle, aunt, nephew, cousin, son-in-law and daughter-in-law, considering there is no definition on 'immediate family members' while only 'parents, spouse, child' are suggested.

Moreover, it is an established practice for local developers to set up a subsidiary company to act as the vendor of a particular development.[23] Does the requirement govern the vendor company only, or include its holding company/parent company? Legislator Lee Wing-tat believed that a developer could avoid legal sanctions by appointing low-ranked staff as directors of a subsidiary that oversees the developments (SCMP 2011). Better if the rules were drafted to govern 'transactions which involve directors of boards of the vendor company and its parent/holding companies (if any), their immediate family members, and any company solely or jointly owned by them'.

It is worth noting that a holding company is loosely defined in the *Ordinance* as within the meaning of the *Companies Ordinance* (Cap 622).[24] Section 2(7) of the Companies Ordinance states that 'a reference in this Ordinance to a holding company of a company shall be read as a reference to a company of which that last-mentioned company is a subsidiary'.

En-bloc sale

An *en-bloc sale* or a *bulk sale* is a transaction of two or more units, in which the deal is based on 'an aggregate amount of considerations instead of a flat-by-flat amount'. In such circumstances the developer should 'simply show the total number of flats involved, the aggregate amount of considerations and the date of signing the PASP/ASP'.[25] This is critical because each single flat is not valued on an individual basis in a bulk sale.

The rational of the rule can be best explained against the practice that in some cases the vendor may have 'deliberately disclosed transaction prices that were at a record high without disclosing other transaction prices that might be lower than the expected market price' (Goo 2010). As a famous case-study, 'In the sale of *Arch* in May 2005, a penthouse of over 5,000 square feet had been sold at a record-high price of over HK$30,000 per square foot unit since 1997; but the transaction was later reported to be bundled with three four-bedroom apartments in the same development project that were priced below the market price' (Chan et al. 2015).[26]

A more recent illustration is the record-setting transaction at *39 Conduit Road* in 2009, where an agreement for sale and purchase of 439 million was entered into for a duplex at HK$ 71,280 per square foot of gross floor area or HK$ 88,000 per square foot of saleable area. The headline spread through town quickly, the public were astonished at the new record of the property price in the region's history, and an atmosphere was soon created. *39 Conduit Road* immediately established itself as the new legendary landmark luxury property in Hong Kong, ready to ask for HK$100,000 per square foot for the apartment on the top floor (SCMP 2009a).

Later it was revealed that the duplex could have been sold to one purchaser together with other units of the development.[27] It may well be that the price was achieved only because it was linked to other sales within the development. Hence no more ink needs to be spilt on whether the breath-taking price truly reflected the value of the duplex even if the sale were successfully completed.[28] The grand image was torn down when the record-setting transaction was cancelled, together with the transactions of another 19 flats sold in October. All of them collapsed upon the extended deadline of completion (SCMP 2010b). The drama demonstrated how early and fundamentally developers are able to mislead the market by not disclosing bulk sale information.

Bulk sale still occurs from time to time after the commencement of the *Ordinance*. The Council noticed in a 2014 sale that the vendor bundled sales of a principal flat and its adjacent open studio flat: the studio cannot be purchased unless with the principal flat (CC 2014). In terms of the purchasers' right to selection, this practice may be questionable in the sense that a purchaser may, in the example above, be interested in purchasing the open studio flat alone. But in terms of the purchasers' right to information about transaction price, such details are requested under the *Ordinance* to be disclosed with the adoption of the Register. An example of the indication of a bulk sale by the Register after the implementation of the *Ordinance* is contained in the cited page 10 of the Register of Transaction in the sale of *Alassio* (see Table 12.4 above). The Register suggests that Unit E on the twenty-second floor and Unit E on the twenty-third floor were sold together for the price of HK$35,027,000.

Discounted transaction

Another type of transaction is what might be called a *discounted transaction*, which essentially concerned two related sales: a sale with a discounted sale within one transaction. Suppose an apartment is sold with a parking space as a free gift, or an apartment and a parking space are sold together to one purchaser but when the price is disclosed, the parking space is not mentioned. Or worse, the parking space is sold to the purchaser in a separate contract outside the agreement for sale and purchase but at a nominal value, say HK$1. In these cases, the disclosed price reflects the total value of the apartment and the parking space; but the public, not knowing the involvement of the parking space in the deal, is likely to regard the transaction price as representing the value of the apartment only. This would send out misleading information as to the true value of the property.

The practice is now regulated by the *Ordinance*: developers are to disclose 'any discount on the price, any gift, or any financial advantage or benefit, made available in connection with the purchase' in the column 'the terms of payment' in the Register.[29]

In the case of car parking spaces, regardless of whether the parking space is sold or given to the purchaser, as long as the property is sold with the parking space under one contract, such fact must be indicated in a specific column the Register of Transaction.[30] As discussed in Chapter 3, the area of the parking space in not calculated in the saleable area, therefore when a parking space is sold with the property under one contract, the unit rate of the residential unit which is based on the saleable area would look much higher than that of a similar unit sold individually in the same development. Thus the disclosure of the information is critical for purchasers to assess the real value of the properties for sale.

Collapsed transaction

After the signing of the ASP, the sale may be aborted in two principal ways. On the one hand, the transaction may collapse if the developer fails to complete the construction on the agreed date (as stipulated in clause 4(c) of the standard ASP enclosed in Schedule 5 of the *Ordinance*); or fails to obtain any extension under clause 10, in which case the purchaser may elect to rescind the ASP.[31] If the purchaser chooses to wait for completion, there is another chance that the purchaser may rescind the agreement at her option – if the developer fails again to complete construction within six months after the agreed date stipulated in clause 4(c) or any other extended date under clause 10.[32] Non-completion or late completion however seldom occur in recent years: the Consent Scheme has been proven to be effective to check the financial ability of developers.[33]

On the other hand, the transaction may be cancelled at any time when the purchaser so requests or fails to perform her duty as agreed in clause 3(b) of the standard ASP: this could take place if the purchaser, after signing the PASP, does not sign the ASP; or when she fails to advance a second part of deposit within 60 days of signing the ASP; it may also occur at a much later time, for example when she fails to pay off the balance – usually being 85 per cent or 80 per cent of the purchase money depending on different payment methods – within 14 days after the developer notifies her in writing that the developer is in a position validly to assign the property.[34]

The lead time between the cancellation of the transaction and the disclosure of the information used to be five working days.[35] In 2010, the Transport and Housing Bureau suggested releasing the information within 24 hours (SCMP 2010c). On a similar footing, the Steering Committee (2011) proposed the time be shortened to within one working day. In the end the Legislative Council endorsed the proposal of one working day. Thus if the transaction is terminated under section 53(3), i.e., the purchaser did not proceed to enter into the ASP with the owner within five working days after the date on which the PASP is entered into, the vendor has to indicate that information in the Register of Transactions by the sixth day.[36] This applies to cancellation of the ASP that occurred after the completion of registration of the respective ASP in the Land Registry.

Information on collapsed transactions reveals the market's revised evaluation of the property, for most cancellations are due to the purchaser's choice to extract herself from the sale – at the cost of 5 per cent of the purchase money before 13 August 2010 or after the commencement of the *Ordinance* (or at 10 per cent between 13 August 2010 and 29 April 2013)[37] – than to pour in millions more dollars to complete the sale. This usually happens at the time of a market crash or where the purchase price turns out to be irrational.

What occurred at *39 Conduit Road* is a case in point. 25 flats were reported to be sold in October 2009, among which was the record-setting duplex sold at HK$ 439 million (SCMP 2010d). If all or most of the 25 transactions had been completed, then the purchase price could have been said to be reflective of the market's judgement on the development. However, only one transaction was successfully completed upon the deadline in March 2010 (SCMP 2010e). The developer then extended the deadline for completion to 16 June 2010, by which time only another four sales were completed. The developer had to conclude that the other 20 transactions including that for the multi-hundred million dollar duplex were cancelled (SCMP 2010d). As might have been anticipated, the collapse of the legend was followed by a price revision in subsequent sales of the residential units in the development.

Although this rule has its origin in the luxury market, its significance extends to the mass market, where price exaggeration seldom attracts media coverage and could always be nicely dressed by the optimistic statements by developers and real estate agents.

Conclusion

The majority of measures on compulsory disclosure of past transaction information imposed by the Lands Department Consent Scheme and endorsed by the *Residential Properties (First-hand Sales) Ordinance* are appropriate and, as practice suggests, have been effective in promoting transparency and eliminating information asymmetry between developers and purchasers.

As a celebrated improvement, the newly designed Register of Transactions provides comprehensive information on details of non-typical transactions: e.g., en-bloc sale, related party transactions, discounted transactions and collapsed transactions. The arrangement complements the requirement to disclose transaction details to the public upon the signing of PASP within 24 hours.

All in all, the new regulation ensures accurate and timely disclosure of transaction information in sales of first-hand residential properties. The arrangement on the amount of forfeiture, however, should be revised, together with the lead time between the signing of the PASP and ASP.

Notes

1 An earlier version of this chapter was published by LexisNexis as an article in the *Australian Property Law Journal*. The article may be cited as Devin Lin, Regulation of Sales Arrangements and Disclosure of Transaction Price in Off-Plan Sales in Hong Kong (2013) *Australian Property Law Journal*, Volume 21 at 251.
2 Clause 24 in the standard form of agreement for sale and purchase in LACO Circular Memorandum No. 66.
3 As prescribed in the Payment Terms in the price lists of the Hermitage; Clause 3, 4 (6), 5 (1) (2) and Schedule 5 in the standard form of agreement for sale and purchase in LACO Circular Memorandum No. 66.
4 Section 5, Land Registration Ordinance.
5 LACO Circular Memorandum No. 63. See the Payment Method of the Oceanaire, which provides that 10 per cent of the purchase price must be paid upon the execution of the preliminary agreement for sale and purchase; the sale was started on 2 October, 2010. www.oceanaire.com.hk/popup/payment_method.pdf .
6 Section 52(1), Part 2 - Division 7, Residential Properties (First-hand Sales) Ordinance, A2399.
7 A preliminary agreement for sale and purchase to sell a second-hand property was so held by Godfrey J.
8 Lam Tam Yi v Chak Wai Man [1993] 1 HKC 537.
9 Section 1, 'Warning to Purchasers – Please Read Carefully!': Rule 5C of the Solicitors' Practice Rules – Approved Forms A1 and A2 (for Consent Scheme), Approved Forms

B1 and B2 (for non-Consent Scheme), Section 12 in Chapter 24, Practice Directions, Guide to Professional Conduct ,Vol. 2, the Law Society of Hong Kong.

10 Section 53(2), Part 2–Division 7, Residential Properties (First-hand Sales) Ordinance, A2401.

11 Ibid., clause 7, Part 1 of Schedule 4, A2561.

12 Clause 7, Part 1 of Schedule 4, Residential Properties (First-hand Sales) Bill, March 2012, C805.

13 Section 53(2)(3), Part 2 – Division 7, Residential Properties (First-hand Sales) Ordinance, A2401.

14 Case No.: KTS21568–572、595–599、600–608/15.

15 REDA Guidelines on 23 November, 2009. Now the rule is in section (g) in LACO Circular Memorandum No. 62. This was first suggested by Alice Lee and S H Goo in their conference paper *The Sale and Purchase of Uncompleted Flats in Hong Kong*, presented in an International Conference on December 16th, 2008 by the Faculty of Law, University of Macau; see S. H. Goo, Regulation of Sale of Off-the-plan Property, *The Conveyancer and Property Lawyer*, Issue 2, 2010, at page 136.

16 Annex A to REDA Guidelines on August 10 2010.

17 Section 59(1), Part 2 – Division 8, Residential Properties (First-hand Sales) Ordinance, A2409.

18 Ibid., section 59(2),(3) and(4), A2409–2415.

19 Ibid., section 59(5), A2415.

20 Ibid., section 60(1),(2) and (3), A2417–A2419.

21 Section 2 in REDA Guidelines on June 1, 2010; Section (g) in LACO Circular Memorandum No. 62. Note 5 in Annex A to REDA Guidelines on 1 June 2010.

22 Section 59(7), Part 2 – Division 8, Residential Properties (First-hand Sales) Ordinance, A2415.

23 For example, in the sale of *Hermitage*, the Vendor is a 'Best Profit Limited' established by Sino Land Company Limited and Nan Fung Development Limited as Parent / Holding companies.

24 Section 2(1), Residential Properties (First-hand Sales) Ordinance, A2297.

25 Section 2, REDA Guidelines on 1 June 2010.

26 See also Goo, S. H. (2010) Regulation of Sale of Off-the-plan Property, *The Conveyancer and Property Lawyer*, no. 2, pp. 133–136.

27 Yvonne Liu, Flats' purchasers missed out on millions, *South China Morning Post*, 14 November 2009. It was later confirmed that about four purchasers were involved in the 24 flat sold in October whose transactions were not completed by March, 2010; see Paggie Leung and Gary Cheung, Conduit Road sales will be 'done by July', *South China Morning Post*, 25 March 2010. 20 of the 24 transactions were later cancelled in July.

28 The sale of the duplex collapsed on 16 June 2010. See The long and winding deals at 39 Conduit Road, *South China Morning Post*, 16 June 2010.

29 Section 59 (1)(g) and (2)(a)(v), Part 2 – Division 8, Residential Properties (First-hand Sales) Ordinance, A2411.

30 Ibid., section 59(1)(b) and (2)(a)(ii), A2409–A2411.

31 Ibid., Clause 6, Part 1 of Schedule 5, A2585. See also section 4(3) in the standard form of agreement for sale and purchase in LACO Circular Memorandum No. 66.

32 Ibid., Clause 7, A2585–A2587. See also Clause 4(4)(c) in the standard form of agreement for sale and purchase in LACO Circular Memorandum No. 66. For a detailed discussion, see Chapter 8.

33 See section 2, 3 and 4, Part II in the Annex to LACO Circular Memorandum No. 40.

34 Clause 15, Part 1 of Schedule 5, Residential Properties (First-hand Sales) Ordinance A2591. See also clause 5(2) in the standard form of agreement for sale and purchase in LACO Circular Memorandum No. 66. Such notification should be made within one month of the issue of the Consent to Assign or the Certificate of Compliance, see Clause

14. Genuine purchasers who do wish to complete the deal may however apply to the developer to delay completion of the sale and usually three extra weeks would be granted; see Celine Sun and Gary Cheung, Suspect property deals will be probed, Tsang says, *South China Morning Post*, 21 March 2010.

35 Note 7 in the Annex to REDA Guidelines on 10 August 2010.

36 Section 59(3), Part 2 – Division 6, Residential Properties (First-hand Sales) Ordinance, A2413–A2415. See also Section (A) and Note 1 in Annex J to the Report of the Steering Committee on Regulation of Sale of First-hand Residential Properties by Legislation, October 2011.

37 B18 in the Annex to LACO Circular Memorandum No. 68, 22 March 2012. The 10 per cent of the total purchase price as forfeiture came into effect in September 2010; see B17 in the Revised Annex I to LACO Circular Memorandum No. 62 in LACO Circular Memorandum No. 63.

References

AD (2016) 同珍富雅閣違規罪名成立　罰款72萬, 3 August 2016, *Apple Daily*, http://hk.apple.nextmedia.com/realtime/finance/20160803/55447446

Black, F. (1986) Noise, *The Journal of Finance*, Vol XLI, No.3, July 1986, pp. 529–534.

CC (2014) Study on the Sales of First-hand Residential Properties, pp. 17–89, 11 November 2014, Consumer Council, www.consumer.org.hk/ws_en/competition_issues/reports/20141111.html.

Chan, H.S., Chan, Y.K., Cheng, W.S., and Sze, K.W. (2015) Regulating the Sale of First-hand Residential Properties in Hong Kong: a Study of Policy and Administrative Dynamics, Capstone project report submitted in partial fulfilment of the requirements of the Master of Public Administration, Department of Politics and Public Administration, The University of Hong Kong, p. 42.

Goo, S. H. (2010) Regulation of Sale of Off-the-plan Property, *The Conveyancer and Property Lawyer*, no. 2, pp. 133–136.

Goo, S. H. and Lee, A. (2015) *Land Law in Hong Kong*, 4th edn, LexisNexis Butterworths, Chapter 2.

HKET (2016) 富雅閣涉違規賣樓　表證成立, 3 June 2016, *Hong Kong Economics Times.*

Lands D (1999) Legal Advisory and Conveyancing Office Circular Memorandum No. 40, Lands Department Consent Scheme, Legal Advisory and Conveyancing Office, Lands Department, 28 May 1999.

Lands D (2010a) Legal Advisory and Conveyancing Office Circular Memorandum No. 62, Lands Department Consent Scheme, Legal Advisory and Conveyancing Office, Lands Department, 2 June 2010.

Lands D (2010b) Legal Advisory and Conveyancing Office Circular Memorandum No. 63, Lands Department Consent Scheme, Legal Advisory and Conveyancing Office, Lands Department, 1 September 2010.

Lands D (2011) Legal Advisory and Conveyancing Office Circular Memorandum No. 66, Lands Department Consent Scheme, Legal Advisory and Conveyancing Office, Lands Department, 11 November 2011.

Lands D (2012) Legal Advisory and Conveyancing Office Circular Memorandum No. 68, Lands Department Consent Scheme, Legal Advisory and Conveyancing Office, Lands Department, 22 March 2012.

Lee, A. and Goo, S. H. (2008) The Sale and Purchase of Uncompleted Flats in Hong Kong, The International Conference *The Judicial Reform of Macau in the Context of Globalization* on December 16th, 2008, the Faculty of Law, the University of Macau.

Merry, M. (1993) Preliminary Agreements for the Sale of Land: Recent Development, *Law Lectures for Practitioners*, p. 187.

Merry, M. (2008) Protection of Purchasers of Uncompleted Residential Flats – The Hong Kong Experience, *HKU-NUS*-SMU Symposium Paper, November, pp. 10–11.

REDA (2006) REDA Guidelines for Sales Descriptions of Uncompleted Residential Properties, Real Estate Developers Association of Hong Kong, 1 June 2006.

REDA (2009) REDA Guidelines for Sales Descriptions of Uncompleted Residential Properties, Real Estate Developers Association of Hong Kong, 27 November 2009.

REDA (2010) REDA Guidelines for Sales Descriptions of Uncompleted Residential Properties, Real Estate Developers Association of Hong Kong, 10 August 2010.

REDA (2012) Residential Properties (First-hand Sales) Bill, Press Release, 30 May 2012, http://reda.hk/2012/05/30/residential-properties-first-hand-sales-bill/.

SC (2011) Report of the Steering Committee on Regulation of Sale of First-hand Residential Properties by Legislation, The Steering Committee on Regulation of the Sale of First-hand Residential Properties by Legislation, October 2011.

SCMP (2009a) Lai See, *South China Morning Post*, 21 October 2009, Hong Kong.

SCMP (2009b) Flats' Purchasers Missed Out on Millions, *South China Morning Post*, 14 November 2009, Hong Kong.

SCMP (2010a) 39 Masterpiece Flats Sold to 'VIPs' before Public, *South China Morning Post*, 11 March 2010, Hong Kong.

SCMP (2010b) Record Mid-levels Sales Fall through, *South China Morning Post*, 16 June 2010, Hong Kong.

SCMP (2010c) Flat-sale Rules Aim to Increase Transparency, *South China Morning Post*, 11 August 2010, Hong Kong.

SCMP (2010d) The Long and Winding Deals at 39 Conduit Road, *South China Morning Post*, 16 June 2010, Hong Kong.

SCMP (2010e) Henderson's Lee Says Transactions Are Genuine, *South China Morning Post*, 20 March 2010, Hong Kong.

SCMP (2010f) Suspect property deals will be probed, Tsang says, *South China Morning Post*, 21 March 2010, Hong Kong.

SCMP (2010g) Conduit Road Sales Will Be 'Done by July', *South China Morning Post*, 25 March 2010, Hong Kong.

SCMP (2011) Steep Fines to Stop Deposit Ploy on Flats, *South China Morning Post*, 11 October 2011, Hong Kong.

SRPA (2013) Guidelines on Register of Transactions, the Sales of First-hand Residential Properties Authority, 5 April 2013. www.srpa.gov.hk/files/pdf/guidelines/Guidelines_on_Register_of_Transactions_Eng.pdf

The Vendor of Alassio (2016) Register of Transaction, viewed 4 July 2016, www.alassio.com.hk/pdf/register_of_transactions.pdf

Webb, D. (2009) A Cooling-off Period for New Home Sales, 28 October 2009, https://webb-site.com/articles/property888.asp.

Yiu, C.Y., Wong, S. K. and Chau, K. W. (2009) Transaction volume and price dispersion in the presale and spot real estate markets, *Journal of Real Estate Finance and Economics*, vol. 38, no. 3, pp. 241–253.

13 Information channels[1]

Introduction

Chapters 3 to 12 explored various aspects of the first-hand residential units on sale as well as of the sale activities, i.e., the issuance of price lists, the signing of agreement for sale and purchase, and the disclosure of the transaction information and so on. The discussion reveals the *types* of information that a sale of first-hand residential property requires disclosure of. This chapter discusses the various channels through which all the key information is disclosed to the general public: the sales brochure, advertisement, the sales office, the website designated by the vendor for the development, etc.

Malcolm Merry (2008) vividly describes the roles of the sales brochure, advertisement and sales office in contributing to the sales campaigns:

> [T]he selling of flats in large developments has become very big business. Prior to the launch of the flats, advertisements appear in Hong Kong's numerous newspapers, sometimes taking up the whole front page or entire supplements, lauding the new estate and containing artist's impressions which bear only a tenuous relationship with the eventuating reality. Long and imaginative advertisements appear on television, often featuring celebrities and actors, and aimed it seems at creating a style or mood with which the estate wishes to be associated. Opulent brochures are produced which contain plans which sometimes curiously omit inconvenient features, such as cemeteries, in the vicinity of the development. Space is devoted to mock-ups of the flats in commercial centres associated with the developer's group and the centre and its environs is flooded with staff of the estate agencies, mostly young, earnest and dressed in similar dark suits. Representatives of several banks will be in attendance, ready to explain to would-be purchasers their rival mortgage products. For more expensive properties the promotion may be accompanied by refreshment and souvenirs and even entertainment.

In a 1997 off-plan sale of a development in Tai Po, misleading information was given in sales brochures, newspaper advertisements, and a scale model placed in the sales centre. *Behrens Ng Mo Chee Cindy & Others v Credit World Ltd* tells the story of 18 purchasers-turned-owners of 11 residential units situated on the podium level of the estate *Grand Palisades*. The owners, after moving in, were asked by the Owners' Committee to open the podium gardens for the common use of all the residents of the development. According to the Owners' Committee, the podium gardens were part of the common area of the development. Such conclusion was fundamentally different from what the purchasers had been informed in the sale, where they were assured by the sales representatives that the podium gardens would be for the exclusive possession of the respective unit owners. The statement was supported by a to-scale model of the building displayed in the sales office indicating that every podium garden was fenced and every podium garden linked to the respective podium unit could be accessed only through the door from inside the podium unit. A picture of the scaled model was contained in the newspaper advertisements by the developer.[2] The judge in the case expressed the view that the model and the sales brochure constituted *misrepresentation* in terms of the ownership of the podium gardens:

> [T]hese transactions were sale and purchase of uncompleted flats in a development under the Consent Scheme. Thus what was presented by the model and in the brochure must be the best evidence of what the vendor represented as the final product it was offering to sell. If the plaintiffs indeed were able to prove that this representation was operative, it is an actionable misrepresentation, although it is not the only misrepresentation.[3]

The drafting and publication of the sales brochure, advertisement as well as the construction of sales office constitute the main body of the *Residential Properties (First-hand Sales) Ordinance* (the *Ordinance*). The division of the piece of legislation clearly indicates the significance assigned to the supervision and regulation of the issue of sales brochure (Division 2 of Part 2), advertisement (Part 3), and show flats (Division 4 of Part 2).

The discussion starts with the sales brochure, the channel of paramount significance in any first-hand sale. The structure and contents of the sales brochure stand at the centre of the regulatory regime, and the importance of clear, accurate and comprehensive information to be provided in the sales brochure has been consistently emphasized throughout the legislation.

The sales brochure

A tradition created by Dr Fok

The very first sales brochure is believed to have been issued by Dr Fok in the first sale of uncompleted flats in Hong Kong in 1954: the 'Sales Brochure for the Subdivided Sale of the New Building at Public Square Street in Yau Ma Tei, Kowloon' (or in Chinese, '九龍油麻地公眾四方街新樓分層出售說明書') contained information in Chinese including a description of the environment, a location map, floor plans, section plans, fittings and finishes, prices, methods of sale and payment methods. According to the biography of Dr Fok, the reason to issue the little pamphlet for the sale was to boost the confidence of the purchasers and ease the burden of salesmen to entertain enquiries by prospective purchasers (Leng 2010).[4] The tradition of issuing a sales brochure has been observed by all the subsequent developers. Fifty-nine years later, upon the commencement of the *Ordinance* in 2013, the tradition has been made into a statutory duty: developers in Hong Kong must issue sales brochures in sales of first-hand residential properties.[5]

Redefining sales brochure in 2010

In 2010, the Hong Kong Museum accepted a donation by a Hong Kong citizen of 300 sales brochures issued from 1967 to 1997 by local developers. According to the media, the collection displays a clear tendency of allowing more and more levity in making sales brochures (AD 2010). The period 1967–1997 represents the first three decades of off-plan sales in Hong Kong. Such tendency continues in the next two decades. Brochures issued by local developers remained succinct and economical till the 1990s. The sales brochure for the *Pictorial Garden Phase 3* printed in February 1992, for example, only had eight pages in all. When it came to the millennium, sales brochures bulked up. Photos, computer-generated pictures, artistic impressions, all crept into the little pamphlet. The tendency was stopped to a certain extent in 2009, when REDA redefined the sales brochure as the booklet with 'all information as required under the Lands Department Consent Scheme and the consent letter issued to the developer'. From then, developers are required to separate promotional materials from the sales brochure.[6] Thus in the sale of *Yoho Midtown* in early 2010, the developer issued two booklets: one was the sales brochure, the other was titled advertisements.

The *Ordinance*, on the other hand, does not incorporate the definition given by the Consent Scheme or try to define the sales brochure itself. Instead, it simply describes the sales brochure as a 'publication prepared by the vendor for the development or the phase'.[7]

This simplicity is complemented by the great number of rules stipulating how useful information should be set out in the brochure. The majority of rules are consolidated in Division 2 of Part 2 of the *Ordinance* and Schedule 1 'Information in Sales Brochure' to the *Ordinance*. As an illustration on the degree of regulation under the new legislation, detailed requirements on the size of the letters and characters of the title of the brochure are all present in the *Ordinance*, i.e., they must not be smaller than the size of the same letters in 18 point Times New Roman typeface or 180 point '新細明體' typeface.[8] Such detailed requirement is not very commonly seen in a legislative instrument.

Section 25 of the *Ordinance* creates a statutory duty on developers to prepare a publication for the development entitled 'sales brochure' (or '售樓說明書' in Chinese). The vendor of *Full Art Court*, who had no idea that the new legislation applies to the development (which was completed in 1998) in terms of the transaction of some unsold apartments, did not prepare an official sales brochure to prospective purchasers when offering to sell some residential properties in 2014 (HKET 2016). In the end, the vendor was held guilty under the *Ordinance* for the ignorance in a verdict handed down by the Kwun Tong Magistrate Court in August 2016 (AD 2016a).[9]

If a development is divided into phases, one sales brochure must be prepared for each phase. Developers will face a fine of up to HK$ one million in breach of this duty.[10] Sales brochures must be printed bilingually[11] and must state the date on which they are printed.[12]

Estate agents cannot use the title 'sales brochure' in any promotion materials that are made by themselves: only the persons in the shoes of the vendor can prepare and make publication of sales brochures.[13]

Developers are required to make the sales brochure available no less than seven calendar days before the sale commences.[14] The *Ordinance* extends the seven-day requirement to project websites: the electronic copy of sales brochure must be uploaded onto the project website at least seven calendar days before the sale commences.[15] The SRPA (2013a) further clarifies that the date of sale itself is excluded from the counting of the seven days.

Contents of sales brochure

In general the contents of the sales brochure are not part of the agreement for sale and purchase, unless the agreement expressly incorporates the contents enclosed in the brochure. Some argue that purchasers will be better protected if the brochure forms part of the agreement (Fan 2005). The same opinion cannot be inferred from respective provisions in the *Ordinance*. This means the claim against any untrue or misleading information contained in the sales brochure by an aggrieved purchaser should be based principally on misrepresentation rather than breach of contract.[16]

The standard of accuracy for any information set out in the sales brochure by the *Ordinance* is 'accurate in every material respect' as at the date on which it is printed or of the last examination.[17] Against such standard the occurrence of misstatement, misdescription or misinformation in the literature and graphics is not tolerated.

According to the *Ordinance*, the sales brochure must begin with the steps that a purchaser is advised to take for her own protection before deciding to purchase a residential property in the development (the first part of the brochure).[18] After that, the brochure must set out the following: information on the development; information on the vendor and the others involved in the development; the relationship between the parties involved in the development; information on the design of the development; information on the property's management; a location plan of the development; an aerial photograph of the development; the outline zoning plan or development permission area plan or a plan by virtue of section 25(7) of the *Urban Renewal Authority Ordinance* (Cap 563); a layout plan of the development; floor plan of the residential properties in the development; the area of the residential properties in the development; a summary of the preliminary agreement for sale and purchase; a summary of the latest draft of deed of mutual covenant; a summary of the land grant; information on facilities, open space or any part of land for public use.[19]

Developers may choose to include in the sales brochure the following two subjects: previous aerial photograph and other common facilities that are not required to be listed in section 19 of the *Ordinance*.[20]

Examination and revision

Once the sales brochure is made available to the public, the SRPA and online, the vendor can revise the sales brochure whenever it thinks necessary (SRPA 2013b). As, in some cases, a sale of first-hand residential properties will continue for months, to ensure the accuracy of the information contained in the sales brochure, section 17(1) of the *Ordinance* requests vendors to examine the sales brochure to ascertain the information set out therein is accurate as at the date of the examination. Then, as explained in the *Guidelines on Sales Brochure* issued by the SRPA (2013c), section 25(9) of the *Ordinance* stipulates that a reference to the sales brochure for the development is a reference to the sales brochure for the development printed, or examined under section 17(1) of the *Ordinance*, within the previous three months. Lastly, section 22(1)(b) prescribes that the sales brochure must disclose the date of each examination; if revision of any kind is made during the examination, the sales brochure must indicate the revised part.

If there are changes regarding the information set out in the sales brochure, the vendor is under a duty to revise the sales brochure to reflect the change and notify in writing the SRPA of the change within three working days after the date of the revision.[21] Shortly before the commencement of the *Ordinance*, the SRPA further suggested in April 2013 that in case an examined and revised brochure is necessary to replace the original sales brochure in a sale, the sale activities do not need to be suspended for another seven days after the making available of the examined and revised sales brochure (SRPA 2013b).[22]

The application of the above provisions was tested in the sale of *City Point* in May 2014. The first version of the sales brochure of *City Point* was printed on 24 April 2014 and made available to the public on 14 May 2014. By the time the sales brochure was printed, a site nearby was indicated as 'Industrial' ('I') in accordance with the then draft Kwai Chung Outline Zoning Plan. The site was situated within 500 metres from the boundary of that development and therefore was included in the location plan and outline zoning plan in the sales brochure according to section 8(2)(b), Schedule 1 – Part 1 of the *Ordinance*. In the first version of the sales brochure, the site was labelled as a 'public carpark', reflecting the fact that the site then was used as a public carpark. The Town Planning Board (TPB) announced amendments to the draft Kwai Chung Outline Zoning Plan on 9 May 2014, which contained the rezoning of the site to 'Other Specified Uses' ('OU') annotated 'Columbarium' for a proposed public columbarium development (SRPA 2014a). According to section 6(3), Part 1 of Schedule 1 of the *Ordinance*, columbarium must be shown in the location plan of the development in the sales brochure if the site is situated within 250 metres from the boundary of the development.

The question is whether the vendor has contravened the *Ordinance* if the proposed columbarium development is not shown on the 'location plan of the development' in the *first* version of the sales brochure of *City Point* made available on 14 May 2014. The following analysis would suggest that the vendor did not. To start, the information as enclosed in the location plan and outline zoning plan was accurate by the time it was printed, i.e., 24 April 2014; therefore it complied with section 22(2)(a). After making available the brochure, the duty of examination under section 17(1) would arise and section 17(2) stipulates that any inaccuracy identified at an examination must be corrected by a revision to the sales brochure for the development: this clearly suggests that revision must be made to the sales brochure to reflect the rezoning of the site as announced in the TPB on 9 May 2014. However, according to section 25(9), the vendor must conduct the examination within three months: as the first version of the brochure was made available on 14 May 2014, the latest acceptable date of examination in this case would be 13 August 2014. In other words, in this case the vendor is allowed to correct the information in the sales brochure by way of a revision on or before 13 August 2014. In the end the vendor revised the location plan and the outline zoning plan in the sales brochure on 27 May 2014. It should be added that once an examination takes place, section 22(2)(b) will apply, i.e., the information set out in the sales brochure for the development must be accurate in every material aspect as at the date of last examination.

The incident raises the question: if revision is requested due to change of external circumstances that are beyond the control of the vendor, how many days the vendor can have before making available the revised version of the sales brochure after the change takes place? As a result of thorough discussion in the Bills Committee (LC 2012), a three-month period for examination and revision has been set out in the *Ordinance*. A shorter period though, e.g., 30 days, may appear to be more practical to ensure the timely correction of inaccurate information in the sales brochure had material change of external circumstances occurred.

Advertisements

Unlike any presentation in the highly structured sales brochure, advertisement gives a more pleasant, elaborate and artistic presentation of the property. Since the separation of sales brochure from advertisement in 2010, the regulatory framework has applied different standards to the two types of sales literature. Compared to sales brochure, more freedom and licence is retained in the design of advertisements. Yet this is not to say the advertisement goes without restriction.

Advertisements have the highest potential to affect prospective purchasers: they are more eye-catching than the sales brochure; they can be played on a repeating basis in multi-media including television, radio, internet, buses, elevators and newspapers, attracting a large audience. Save those distributed in the sales office or displayed on the project website, advertisements can catch the attention of a prospective purchaser when she is in an environment without immediate reference to the sales brochure, i.e., where she may place a heavier reliance on the contents of the advertisement.

Therefore, a bottom line needs to be drawn.

General requirements

It seems that the persuasion power of advertisement is well understood by the government and the legislature. The *Ordinance* not only entertained the proposal by the Steering Committee to include a provision 'prohibiting the inclusion of any false or misleading information or description in advertisements in all forms that are produced by or on behalf of the developers',[23] but has gone much further to make it an *offence*: 'if a person publishes or causes to publish an advertisement containing information that is false or misleading in a material particular who knows or is reckless as to whether the information is false or misleading.' The person who commits the offence will be liable on conviction on indictment to a fine of HK$ 5,000,000 and to imprisonment for seven years or on summary conviction to a fine of HK$ 1,000,000 or to imprisonment for three years.[24]

In addition, the Steering Committee (2011) further suggested developers should be designated as the *source* of the advertisements, i.e., developers should be made ultimately responsible for any advertising materials that originate from their own materials. Accordingly, the Committee suggested that advertisements bear the name of developers. The *Ordinance* does not explicitly appoint the developers as the source of the advertisement, but it requires that, in case an advertisement is published by the vendor or by another person with the consent of the vendor, the advertisement must state the fact.[25]

The Steering Committee (2011) also suggested that the proposed legislation should impose a duty upon developers to remind prospective purchasers to refer to the sales brochure, and ensure that information given in advertisements in all forms is consistent with the information given in the sales brochure. This is accepted by the *Ordinance*. In cases of moving visual advertisement, the advertisement should bear a reasonably legible statement 'Please refer to the sales brochure for details'; in cases of advertisements comprising solely sound broadcasting, it should contain a reasonably audible announcement of the aforesaid statement; any other advertisement must contain a notice to the effect that a prospective purchaser is advised to refer to the sales brochure for any information on the development.[26]

Last, the Steering Committee suggested that developers should not quote information on gross floor area per flat and unit price based on the gross floor area in advertisements (SC 2011). This again is accepted by the Legislative Council. The *Ordinance* stipulates that an advertisement must not give information on the unit price of any specified residential property otherwise than by reference to the saleable area of that property.[27]

In the year 2016, the vendors of the phase *Graces* in *Providence Bay* and the vendor of *Ocean One* were held by the Kwun Tong Magistrate Court in two verdicts handed down in November respectively that the advertisements had false or misleading information regarding price information (AD 2016b and 2016c).[28] Despite the recent ground-breaking development in case law under section 70 of the *Ordinance* in 2016, it remains uncertain as to just exactly what constitutes 'information that is false or misleading in a material particular'. It was argued that an advertisement could be misleading if it contained information or description relating to the clubhouse facilities and the housing estate using a so-called 'life-style concept' in brochures and newspaper (Goo 2010).

At this moment whether advertising a concept that bears no apparent relation to the property will or not violate section 70 remains to be fleshed out by further case law.

Printed advertisements

The distribution of printed advertisements and promotional materials has been subject to the regulation under the Consent Scheme since October 2009.[29] Now the *Ordinance* specifies printed advertisements as advertisements in a newspaper, by the display of posters, notices, signs, labels, showcards or good, or by the distribution of circulars, brochures, catalogues, or any other materials.[30]

For information to be included in printed advertisements, reference is made to the standard Consent Letter and Annex IV to LACO Circular Memorandum No.62.[31] The former required a clear and legible disclosure of the following information: the names of the Developer and its parent or holding company or companies; the names of the Authorized Person registered with the Building Authority; the name of the main superstructure contractor for the Development registered with the Building Authority; the name(s) of all the solicitors firm(s) acting for the Developer in the sale of the Units; the name of the mortgagee bank/ the name of the bank which has given an undertaking to provide finance to complete the Development; various statements disclosing any personal/ contractual/institutional relationships between the Authorized Person, a partner of the solicitors firm, the main superstructure contractor and the developer or a director/a secretary of the Developer or the parent or holding company of the Developer (Lands D 2011).[32] At the same time, REDA Guidelines issued on 7 October 2009 and LACO Circular Memorandum No. 62 stipulated that printed materials should include: all information required under the consent letter; the name of the district where the development is located; the postal address of the development; the website address of the development (REDA 2009; Lands D 2010). After the commencement of the *Ordinance*, the two requirements are jointly provided in Part 3.[33]

If the advertisement contains a picture, image, drawing or sketch showing an *artistic impression* of the development and surrounding areas, the advertisement needs to contain a statement saying: 'The photographs, images, drawings or sketches shown in this advertisement/promotional material represent an artist's impression of the development concerned. They are not drawn to scale and may have been edited and processed with computerized imaging techniques.

Prospective purchasers should make reference to the sales brochure for details of the development. The vendor should also advise prospective purchasers to conduct an on-site visit for a better understanding of the development site, its surrounding environment and the public facilities nearby.'[34]

Understandably, the *Ordinance* does not discuss whether a certain degree of reality should be reflected in the drawing. Given the nature of advertisement, it is not advisable to define a degree of reality in the legislation; in fact, it is technically impossible. However, this is not to say the legislation should then be considered as to allow any form of artistic impression without a bottom line. On the contrary. All artistic impressions will be judged on a case-by-case basis to see if the drawing is misleading and is a misrepresentation of the actual environment. Some artistic impressions were found extremely idealistic; one common practice, as observed by Merry (2008), is the replacement of nearby existing buildings with spacious lawns and verdant trees. On a case-by-case basis, there is a real possibility for such practice to be regarded as misleading under the *Ordinance*.

The *Ordinance* also gives detailed requirements at section 73(8) regarding the size and font of English letters or Chinese characters or numbers to be used in statements contained in an advertisement. In 2016, the Court held that the vendor of *Ocean One* commits an offence under the *Ordinance* by failing to use the specified font size in advertisements (SCMP 2016).

Location and environmental features are the favoured theme for advertisements of sales of first-hand properties. However, little do the *Ordinance* and the Consent Scheme touch on how such information should be presented in advertisements. The requirements on disclosure of environmental features only apply to sales brochures; while the location plan and outline zoning plan may be informative on the prominent environmental features around the estate, their academic nature requires some degree of relevant knowledge and technique (coupled with some patience, perhaps) to extract the information from the graphic presentations: a commitment more than most prospective purchasers will be willing to undertake. In contrast, it is much easier for unchecked information to find the way into a prospective purchaser's mind through eye-catching and easy-to-read advertising texts. For example, artistic maps depicting only positive features and facilities around the development are still seen. Undeniably, a certain tendency towards exaggeration and misrepresentation remained in advertisements after the introduction of additional measures to the Consent Scheme in June 2010 till the time of the *Ordinance*.

Advertisements on television and radio

Before 2012, the Broadcasting Authority was empowered by the *Broadcasting Authority Ordinance* (Cap 391) to regulate advertisements on television and radio.[35] With the taking into effect of the *Communications Authority Ordinance* (Cap 616), the Communications Authority was established on 1 April 2012 as a unified regulatory body overseeing the converging telecommunications and broadcasting sectors. The new Authority has issued two Generic Codes of Practice on television advertising standard and radio advertising standard respectively in 2013.[36] It must be first pointed out that these Generic Codes of practice regulate the acts of service licensees (e.g., TVB and RTHK) other than the authors of the advertisement (e.g., developers), therefore there is no direct comparison with the *Ordinance*. Nonetheless for our discussion on consumer protection, the standards prescribed therein are worth exploring.

Take the television advertising standard as an example: the Communications Authority (2013) requests, as a general principle, that 'television advertisement must be legal, clean, honest and truthful'.[37] The Generic Code does not define what is 'legal', 'clean' or 'honest', but regarding 'truthful presentation', it further states that 'No advertisements may contain any descriptions, claims or illustrations which expressly or by implication depart from truth or mislead about the product or service advertised or about its suitability for the purpose recommended.'[38] Against such a standard a TV commercial of a 2011 presale in Hong Kong contains photos of geographic features out of Hong Kong might have departed from being a truthful presentation.[39] On a similar vein, in 2009, the TV commercial of *Lake Silver* also attracted criticisms for the use of computer-generated sceneries of forests and lakes (SCMP 2009a; Goo 2010).[40]

The general principle, of course, can be vague and abstract, for it covers advertisements of all kinds of products and services; but the Generic Code has specific requirements for 'Real Property Advertising'. Paragraph 39 imposes a general duty of care on the licensee to ascertain that 'any descriptions, demonstrations and claims of a specific nature with regard to real property advertisements have been adequately substantiated by the advertisers'. Section (a) of paragraph 39 provides, that 'no claims may expressly or by implication misrepresent the location, size and value of the real property and the available transport facilities'; section (b) provides 'the lowest selling price of a real property should be stated as such and should not give an impression that it is the average price'; and section (d) says that 'advertisements must not offer any furniture, home appliances or any other goods as "free gifts" unless such items are supplied at no cost or no extra cost to the recipient.'[41]

The general duty prescribed by the Code, i.e., *to ascertain that any descriptions, demonstrations and claims of a specific nature with regard to real property advertisements that have been adequately substantiated,* could serve as a very helpful guideline in the consideration of regulating advertisements distributed by vendors as well.

In addition, the Generic Code requests that all advertising material must comply with the laws of Hong Kong.[42] This should direct the stakeholders' attention to the relevant requirements on advertisement in first-hand sale of residential properties in the *Ordinance* after April 2013.

Advertisements by estate agents

In sales of first-hand properties in Hong Kong, the role played by real estate agents in presenting the properties to perspective purchasers is so engaging that it is an understatement to merely describe it as *proactive*. More than often the agents will supply with their clients and would-be clients printed materials on the property on sale. Section 44(1) of the *Estate Agents Ordinance* (Cap 511) empowers the Estate Agents Authority to regulate advertising by licensed estate agents.[43] Section 44(2) prohibits the inclusion by licensed estate agents in advertisements, statements or particulars which are false or misleading in a material particular.

Estate Agents Authority has been regulating the advertisements produced by agents via its Code of Ethics and Practice Circulars, both persuasive in nature (EAA 2007). The effectiveness of the regulation was questioned in the incident regarding the sale of *Icon* in 2011, where complaints were directed to the misleading materials given by real estate agents for a Non-Consent Scheme sale of uncompleted flats (Standard 2011).

Now, with the enactment of the *Ordinance*, the question is whether all the promotional materials, i.e., those produced by the vendors and those duplicated by estate agents, are subject to the regulation of the new legislation. The answer should be yes. According to section 69, the *Ordinance* applies to *an advertisement purporting to promote the sale of any specified residential property*. The *Ordinance* does not stipulate that only the vendor can publish advertisement of the property, nor does it designate the vendor as the only source of the advertisement. Thus if a real estate agent produced and distributed an advertisement of the property containing misleading or false information on its own, the agent may be made liable under section 70(1) of the *Ordinance*, which stipulates that *a person commits an offence if the person publishes an advertisement containing information that is false or misleading in a material particular or causes such an advertisement to be published* and *that person knows that, or is reckless as to whether, the information is false or misleading in the material particular*.

In some mega sales, developers may issue training materials for the purpose of internal training for employees or estate agents commissioned by the sale. These materials are not originally intended to be distributed to the public by the developers. As a result, statements or presentation of a more casual or exaggerated nature may be contained in these materials, together with information, illustration or presentation that are not to be included in the sales brochure or advertisement. The Consumer Council noted in its 2014 study that some training materials were distributed to purchasers by estate agents together with advertisements published by the developers (CC 2014). The solution would be to prohibit the distribution of such materials to perspective purchasers by the issue of a Practice Circular by the Estate Agent Authority. Meanwhile, it should be highlighted that the *Ordinance* applies to any material purporting to promote the sale of any specified residential property; therefore there is a possibility that, depending on the facts of the case, respective provisions in the *Ordinance* may apply to these training materials too.

Show flats

A show flat is a model flat built by developers to illustrate the internal dimensions of a unit. The *Ordinance* defines a show flat as a property unit, or a structure resembling a property unit, that depicts the residential property for viewing by prospective purchasers or by the general public.[44] Being an 1:1 scale three-dimensional illustration or mock-up of the residential flat, the show flats should be the most ideal place for a purchaser to learn the information about the floor area and internal structure of the flat on sale, but there used to be an era where the media had advised purchasers to avoid show flats – if they wished to have an accurate idea about how the flat would look once completed (SCMP 2009b). Decorated show flats or modified show flats constructed in the sales centres had been a minefield of misrepresentation and misdescription. The landmark report by the *South China Morning Post* based on an investigation into the show flats created by five major developers in late 2009 revealed the common perception-altering tricks that took place in the show flats: the use of small and extra-shallow furniture; doing away with the front door and encroachment on public space outside; replacing solid walls that are 10cm or so thick with glass partitions less than 2.5cm thick; removing walls separating bedrooms; feature a ceiling at least 15cm higher than the height of the ceiling in the development; missing out balcony railings (SCMP 2009b).

All of these are not isolated phenomena. Everything is perfectly blended into the posh appearance of the show flats created by leading interior designers. Purchasers could be easily taken away by the charming appearance of the show flats without realizing that they did not accurately reflect the internal dimensions of each compartment of the flat. This remained the case until June 2010, where a weighty part of LACO Circular Memorandum No. 62 was dedicated to the construction of show flats.[45] Now this part of regulation is consolidated in Division 4 of Part 2 of the *Ordinance* under the title 'Show Flats for Uncompleted Development or Phase'.

The practice of creating show flats in sales offices has been popular for decades. With their scrumptious appearance, model flats have been considered the major attraction of the campaign (Merry 2008). The following discussion answers questions on why show flats should be allowed by the legislation and how the legislation ensures that they are built to assist, rather than mislead or confuse, the prospective purchasers.[46]

Necessity to create show flats

Are developers under a duty to set up show flats for the reference of prospective purchasers? The question may be purely academic, for seldom is it not in the interests of developers to create such flats to promote the sale.[47] But this does not justify a statutory duty to create show flats in sale of first-hand residential properties by the vendor, given the cost of the construction of show flats is substantial (much more expensive than issuing sales brochures). The Consent Scheme does not make it mandatory for vendors to present the property by way of constructing show flats. The answer is explicitly given in the negative by the *Ordinance*, viz., 'the vendor is not required to make any show flat available for viewing by prospective purchasers or by the general public'.[48]

Yet still, the provision of show flats should be encouraged, especially for the sale of uncompleted flats. As long as there are rules that effectively eliminate misrepresentation, a model flat will serve the purpose of enhancing transparency and promoting consumer protection, for it makes the most illustrative and perceivable presentation on the size, dimension, internal structure, fittings and finishes of the actual flat. In 2014, the Consumer Council raised the issue that only a very limited number of show flats were made available for viewing: sometimes the mock-ups available are not the type of units covered in the price lists (CC 2014). It seems that the Council is of a very encouraging view for the provision of show flats for the better information of the purchasers at sales offices.

It must be highlighted that only the show flats set up in sales of uncompleted flats are subject to the requirement of Division 4.[49] In case of a sale of completed residential properties, the vendor is not obliged to create show flats although she shall feel free to do so. If she decided to do so, such flats were not subject to the regulation of Division 4 (SRPA 2013d). However, in this case the *Ordinance* does impose a duty on the vendor to make the respective residential property available for viewing. An alternative way to fulfil the duty is to let the purchaser to view a comparable residential property in the completed development if it is not reasonably practicable for the specified residential property to be viewed by the person. In case it is not reasonably practical for any comparable residential property to be viewed by the person, the vendor must acquire the purchaser's written agreement not to require the vendor to make the viewing available before the vendor can sell the specified residential property to the purchaser.[50]

The 2014 survey suggested that the statutory requirement might not be fairly implemented by vendors, as less than 40 per cent of the respondents had the chance to view a comparable property in sales of residential properties in completed development (CC 2014). In the sale of *Mont Vert Phase I*, the vendor had issued a 'No Viewing Agreement' and required registrants who have submitted Registration of Intent before a certain date to submit to the vendor the signed 'No Viewing Agreement' in order to be eligible for the balloting. The effect of the 'No Viewing Agreement' was that the purchaser would gave up the right to view the specified or comparable property in the development before entering into the preliminary agreement of purchase and sale with the vendor. According to the SRPA (2014b), the arrangement constituted 'a serious departure from the spirit of the *Ordinance* which requires that vendors must make the residential property which a person intends to purchase available for viewing by that person before the vendor sells the residential property to that person'.[51] The Consumer Council also commented such practice was in opposition to the principle of transparency as espoused by the *Ordinance* (CC 2014).

The SRPA could have further pointed out that the written consent by the purchaser can only exempt the vendor from performing the duty where it is *not reasonably practicable* for the specified residential property to be viewed *and*, at the same time, it is not reasonably practicable for any comparable residential property to be viewed – note the word 'and' at the end of section 44(2)(a). In other words, the written consent is relevant only if the vendor can prove that viewing of neither the specified nor the comparable residential property in the development is *reasonably practicable*. Thus requiring the intended purchasers to return an agreement to not view any property in the development without proving the impracticability of viewing is clearly in contravention of section 44 of the *Ordinance*.

In this case, the vendor's intention to set up show flats for the purchasers' reference was regarded by the SRPA as an irrelevant factor to discharge the burden under section 44.[52]

Unmodified and modified show flats

According to the 2014 Survey by the Consumer Council, following 'units available for selection at the time of sale' and 'sales brochures and price lists prepared by developers', 'Unmodified show flats' was regarded by most respondents as among the top three important items at the sales office (CC 2014). The concept of an unmodified show flat, however, was first introduced to the regulatory regime by LACO Circular Memorandum No. 62 in 2010. Before that, all the show flats were modified.

According to LACO Circular Memorandum No. 62, a show flat is an unmodified show flat if it is a model flat 'showing the same conditions of the actual unit', which must present all the non-structural internal walls/partitions, fittings and finishes and complementary appliances 'in exactly the same way as they will be featured in the actual unit' (Lands D 2010). A more detailed description is given by section 36 of the *Ordinance*, which stipulates that a show flat of a residential property is an unmodified show flat of the residential property if (a) any bay windows, air-conditioning plant room, balconies, utility platforms and verandahs in the show flat are the same as those in the residential property as depicted in the sales brochure for the development; (b) the dimensions of the show flat, and of any bay windows, air-conditioning plant room, balconies, utility platforms and verandahs in the show flat are the same as those specified in relation to the residential property in the sales brochure; (c) the show flat is provided with a ceiling in such a way that the floor-to-ceiling height of the show flat does not exceed the corresponding projected height of the residential property; (d) the internal partitions in the show flat are the same as those specified in relation to the residential property in that sales brochure; and (e) the fittings, finishes and appliances in the show flat must be the same as those in the residential property.[53] Section 40 further prescribes that the vendor must provide enclosing walls and boundary walls for, and internal partitions and doors in an unmodified show flat in the same way as they will be provided in the residential property as depicted in the sales brochure for the development.

The *Ordinance* does not address whether furniture can be displayed in an unmodified show flat. Ideally not, as an unmodified flat should be constructed in such a way that it resembles *in every material aspect* the residential property that which is to be handed over to purchasers upon delivery. Therefore no furniture should be allowed to be displayed in an unmodified flat.

The *Ordinance* gives a similar definition of modified show flats at section 37, yet the requirements for internal partitions and fittings, finishes and appliances as enclosed in section 36(1)(d) and (e) do not apply to modified show flats. Section 41(2) then suggests that the vendor must provide enclosing walls and boundary walls for, and internal partitions and doors in a modified show flat in the same way as they will be provided in the residential property as depicted in the sales brochure for the development, save where subsection (3) applies, i.e., if by virtue of section 41(3) of the *Buildings Ordinance* (Cap 123), the partition or the door may be removed from the residential property without the approval of the Building Authority, then the vendor is not required to provide an internal partition or door in the show flat. In this case, the vendor needs to mark a solid line on the floor of the show flat showing the position and thickness of the partition; at the same time, the vendor must display a plan of the residential property that is reasonably visible to any person entering the show flat, showing the layout, orientation and thickness of all the internal partitions in the residential property.[54] For fittings and finishes, the vendor must display a notice in the modified show flat setting out which of the fittings, finishes and appliances are to be included and which will not be included.[55]

Still, there are additional requirements. For both modified and unmodified show flats, the vendor must provide any balcony, utility platform or verandah with boundary walls or parapets.[56] In case a passageway or door is provided through an enclosing or boundary wall of the show flat as a means of escape for the purposes of regulation 41(1) of the *Building (Planning) Regulations* (Cap 123 sub leg F.), the vendor must provide a solid line on the floor showing the position and thickness of the enclosing or boundary wall and display a notice which is reasonably visible to any person entering the show flat, stating that there is no such passageway or door in the residential property.[57]

The next question is: should each modified show flat be accompanied by an unmodified show flat of the same size and international partition and vice versa? LACO Circular Memorandum No. 62 set out the rules on the provision of unmodified flats as follows: the developer should provide at least one unmodified show flat in the sales office; if the developer intends to set up modified flats as well, then one of the modified show flats must mirror the unmodified unit in type and size, i.e., *the mirrored show flat* (Lands D 2010). In other words, the vendor only needed to create one unmodified show flat in one presale under the Consent Scheme. The weakness of such an arrangement is apparent: purchasers interested in units of another size and internal structure might find little assistance from the unmodified unit and still be left uninformed. Given the unappealing appearance of the unmodified flat (which is always in contrast with the modified flats), it would be difficult to imagine that a developer would willingly set up a second unmodified flat.

In *Law Lectures for Practitioners 2010*, it was argued for the first time that it would be ideal if *every* modified flat were accompanied by an unmodified mirrored flat in size and type (Lin 2012). In November 2011, the Steering Committee recommended that no modified show flat can be built without an unmodified show flat of the same type/size (SC 2011).[58] The *Ordinance* reconciles the suggestions, prescribing at section 38 that if a modified show flat is to be set up by the developer, she must first set up an unmodified show flat of the residential property; but the developer is not required to set up a modified show flat of the same residential property in case she only intends to set up an unmodified flat of that residential property.

In relation to the unmodified flat, the Consent Scheme was silent on whether the paired modified and unmodified flats should stand next to each other in the sales office. In practice, the answer is usually no. It can be difficult to blend an unmodified flat into the delicate and luxury atmosphere of the rest of the sales office. Then in the sales office of *Hermitage* (one of the first presales after the issue of LACO Circular Memorandum No. 62) in 2010, one unmodified flat was built at the very entrance of the sales office on the lower floor; all the four modified show flats were on the upper floor including the one mirroring the raw flat.

The Consumer Council believed the purpose of construction pairing show flats cannot be achieved if a prospective purchaser cannot make a direct comparison if the unmodified show flat and the corresponding modified show flat were not situated next to each other (CC 2014). The legislation should require that each unmodified flat and its mirroring flat be located next to each other in the sales office.

Measurements and photo-taking

A celebrated improvement required by LACO Circular Memorandum No. 62 was that show flats must be open for viewers to take measurements and photographs.[59] For show flats first open to the public on or after 1 June 2010, only crowd management concerns could justify the prohibition on photo-taking. The crowd management exception applied only when there are genuine crowd management concerns. The developer was under a duty to 'clear any hurdles for allowing show flat visitors to take photos or make videos' with the designers before the service is engaged.[60]

The *Ordinance* has given more protection to the works of interior designers. According to the *Ordinance*, developers must not restrict any person who views the show flat from taking measurements, taking photographs or making video recordings of an unmodified show flat; this means that developers could refuse viewers to take photos or make video recordings of a modified show flat. But for modified show flats, only the right of taking measurement in modified show flats is upheld by the *Ordinance*; the view shall not take photos or make video recordings of the show flat.[61] The 2014 survey revealed that after the commencement of the *Ordinance*, still a portion of visitors (i.e., 23.6 per cent of the respondents) to the show offices were stopped by the on-site staff from taking photos or videos or taking measurement at unmodified show flat (CC 2014).

Website designated by the vendor for the development

In the era of e-commerce, webpages on the internet have become a major information channel to promote any business including sales of residential properties. The website designated for a particular sale of development is unique for two reasons: firstly, it is much more accessible by the public than the sales office; and secondly, information published on the website can be updated on a daily basis. The *Ordinance* has clearly acknowledged the unique role of the website established by a vendor in a sales campaign for timely disclosure of updated information, even though the legislation does not contain a provision stating to the effect that vendors are under a statutory duty to establish a website for a sale of first-hand residential properties.

There are however a number of requirements in the *Ordinance* concerning disclosure of information on the website. For example, section 47(1)(b) stipulates that at least three days before the date of sale developers must make available on the website the information on sales arrangement of the development.[62] Section 47(3) further adds that the information must be published in such a manner that the information is reasonably visible to any person browsing the website. Notably the website is the only platform the *Ordinance* chooses for disclosure of the above information. Such detail alone may be sufficient to imply a duty to set up a website for each presale by developers. Similarly, section 32(3) requests that during a period of at least three days immediately before a date of the sale, the vendor must make a copy of the relevant price list available for inspection on the website.

The importance of the website is stressed again in section 49, which demands the latest draft of every deed of mutual covenant in respect of the specified residential property and the aerial photograph of the development be uploaded to the website on the date of the sale for inspection.[63] According to section 20(3) of the *Ordinance*, the sales brochure for the development must set out the address of the website designated by the vendor for development for the purpose of Part 2 of the *Ordinance*.[64] At the same time, electronic copies of the sales brochure are to be made available for inspection on the website at least seven days before the date of the sale.[65] In a nutshell, the sales brochure and the website must make reference to each other.

All in all, it can be inferred from various provisions of the *Ordinance* that developers are requested to set up the website designated by the vendor for the development for the publication of sales brochure, price list and other information regarding the sale. For phased development, each phase of the development should establish its own website; this view could be inferred from section 27(1) which suggests that each phase should issue its own sales brochure. Exemption perhaps should be made for vendors of specified New Territories developments, which usually concerns only one house of three flats, or several houses. Developments consisting of less than 50 flats can also be exempted from the burden. Other than that, the duty should be imposed upon all developers including the Housing Authority and the Housing Society, although for the Housing Authority, according to section 65, Divisions 2, 3, 4, 5, 6, 7 and 8 of Part 2 of the *Ordinance* do not apply if the development is constructed by the Housing Authority. Still the Housing Authority would follow the provisions of Part 2 of the *Ordinance* as far as possible in the sale of first-hand residential properties. The contents of the website should be regulated in a similar way as those contained in the sales brochure.

It will be appropriate that a project website includes the following information sections: (a) notes to purchasers of first-hand residential properties; (b) basic information of the development; (c) an electronic copy of the sales brochure; (d) an electronic copy of the most up-to-date deed of mutual covenant; (e) a most update-to-date aerial photo of the development; (f) price lists; (g) register of transaction; (h) sales arrangement; (i) floor plans; (j) area schedule of units; (k) floor plan of the car park; (l) matters relating to the preliminary agreement for sale and purchase; (m) salient points of the land grant conditions; and (n) government, institutional or community facilities, public open space and public facilities.

In addition, it would be ideal if the links to the following webpages are conspicuously displayed on the website: (a) the website of SRPA and the webpage of the sales of first-hand residential properties electronic platform – an electronic database of information and statistics on the residential property market in Hong Kong established under section 89 (1) of the *Ordinance*,[66] i.e., the Sales of First-hand Residential Properties Electronic Platform (to be discussed below); (b) the Legislative Council; (c) the Lands Department; (d) the Law Society of Hong Kong; (e) the Consumer Council; (f) the Estate Agents Authority; (g) the Hong Kong Institute of Surveyors; (h) the Real Estate Developers Association of Hong Kong; (i) the Education Bureau; and (j) the MTR Corporation. For pre-sales of flats under the Home Ownership Scheme, the website should provide a link to the official website of the Housing Authority.

Finally, wherever an unexpected situation occurred or novel issues regarding information disclosure arose during a sale, developers' response in these circumstances may help prospective purchasers to get a better picture of the sale and the property on sale. The high reference value of a timely update on the vendor's explanations or response may suggest that a new requirement to be added into the *Ordinance*: answers, comments, announcements or press releases relating to the property on sale by the vendor during the sale should be published on the website designated by the vendor for the development in a timely manner.

The sales of first-hand residential properties electronic platform

On top of all the traditional channels, the legislation has introduced one more official information channel upon its commencement: the Sales of First-hand Residential Properties Electronic Platform (SRPE).[67] As a centralized electronic database, the SRPE keeps, for public inspection, all the sales brochures, price lists, and registers of transactions of individual first-hand residential developments submitted by developers to the Authority after the operation of the *Ordinance* began (SRPA 2013b).

At SRPE, the purchaser can search for all residential developments the sale of which is subject to the *Ordinance*. The website provides four search paths to allocate the development, i.e., by Broad District and/or Sub Area in Outline Zoning Plans/Development Permission Area Plans, by the Name of Development, by the Street Name and Street Number and by the Lot Number. Once the development is identified, the platform will present links for the purchaser to download the sales brochure (and the examination record), the register of transactions and price lists. It also provides information including the address of the website designated by the vendor for the development and the dates of first printing and examination of the sales brochure.

As the official platform established and administrated by the SRPA, the SRPE enables a purchaser to verify the documents claimed to be sales brochures, price lists and register of transactions published by developers as well as the website designated by the vendor. In this way it extinguishes the possibility of fraudulent misrepresentation on, say, a sale of uncompleted flats in a development that does not exit. Therefore it provides extra protection to purchasers.

The usage and utilization of SRPE by the public, however, was less than 10 per cent according to the survey conducted by the Consumer Council in 2014 (i.e., only 7.5 per cent of the survey respondents had used SRPE). Thus it was advised that 'more effort could be put into making the service more comprehensive, and therefore more valuable in terms of information, as well as more widely known.' Overall, the Council regards the establishment of SRPE 'a positive step towards the development of a comprehensive and interactive information platform for use by the general public' (CC 2014).

Conclusion

Radical changes have been introduced into the regulatory regime of the sale of first-hand residential properties in Hong Kong after the reform of the Consent Scheme in 2010 in regards to the drafting and issuance of sales brochures, the contents and distribution of advertisements, and the construction and presentation in the show flats. The *Ordinance* further recognizes one more official information channel, i.e., the website designated for the sale by the vendor, and requests timely update of information on transaction volume/price, revision of price lists and sales brochure. The legislative purpose of the *Ordinance*, i.e., to enhance transparency in the first-hand real estate market, is achieved by regulating the contents and publication of the sales brochure, advertisements as well as the establishment of show flats and the project websites. Among the four major information channels, the show flats and the sales brochure remain the most regulated areas with the advertisement the least. Much effort is needed to extend the regulation into advertisements to maintain a cohesive standard among the channels.

At the same time, more attention should be given to the practice of disseminating unauthorized information through unofficial channels. The Consumer Council's study in 2014 revealed that in practice, materials containing unofficial pricing information, units available for sale and sold, etc., that were supposedly intended for internal training were distributed by real estate agents together with the official price lists, advertisements and sales brochures which are prepared by the developers. Moreover, estate agents may send these types of unofficial information via WhatsApp or Wechat messages to prospective purchasers (CC 2014). The law should prohibit dissemination of unverified or unauthorized information to purchasers by agents via phones or in hard copies.

Furthermore, since 24 October 2013, the SRPA has invited the public to call the Authority in case of receiving false or misleading information on the prices of first-hand residential properties via mobile phones before the vendors of those properties made available to the public the price lists (SRPA 2016). For a more effective interaction with the public, the Authority could consider providing at the same time a mobile number with an official WhatsApp account and an official Wechat account so anyone who receives such information can conveniently forward them to the official account of the SRPA via WhatsApp or Wechat.

Notes

1 Part of the chapter's discussion on the Consent Scheme was included in the lecture manuscript entitled 'The New Rules for Sales of Uncompleted Flats' in the book *Law Lectures for Practitioners 2010* by Hong Kong Law Journal Ltd & Faculty of Law, the University of Hong Kong.
2 [1999] HKCU 653.
3 By Mr Justice Anthony To, HCA004404A/1999.
4 Henry Fok Ying Tung and L X, *Henry Fok Tells His Story*, 3rd Edition, 2010, pp. 46–56. The context of the sales brochure (in Chinese) is enclosed in the book at pp. 58–60.
5 Section 15(1), Part 2 – Division 2, *Residential Properties (First-hand Sales) Ordinance*, A2331.
6 A1 in Annex to LACO Circular Memorandum No.68; firstly implemented by REDA Guidelines issued on 7 October 2009.
7 Section 2 (1), Part 1 – Division 2, *Residential Properties (First-hand Sales) Ordinance*, A2301.
8 Ibid, section 18, Part 2 – Division 2, A2333.
9 Case No.: KTS21568–572、595–599、600–608/15.
10 Section 15, Part 2 – Division 2, *Residential Properties (First-hand Sales) Ordinance*, A2331.
11 Ibid., section 24, A2347.
12 Ibid., section 22(1)(a), A2343–A2345.
13 Ibid., section 16, A2331.
14 Ibid., section 25(1), A2349. See also paragraph (a) in LACO Circular Memorandum No. 62; Paragraph 4.3, Report of the Steering Committee on Regulation of Sale of First-hand Residential Properties by Legislation, October 2011, p. 14.
15 Ibid., section 25(3), A2349.
16 More discussion see Chapter 14.
17 Section 22(2), *Residential Properties (First-hand Sales) Ordinance*, A2345.
18 Ibid., section 19, Part 2 – Division 2, A2333.
19 Ibid., section 21, Part 2 – Division 2, A2341 and section 29, Part 3 of Schedule 1, A2547.
20 Ibid., sections 30 and 31, Part 4 of Schedule 1, A2547–A 2549.
21 Ibid., section 17, *Residential Properties (First-hand Sales) Ordinance*, A2331–A2333.
22 'When an examined and revised sales brochure has been made available to the public, as long as the original version and the examined and revised version have been made available without interruption for a period of at least 7 days before the commencement of the sale of the development, there is no need for the development to wait for another 7 days after the making available of the examined and revised sales brochure before it could be put up for sale.' The Sales of First-hand Residential Properties Authority, SRPA's response on Sales Brochures and Ordinance, *Press Releases*, 26 April 2013, www.info.gov.hk/gia/general/201304/26/P201304260683.htm

23 Paragraph 8.13(a), Report of the Steering Committee on Regulation of Sale of First-hand Residential Properties by Legislation, October 2011.
24 Section 70, Part 3, *Residential Properties (First-hand Sales) Ordinance*, A2429.
25 Section 71(1) Part 3, *Residential Properties (First-hand Sales) Ordinance*, A2429.
26 Ibid., section 72 (2), (3), (4) and (5), Part 3, A2433. See also paragraph 8.13(d), Report of the Steering Committee on Regulation of Sale of First-hand Residential Properties by Legislation, October 2011, p. 40.
27 Ibid., section 71 (4), Part 3, A2431.
28 For Ocean One, Case No.: KTS8512-8517/2016; for Graces, Case No.: KTS15705–15719/2016.
29 The rules were first shown in a 'Proposal on Advertisement' in REDA Guidelines on 7 October 2009; then in Annex IV of LACO Circular Memorandum No. 62.
30 Section 73(1), Part 3, *Residential Properties (First-hand Sales) Ordinance*, A2435.
31 Extracts of the two documents are provided in Annex K to the Report of the Steering Committee on Regulation of Sale of First-hand Residential Properties by Legislation, October 2011.
32 Items 20 and 21, the *Standard Consent Letter* as revised on 1 September 2011, Lands Department.
33 See section 73(2) and (3), Part 3, *Residential Properties (First-hand Sales) Ordinance*, A2435.
34 Ibid., Section 74, A2441–A2443. See also Appendix I and II in Annex IV to *LACO Circular Memorandum No. 62*.
35 Section 9(1)(d), Broadcasting Authority Ordinance (Cap 391).
36 Generic Code of Practice on Television Advertising Standards: www.comsauth.hk/filemanager/common/policies_regulations/cop/code_tvad_e.pdf; Radio Code of Practice on Advertising Standards: www.coms-auth.hk/filemanager/common/policies_regulations/cop/code_radioad_e.pdf.
37 Paragraph 1, Chapter 3, Generic Code of Practices on Television Advertising Standards, Communications Authority, January 2013, p. 8.
38 Ibid., paragraph 9, Chapter 3, p. 9.
39 TV Commercial for the sale of *Festival City* aired in November and December 2011.
40 'The TV advertisement shows the long and winding road on the coast of south of France and the two-storey pink Villa Ephrussi de Rothschild and large garden with beautiful maze formed by hedges. There is no such villa or maze in the estate.' See S. H. Goo, Regulation of Sale of Off-the-plan Property, *The Conveyancer and Property Lawyer*, Issue 2, 2010, p. 139. See also Ng Kang-chung, TV stations rapped over misleading Sino Land ad, *South China Morning Post*, 3 November 2009.
41 Paragraph 39, Chapter 6, Generic Code of Practices on Television Advertising Standards, Communications Authority, January 2013, pp. 28–29.
42 Ibid., Paragraph 3, Chapter 3, Communications Authority, January 2013, p. 8.
43 'The Authority may, with the approval of the Secretary, by regulation regulate advertising by licensed estate agents to whom the regulations apply in such manner as appears to the Authority to be appropriate'; section 44(1), Estate Agents Ordinance (Cap 511).
44 Section 12, Part 2 – Division 1, *Residential Properties (First-hand Sales) Ordinance*, A2327.
45 Annex III to LACO Circular Memorandum No.62; first published in Measure (3) and Annex B in REDA Guidelines in June 2010.
46 For discussion on how internal structures and fittings/finishes should be presented in show flats, see Chapter 5.
47 As a rare example, the sale of the *Emerald 28* in 2009 proceeded without setting up any show flat in the sales office.
48 Section 38(1), Part 2 – Division 4, *Residential Properties (First-hand Sales) Ordinance*, A2377.

49 Ibid., section 38(2).
50 Ibid., section 45 (1) (2).
51 See the Press Release by the Sales of First-hand Residential Properties Authority, SRPA advises prospective purchasers of Mont Vert Phase I not to easily give up their right to view the properties they intend to purchase, *Press Release*, 17 July 2014. www.info.gov.hk/gia/general/201407/17/P201407171205.htm.
52 'The SRPA wishes to emphasise that, when offering to sell completed first-hand residential properties, vendors should not take it as an excuse that since they have made available show flats for viewing by prospective purchasers, they therefore do not have to make available the residential properties which prospective purchasers intend to purchase, or comparable residential properties, for viewing by the prospective purchasers.' See ibid.
53 Section 36, Part 2 – Division 4, *Residential Properties (First-hand Sales) Ordinance* A2371–A2373.
54 Ibid., section 41(4)(6), A2381–A2393.
55 Ibid., section 41(5), A2383.
56 Ibid., section 39(2), A2379.
57 Ibid., section 39(4), A2379.
58 'There should first be an unmodified show flat to be provided for any type/size of units before a modified show flat of that same type/size of units can be provided.' Paragraph 9.15(a), Report of the Steering Committee on Regulation of Sale of First-hand Residential Properties by Legislation, October 2011, page 49.
59 Section 12 in Annex III to LACO Circular Memorandum No. 62. The rule was originally implemented by REDA Guidelines on 27 April 2010.
60 Ibid., section 12(c).
61 Section 42(1)(2), Part 2 – Division 4, *Residential Properties (First-hand Sales) Ordinance* A2383–A2385.
62 Ibid., section 47(1)(2), Part 2, A2391.
63 Ibid., A2395;
64 Ibid., section 20(3), Part 2 – Division 2, A2341. For example, in the sale of *Mount Nicholson Phase 1*, the sales brochure states the website address for the Phase on page 243.
65 Ibid, section 25(3), A2349. See also Paragraph 5.2, Report of the Steering Committee on Regulation of Sale of First-hand Residential Properties by Legislation, October 2011, page 49; section 8 in REDA Guidelines on 1 June 2010.
66 Ibid., section 89(1), Part 6 – Division 1, A2477. See also paragraph 16.1, Report of the Steering Committee on Regulation of Sale of First-hand Residential Properties by Legislation, October 2011, p. 75.
67 The Sales of First-hand Residential Properties Electronic Platform, www.srpe.gov.hk/opip/default.htm.

References

AD (2010) '市民捐贈300份　成歷史見證 30年樓書　由平實到浮誇', *Apple Daily*, 17 June 2010. http://hk.apple.nextmedia.com/news/art/20100617/14144102
AD (2016) 同珍富雅閣違規罪名成立　罰款72萬, 3 August 2016, *Apple Daily*, http://hk.apple.nextmedia.com/realtime/finance/20160803/55447446
AD (2016b) Ocean One廣告誤導罰36萬, *Apple Daily*, 11 November 2016.
AD (2016c) 海鑽開售前刊誤導性廣告　發展商遭罰款20萬, *Apple Daily*, 24 November 2016. http://hk.apple.nextmedia.com/realtime/news/20161124/55958817

CA (2013a) Generic Code of Practice on Television Advertising Standards, Communications Authority, January 2013, www.comsauth.hk/filemanager/common/policies_regulations/cop/code_tvad_e.pdf.

CA (2013b) Radio Code of Practice on Advertising Standards, Communications Authority, January 2013, www.coms-auth.hk/filemanager/common/policies_regulations/cop/code_radioad_e.pdf.

CC (2014) Study on the Sales of First-hand Residential Properties, pp. 23–115, 11 November 2014, Consumer Council, www.consumer.org.hk/ws_en/competition_issues/reports/20141111.html.

EAA (2007) Code of Ethics, Estate Agents Authority, www.eaa.org.hk/Compliance/Codeofethics/tabid/100/language/en-US/Default.aspx.

Fan, C.S. (2005) The Consent Scheme in Hong Kong: Its Evolution and Evaluation – Home Purchaser Behaviour in Housing Society's Property Transactions Before and After the Asian Financial Crisis, Ph.D Thesis, Department of Real Estate and Construction, Faculty of Architecture, the University of Hong Kong, September 2005, p. 81.

Goo, S. H. (2010) Regulation of Sale of Off-the-plan Property, *The Conveyancer and Property Lawyer*, no. 2, pp. 139–140.

HKET (2016) 富雅閣涉違規賣樓 表證成立, 3 June 2016, *Hong Kong Economics Times.*

HTB (2011) Residential Properties (First-hand Sales) Bill, Annex A to the Public Consultation on the Proposed Legislation to Regulate the Sale of First-hand Residential Properties, the Housing and Transport Bureau, November 2011.

Lands D. (2010) Legal Advisory and Conveyancing Office Circular Memorandum No. 62, Lands Department Consent Scheme, Legal Advisory and Conveyancing Office, Lands Department, 2 June 2010.

Lands D. (2012) Legal Advisory and Conveyancing Office Circular Memorandum No. 68, Lands Department Consent Scheme, Legal Advisory and Conveyancing Office, Lands Department, 22 March 2012.

LC (2012) Administration's Response to Issues Raised by Members at the Bills Committee Meeting held on 31 May 2012, LC Paper No. CB(1) 2120/11–12(02), Legislative Council, June 2012, www.legco.gov.hk/yr11-12/english/bc/bc04/papers/bc040607cb1-2120-2-e.pdf

Leng, X. (2010) *Henry Fok Tells His Story*, 3rd edn, pp. 46–56. 《世紀回眸：霍英東回憶錄》霍英东口述，冷夏執筆，香港名流出版社，第三版.

Lin, D. (2012) The New Rules for Sales of Uncompleted Flats, Law Lectures for Practitioners 2010, Cheng, M.L., Jen, J. and Young, JYK (Eds.), Hong Kong Law Journal & Faculty of Law, the University of Hong Kong, pp. 78–118.

Merry, M. (2008) Protection of Purchasers of Uncompleted Residential Flats – The Hong Kong Experience, *HKU-NUS-SMU Symposium Paper*, pp. 4.

REDA (2009) Guidelines for Sales Descriptions of Uncompleted Residential Properties, The Real Estate Developers Association of Hong Kong, 7 October 2009.

SCMP (2009a) TV Stations Rapped over Misleading Sino Land Ad, 3 November 2009, *South China Morning Post*, Hong Kong.

SCMP (2009b) See-through Walls but No Transparency in Show Flats, 7 December 2009, *South China Morning Post*, Hong Kong.

SCMP (2016) Ground broken: Hong Kong property developer fined HK$200,000 for sales malpractice, 19 July 2016, *South China Morning Post*, Hong Kong. www.scmp.com/news/hong-kong/law-crime/article/1991764/ground-broken-hong-kong-property-developer-fined-hk200000

SC (2011) Report of the Steering Committee on Regulation of Sale of First-hand Residential Properties by Legislation, The Steering Committee on Regulation of the Sale of First-hand Residential Properties by Legislation, October 2011.

SRPA (2013a) SRPA's Response to Media Enquiries on Counting of Seven-day and Three-day Period under the Residential Properties (First-hand Sales) Ordinance, *Press Releases*, the Sales of First-hand Residential Properties Authority, 6 June 2013, www. info.gov.hk/gia/general/201306/06/P201306060603.htm.

SRPA (2013b) SRPA's Response on Sales Brochures and Ordinance, *Press Releases*, the Sales of First-hand Residential Properties Authority, 26 April 2013, www.info.gov.hk/ gia/general/201304/26/P201304260683.htm.

SRPA (2013c) Guidelines on Sales Brochure, the Sales of First-hand Residential Properties Authority, 5 April 2013, para 8, p3. www.srpa.gov.hk/files/pdf/guidelines/Guidelines_ on_Sales_Brochure_Eng_20140826.pdf

SRPA (2013d) SRPA's Response to Media Enquiries on Development at Yuk Yat Street, *Press Releases*, the Sales of First-hand Residential Properties Authority, 24 June 2013, www.info.gov.hk/gia/general/201306/24/P201306240588.htm.

SRPA (2014a) SRPA Advises Prospective Purchasers on Proposed Columbarium Development near City Point, *Press Releases*, the Sales of First-hand Residential Properties Authority, 15 May 2014, www.info.gov.hk/gia/general/201405/15/ P201405150750.htm.

SRPA (2014b) SRPA Advises Prospective Purchasers of Mont Vert Phase I Not to Easily Give up Their Right to View the Properties They Intend to Purchase, *Press Releases*, 17 July 2014, www.info.gov.hk/gia/general/201407/17/P201407171205.htm.

SRPA (2016) On Suspected Dissemination of False/Misleading Information, the Sales of First-hand Residential Properties Authority, July 2016.

The Standard (2011) *$10m flat sale row sparks heat over legal loopholes*, 17 January 2011.

The Vendor of City Point (2014) Examination Record, Sales Brochure, www.citypoint. com.hk/CITYPOINT/brochure/CityPointSBExaminationRecord.pdf.

The Vendor of Festival City (2011) Advertisement, 2011.

The Vendor of Pictorial Garden Phase 3 (1992) Sales Brochure, 1992.

The Vendor of Mount Nicholson Phase 1 (2016) Website of the Phrase, Sales Brochure, p. 243, www.mountnicholson.com.hk/brochure.

14 False or misleading information and misrepresentation

Introduction

From Chapters 3 to 12, the discussion has presented a detailed analysis on how the *Residential Properties (First-hand Sales) Ordinance* (the *Ordinance*) regulates sales descriptions on a variety of aspects of the first-hand residential properties on sale while promoting information disclosure in the selling process. In the sequence as it appears in this book these aspects include: the internal floor area; the layout and internal partitions; fittings and finishes; location and environmental features; the floor number; date of completion; lease term; salient points of the Deed Mutual Covenant and the land grant conditions; price lists; sales arrangement; the preliminary agreement for sale and purchase and the agreement for sale and purchase; and past transaction records. The *Ordinance* requires in general that any information regarding the property and the transaction must be accurately disclosed in the sale of first-hand residential properties. Chapter 13 then discusses how, when and where such information is to be disclosed to reach prospective purchasers. All these set the stage for a discussion on penalties and remedies for misrepresentation in the course of sales of first-hand residential properties: finally, we have arrived at the most revolutionary part of the *Ordinance*.

The *Ordinance* has, in its Parts 2 and 3, set a precedent to attach criminal liabilities to commission of practices in sales of first-hand residential properties that fail to comply with respective requirements enclosed in the legislation. As discussed in Chapter 13, section 70 creates the offence of 'publishing an advertisement containing information that is false or misleading in a material particular'. Other examples are section 15(3), section 16(2), section 17(4)(5) and section 18(4) in regard to the preparation of a sales brochure. For the first time in the history of Hong Kong, non-compliance with measures that originally were designed to enhance transparency in sales of first-hand residential properties may attract criminal liabilities. To start with, the certainty of punishment by criminal law may have the clearest deterrent effect, but criminal liability is not the only thing worthy of discussion.

A startling feature of the new legislation lies in Part 4 of the *Ordinance*, which encloses the provision on another two offences: *misrepresentation* at section 76(1) and *dissemination of false or misleading information* at section 78(1).[1] Although it remains the case by the end of 2016 that no vendor has ever been prosecuted under either section 76 or section 78, these two offences perhaps have a much wider scope of applicability compared to other offences under the *Ordinance* in catching various questionable commercial practices. In comparing the established rules in the common law to sections 75, 76 and 77 of the *Ordinance*, this chapter reveals how the *Ordinance* has reformulated and forcefully expanded the common law rules on misrepresentation in the specific context of sale of new residential properties. To better understand the impact of these new provisions in preventing the making and inclusion of misleading statements in the sales literature, it is necessary to investigate the effectiveness of the common law doctrine of misrepresentation in catching misleading statements and sales description in property transactions (in particular in off-plan sales) in Hong Kong.

Misrepresentation at common law

A significant part of the English contract law deals with the consequences of making a statement in pre-contractual negotiations. Depending on the extent the maker of a statement accepting liability for the truth of that statement, the common law categorizes a misleading statement made by one party to the other party when entering into a contract into the following four types of statements recognized by common law with regards to a misleading statement made by one party to the other party when entering into a contract: a *mere puff*, a *warranty* or a *condition* or *promise*, a *collateral contract* and a *representation/statement*. A *mere puff* gives rise to no liability.[2] If the court considers the statement a *warranty*, *condition* or *promise*, it will regard the statement as part of the contract, considering that the maker of the statement has accepted (or appears to have accepted) an obligation to do or not to do something.[3] This will potentially give rise to civil liability under contract law – normally an award of damages. The result is the same if the court finds that the parties have entered into a *collateral contract*.[4]

But if the court takes the view that the maker of the statement merely asserts the truth of a given state of facts, then it is likely that the court will regard the statement as a *representation*.[5] While the specific circumstances of each case will determine the outcome of that particular case, considerations of consumer protection may play a role in reaching the decision.

The doctrine of misrepresentation applies to statements of the last kind: a *representation* is a statement more than a *mere puff*, in the sense that the maker of a representation does assert the truth of a fact in the statement, yet less than a *warranty* or *condition*, i.e. the maker of the statement did not appear to accept any obligation to do or not to do something. The representation will constitute a *misrepresentation* if it is a false statement of fact that has been relied upon by the other party to enter into the agreement; this will enable the misrepresentee to claim damages, and, in case of fraud, to rescind the contract. This position derives from both common law rules and the *Misrepresentation Ordinance* (Cap 284).[6]

The doctrine has been applied to many disputes concerning misstatements given by developers/estate agents or misdescriptions in sales brochures/

advertisements in off-plan sales in Hong Kong. While a large body of case law shows that the doctrine has been effective in catching statements made in commercial activities where a contract is entered into or can be implied, the latest court decision in Hong Kong may suggest the limitation of the doctrine in its operation in statements made in sales brochures or advertisements in sales of first-hand residential properties.

A statement

If one claims that she has been misled by a statement made by the developer to enter the agreement for sale and purchase, the court will first decide whether the statement amounts to a *representation*. If in the court's opinion the statement is too vague or too general to imply any suggestion, it will not attach any contractual effect to the statement, even if the statement is enticing *per se*. In *Dimmock v Hallett*, the court found that a statement that the land on sale was 'fertile and improvable land' was a mere puff.[7] The distinction, as remarked by Edwin Peel (2007), is between 'indiscriminate praise' on the one hand, and 'specific promises or assertions of verifiable facts' on the other. This means that a purchaser of an uncompleted flat probably cannot succeed in her claim if the statement under concern is evaluative in nature. For example, there is not much chance that statements like 'the view is fantastic', 'it's a very prestigious location', or 'the price is not high at all' would be held as misrepresentation, even if the view appears boring, the location requires a mini bus shuttle to the nearest traffic centre and the price turns out to be sky-high.

   A statement of the sort concerned here can be given either orally or in writing; and if in writing, either in words or in graphic patterns. A floor plan was held to be a misrepresentation in *Balchita Ltd v Kam Yuck Investment Co Ltd & Anor*,[8] so was a tenancy plan which gave the impression that a yard was part of the property for sale in *Green Park Properties Ltd v Dorku Ltd*.[9] In *Cheng Kwok Fai v Mok Yiu Wah Peter*, a sketch drawn by a real estate agent showing the area as 950 square feet (of a flat in fact only 846 square feet) was also held to be a misrepresentation.[10]

A statement of fact

If it is a statement, the court then needs to consider whether it is *a statement of fact*, or *a statement of opinion or belief*, for only a statement of fact can contain a positive assertion that the fact is true.

   In *Bisset v Wilkinson*,[11] Bisset, who intended to sell some land to Wilkinson, made a statement that 'the land had a carrying capacity of 2000 sheep'. The Privy Council held that the statement was not actionable, as a statement of *belief* rather than of *fact*. In reaching the decision the Privy Council gave special consideration to the fact that both parties were aware at the time of contracting that the appellant had never carried on sheep-farming upon the land in question.[12] The court would otherwise hold the statement as of a fact if such statement was made 'by an owner who has been occupying his own farm'.[13] This is to be contrasted with *Smith v Land & House Property Corporation*, where a statement that the hotel on sale was let to a 'most desirable tenant' was held to be a statement of fact. The judge noted that the relation between the landlord and tenant was a fact known by the statement maker but unknown to the other party. Bowen LJ said: 'if the facts are not equally known to both sides, then a statement of opinion by the one who knows the facts best involves very often a statement of a material fact, for he impliedly states that he knows facts which justify his opinion.'[14] In *Esso Petroleum Co Ltd v Mardon*, emphasis was given to 'special knowledge or skill possessed by the man who made the statement' by Lord Denning as a key factor in determining whether it was a statement of fact or a statement of opinion.[15]

In the pre-contract negotiations of a pre-sale between a developer and a purchaser, the developer is the party who professes special knowledge of the development and the sale; to a lesser extent so are estate agents. Thus a representation about the property or the sale by developers and agents is very likely to be held as a statement of fact at common law.

A statement of an existing fact

As a general rule, the statement must refer to a fact which exists at the time the statement is made; as pointed out by *Treitel on the Law of Contract*, 'representation as to the future does not, of itself, give rise to any cause of action unless it is binding as a contract' (Peel 2007). This is the trickiest part of applying the doctrine to off-plan sales, for many statements may be made when the development concerned is still in construction – i.e. about a physical entity which does not exist at the time the statement is made.

Balchita Ltd v Kam Yuck Investment Co Ltd & Anor concerned a sale of uncompleted shops in the early 1980s in Hong Kong.[16] In that case the property in question was on the ground floor. The sales brochure was issued *after* the construction of the ground floor was completed. The ground floor plan contained in the brochure was considered as misleading by the judge. Kempster J concluded that the ground floor plan was a representation as to an existing fact.[17] Would the outcome of the case have been different if the sales brochure was issued *before* the construction of the floor under concern was completed? Does this imply that the common law will not regard a misleading floor plan in a sales brochure a statement of existing fact if by the time the sales brochure is issued (e.g. the date it is made available to the public as under section 25 of the *Ordinance*) the floor concerned was still 'in the air'?

Three decades ago, the House of Lords held in *British Airways Board v Taylor* that 'an assertion of existing fact and a promise of future conduct may be found in one and the same statement'.[18] In 2002, a developer in England was held liable under the *Property Misdescriptions Act* for making a misleading statement of an existing fact by displaying and showing purchasers a picture of a townhouse on the wall of its site office which exhibited features different from the ones planned to be built. As Simon Brown LJ concluded:

[i]t seems quite obvious that by showing prospective purchasers pictures of a Maidstone design and the show house itself, the respondents were stating that that was how they proposed to build the houses. That, in other words, was their present intention and so far as they knew nothing stood in the way of it.[19]

Recent developments in English law shows a tendency to include statements as to the future into the operation of the doctrine. In *BskyB Ltd v HP Enterprise Services UK Ltd*, one supplier gave over-optimistic opinions about its ability to deliver a project on tendering for it; the supplier won the project but failed to complete the project by the deadline; the court ruled that the supplier should be liable for misrepresentation if it did not carry out a proper analysis of the time needed to complete the project or had no reasonable grounds for the timeline put forward.[20]

The latest development in case law in Hong Kong may suggest a totally different perspective. In *Yang Dandan v Hong Kong Resort Co. Ltd*, the statement of '*Mid-rise Residential Development Area Under Planning*' (or in Chinese, '籌劃中中座發展項目') was held by Hon Kwan JA in the Court of Appeal as 'not a statement of present fact but of future intention' for 'It concerned a development under planning and not yet materialized', where the Judge reiterated that 'A statement of future intention is not an actionable misrepresentation'.[21]

It is noteworthy that the Court of First Instance expressed the view that the plaintiff might have a stronger case if she could formulate her case to be a fraudulent or reckless misrepresentation of the *present* intention of the developer.[22] This implies that the Court could hold the developer liable for misrepresentation if the plaintiff argues that the statement is not a true reflection of its then *present belief or plan* for its future conduct, i.e., to build a high-rise development.

Falsity

Falsity remained a most critical yet perhaps least illustrated requirement by the case law until perhaps the case of *Yang Dandan v Hong Kong Resort Company Limited*.

To start with, the representation must be untrue to be actionable in contract law.[23] But little has been elaborated in case law on what amounts to a *false* statement, in particular, whether a misleading statement is a false statement. A crucial difference between the doctrine of misrepresentation on the one hand and the repealed UK *Property Misdescriptions Act 1991* (the *PMA*) and *The Consumer Protection from Unfair Trading Regulations 2008* (the *CPUTR*) on the other, is that the doctrine of misrepresentation operates only upon *false* statements, whereas the *PMA* and *CPUTR* catch both *false* and *misleading* statements (or behaviours). While it can be said that all untrue statements are misleading, the reverse of the statement, i.e., all misleading statements are untrue, is not true. There seems to be a grey area out of the reach of the common law doctrine of misrepresentation: statements which are not false but just ambiguous, i.e. partially true or misleading.

For example, in *Chan Yeuk Yu & Another v Church Body of the Hong Kong Sheng Kung Hui & Another*, the express representation in the sales brochure of a luxury flat development, Deer Hill Villas in Tai Po, advertised the area in the vicinity of the development as 'regal surroundings for the select few'. These words occupied a single page 'in a very expensive looking and glossy brochure'. Burrell J ruled that the words were not misleading or exaggerating:

> [T]he 'select few' is plainly a reference to the small number of people who have $20–$30m to spend on a residential flat. The 'regal surroundings', equally plainly, is a reference to the atmosphere intended to be created when being in the entire development. The plaintiffs do not contend it should be like a palace for royalty but that by the use of such words the property, by implication, would be constructed to a very high standard of luxury.[24]

It has long been debated in academia that the tellers of *half-truths* may be held liable for misrepresentation. In *Nottingham Patent Brick and Tile v Butler*, the statement by the solicitor acting for the vendor of a property (where restrictive covenants affected the land but not to the solicitor's knowledge, who had failed to check the position) that 'he was not aware of any restrictive covenants affecting the land under negotiation' was held to be a misrepresentation and the purchaser was entitled to rescind the agreement.[25] Two modern comments on the case provide insightful observations to the outcome of the case and the rule regarding half-truths. According to Mindy Chen-Wishart (2010), the solicitor was liable because he failed to add that the reason he was not aware of any restrictive covenants was because he had not bothered to check; in these circumstances even if what he said was literally true, he omitted important qualifications which distorted the representee's assessment of the proper weight to be attached to the statement: in other words, he failed to make clear that the implication (that the property under negotiation was free of any restrictive covenants) which was likely to be drawn by the purchaser could not in fact be drawn. According to the Law Commission and the Scottish Law Commission of the United Kingdom, the solicitor's representation though literally true was misleading and false as a whole, for it implied that the solicitor had at least checked whereas he had not: a half-truth carries the implication that the rest of what the defendant knows (and that he has omitted to say) does not invalidate what was said. It is this omission that makes what was actually said false (LCUK & SLC 2011).

Meanwhile, the English law offers the view that ambiguity will probably not save a statement from being untrue. In *The Siboen and the Sibotre*, a statement made so ambiguously that a reasonable person would extract from it a meaning which was untrue to the knowledge of the maker of the statement was held to be a fraudulent misrepresentation, even if on the true construction the statement bore a meaning that was true (Peel 2007).[26]

Finally in 2015 and in 2016, the issue of *falsity* in the sale of first-hand residential properties has been thoroughly discussed in the case of *Yang Dandan v Hong Kong Resort Co. Ltd.* In that case, the sales brochure of the *Chianti* (Author: the sale of the *Chianti* took place in 2008 and it was until 2009 that promotional materials were required for the first time to be excluded from the contents of the sales brochure, see previous chapter) contains various graphic and verbal statements as to the sea view of the development such as '*Premium Waterfront Residence at Discovery Bay*' (or in Chinese, '矜貴愉景灣稀世海隅豪宅').[27] Among all these statements, two statements, if viewed together, may imply a height difference between the development on sale on one hand (named by the vendor as '*Chianti*') and the development under planning on the other (later named by the vendor as '*Amalfi*'): one, '*Chianti, five blocks of waterfront high-rises*' (or in Chinese, '尚堤5幢臨海大宅'), which is to be contrasted with another statement '*Mid-rise Residential Development Area Under Planning*' (or in Chinese, '籌劃中中座發展項目'). When the construction of the *Amalfi* was completed, *Amalfi* turned out to be of almost the same height as the *Chianti*, as part of the sea view previously enjoyed by the owner of a duplex on the top two floors of the *Chianti* were obstructed by the *Amalfi*. Then the counsel for the owner argued that in this case at least one of the two statements must be untrue, as 'A reasonable-minded reader of the brochure in the position of the Plaintiff would understand that there was a significant enough contrast in heights between the buildings in Chianti and those in Phase 14 with the use of the contrasting descriptions "high-rises" and "mid-rise residential development", otherwise the difference of descriptions serve no sensible purpose.'[28]

However, either the Court of First Instance or the Court of Appeal held any of the two statements were *untrue*. The judge of the Court of First Instance held that a statement, when enclosed in the sales brochure, must be interpreted in the context of the entire sales brochure. The Judge then paid attention to two disclaimers on the same page of the statement: '*Mid-rise Residential Development Area under Planning*', which say that 'all information and photos are for reference only' and that 'the developer reserves the right to make modifications and changes to the future development without prior notice'. Then, to interpret the statement in the context of the page, the Judge arrived at the conclusion that 'The disclaimers in the Brochure were so clear that a reasonable reader of the Brochure even with lesser commercial and education background could not possibly regard the Amalfi's Description as any definitive statement of fact'.[29]

At the Court of Appeal, when considering whether the statements were true or false, Hon Kwan JA distinguished the statements from their implication:

> Assuming that the Amalfi Description ('Mid-rise Residential Development Area Under Planning') would convey to a reasonable person in the position of the plaintiff (a highly educated person who knew that the Property is on the 16th and 17th storeys of Block 5) there would be a difference in height between a mid-rise development (Amalfi) and a high-rise development (Chianti), it is a quantum leap to deduce from this that (1) the difference in height would be significant or sufficiently significant; or (2) the sea view would not be obstructed (this would depend on a number of factors including the orientation of the unit, the relative distance of the unit from the mid-rise development under planning, the topography of the sites); or (3) there would

be unobstructed sea view continuously in future (there was nothing in the advertisements or the Brochure to suggest permanence of any view, as accepted by the plaintiff [25]).[30]

A similar view was expressed by the Court of First Instance below when the Judge observes that 'Even without the disclaimers and the uncertainty element of the Amalfi's Description, in my view, a high-rise building is not necessarily significantly taller than a mid-rise building. Even if there is a significant difference in height, which in itself is not amenable to exact definition, it is possible that the sea view of a high-rise building could still be obstructed by a mid-rise building. It very much depends on the relative distance between the harbor/sea and the buildings'.[31]

As such, the Courts concluded that the statements, despite the *high-rise* and *mid-rise* contrast, are not false (and therefore no actionable misrepresentation). This is a critical finding that we shall revisit in the later discussion of this chapter on misrepresentation under the *Ordinance*.

Materiality

The statement in question cannot be a misrepresentation at common law if it is not material: it should have influenced the other person in such a way that her judgement on whether and on what terms to enter into the contract was affected by the statement; or that she entered into the contract without making inquiries which she would have otherwise made if she hadn't been influenced by the statement (Peel 2007).

One Hong Kong case has illustrated the requirement of materiality in property transactions. *Green Park Properties Ltd v Dorku Ltd* concerns a sale of a shop over 2,000 sq. ft. with a back yard of about 72 sq. ft.[32] The yard was part of the common area of the building but the tenancy plan gave the impression that the yard was part of the property. In the Court of First Instance, Cheung J concluded that the representation was material, even though the yard made up only approximately 3 per cent of the contract value. The judge, believing that every part of a property has value to its owner, found that the yard appeared to form part of the property to be sold and that it affected the overall size and value of the property. Similarly, in *Donnelly v Weybridge Construction Ltd (No.2)*, a case concerning an off-plan sale in London, the presentation of limestone flooring throughout the flats in advertisements was held an actionable misdescription, even though the item was worth less than 5 per cent of the value of the flat.[33]

In *Balchita Ltd v Kam Yuck Investment Co Ltd & Anor*, the court regarded as material a graphic representation suggesting that the shops for sale were at street level but in fact they were below street level, as 'differences in level materially affected the description and value of the shops in question'.[34]

Inducement

In *Win Wave Industrial Ltd v Gosbon Industries Ltd & Ors*, a false statement was made about the permitted use of the property. Leung J concluded that the statement was an inducement to the purchaser, after accepting the purchaser's claim that 'if she had known that the user of the property was still restricted to a bowling centre, she would not have committed to the deal'.[35] In *Balchita Ltd v Kam Yuck Investment Co Ltd & Anor*, dotted lines were used by the vendor to imply stairs in the floor plan; the judge observed that 'The probability of the dotted lines indicating staircases was less than the probability that they indicated concealed or overhanging objects or other objects outside the ground floor area.' Thus the ground floor plan was an inducement to the plaintiff to sign the sale agreement, which the plaintiff was then entitled to rescind. In reaching this conclusion, the judge was satisfied that the plaintiff would not have entered into the provisional agreement for sale and purchase if he had appreciated that the dotted lines in question indicated staircases.[36] These two cases indicate that the courts, albeit inexplicitly, seemed to adopt a *but-for* test to determine inducement: the claimant has to prove that she would not have entered into the contract *but for* the misrepresentation.

However, it is evident in another line of cases that the courts will be prepared to treat a case as easily over this hurdle if they find the misleading statement a material one. 'If it is a material representation calculated to induce him to enter into a contract, it is an inference of law that he was induced by the representation to enter into it', as stated in *Redgrave v Hurd*.[37] The spirit of this approach was observed by both the Court of First Instance and the Court of Appeal in delivering judgment in *Green Park Properties Ltd v Dorku Ltd*. In the Court of First Instance, Cheung J cited *Chitty on Contracts* to the point that 'where a person seeks to rescind a contract on the ground of misrepresentation, it is not necessary for him to prove that if the misrepresentation had not been made, he would not have made the contract; it is sufficient if there is evidence to show that it was materially influenced by the misrepresentation.'[38] In the Court of Appeal, Le Pichon JA, citing *Smith v Chadwick*, indicated that 'once it is proved that a false statement was made which was likely to induce the contract, and that the representee entered the contract, it is a fair inference of fact (though not an inference of law) that he was influenced by the statement.'[39]

Reliance

A purchaser's reliance on the representation is closely associated with the nature of the representation as an inducement. The flow of arguments in most judgments suggests that the requirements to prove *inducement* and *reliance* are in fact not two but one.[40] Reliance is genuinely proved if the representation has induced the purchaser to enter into the agreement with the seller (Peel 2007).[41] However, three scenarios will vitiate reliance, viz. that the purchaser possessed knowledge of the real facts/truth; that the purchaser would have entered into the contract even if she had known the truth; or that she relied on her own information.[42] Showing reliance is not necessary in case of fraud.[43]

In *Yang Dandan v Hong Kong Resort Company Limited*, the Court of Appeal held that there was indeed no reliance by the owner of the duplex at the top floor of *Chianti* on the statement of the 'Mid-rise Residential Development Area Under Planning', where the Court suggested that reliance must be objectively assessed from the perspective of a reasonable person, i.e., 'what a reasonable person would have understood from the words used by looking at the nature and content of the statement, the context in which it was made, the characteristics of the maker and the person to whom it was made, and the relationship between them'. Weighty consideration was given to the disclaimers, i.e., statements to remind the reader that 'all information and photos are for reference only' and that 'the developer reserves the right to make modifications and changes to the future development without prior notice'. The Court held that in the circumstances a reasonable person was not entitled to rely on the statement. As per Hon Kwan JA: 'Where the statement is accompanied by a qualification or explanation, this may indicate to a reasonable person that the representor was not assuming responsibility for the accuracy or completeness of the statement or was saying no reliance can be placed on it.'[44]

Fraud and negligence

Hong Kong law makes a distinction between misrepresentations that are made fraudulently and those made negligently or innocently. Fraud is proved when it is shown that a false representation has been made *knowingly* or *without belief in its truth* or *recklessly, careless (as to) whether it be true or false*. The motive of the maker of the fraudulent statement is immaterial, nor is the fact whether the purchaser had relied on the representation.[45] The claimants are entitled to rescind the contract and claim damages in tort for deceit for any loss directly flowing from the fraud (even if the loss could not have been foreseen).[46]

On the other hand, a negligent misrepresentation involves a statement not made fraudulently but carelessly. English law recognizes a common law duty of care in the tort of negligence which can be owed by a person who makes a statement then reasonably relied on by the other party to take reasonable care that the representation is accurate and to be liable in damages for resulting losses. This was established in *Hedley Byrne & Co Ltd v Heller & Partners Ltd.*[47] This duty of care often arises where the representor acts in a professional capacity and/or the statement or representation was made for a particular purpose; in other words, there is a special relationship as between the maker of the statement and the person to whom the statement is made. And it is not necessary that the two parties are in a contractual relationship (Peel 2007).

There are two causes of actions for negligent misrepresentation: one arises from the breach of a duty of care under common law; the other is a statutory cause of action under section 3(1) of the *Misrepresentation Ordinance* (Cap 284) (the *MO*). At common law, the burden of proof lies on the shoulders of the claimant to prove that the statement was false and had induced her to enter into the contract. Having proved that, the claimant is entitled to rescind the contract and recover all the damages the kind of which is *reasonably foreseeable* arising from the breach of duty.[48] The basis on which damages are assessed is to put the victim of the statement into a position in which she would have been had the representation not been made.

The *Misrepresentation Ordinance* is not a statutory codification of the common law rules on misrepresentation. The better view is to see it as a parallel vehicle with distinctive qualities of its own. Section 3(1) of the *Misrepresentation Ordinance* provides a more *purchaser-friendly* route to claim damages for negligent misrepresentation. Under section 3(1), liability occurs as long as the following two conditions are met: first, a misstatement is made; second, the representor and the representee are in a contractual relationship. There is no requirement of any *special relationship*; whether the purchaser has relied on her own judgement or has been advised by her own experts is irrelevant, so is whether it is reasonable for the representor to assume that the purchaser has been backed up by her own professional advice. Then, for some cases, where no duty of care at common law, liability can rise under the *Misrepresentation Ordinance* even if it is hard to establish a *Hedley Byrne* duty of care at common law (Peel 2007).

As such, the *Misrepresentation Ordinance* has a slightly broader application than the common law doctrine. It well fits with sales of first-hand residential properties: a developer could be made liable for a misstatement even if the statement is made by her agents.[49] At the same time, despite the fact that agents employed by developers solicit and escort purchasers during the sales campaign without entering into an agency agreement with any prospective purchasers and that they collect commission from developers only, there is an established contractual relationship between the agents and the prospective purchasers. Thus purchasers can sue the agents for misrepresentation under section 3(1) of the *Misrepresentation Ordinance*.

The statute also reverses the burden of proof: at common law the purchaser must prove that she has relied on the statement to enter into the contract; whereas under the *Misrepresentation Ordinance*, the maker of the statement will be liable unless she can prove that she had reasonable grounds to believe and did believe up to the time the contract was made that the facts represented were true.

If a misrepresentation is established under the *Misrepresentation Ordinance*, section 3(1) enables the misrepresentee to recover all the losses, even if those losses were unforeseeable, provided that they were not otherwise too remote: i.e., all losses flowing from the misrepresentation.[50] Consequential losses are also recoverable under section 3(1).[51] The purchaser is also entitled to rescind the contract. In addition, on a discretionary basis damages may be awarded in lieu of rescission under section 3(2) if the court or arbitrator found it equitable that the contract subsists, having regard to the nature of the misrepresentation and the loss that would be caused by it if the contract were upheld, as well as to the loss that rescission would cause to the other party.[52]

As indicated by *Yang Dandan v Hong Kong Resort Company Limited*, the degree of *purchaser-friendly* by the *Misrepresentation Ordinance* appears to be limited for flat purchasers. As discussed earlier, the plaintiff failed to establish misrepresentation under section 3(1) of the *Misrepresentation Ordinance* due to the high threshold of the requirement of falsity.

Common law sometimes makes a further distinction between *negligent misrepresentation* and *innocent misrepresentation*. An innocent misrepresentation is one which is neither fraudulent nor negligent. The case *Derry v Peek* indicates that the court will consider the misrepresentation as being innocent if it is convinced that the representor had reasonable grounds for believing her false statement was true.[53]

Entire agreement clause and disclaimer

In commercial practices, statements can and often are given in pre-contractual negotiations which may lead up to the conclusion of the contract. The doctrine of misrepresentation provides that these statements are actionable if they meet the conditions of falsity, materiality, inducement and reliance. But vendors, who are aware of the risk of misrepresentation yet nevertheless enthusiastic in advertising and promoting the properties, may later insert a term into the agreement suggesting that the agreement for sale and purchase supersedes all prior representations, in order to exempt themselves from any liability for making the statements. For example, in *Green Park Properties Ltd v Dorku Ltd*, clause 12 of the provisional agreement for sales and purchase said: 'This agreement supersedes all prior negotiations, representation, understanding and agreements of the parties hereto.' The clause is sometimes called an '*entire agreement clause*'. Section 4 of the *Misrepresentation Ordinance* provides that such a term shall be of no effect except in so far as it satisfies the 'requirement of reasonableness' as stated in section 3(1) of the *Control of Exemption Clauses Ordinance (Cap 71)* that the term was a *fair* and *reasonable* one. Clause 12 was held to be of no effect in *Green Park Properties Ltd v Dorku Ltd* by Cheung J in the Court of First Instance, who found the vendor knew that the yard was 'not included as part of the property' but, without advising the agents of the fact in advance, nevertheless allowed the agents to show the property to the purchasers.[54] In the Court of Final Appeal, Litton NPJ said:

> the reasonableness test is satisfied if the judge concludes that the term was fair and reasonable having regard to the circumstances which were, or ought reasonably to have been, known to or in the contemplation of the parties when the agreement was made. What might those circumstances be? In this case they would include the circumstances surrounding real estate dealings in Hong Kong known to both parties bearing on whether it was fair and reasonable for a term like cl.12 to be included in a standard form of provisional agreement put forward by real estate agents for the parties.[55]

In *Win Wave Industrial Ltd v Gosbon Industries Ltd & Ors*, a similar clause (Cl 13) was inserted into the agreement for sale and purchase: it 'superseded all prior negotiations, representation, understanding and agreements of the parties'. In that case, the vendor, who told the purchaser that the property was for commercial use, did not disclose that the property was actually restricted to use as a bowling centre. The court found the statement by the vendor a fraudulent misrepresentation, and 'once fraudulent misrepresentation is established on the part of a party to the agreement, that party cannot rely on an entire agreement clause like the present one'.[56]

An opposite view on the reasonableness of entire agreement clause was expressed by Gerald Godfrey in *Cheng Kwok Fai v Mok Yiu Wah Peter*. In this case the agreement for sale and purchase contained clause 20: 'This agreement sets out the full agreement between the parties. No warranties or representations express or implied are or have been made or given by the vendor or by any person on his behalf relating to the property or to the user thereof or the possibility of any redevelopment thereof and if any warranty or representation express or implied has been made the same is withdrawn or deemed to have been withdrawn immediately before the parties entered into this agreement unless made in writing and expressed to survive this agreement.' Gerald Godfrey expressed the view that even if the court held the vendor liable for the misrepresentation of the agent (which the court did not) the vendor could still rely on the clause, because the purchaser relied entirely on the sketch of the property supplied by the agent who was acting for both parties; the vendor, on the other hand, did not do anything to mislead the purchaser. Note that such a view was against the background that the purchaser could have arranged for the flat to be measured or insisted on having a statement about its area incorporated into the contract.[57]

Misrepresentation by estate agents

The pre-contract negotiation of sales of uncompleted flats usually involves three parties: the vendor (developer), the purchaser and the estate agents. Statements can be made directly by the vendor to the purchaser; but they can also be passed to the purchaser from the agent on behalf of the developer – either orally, by conduct or in written form such as pamphlets printed by agents based on the information and design of the sales brochures published by developers. The tri-party situation gives rise to three questions. First, if a misleading statement is made by the developer and passed to the purchaser by the agent, will the developer be liable for this misrepresentation? Second, will the agent be held liable? Third, if the agent made a misstatement on her own, would the developer in this case be held liable for it?

The first question is answered in *Pilmore v Hood*. A vendor of a public house made a false statement that the pub made £180 a month; the statement was made only to one interested purchaser, who passed the statement to the end purchaser, by whom the statement on the receipts of the pub was acted upon. In the case the court found that the vendor was on (*constructive – by the author*) notice of the fact that the statement that he fraudulently made to the intended purchaser had been passed to the real purchaser. Lord Tyndal, considering such notice to the vendor was 'an important ingredient in the case', remarked that: 'We decide that he is responsible in this case for the consequences of his fraud, whilst the instrument was in the possession of a person to whom his representation was either directly or indirectly communicated, and for whose use he knew it was purchased.'[58]

In contrast, a vendor of a complex with hundreds of units and the agents who are engaged in the sale stand much closer to the prospective purchasers than a vendor of one public house and one purchaser in between. In these mega pre-sales that happen once or twice a month in Hong Kong, the agents are the professional propagandists employed by developers to market the projects; they are coached by the developers in terms of selling points of the development. Many a statement made by the agents are created and intended by the developers. Applying *Pilmore v Hood* to sales practices in Hong Kong, developers are responsible for misleading statements made by agents, as it is not difficult to establish that developers have actual or constructive notice of the fact that the statements are communicated to the prospective purchasers via estate agents. According to Edwin Peel (2007), contract law will make the maker of the statement liable even if she did not make the statement directly to the person who later contracted with her, as long as she *intended* to bring the result to the contracting party.[59] As such, if developers distribute training materials to agents which contain exaggerated statements and the agents then distribute these materials to prospective purchasers, with or without other authorized materials produced by developers, developers may be held liable for misrepresentation at common law if they do not effectively prevent agents from distributing these materials.

Then, should the agents be liable for the misstatements they pass to the prospective purchasers that were originally made by developers? *Win Wave Industrial Ltd v Gosbon Industries Ltd & Ors* dealt with a sale of a property which used to be a bowling centre, where the agents acting for the vendor Gosbon told the representatives of the purchaser 'the property could be converted from bowling alley use to general commercial use; the property could be used for restaurants, clubs, supermarkets and fitness clubs in the future'. These statements were originally given by Gosbon to the agents. At the time, Gosbon's application to change of user of the property had yet to be approved: the property could not be used for general commercial purposes right away. In that case the agent Miss Leung called the vendor to confirm whether the user had been changed. She got an affirmative answer and some documents, including a letter from the District Lands Office stating that the District Lands Office had no objection to the application for change of user. Then the agent made the same representations to the purchaser Win Wave. The court found that the situation gave rise to a duty of care owed by the agents to the purchaser, even though strictly speaking, they were only agents for the vendor, because in passing the information to the purchaser, they knew or ought to have known that the purchaser was relying on their experience and skill to pass on accurate and reliable information about the property. The agents were held liable for Gosbon's fraudulent misrepresentation and therefore vicariously responsible for Win Wave's loss.[60]

The yardstick is high against which the reasonable care and skill expected of a licensed estate agent is measured. There is no absolute immunity to be granted to a professional agent in case of misrepresentation originally made by the vendor. Agents who wish to be immune from the developer's statements have to ensure that the information they pass to the prospective purchasers is accurate and reliable. If the court regards the statement as false, the tendency to hold agents liable is compelling.

An even more difficult question arises where a misstatement is created and made to a potential purchaser by an agent. Will the developer, who is neither the creator nor the passer-on of the statement, be liable for the statement? Although developers are seen to be the source of many misleading statements, particularly those enclosed in the sales brochure, advertisement and show flats, a large number of oral misstatements owe their origin to the agents, who are as eager as the developers to close the deal. In these cases the agents are undoubtedly liable, but will their exaggerated descriptions affect the developers?

In this scenario the current outcome in Hong Kong law appears highly fact-specific. Developers will be affected if the court finds that the agent is acting as the agent of the vendor for the purpose of making representations (no matter whether the agent is engaged by the vendor or by the purchaser or in a dual agency situation). The authority is the celebrated judgment of *Cheng Kwok Fai v Mok Yiu Wah Peter*, in which Gerald Godfrey with striking clarity 'dissected the issue to the bone'.[61] He first contrasted the position of an estate agent in Hong Kong with that of one in England, where he said that 'An agent in Hong Kong acts as a broker', because here in Hong Kong agents bring together the vendor and purchaser and take commission from one or both of them. Then he stated the general rule of Hong Kong law regarding the vendor's liability for a misleading statement made by the agents: 'No doubt, in some cases even in Hong Kong, a misrepresentation made by an agent to a purchaser will, on the facts, be held to have been made on the vendor's behalf.' He went on to consider the facts, where the purchaser had relied on a sketch supplied by the agent suggesting that the flat was 950 square feet. He held that:

> [T]hey had not given the agent any actual authority to represent to the purchaser that its area was 950 sq. ft. or to produce the sketch to him. Nor, in my judgment, did they confer on the agent, merely by appointing it to act as their agent for the purpose of selling the flat, any apparent (or ostensible) authority to supply the purchaser with the sketch, not from any document given to the agent by the vendors, but from the agent's own records. In my judgment, when the purchaser asked the agent for a plan and was supplied with one from the agent's own records, the agent was acting on behalf of the purchaser, not the vendors.[62]

Gerald Godfrey stressed that the court should not get lost in the contractual relationship between the vendor, purchaser and agents, but instead should investigate what had happened in order to determine the source of the statement. The *ratio* was then applied in a case concerning misrepresentation on a stigmatized flat in *Jopard Holdings Ltd v Ladefaith Ltd & Anor*, where Recorder B Yu SC reaffirmed that 'whether a misrepresentation made by an agent to a purchaser will be held to have been made on the vendor's behalf is essentially a question of fact'.[63]

Misrepresentation as a cause of action

The cases cited above prove how the concept of misrepresentation can successfully provide remedies to purchasers in Hong Kong: the courts adopt a generally supportive approach to the more vulnerable party, i.e. the property purchaser, the tenant, the misrepresentee. All in all, the doctrine of misrepresentation offers four possible causes of actions for a flat purchaser to seek redress for misstatements made by developers and real estate agents: (a) fraudulent misrepresentation; (b) negligent misrepresentation at common law; (c) negligent misrepresentation under the *Misrepresentation Ordinance*; and (d) innocent misrepresentation.

But in order to make a successful claim, the purchaser has to prove that the statement is untrue, factual, material, relied upon and has induced her to enter into the agreement. At the same time, as discussed earlier, it is doubtful how much teeth this doctrine has to catch misleading statements or presentations which are not exactly untrue. Another disadvantage is its incapability of handling *omissions*. The general rule at common law is that an omission cannot count as a misrepresentation.[64] At common law, the doctrine of misrepresentation does not challenge the doctrine of *caveat emptor*, or the rule of non-disclosure. Lord Atkin described the rule in *Bell v Lever Bros Ltd* as 'the failure to disclose a material fact which might influence the mind of a prudent contractor does not give the right to avoid the contract'.[65] The doctrine of misrepresentation does not itself encourage developers to disclose any information, and if developers and agents conceal any critical information about the property or the sale, the doctrine cannot help purchasers who would claim that had they known the fact they would not have bought the flats. A third disadvantage is that it operates solely on a remedial basis: it cannot punish developers for making false or misleading statements at large; the application of the doctrine depends on claims brought by individual purchasers; the remedies may only be available for a purchaser if she goes through all the trouble to take the case to the court (and the court in the end holds in her favour).

Misrepresentation under the Ordinance

The above discussion reveals the following conclusion for the common law doctrine of misrepresentation (including the *Misrepresentation Ordinance*): firstly, it only operates on pre-contract statements of an existing fact: thus the doctrine is not helpful if a purchaser is misled by a promise or a statement regarding the future. Secondly, it only operates on pre-contract statements that are false: a statement that is not necessarily untrue will not give rise to liability of misrepresentation at common law. Thirdly, it does not exclude the principle of *caveat emptor*: the doctrine does not impose a duty on the shoulder of vendor to disclose information and therefore is not applicable in case of omission of material information. Lastly, it attaches civil liabilities for misrepresentation. The *Residential Properties (First-hand Sales) Ordinance*, on the other hand, not only smashes the spirit of *caveat emptor* into pieces by demanding compulsory information disclosure in sales brochures, price lists etc., but takes misleading commercial statements and sales description in first-hand residential property sales out of the jurisdiction of contract law by creating three offences at criminal law: (a) publishing an advertisement containing information that is false or misleading in a material particular (more discussion in Chapter 13)[66]; (b) misrepresentation[67]; and (c) dissemination of false or misleading information.[68]

Misrepresentation

The *Ordinance* makes a distinction between *fraudulent* misrepresentation and *reckless* misrepresentation. Section 75(1) recognizes three types of statement as fraudulent misrepresentation. The first is a statement that is false, misleading or deceptive to the person's knowledge when the statement is made.[69] Statements of such type may also be held as fraudulent misrepresentation at common law.

The second is a *promise* that when being made, either to the knowledge of the maker of the promise it is incapable of being fulfilled or the maker has no intention of fulfilling the promise.[70] This remarkably extends the range of statements from being a statement of existing fact under common law to statements as to the future and statements of intention.

In *Yang Dandan v Hong Kong Resort Company Limited*, the statement that suggested the *Amalfi* would be a mid-rise development is held as a statement of future fact or intention. Hon Kwan JA held that such a statement 'is simply a prediction or a promise, not a representation' and 'if one party wishes to hold the other liable in the event that the prediction is not borne out by the facts as the future finds them or if the promise is not kept, the remedy at law is not in pre-contractual misrepresentation'.[71] In this regard, with the *Ordinance*'s explicit inclusion of the word *promise*, it seems what cannot be caught as misrepresentation at common law, i.e., a *promise* (which is common in the form of description of planning intention in first-hand sales of residential properties) will now, in case of applicability, be caught by section 75(1).

In this regard reference shall be made to a similar provision in the *Property Misdescription Act* (the *PMA*). Research on the *PMA* suggests that a developer might constitute an offence under the PMA if she has been shown in the sales brochure that the estate or apartments will have an uninterrupted sea view but fails to mention that planning permission has been given for development which upon completion of construction may obliterate the view (Goo 2010).

The third recognized type of statement by the new legislation fills a gap in the common law. The *Ordinance* extends criminal liability to statements which are traditionally recognized as non-actionable *omissions*, treating a statement as

244 Refalse or misleading information

fraudulent if the maker intentionally omits a material fact from the statement and as a result the statement is rendered false, misleading or deceptive.[72] This sub-section alone puts the provision in a much more helpful position to purchasers than that of the doctrine of misrepresentation: the latter is incapable of bypassing the rule of non-disclosure to provide any remedies for purchasers misled by silence or omission. Under this limb of the rule, developers will be liable for misrepresentation if they conceal a negative environmental feature in an artistic illustration of the environment.

Additionally, section 75(2) recognizes statements that are made recklessly as potentially actionable misrepresentations.[73] A reckless misrepresentation is a *statement* that is false, misleading or deceptive; or a *promise* that is incapable of being fulfilled; or being a statement when made the person who makes the statement recklessly omits a material fact from the statement, rendering the statement false, misleading or deceptive. This offence has an even lower threshold than that of fraudulent misrepresentation: neither the *knowledge* nor the *intention* of the maker is relevant. The key is to show that the statement is false, misleading or deceptive. In order to prosecute a developer, this is indeed the easiest route. The only thing the prosecution needs to prove would be *inducement* under section 76(1).

Although a clear distinction is made by the *Ordinance* between a fraudulent misrepresentation and a reckless misrepresentation, the legislation does not elaborate on the difference between the two. Misunderstanding the difference may cause certain confusion, especially when a cross-reference is made to the common law doctrine. At common law, a fraudulent misrepresentation is a false representation that is either knowingly untrue, or where the representor has no belief in its truth, or is reckless as to its truth.[74] Thus, according to the terminology of the common law, a fraudulent misrepresentation can be made recklessly and a reckless misrepresentation can be made fraudulently. It is therefore very helpful to distinguish the concept of 'fraudulent misrepresentation' at common law from the concept of 'fraudulent misrepresentation' as contained in section 75(1) of the *Ordinance*. Then the meaning assigned to the word 'fraudulent' and 'reckless' by the *Ordinance* must be understood in the context of the *Ordinance* itself: i.e. sections 75(1) and 75(2). The key is in the word 'intention' in section 75(1)(b) which is missing in 75(2)(b), as well as the word 'intentionally' in section 75(1) (c), missing in 75(2)(c). It is most likely that under the *Ordinance* the term 'fraudulent misrepresentation' refers to a misstatement that is intentionally made, whereas the term 'reckless misrepresentation' a misstatement that is recklessly made. To translate into the language of common law, therefore, a 'reckless misrepresentation' under the *Ordinance* refers to a 'fraudulent misrepresentation that is made recklessly'.

The subtle difference between the concepts of 'fraudulent misrepresentation' and 'reckless misrepresentation' may suggest that both sections 75(1) and 75(2) can simultaneously be relevant to the making of a single statement.

Then section 76(1) provides that it is *an offence* to make a fraudulent misrepresentation under section 75(1) or a reckless misrepresentation under section 75(2) for the purpose of inducing another person to purchase any specified residential property. According to section 76(2), a person will be liable on conviction on indictment to a fine of HK$ 5,000,000 and to imprisonment for seven years or on summary conviction to a fine of HK$ 1,000,000 and to imprisonment for three years if the court is satisfied that the fraudulent misrepresentation or the reckless misrepresentation was made for the purpose of inducing another person to purchase any specified residential property.[75]

In case of successful prosecutions, the penalties imposed by section 76 will be levied by the government. This raises the issue of compensation for the victims of the misrepresentation: the purchasers. In this sense the draft *Bill* (HTB 2011) which concerned criminal liability for misrepresentation only (i.e., Clause 55 in Part 4) was *incomplete* for introducing the offence of misrepresentation without providing any remedies for purchasers. Such omission essentially resembles the position under the now repealed *PMA*, whose major weakness was considered as not providing a civil remedy (Goo 2010).

The deficiency of the draft *Bill* was spotted by the Bills Committee (LC 2012), who demonstrated much sympathy and a clear view that the maker of the misrepresentation should not only bear criminal liability but also be made liable, under the legislation, for any pecuniary loss the purchaser has sustained as a result of reliance on a misrepresentation. Section 77 entitled 'Misrepresentation: civil liability' is added to the *Ordinance*, which sets out the civil liability of the person who makes the misrepresentation: i.e., pay compensation by way of damages to the other person for any pecuniary loss that the other person has sustained as a result of reliance by the other person on the misrepresentation.[76] Section 77(3) further provides that the purchaser can assert civil liability under section 77 even if the maker of the statement has not been charged with or convicted of an offence under section 76(1).

The meaning of misrepresentation at common law and under the Ordinance

What amounts to misrepresentation? Now the common law and the *Ordinance* have given different answers.

With the discussion on the element of falsity above, the following conclusion could be drawn from the 2016 decision in *Yang Dandan v Hong Kong Resort Company Limited* that to establish misrepresentation at common law, the statement enclosed in the sales brochure or advertisement, viewed from the entire sales brochure or advertisement, must be untrue. The contrast brought by the words *mid-rise* and *high-rises* adopted in the statements in the sales brochure of *Chianti* did not in the opinion of the Courts render the statement as untrue, for a development described as high-rise does not have to be necessarily significantly taller than one described as mid-rise.[77] As such, there is no actionable misrepresentation under common law, for the requirement of falsity is not met.

The *Yang Dandan* case has shown the degree of difficulty in convincing the Courts that a statement enclosed in the sales literature is untrue. But a statement which is not completely false – perhaps because of the vogue wording or the disclaimers – may still have the potential to mislead a purchaser, inter alia, *misleading*. It is indeed more difficult to prove the statement is false than to prove the statement is, simply, misleading. As evident in the 2016 court decision, the common law rule seems to suggest that misrepresentation applies to *false* statements only, and such position is not yet to be expanded to include misleading statements, at least not by the Courts in Hong Kong. As such, what the judges did not discuss in the case is whether the use of the words mid-rise to describe the development under planning is nevertheless misleading when, at the same time, the development on sale is described as high-rise?

In contrast, the *Ordinance* suggests a much broader scope for misrepresentation under the *Ordinance*. Section 75(1) operates on a statement that is either *false*, *misleading* or *deceptive*. The wording itself suggests that a misleading statement does not have to be false yet still could be held as misrepresentation. Thus a developer may be held liable under section 75(1) for a statement which, by the common law standard, is not untrue, but nevertheless misleading.

On a similar vein, the offence of dissemination of false or misleading information under 78(1) of the *Ordinance* (to be discussed below) as well as the offence of containing false or misleading information in advertisement under 70 of the *Ordinance* concerns both *false* information and *misleading* information.

With all these provisions ready for application to sale of first-hand residential properties after April 2013, the *Yang Dandan* case would probably have a different outcome if the sale of the *Chianti* happened after the implementation of the *Ordinance*. This is because if the case is premised on the common law doctrine, the purchaser has to prove that the statement is untrue in order to hold the vendor liable for misrepresentation; whereas if the case is premised on the *Ordinance*, the vendor will be held liable if in the opinion of the Court the statement is untrue, *or*, even not completely untrue, misleading or deceptive.

Dissemination of false or misleading information

Beyond misrepresentation itself, a person will commit an offence under section 78(1) if she disseminates, or authorizes, or is concerned in the dissemination of information which is false or misleading as to a material fact or through the omission of a material fact, provided that the material fact is likely to induce another person to purchase any specified residential property; the corresponding *mens rea* is that the person knows the information is false or misleading or is reckless as to whether the information is false or misleading.

It should be highlighted that 'the person' under sections 76(1) or 78(1) is not confined to the vendor company and its officers. It includes estate agents who may or may not be directly employed by the vendor for the sale. Beyond that, it indeed can be any person from the public.

Then the question is, whether the offence under 78(1) and the one under 76(1) are mutually exclusive. If, for example, an estate agent makes a false statement to a purchaser based on what she has been told by the vendor, will the agent commit an offence under section 78(1), i.e. disseminate or authorize the dissemination of false or misleading information, or 76(1), i.e. make a fraudulent misrepresentation or a reckless misrepresentation for the purpose of inducing another person to purchase any specified residential property, or both?

To figure out the correct answer, we need to ascertain the meaning of the words 'make' in section 76(1) and 'disseminate' in section 78(1) in the context of the *Ordinance*. The meaning of the word 'disseminate' is defined by section 78(3) as to mean *circulate* or *disclose*.[78] These two words do not just suggest 'create or invent'; they can surely refer to activities of making available something that has been created or invented by someone else. By contrast, the word 'make' conveys a strong sense of creativity and originality, i.e., an authorship of the statement. In other words, it is most likely that the *Ordinance* intends section 76(1) to apply to the maker of the statement while section 78(1) applies to the broadcaster or messenger of the statement.

The above conclusion is supported by the fact that for the offence under section 78(1) a number of defences are recognized by Part 5 of the *Ordinance* (to be discussed below) while no statutory defence is provided for the offence under section 76(1). The design indicates that the contravention of the provision under 78(1) can be excused in certain circumstances: for example, the one who disseminates or publishes may not know the contents are misleading. The one who commits an offence of *making* a fraudulent or reckless misrepresentation must know the contents are false, misleading or deceptive.

Thus an estate agent who makes a false statement to a purchaser based on what she has been told by the vendor will be most likely committing an offence under section 78(1), with the vendor being held guilty under section 76(1). This suggests that under the *Ordinance* it is no longer critical to distinguish between a misrepresentation made by the vendor via the agent and a misrepresentation made by the agent on behalf of the vendor.

On the other hand, if the agent had exaggerated a true statement originally made by the vendor into a false statement, then the agent would herself be committing an offence under section 76(1).

Under the design by the Steering Committee, 'dissemination of false or misleading information' included publishing an advertisement containing false or misleading information. This is evident from the fact that the Steering Committee only proposed two offences at the beginning: *misrepresentation* and *dissemination of false or misleading information* (Steering Committee 2011).

In the draft *Bill* (HTB 2011), however, the Transport and Housing Bureau created an independent offence of 'publishing an advertisement containing information that is false or misleading in a material particular' at clause 50, Part 3, which later became section 70 of the *Ordinance*. The significance of adding the third offence is yet to be explored when a claim set in train the potential application of sections 70 and 78 at the same time. By the end of 2016, a number of developers had been prosecuted and held guilty under section 70 but none under 78. It can be anticipated that the distinction may soon be discussed by the case law.

Capacity

Either a corporation (e.g. a developer or a subsidiary company set up by the developer to make sales) or an individual person can commit offences under the *Ordinance*. In terms of corporate crime, who may be held liable under the *Ordinance*? Section 84 provides that if, *actus reus* wise, the commission of the offence was aided, abetted, counselled, procured or induced by an officer of the corporation or of a holding company, and *mens rea* wise the offence was committed with the consent or connivance of or was attributable to any recklessness on the part of an officer, then both the officer and the corporation commit the offence. The *officer* includes director(s), secretary or manager of the company.[79]

Statutory defences

Part 5 of the *Ordinance* provides a number of defences against the charge in section 78(1), i.e. *disseminating or authorizing or being concerned in the dissemination of false or misleading information*, or section 70, i.e. *publishing or causing to be published an advertisement containing information that is false or misleading in a material particular*. For example, section 78(1) does not apply to people engaged in the printing or distribution of the sales brochure or advertisements, e.g. employees of the printing company which is commissioned by the vendor to print the sales brochure. In this case, the defence in section 81(1) will arise, i.e. the issue or reproduction of the information or advertisement takes place in the ordinary course of a business, the principal purpose of which is issuing or reproducing materials provided by others.

Given the maker of the misrepresentation must know and understand the contents of the statement when committing the offence, there is no statutory defence for the offence of making a fraudulent misrepresentation or a reckless misrepresentation for the purpose of inducing another person to purchase any specified residential property.

Time limit for prosecution of offences

Two trigger points for the prosecution period were raised and considered by the Steering Committee: *the date of commission of the offence* and *the date of discovery of the offence*. The time limit for prosecution for the former is normally three years and the latter one year. The Steering Committee (2011) decided to choose 'the date of commission of the offence' as the single trigger point. Section 85 stipulates that proceedings in respect of an offence under the *Ordinance* must be brought within three years after the commission of the offence.

Conclusion

With the full operation of the *Ordinance*, the same statement by a vendor of first-hand residential property that is regarded as misrepresentation by the common law and therefore gives the misrepresentee the right to rescind the contract may now spontaneously commit a criminal offence under the *Ordinance*.

At the same time, with the recognition of both civil liability and criminal liability for making a fraudulent misrepresentation or a reckless misrepresentation for the purpose of inducing another person to purchase any specified residential property, the *Ordinance* has expanded the common law rules on misrepresentation considerably in the specific context of first-hand sales of residential properties. It is wide-ranging in its capability of catching applications of a rich variety of false, misleading or deceptive statements which are not caught by the traditional common law rules, i.e. promises and omissions. Compared to the requirements at common law and under the *Misrepresentation Ordinance* to establish an actionable misrepresentation, section 77 – alone or together with section 76 – represents a much more straightforward cause of action for a purchaser who has relied upon a false or misleading statement made by the vendor or the estate agents in a sales brochure, advertisements, show flats, a project website or during a site visit.

It may still be a premature discussion for this edition of this book on this part of the legislation, as by the time the final transcript for publication was prepared, no vendor had been convicted of an offence under section 76 or section 78 or held liable under section 77. This fact may suggest that, with the creation of offence of misrepresentation and other likely offences, the *Ordinance* has exhibited a high level of deterrent effect. At the same time, the 2016 Court of Appeal decision in *Yang Dandan v Hong Kong Resort Co Ltd* has timely confirmed that the common law doctrine of misrepresentation appears to be out of reach for an annoyed purchaser of first-hand residential properties due to the high threshold of the requirement of falsity. Although the new legislation is not discussed in the judgments by either the Court of First Instance or the Court of Appeal (as the sale took place before the commencement of the *Ordinance*), the difficulty the Courts encountered in holding the statements as misrepresentation at common law however seems to suggest an unparalleled advantage of the *Ordinance* for future aggrieved purchasers, which, besides false statements and information, is ready to operate on statements and information that are either misleading or deceptive.

Notes

1 See Part 4, *Misrepresentation, and Dissemination of False or Misleading Information etc.*, *Residential Properties (First-hand Sales) Ordinance*, A2447–A2451.
2 *Dimmock v Hallett* (1866) 2 Ch App 21.
3 *Oscar Chess Ltd v Williams* [1957] 1 WLR 370; *Esso Petroleum Co Ltd v Mardon* [1976] QB 801.
4 *Mann v Nunn* (1874) 30 LT 526; *Heilbut, Symons & Co v Buckleton* [1913] AC 30, where Lord Moulton remarked that 'such collateral contract must from their very nature be rare'.
5 *Smith v Land & House Property Corporation* (1884) 28 Ch D 7.
6 See also section 50 of the *Consumer Rights Act 2015* (UK), which under conditions converts all pre-contractual statements relied on into enforceable terms of a Business-to-Customer contract.
7 (1866-67) LR 2 Ch App 21.

8 [1983] 2 HKC 333 at 337.
9 [2000] 2 HKLRD 400 at 413.
10 [1990] 2 HKLR 440.
11 [1927] AC 177.
12 'In ascertaining what meaning was conveyed to the minds of the now respondents by the appellant's statement as to the two thousand sheep, the most material fact to be remembered is that, as both parties were aware, the appellant had not and, so far as appears, no other person had at any time carried on sheep-farming upon the unit of land in question.' Lord Merrivale, *Bisset v Wilkinson* [1927] AC 177, pp. 183–184.
13 'In ordinary circumstances, any statement made by an owner who has been occupying his own farm as to its carrying capacity would be regarded as a statement of fact...' Sim J, cited by Lord Merrivale in *Bisset v Wilkinson* [1927] AC 177, p. 184.
14 (1884) 28 Ch D 7.
15 'If a man, who has or professes to have special knowledge or skill...makes a representation by virtue thereof to another... with the intention of inducing him to enter into a contract with him, he is under a duty to use reasonable care to see that the representation is correct, and that the advice, information or opinion is reliable'; [1976] QB 801.
16 [1983] 2 HKC 33.
17 'By 11 August 1980, Kam Yuck Building had reached first floor level and therefore any representation made in relation to the ground floor was a representation as to existing fact.'. Ibid., at p. 337.
18 [1976] 1 All ER 65; per Lord Edmund-Davies.
19 *Lewin (Trading Standards Officer) v Barrett Homes Ltd* [2002] 03 EG 132; for a detailed analysis, see Goo, S. H. (2010) Regulation of Sale of Off-the-plan Property, *The Conveyancer and Property Lawyer*, no. 2, pp. 140–141.
20 [2010] EWHC 86.
21 As per Hon Kwan JA, paragraph 63, [2016] HKEC 1722.
22 Paragraph 41, [2015] HKEC 2050.
23 *Avon Insurance Plc v Swire Fraser Ltd* [2000] 1 All ER 573, paragraphs 15 to 17, by Rix J.
24 [2001] 1 HKC 621.
25 [1886] 16 QBD 778.
26 [1976] 1 Lloyd's Rep. 293, p. 318. 'In such a case, it is no defence for the representor to show that, on its true construction, the statement bore a meaning that was in fact true'. See Edwin Peel, *Treitel* on the *Law of* Contract, 12th edition, paragraph 9–012, Thomson Sweet & Maxwell, London 2007, p. 366.
27 For a summary of the presentations, see para. 30–40 of the judgment, [2016] HKEC 1722.
28 Ibid., cited by Lam Hon VP at paragraph 41.
29 As per Kwan JA, paragraphs 44–46, [2015] HKEC 2050.
30 As per Hon Kwan JA, paragraph 58, [2016] HKEC 1722.
31 Paragraph 51, [2015] HKEC 2050, cited in [2016] HKEC 1722.
32 [2000] 2 HKLRD 400; for a thorough analysis of the case, see Judith Sihombing and Michael Wilkinson, A Student's Guide to Hong Kong Conveyancing (6th Edition), LexisNexis Hong Kong, 2011, pp. 766–767.
33 [2006] EWHC 2678.
34 [1983] 2 HKC 33, p. 340.
35 [2009] HKCU 592, paragraph 42.
36 Ibid., pp. 338–339.
37 (1881) 20 Ch D 1.
38 [2000] 2 HKLRD 400; see also *Chitty on Contracts* (28th edn), paragraph 6-039.
39 [2001] 1 HKLRD 139.

40 For example, see Leung J in *Win Wave Industrial Ltd v Gosbon Industries Ltd & Ors* [2009] HKCU 592.
41 'The person to whom the misrepresentation was made must have relied on it in the sense that it must have induced him to enter into the contract,' Edwin Peel, *Treitel* on the *Law of* Contract, 12th edition, paragraph 9-017, Thomson Sweet & Maxwell, London 2007, p. 369.
42 Ibid; *Chase Manhattan Equities Ltd v Goodman* (1991). BCC 308. 5.
43 *Redgrave v Hurd* (1881) 20 Ch D 1.
44 As per Hon Kwan JA, paragraph 67, [2016] HKEC 1722.
45 *Derry v Peek* (1889) LR 14 App Cas 337, per Lord Herschell.
46 *Doyle v Olby (Ironmongers) Ltd* [1969] 2 QB 158.
47 [1964] AC 465.
48 *Overseas Tankship (UK) Ltd v Morts Dock and Engineering Co Ltd, The Wagon Mound (No 1)*[1961]UKPC 1.
49 *Gosling v Anderson* (1972) 223. E.G. 1743.
50 *Royscot Trust Ltd v Rogerson* [1991] EWCA Civ 12.
51 *Thomas Witter Ltd v TBP Ltd* [1996] 2 All ER 573.
52 *William Sindall Plc v Cambridgeshire County Council* [1994] 1 WLR 1016.
53 (1889) LR 14 App Cas 337.
54 [2000] 2 HKLRD 400.
55 (2001) 4 HKCFAR 448.
56 [2009] HKCU 592.
57 [1990] 2 HKLR 440.
58 5 Bing. N. C. 97.
59 '*where A makes a misrepresentation to B which later comes to the notice of C and induces C to contract with A. If A intended to bring about this result he is liable to C.*' Edwin Peel, *Treitel on the Law of Contract*, 12th edition, paragraph 9-035, Thomson Sweet & Maxwell, London 2007, p. 380.
60 [2009] HKCU 592, paragraph 90, 92, 105, and 111.
61 'An early example of his trenchant insights can be seen in the case of Cheng Kwok Fai v Mok Yiu Wah [1990] 2 HKLR 440 where the position of a real estate agent in Hong Kong was contrasted with that of one in England. In a short judgment of barely five p.s, the issues were dissected to the bone; and the findings led to a convincing conclusion.' Henry Litton, In Memoriam - Gerald Godfrey, *Hong Kong Lawyer*, January 2008.
62 [1990] 2 HKLR 440.
63 [2005] 1 HKLRD 317.
64 *Smith v Hughes* (1871) LR 6 QB 597.
65 [1932] AC 161, at p. 227.
66 Section 70(1), Part 3, *Residential Properties (First-hand Sales) Ordinance*, A2429.
67 Ibid., section 76(1), A2447.
68 Ibid., section 78(1), A2451.
69 Ibid., section 75(1)(a), Part 4, A2445.
70 Ibid., section 75(1)(b).
71 As per Hon Kwan JA, paragraph 66, [2016] HKEC 1722.
72 Section 75(1)(c), Part 3, *Residential Properties (First-hand Sales) Ordinance*, A2429.
73 Ibid., section 75(2).
74 *Derry v Peek* (1889) LR 14 App Cas 337, per Lord Herschell.
75 Ibid., section 76 (1) and (2), A2447.
76 Section 77(2), Part 4, *Residential Properties (First-hand Sales) Ordinance*, A2447.
77 Paragraph 51, [2015] HKEC 2050, cited in [2016] HKEC 1722.
78 Section 78(3), Part 4, *Residential Properties (First-hand Sales) Ordinance*, A2451.
79 Ibid., section 85(3), A2469.

References

Chen-Wishart, M. (2010) *Contract Law*, Oxford University Press, 3rd edn, p. 235.

Goo, S. H. (2010) Regulation of Sale of Off-the-plan Property, *The Conveyancer and Property Lawyer*, Issue 2 , p. 140–142.

HTB (2011) Residential Properties (First-hand Sales) Bill, Annex A, Public Consultation on the Proposed Legislation to Regulate the Sale of First-hand Residential Properties, The Housing and Transport Bureau, November 2011, pp. 48–54.

LC (2012) Bills Committee on Residential Properties (First-hand Sales) Bill, Paper for the House Committee, 15 June 2012, LC Paper No. CB(1) 2192/11–12, pp. 29–30, the Legislative Council, Hong Kong. www.legco.gov.hk/yr11-12/english/hc/papers/hc0608cb1-2192-e.pdf

LCUK & SLC (2011) *A Joint Consultation Paper on Consumer Redress for Misleading and Aggressive Practices,* The Law Commission and the Scottish Law Commission, 12 April 2011, pp. 60–61.

Litton, H. (2008) In Memoriam – Gerald Godfrey, *Hong Kong Lawyer*, January 2008.

Peel, E. (2007) *Treitel on the Law of Contract, 12th edn,* Thomson Sweet & Maxwell, London, pp. 362–380.

SC (2011) *Report of the Steering Committee on Regulation of Sale of First-hand Residential Properties by Legislation*, The Steering Committee on the Regulation of the Sale of First-hand Residential Properties by Legislation, October 2011, p. 68.

Sihombing, J. and Wilkinson, M. (2011) A *Student's Guide to Hong Kong Conveyancing*, 6th edn, LexisNexis Hong Kong, pp. 766–767.

15 Regulation by legislation

Under the *Residential Properties (First-hand Sales) Ordinance* (the *Ordinance*), there are about 120 offences in total. Chapter 14 revealed the efficiency and deterrent effect of the *Ordinance* with the creation of criminal offences, including the one of *misrepresentation* at section 76 and the one of *dissemination of false or misleading information* at section 78. What is the relationship between these two offences and the remaining ones? This question will be answered by this chapter. At the same time, our discussion on the common law doctrine of misrepresentation in the previous chapter suggests an apparent advantage of the *Ordinance* over the corresponding common law doctrine in establishing misrepresentation in the sale of first-hand residential properties, where the new law has attached criminal (and civil) liability to not only false but also misleading or deceptive statements. But with the worldwide trend of consumer-protection-oriented legislation since the millennia, the *Ordinance* is not the only legislation in existence that operates on false, misleading and deceptive statements in commercial transactions. Does the young *Ordinance* possess any advantage over parallel legislation in other jurisdictions? This is the second question to be answered by this chapter. Attention will then be paid to the common approach exhibited by the modern consumer protection legislation altogether: to criminalize misrepresentation in commercial practices. The question following such an observation is whether it is justifiable to engage criminal law to regulate commercial practices, especially in a free economy like Hong Kong for the sake of better consumer protection. Finally, as the *Ordinance* has its origin in an administrative scheme, before we give our final comments on the effectiveness of the new regulatory regime based on the implementation of the *Ordinance* from 2013 onwards, we need to explore the significance of resorting to the law to regulate certain unfair commercial practices in sales of first-hand residential properties, i.e., the meaning of legislation and codification.

One ordinance, two approaches

The previous 14 chapters of this book have given a detailed account of how the *Ordinance* has evolved from, and moved beyond, the Consent Scheme: the new legislation not only codifies all the major transparency-enhancement measures of the Consent Scheme but also introduces two new offences, i.e., misrepresentation and dissemination of false or misleading information, in Part 4. The creation of new offences, plus codification of almost the entire Consent Scheme's measures regarding disclosure of information, is worthy of much study.

Perhaps with the only exception of section 70, which prescribes the offence of *publishing or causing to be published an advertisement containing information that is false or misleading in a material particular*, there is an obvious contrast between the rules contained in Parts 2 to 3 of the *Ordinance* (e.g. the price list must set out the name and location of the development; the owner may only sell the specified residential property at the price of that property specified in the price list; the vendor must not restrict any person from taking measurements, taking photographs or making video recordings of the residential property) and those in Part 4 (i.e. sections 76 and 78) on misrepresentation and dissemination of false or misleading information. The former are very specific and instructional. At a first glance, the rules in Part 4 seem to be much more general in their wording and therefore seem to imply a much wider scope of reach than those in Parts 2 and 3.

When the new offences on misrepresentation and dissemination of false or misleading information were first suggested in the Steering Committee's Report (SC 2011), the relationship between these provisions and other parts of the legislation was not entirely clear. Are they concluding provisions which define all the other rules, or do they add extra requirements to the first three parts of the *Ordinance*? If they are concluding provisions, sitting above the requirements in Parts 2 to 3 of the *Ordinance*, then a breach of any other requirement in Part 2 or Part 3 would, subject to few exceptions, constitutes either the offence of misrepresentation or that of dissemination of false or misleading information. Given the fact that detailed provisions on penalties are provided for contravention of every major rule in Parts 2 to 3, it becomes clear that Part 4 is intended as *additional* to the other rules on sales brochures, price lists, show flats, advertisements, registers of transaction, sales arrangements, etc. Thus only actions (or omissions) which are in contravention of the provision in sections 76 and/or 78 can give rise to the respective criminal and civil liabilities. In this sense, Part 4 appears to take the role of 'safety-net provisions', designed to catch wrongdoings in the sales process which are not covered by the more precise offences addressed by earlier parts of the *Ordinance*.

The conclusion is supported by the fact that, with the exception of section 70, the *Ordinance* has provided different defences for offences under Parts 2 and 3 on one hand and Part 4 on the other. Section 79 provides a statutory defence for an offence under Part 2 or Part 3 (other than section 70) that the person took all reasonable precautions and exercised all due diligence to avoid the commission of the offence by that person. This defence is not available for the offence under section 78(1), i.e., *disseminating, or authorizing or being concerned in the dissemination, of false or misleading information*, or the offence under section 70, i.e., *publishing or causing to be published an advertisement containing information that is false or misleading in a material particular*. For these two offences, a number of defences are made available in Part 5 of the *Ordinance*. No defence is provided for the offence under section 76(1), i.e., *misrepresentation*.

But that does not completely rule out the possibility that a particular sales practice could contravene an offence in the early parts of the *Ordinance* and, at the same time, attract criminal liability under sections 76 and/or 78. Equally, compliance with all the requirements set out in the earlier parts of the *Ordinance* does not guarantee immunity from prosecution under sections 76 and/or 78. For example, a fraudulent or reckless misrepresentation for the purpose of inducing a property transaction can be made orally in contractual negotiations, while Parts 2 and 3 of the *Ordinance* primarily focus on written or material information and description (e.g. sales brochures, advertisements and show flats).

Essentially, the *Residential Properties (First-hand Sales) Ordinance* adopts two approaches to regulate information asymmetry and sales misdescription: first, to give detailed guidelines to vendors in the provision of sales brochures, advertisements, price lists, a register of transactions etc.; second, to impose general criminal liability in cases of misrepresentation or dissemination of false or misleading information in sales of first-hand residential properties.

The Property Misdescriptions Act 1991

To better explain the dual-approach pattern of the *Ordinance*, comparison can be made with the UK *Property Misdescriptions Act 1991 (the PMA)*, a parallel legislation adopted to regulate the same issues as the *Ordinance*: vendors and real estate agencies making false or misleading statements about specified aspects of land and buildings. Now repealed by *The Property Misdescriptions Act 1991 (Repeal) Order 2013*, this legislation ceased to be in force from October 2013 and has been replaced by European measures concerning unfair business-to-consumer commercial practices (i.e. the *Consumer Protection from Unfair Trading Regulations 2008*, discussed below) and on misleading and comparative advertising, now implemented in the UK. Yet a study on the application of the *PMA* in the UK before 2013 is still necessary for the purpose of discussing the effectiveness of the *Ordinance*; and it may acquire greater relevance in the near future against the background that the UK voted to leave the European Union in the Referendum in June 2016. It was argued that with the *PMA* (under which misrepresentation may also attract criminal liability) and *the Estate Agents Act 1979* sales practices in property transactions were much more effectively regulated in the United Kingdom than in Hong Kong then (Goo 2010).

Under the *PMA*, it is *an offence* for professionals involved in either estate agency or the property development business to make *false* or *misleading* statements about specified aspects of land and buildings.[1] A statement is only a false statement under the statute if it is false to a material degree.[2] A misleading statement arises if it is reasonable to expect a reasonable person to infer from it, or from any omission from it, something that is false.[3] A prescribed matter is a matter relating to land as specified in the *Property Misdescriptions (Specified Matters) Order 1992*. Like the common law doctrine of misrepresentation, the *PMA* operates on statements made up of words, either orally or in writing, as well as statements made by pictures or any other method of signifying meaning.[4] Overall, the wording of the legislation is quite brief and straightforward.

Similar to Part 4 of the *Ordinance*, the *PMA* demonstrated a wide-ranging capability of catching applications of a false or misleading description in real estate transactions. As already mentioned in the previous chapter, one example is *Lewin (Trading Standards Officer) v Barrett Homes Ltd*, where two purchasers were shown a large framed picture of a detached 'Maidstone' house on their visit to the site office of the developer, who offered to sell a house of this type prior to construction; the purchasers believed that the houses being built were the same as those displayed in the pictures. Upon completion, the purchasers discovered that several features displayed by the house in the picture were missing in the real houses (e.g. no gabled roof over one window, no large window above the porch). It was held that the picture on the wall of the sales office was a misleading statement under the *PMA*.[5]

The *PMA* did not impose any positive obligation of disclosure; in other words, the doctrine of *caveat emptor* could arguably still operate in cases to which the *PMA* applied. But the application of *caveat emptor* is much restricted with the implementation of the *Consumer Protection from Unfair Trading Regulations 2008* (the *CPUTR*) in the UK, which suggest that a misleading omission is also unacceptable when dealing with consumers.[6] Even so, we cannot infer a duty of full disclosure of various aspects of the property on sale from these two measures. Thus before October 2013, voluntary sales descriptions of the property made by the vendors and the real estate agents were loosely regulated by the *PMA* in the UK, subject to regulation 6 on 'misleading omissions' in the *CPUTR*; beyond that, there were few governmental regulations to specify what information must be disclosed by the vendor or agents in land transactions.

Overall, the *PMA* filled some of the gaps in the common law rules and provided a short-cut to establish misrepresentation in property transactions. This served as an obstacle against making exaggerated and untrue statements in the course of dealing.

Compared to the *Ordinance*, the *PMA* had a wider scope of application, which covers sales of first-hand and second-hand properties of all sorts: residential, industrial, commercial, etc. The scope of reach determines that the provisions of the *PMA* were general and somewhat vague and abstract. On the other hand, the *Ordinance* focuses exclusively on the sale of first-hand residential properties; with such a clearly-defined narrow scope, the rules can be much more specific and detailed.

To a certain extent, the *PMA* provided simplicity for those who sought its application: it avoided what can be an arduous process of going through many relevant rules and seeing what applies. On the other hand, the *Ordinance* may provide more clarity and give a specific place to look when seeking a remedy. Plus the *Ordinance* provides, by virtue of section 77, purchasers with a civil remedy in case of misrepresentation, whereas the *PMA* only concerns criminal liability and its sanction.

The comparison with the *PMA* suggests that it would be realistic, with the necessary refinements, to extend the scope of application of the *Ordinance* to sales practices by vendors and estate agents in other types of properties. For example, the provisions in Parts 4 and 5 could be useful to regulate sales of second-hand residential, commercial or industrial properties.

The Consumer Protection from Unfair Trading Regulations 2008

Whereas the *PMA* and the *Ordinance* share a similar scope of application, i.e. real estate transactions, the *CPUTR* and the *Ordinance* share a similar understanding on unfair commercial practices.

The *CPUTR* recognizes three types of unfair commercial practices: misleading actions, misleading omissions and aggressive commercial practices. A commercial practice is misleading if it causes or is likely to cause the average consumer to take a transactional decision she would not have taken otherwise by containing false information and therefore is untruthful in relation to certain aspects of the product (e.g. the existence or nature of the product, the main characteristics of the product or the nature of the sales process) or that its overall presentation in any way deceives or is likely to deceive the average consumer in relation to the aspects of the product, even if the information is factually correct.[7]

It is a misleading omission if in its factual context the commercial practice omits or hides material information, or provides material information in a manner which is unclear, unintelligible, ambiguous or untimely, or fails to identify its commercial intent, unless this is already apparent from the context and as a result it causes or is likely to cause the average consumer to take a transactional decision she would not have taken otherwise.[8] It should be highlighted that provision of material information in an *unclear* or *untimely* manner will also constitute a misleading omission under the *CPUTR*. For the *Ordinance*, an untimely disclosure of information is regulated mainly by the specific rules in Parts 2 and 3 and is unlikely to be considered as an operative omission under section 75(1)(c), which only applies where a person who intentionally omits a material fact from the statement, with the result that the statement is rendered false, misleading or deceptive when it is made.

Furthermore, the *CPUTR* looks to a third type of unfair commercial activity: *aggressive commercial practices*. A commercial practice is aggressive if in its factual context it significantly impairs or is likely significantly to impair the average consumer's freedom of choice or conduct in relation to the product concerned through the use of harassment, coercion or undue influence; and it thereby causes or is likely to cause her to take a transactional decision she would not have taken otherwise.[9] Aggressive commercial practice is not recognized by the *Ordinance*: in Hong Kong's sellers' market, aggressive commercial practice by the vendor is not common, but estate agents on the other hand may from time to time exercise undue pressure on their clients to make a quick decision (CC 2014).

Under the *CPUTR*, the offences of committing a misleading act, misleading omission or an aggressive practice are all strict liability offences, i.e. no *mens rea* needs be shown. Furthermore, the *CPUTR* seems to have applied different tests of unfairness where unfair practices affect different types of consumer. For example, in the case of a misleading omission, if the trader could reasonably foresee that particular types of consumers are likely to need information to make an informed decision, or if the practice is directed specifically at particular consumers, then it will be a misleading omission not to provide it – even though it would not be misleading in the case of the average consumer (Willett and Oughton 2010).

In addition, the *CPUTR* provides a list of prohibited unfair commercial practices in Schedule 1, which are considered as *always misleading* and *always aggressive* (Willett and Oughton 2010), some of which are indeed seen in the sales of first-hand residential properties in Hong Kong. For example, 'falsely stating that a product will only be available for a very limited time, or that it will only be available on particular terms for a very limited time, in order to elicit an immediate decision and deprive consumers of sufficient opportunity or time to make an informed choice'; 'promoting a product similar to a product made by a particular manufacturer in such a manner as deliberately to mislead the consumer into believing that the product is made by that same manufacturer when it is not'.

In terms of applicability, the *CPUTR* operates where an unfair commercial practice is conducted by a trader in relation to a consumer, defined in the *CPUTR* as an individual who in relation to that trader's commercial practice is acting for purposes which are outside her business.[10] In contrast, sections 76 and 77 of the *Ordinance* apply to *a person* who makes a fraudulent misrepresentation or reckless misrepresentation for the purpose of inducing *another person* to purchase any specified residential properties. *The person* who makes the fraudulent or reckless misrepresentation does not have to be the *trader* as defined by the *CPUTR*, neither the other person who has been induced by the misrepresentation to purchase a property have to be a *consumer* as defined by the *Regulation*. Thus, if a sales person who works for the vendor buys an apartment for herself based on reliance on the information provided by her employer, she may still be protected by section 77 where the information is misleading. Similarly, section 78 of the *Ordinance* does not operate within a trader-consumer framework alone.

Which one is more effective then: the *CPUTR* or the *Ordinance*? On one side, there is the European Union's broadly defined consumer protection from unfair commercial practices which is currently implemented in all the members of the European Union including the United Kingdom. According to the explanatory note in *The Property Misdescriptions Act 1991 (Repeal) Order 2013*, the *CPUTR* (together with the EU Regulation on misleading and comparative advertising) provides the same protection for consumers as the 1991 Act but in a broader and more modern framework (HP 2013). Arguably the *CPUTR* offers greater protection than the *MPA* to the purchaser of real estate in the UK with its provisions about three types of unfair commercial practices.

That said, the *CPUTR*'s ambitious approach, applying to all fields of activity that involve commercial practices between a trader and a consumer might suggest that it could be ineffective in regulating certain specific practices in the sale of residential properties. For example, the *CPUTR* cannot directly punish a vendor for not using a standard contract with the consumer when it is the norm of the trade to use that standard contract, unless under the route in Regulation 5(3)(b): establishing misleading actions by proving a failure by a trader to comply with a commitment contained in a code of conduct which the trader has undertaken to comply with. In this case, to punish the vendor requires referring to another form of regulation and further proving that the trader has indicated that she is bound by that code of conduct and the commitment is firm and capable of being verified and is not merely aspirational. In contrast, section 54 of the *Ordinance* states that a vendor needs to use a standard preliminary agreement for sale and purchase that contains the provisions set out in Schedule 4; if the vendor fails to do so, she will commit an offence under section 57 even if the preliminary agreement for sale and purchase adopted by the vendor contains no false information or misleading omissions.

Due to its broad scope, the rules in the *CPUTR* do not go into specifics and therefore lack details. This is a key issue with statutes that are intended to be applied to multiple trades: they can be vague and require cases to 'flesh them out'. However, there is no guarantee that the judiciary can generate enough case law to interpret the statute in the context of a specific trade: e.g. commercial practices by developers and real estate in sale of real estate properties. Those seeking to apply it will be left without guidance.

On the other hand, there is Hong Kong's heavy regulation represented by the *Ordinance* with a narrower consumer protection focus on sales of new residential properties. Hong Kong's approach has a limited scope but has greater details: e.g. the rules in Parts 2 and 3 of the *Ordinance*. These requirements can only be formulated by the Administration; they cannot be expected to be generated or formed by the judiciary when applying a statute which briefly discusses unfair, misleading or aggressive commercial practices in general. At the same time, these rules in Parts 2 and 3 of the *Ordinance* are so simple and straightforward that they do not need much case law to further figure out their exact meaning. In this sense, the *Ordinance* may provide more clarity and a stronger position for those wanting to see its application. Yet the true meaning and exact scope of the rules in Parts 4 and 5 of the *Ordinance* do await further illustration in case law.

The UK Consumer Rights Act (CRA) 2015

For the United Kingdom, the regulatory system based on *CPUTR* 2008 was enriched dramatically when the *UK Consumer Rights Act (CRA)* 2015 came into force on 1 October 2015. It has already been thoroughly analysed by Philip Britton (2015) that the CRA has a direct impact on B2C (business to customer) construction contracts. It is very likely that the *Act* is equally influential in the property sector and can affect the property sector by regulating B2C and C2C (customer to customer) property contracts (both first-hand and second-hand). In terms of sale of first-hand residential properties, the *CRA* has a very high potential to apply to agreements for sale and purchase as between a developer and individual purchasers/investors (as opposed to corporate purchasers/investors), as the *CRA* regards individual persons only as consumers.[11] On the other hand, the *CRA* recognizes both individual persons and companies as 'traders' as long as the person is acting for purposes relating to that person's trade, business, craft or profession, whether acting personally or through another person acting in the trader's name or on the trader's behalf.[12] It follows that developers acting as vendors when selling first-hand properties to individual purchasers are traders under the *CRA*.

If *CRA* were applicable to Hong Kong, then the developers would have to consider the *CRA* when drafting the agreement for sale and purchase in first-hand sales, in particular sections 9 to 14, which include the requirements that *goods to be as described* (section 11), *goods to match a model seen or examined* (section 14) and *other pre-contract information included in the contract* (section 12), in addition to sections 61 to 69 on unfair terms.

In this regard it seems that the *Ordinance* has already applied some of the spirits of the *CRA* into the first-hand sale of residential properties in Hong Kong with its regulations on, for example, the contents of sales brochure, the construction of show flats and the provisions to be enclosed in the standard agreement for sale and purchase.

The necessity and significance of criminalization

The common trait of the *PMA* 1991, the *CPUTR* 2008 and the 2013 *Ordinance* is that they all criminalize certain unfair commercial practices, for which civil law already provides remedies to consumers or purchasers (e.g. contract law and tort law). The trend of enforcing transparency-oriented consumer protection measures in the form of criminal law is undoubtedly the most noteworthy aspect of the latest development in consumer protection law worldwide. It was argued that the imposition of critical liability to misrepresentation was essential to the success of the *PMA* (Goo 2010).

The *Ordinance* further accentuates this trend by providing a fast-track in section 77 to establish misrepresentation at civil law, at the same time creating misrepresentation as a criminal offence. It provides compensation by awarding damages to a purchaser who has suffered pecuniary loss based on her reliance on a misrepresentation, punishing the wrong of committing misrepresentation under section 76.

Why is it necessary to regulate unfair commercial practices by using the criminal law? Two perspectives may help to explain the phenomenon. Firstly, criminal law is usually engaged when the impact of an unfair commercial practice may potentially affect the interests of more than one particular consumer on an accidental basis but rather a large group of consumers, or even the public as a whole, in general. As Philip Circus (2011) explained, criminal law deals with those wrongs that are considered to be more than just a question of individual rights. An example of such wrongs in the context of sales of first-hand residential property would be disseminating misleading sales information to influence the public's buying decision, which is argued as 'a wrong that definitely harmed the public interest' (Chan et al. 2015). For Hong Kong, practices in sales of first-hand residential properties, if unregulated, could cause much damage not only to individual purchasers but also to the public at large; this is evidenced by the fact that in recent years a variety of developers' questionable commercial practices have triggered waves of public discussion when reported in the media.

Secondly, private law and public law have different yet complementary roles to play in consumer protection. Private law serves the purpose of providing compensation to the consumer after the harm has occurred, whereas criminal law attempts to prevent unfair practices in the first place. It has long been recognized that criminal provisions are important for consumer protection to emphasize the egregious nature of the conduct and to deter traders from engaging in it (Lo 2008). The particular role criminal law plays in consumer protection can be attributed to the very fact that the primary objectives of criminal law are punishment and the suppression of crime.

The availability of compensation in private law may not be a sufficient factor to deter traders from undertaking unfair commercial practices. An individual consumer may not have the time or money to sue, even if the losses suffered are worth pursuing in a court. It would not be surprising if large numbers of consumers who suffered loss are not in the end compensated. As pointed out by Willett and Oughton (2010), the prospect of an award of damages against traders is by no means a sufficient deterrent as they know they will not always be sued. In contrast, criminal law has a much stronger deterrent effect with a much higher degree of certainty of penalty.

Before the *Ordinance*, non-compliance with those transparency-enhancement measures of the Consent Scheme by developers did not attract criminal liability and the Scheme was not specific enough about the penalty the vendor faced in cases of breach. As for purchasers, a large number of those who had an eye to capital gain of their flats might probably choose to ignore the difference between what was promised and what was delivered. Those who had the determination to take a case to courts are a tiny minority, usually after an attempt to reach a settlement with the developer was unsuccessful. A notable trend was observed that very few cases of complaints on behaviours of estate agents and developers by property purchasers were reported in Hong Kong (Goo 2010). Under such circumstances, in order to deter the occurrence of misrepresentation, a developer must face effective sanctions by the government.

Now contravention of a provision in the *Ordinance* may lead to a fine or imprisonment – irrespective of any loss suffered by a purchaser or any claim made by her. It is the Department of Justice's obligation to consider bringing a prosecution. As explained by the SRPA (2013a), the Authority is responsible for overseeing sales: if it identifies possible breaches of the *Ordinance*, it will consider referring the case to the Department of Justice for the possibility of prosecution. Under the post-2013 regulatory regime, ordinary purchasers are no longer the driving force to condemn the wrong by developers or estate agents, where the government has stepped into the shoes to punish those commercial practices in sales of first-hand properties that are explicitly prohibited by the *Ordinance*.

Quite remarkably, the *Ordinance* has imposed much heavier penalties on offenders than parallel legislation in other jurisdictions. For example, a person who commits an offence of misrepresentation under section 76(1) of the *Ordinance* is liable on conviction on indictment to a fine of HK$5,000,000 (or US$644,700) and to imprisonment for seven years; or on summary conviction to a fine of HK$1,000,000 (or US$128,940) and to imprisonment for three years. Under the *CPUTR*, however, a person who is guilty of an offence if she engages in a misleading action or misleading omission is liable on summary conviction to a fine not exceeding the statutory maximum or on conviction on indictment to a fine or imprisonment for a term not exceeding two years or both.

In a nutshell, the *Ordinance* has expanded the boundaries of public law significantly to be applicable to commercial practices in sales of residential properties. First and foremost, a sale and purchase of a residential property between an individual and a developer is a private law transaction. Legal intervention, if any, regulating the transaction must primarily be in the domain of private law. If necessary, private law will assess the rightness of any commercial practices through the principles of fairness, honesty, consciousness, equality and established rules in contract law. If the commercial practice involves misrepresentation or coercion, the contract may be rescinded, but the wrongdoer will not be put into jail, unless a more serious wrong – such as fraud – is involved.

Governmental controls may be justified if the transactions concerned are between ordinary citizens and large corporations (banks, developers etc.) where there is no equality of bargaining power between the purchaser and the seller. A purchaser is particularly vulnerable when a deal concerns a large sum of money and when professional advice is needed in the decision-making process, e.g. in the sale of mini-bonds, lifelong insurance contracts, or a residential flat costing millions of dollars. This is where regulation of an economic sector and government intervention come in. When hearing the case of *Ocean One*, the Principal Magistrate Ernest Lin expressed the view that: 'For some people, buying a property is about the biggest transaction of their lives' (SCMP 2016).

With the implementation of the *Ordinance*, public law in the form of criminal law has taken over much of the regulation of sales practices of first-hand residential properties; but private law still has the power to provide a monetary remedy for a particular purchaser.

The meaning of legislation and codification

With the enactment of the *Ordinance*, Hong Kong has codified the majority of rules and measures under the Consent Scheme that originally aimed to enhance transparency in off-plan sales only. Now the rules have become law and are applied to all sales of first-hand residential properties. The change of status from administrative measures to law brings a higher certainty of implementation of the rules and of sanction.

The nature of the Consent Scheme was to regulate off-plan sales by giving the Director of Lands power to grant or refuse consent for presales. This was achieved by incorporating restrictive conditions in the land leases. The entire mechanism is vividly explained by Merry (2008):

> A restriction on alienation of any part of the land prior to compliance with all positive obligations in the government grant is included in the covenants of any new grant. Amongst the positive obligations is a covenant to complete buildings on the land by a certain date. The restriction on alienation will be lifted to the extent of allowing sales of (as yet unfinished) flats only upon compliance by the developer with certain conditions and criteria. Where there is no covenant against alienation in the government lease (because it is not a new grant) but the developer wishes to have a modification so as to make redevelopment more profitable, the administration will not only extract a premium but also impose pre-conditions to the modification similar to those required concerning the relaxation of a covenant against alienation. After compliance with those conditions, the developer may sell flats off the plan, or as the Hong Kong jargon has it, pre-sell them. There are further conditions which have to be observed before those sales may be completed.

In *Hang Wah Chong Investment Co. Ltd v Attorney-General*, in considering whether permission was needed to modify a condition limiting building on the land, the Privy Council made it clear that the government was acting in its private capacity as the Crown's agent and not in a public law function in its decision to either grant or withhold consent to modifying the terms of a lease.[13] To Roger Nissim (2008), this essentially meant that 'each lease executed is a private transaction with appropriate contractual rights'; in other words, government leases 'are dealt with in the framework of private law, not public law'.

In *Law Lectures for Practitioners 1990*, Sarah Nield explained the enforcement aspect of the Consent Scheme by elaborating on the consequences for developers should the government act, i.e. withhold consent, seek an injunction to stop the breach of conditions in the lease grant, claim damages or a right of re-entry to the land. According to Nield, if the developer was in breach of the lease conditions, it would have difficulty in obtaining the certificate of compliance, without which the developer could not be in the position to assign a legal interest to the purchaser: section 14(1) of the *Conveyancing and Property Ordinance* (Cap 219) provides that if a person has a right to a government lease of any land upon compliance with any conditions precedent, then, only upon the compliance with the conditions will the equitable interest under that right become a legal estate in that land. This is how the government enforced the rules in the Consent Scheme. In parallel, a purchaser of an uncompleted flat could (and still can) enforce clauses in the lease by relying on clauses such as date of completion, variations in building plans, saleable area, fittings and finishes and building defects in the standard agreement for sale and purchase (Nield 1990).

More recent research on the operation of the Consent Scheme in the last 20 years reveals a more critical view from academia on the enforcement of the measures under the scheme when the government was acting in more of its private capacity. Lee and Goo (2008) remarked that the flourishing and always runaway property market in Hong Kong did not have a sophisticated legally sanctioned regime and consumers were really only protected under the general principles of contract law. To them, enforcement of the Consent Scheme was barely satisfactory and little impact was made by it on consumer protection.

In early 2010, three options were discussed for this area of regulation: (i) self-regulation within a statutory framework, with participation from other stakeholders; (ii) government regulation with participation from stakeholders; (iii) independent regulation by a body separate from both REDA and the Lands Department, with independent regulatory functions and powers (Goo 2010). Part of the third option became reality after the enactment of the *Ordinance*: the Sales of First-hand Residential Properties Authority was set up under section 86(1) to implement the new legislation.[14]

Codification changes the nature of the duties in information disclosure shouldered by the developers and some duties also need to be observed by estate agents. For developers, these duties were essentially contractual under the Consent Scheme: developers had to observe the requirements to enhance transparency closed in LACO Circular Memorandum No. 62 because there would be a clause in the conditions of sale requiring the vendor to comply with the Scheme's requirements. It was by the agreement between the government as the grantor of the lease and the developer as the grantee that the developer agreed to implement the requirements in LACO Circular Memorandum No. 62, in return for consent by the government to sell the flats before completion.

With the arrival of the *Ordinance*, these measures have become statutory requirements. Any sales of both uncompleted and completed flats have to observe the provisions in the *Ordinance* in order to comply with the law (a separate issue from carrying out what has been contractually agreed). Of course, for sales of uncompleted flats, developers still need to comply with other requirements under the Consent Scheme (Lands D 2016). But non-compliance with the requirements in the *Ordinance* can immediately attract a pecuniary penalty and/or imprisonment, a totally different sort of sanction than non-compliance with a requirement under the Consent Scheme could produce. A breach of law is not the same as a breach of contract, or a breach of an administrative requirement. A breach of law will, in general, have more serious consequences for the offender in terms of her ongoing business in that field of activity, as well as the penalty she may face.

In this way, the interests of the purchasers of first-hand properties are much better protected by implementation of the *Ordinance*. Legislation in this case can be considered as more innovative and progressive than the judiciary in order to ensure consumer protection. To quote Mindy Chen-Wishart (2010), 'Judicial conservatism has necessitated legislation aimed at protecting certain vulnerable groups'. The enactment of the *Ordinance* represents a decision by the government and legislature to hold developers legally liable for their misleading sales practices.

It should inhibit developers from exploiting for their own gain the information asymmetry with purchasers, who can now request a full and almost comprehensive disclosure of information on the property and the sale. The consumer may well feel in a stronger position by relying on a statute rather than administrative provisions to protect her position.

The only concern, then, is whether the *Ordinance* unnecessarily restricts business freedom: in a free economy, to subject a private transaction to legislative interference may create a risk of over-protection, over-regulation and be overly restrictive on business freedom.

Under the new regulatory regime, the vendor must use a standard preliminary agreement for sale and purchase, a standard agreement for sale and purchase, a standard template to disclose the information of flat size, a standard template for the price list, a standard structure for sales brochures, a standard template to indicate the status of flats available for selection, a standard template to contain information on sales arrangements, etc.; even the examination and revision records of sales brochures have been given a standard template; and deviation from any of this by a vendor may attract criminal liability. The Administration has been working diligently over the past decades to standardize the sales process, in order to eliminate unfair or misleading practices in off-plan sales. Ultimately, it is the high degree of standardization in terms of disclosure and presentation of information that ensures consumer protection in first-hand sales of residential properties.

The decision could be viewed as a bold move, for standardization of sales practices in the form of legislation in a free economy is arguably controversial. Almost all these measures restrict business freedom to varying degrees. Is it justifiable to regulate sales of first-hand residential properties in such details?

These questions should be answered in the affirmative for a number of reasons. Firstly, the amount of money involved in each transaction is significant for any ordinary purchaser. Buying a flat in Hong Kong means the purchaser committing herself to pay back a mortgage for decades. The conditions of residential property forms an essential aspect of the quality of her everyday life. This alone suggests that the government has a direct interest in monitoring the market for the benefit of citizens.

Secondly, in the absence of regulation, the likelihood that sales persons or estate agents adopt unconscionable misleading or even aggressive selling practices to would-be purchasers is high, as shown by the various malpractices exposed before regulatory measures that were aimed to enhance transparency were incorporated into the Consent Scheme in June 2010.

Thirdly, certain regulation already existed under the Consent Scheme before the commencement of the new legislation – at least for the sale of uncompleted flats. In other words, the commencement of the *Ordinance* does not suddenly create a huge number of new rules or additional obligations for developers beyond those already in force under the Consent Scheme after its reform in June 2010, i.e. the regulatory system based on LACO Circular Memorandum No. 62 (Lands D 2010a, 2010b, Lin 2012). The implementation of these measures continues in the time of the *Ordinance*, although many have been reformulated or restructured when becoming part of the *Ordinance*. In general, the legislation has enhanced the enforceability of the rules by introducing the prospect of criminal liability in case of non-compliance. For some, significant improvement has been brought in reformulating the rules, e.g., provisions of show flats, examination and revision of the sales brochure, the employment of standardized templates of the preliminary agreement for sale and purchase as well as the agreement for sale and purchase, strict timeframe for releasing Register of Transactions, etc.

Conclusion

The *Ordinance*, which sets up a new standard worldwide, brings a significant amount of positive changes in promoting consumer protection and information disclosure in sales of residential properties. Seen from an academic perspective, due to its exclusive focus on information disclosure in sales practices by developers and vendors, it may be considered as a pioneering legislation in the development of *promotional marketing law*, an emerging sub-discipline in the area of consumer protection law.

For the completeness of the argument, it should be pointed out that consumer protection may not be the only motivation behind the evolution of the regulatory regime. Behind the evolution of the Consent Scheme and the enactment of the *Ordinance* are political and economic concerns from the Administration. The timing of the enactment of the *Ordinance* – July 2012 – is critical: in that month, the average home price of the region surpassed its historical peak of 1997. The local market had been over-heated for a considerable time since the finance crisis in 2008 and the situation was worsened when more and more hot money flew into Hong Kong after the third round of Quantitative Easing in the United States. The implementation of the measures regarding information disclosure and sales description by legislation might be one of the government's attempts to cool down the rapidly growing market. In this sense, the significance of the passage of the *Ordinance* through the Legislative Council can be seen as somehow connected to the introduction of special stamp duty in 2010, the implementation of the new 'ten measures to cool down the market' announced by the Chief Executive Mr C. Y. Leung on 30 August 2012 or those 'extraordinary measures under exceptional circumstances' concerning additional special stamp duty on 27 October. 2012 (SCMP 2012) and, perhaps, the need to gain support from voters in the 2012 double election year (Chan et al. 2015).

And so at this volatile point in time, we enter the beginnings of the *Residential Properties (First-hand Sales) Ordinance*.

After three years since its commencement, the 2015 study suggests that the legitimacy of the *Ordinance* is highly accepted by the society. On the issue of effectiveness, the study exhibits a more critical view based on the occurrence of questionable sales practices after the implementation of the *Ordinance*; it calls for a tighter regulatory scrutiny and a zero-tolerance approach by the SRPA to achieve higher efficiency. The study further suggests that the SRPA should be held accountable if developers were found contravening the *Ordinance* deliberately without proper and strict control (Chan et al. 2015).

There is, however, no sign of a developer attempting a deliberate contravention of a provision of the *Ordinance* in its first four years' implementation. As commented by the Authority, developers in Hong Kong have shown great efforts in adapting to the new regulatory regime and complying with the requirements of the *Ordinance* (SRPA 2013b). In the circumstances, it should always be borne in mind that regulation is not intended to deprive developers of their legitimate freedom in running the business; the legislation should also safeguard the freedom of developers, as long as all the requirements are complied with. As observed, since the implementation of the *Ordinance*, strict compliance has been achieved by all the developers with the statutory requirements such as that the area and price per square foot and per square metre of a first-hand residential property must only be presented in terms of saleable area; that the sales brochure must be made available for a period of at least seven days immediately before the date of sale; that the price lists and the sales arrangements must be made available for a period of at least three days immediately before the date of the sale; and that to wait for three days before offering to sell those first-hand residential properties if there are amendments made to the price list(s) and the document(s) containing the sales arrangements of those residential properties (LC 2016).

Meanwhile, the SRPA has adopted a diligent and responsible approach in supervising sales practice by conducting compliance checks on sales materials and issuing guidelines and practice notes to the trade. The Authority also performs the role of public education and consumer protection by issuing timely reminders to the public when spotting questionable sales practices either regarding a particular development or across-the-board.

To conclude, the test for an ideal regime of control to regulate sales of residential properties is whether it is effective in promoting frank, comprehensive, and timely disclosure of accurate and unbiased information to the public, as well as the capacity to inhibit false and misleading sales literature. Once this goal is achieved, any more intervention is unjustified.

Overall, the implementation of the *Ordinance* has been effective in promoting accurate and timely information disclosure and enhancing transparency since its commencement in 2013. With stronger protection now being provided to purchasers of first-hand residential properties by the new legislation, the market has been functioning on a much more transparent and efficient footing.

Notes

1 Section 1(1), *Property Misdescriptions Act 1991*. An estate agency business refers to a business pursuant to instructions received from another person who wishes to dispose of or acquire an interest in land for the purpose of, or with a view to, effecting the introduction to the client of a third person who wishes to acquire or, as the case may be, dispose of such an interest; and after such an introduction has been effected in the course of that business, for the purpose of securing the disposal or, as the case may be, the acquisition of that interest; see section 1(5)(e); see also section 1(1) of the *Estate*

Agents Act 1979. A property development is a business which is concerned wholly or substantially with the development of land and for the purpose of, or with a view to, disposing of an interest in land consisting of or including a building, or a part of a building, constructed or renovated in the course of the business; see section 1(5)(f).

2 Ibid., section 1(5)(a). This coins the definition of a false trade description in the *Trade Descriptions Act 1968*, where a false trade description is defined as 'a trade description which is false to a material degree'; see section 3(1), *Trade Description Act.*

3 Ibid., section 1(5)(b).

4 Ibid., section 1(5)(c).

5 [2002] 03 EG 132.

6 Regulation 6(1), *The Consumer Protection from Unfair Trading Regulations 2008.*

7 Ibid, Regulation 5: a misleading commercial practice also includes marketing of a product (including comparative advertising) which creates confusion with any products, trademarks, trade names or other distinguishing marks of a competitor; or any failure by a trader to comply with a commitment contained in a code of conduct which the trader has undertaken to comply with.

8 Ibid., regulation 6.

9 Ibid., regulation 7.

10 Ibid., regulation 2, Part 1.

11 Section 2(3), *The UK Consumer Rights Act (CRA) 2015.*

12 Ibid.

13 As per Lord Edmund-Davies: It has already been observed that he is by definition also the Building Authority, and he is charged with many duties falling within the public domain, in relation to which it might well amount to an abuse of power were he to demand a premium as a condition precedent to acceding to a suppliant's request. Was the Director, ask the appellants, not operating in the public domain when saddling his approval of the appellants' building plans in 1976 with a demand for an extremely high premium which bore no apparent relation to the terms of the appellants' application? And, in consequence, was he not therefore imposing an insupportable condition on his compliance amounting to an abuse of power? It has to be observed in the first place that it is common ground that the Conditions of Sale operate in lieu of the terms of the contemplated Crown lease which was never granted. Secondly, no difference relevant to the present appeal can be drawn between a lease granted by a public body, or indeed the Crown, and a private lease (Wade, 'Administrative Law', 4th Edn. pp.644). Thirdly, the view expressed by Huggins, J.A. in the Supreme Court that 'The Director of Public Works has many responsibilities besides those imposed by the Buildings Ordinance' appears well established, one of those responsibilities being that of acting as the Crown's land agent. And appellants' counsel did not challenge the conclusion of Huggins, J.A. that '... the Director of Public Works can bind himself in his capacity as the Building Authority without binding himself in his capacity as land agent and vice versa'. [1981] HKLR 336, pp. 341.

14 See section 86(1), Part 6, *Residential Properties (First-hand Sales) Ordinance*, A2473, which provides that a public officer to be appointed for the purposes of implementing the Ordinance; see also Paragraphs 15.1 and 15.7, Report of the Steering Committee on Regulation of Sale of First-hand Residential Properties by Legislation, October 2011, pp. 72 and 74.

References

Britton, P (2015) Adjudication and the 'Residential Occupier Exception': Time for a Rethink?, the revised edition of the joint first prize entry in the Hudson Prize Essay Competition 2014, the Society of Construction Law, www.scl.org.uk

CC (2014) Study on the Sales of First-hand Residential Properties, pp. 31–94, 11 November 2014, Consumer Council, www.consumer.org.hk/ws_en/competition_issues/reports/20141111.html.

Chen-Wishart, M. (2010) *Contract Law*, 3rd edn, Oxford University Press, p. 8.

Chan, H.S., Chan, Y.K., Cheng, W.S. and Sze, K.W. (2015) Regulating the Sale of First-hand Residential Properties in Hong Kong: a Study of Policy and Administrative Dynamics, Capstone project report submitted in partial fulfillment of the requirements of the Master of Public Administration, Department of Politics and Public Administration, The University of Hong Kong, pp. 72, 94–101.

Circus, P. (2011) *Promotional Marketing Law: A Practical Guide*, 6th edn, Bloomsbury Professional 2011, pp. 3.

Goo, S. H. (2010) Regulation of Sale of Off-the-plan Property, *The Conveyancer and Property Lawyer*, no. 2, p. 131, pp. 143–144.

HP (2013) The Property Misdescriptions Act 1991 (Repeal) Order 2013, Consumer Protection 2013 no.1575, House of Parliament, 26 June 2013, p. 4, www.legislation.gov.uk/uksi/2013/1575/pdfs/uksi_20131575_en.pdf.

LC (2016) The work of the Sales of First-hand Residential Properties Authority, Legislative Council Panel on Housing, CB(1)861/15–16(01), April 2016, pp. 2–3.

Lands D (2010a) Legal Advisory and Conveyancing Office Circular Memorandum No. 62, Lands Department Consent Scheme, Legal Advisory and Conveyancing Office, Lands Department, 2 June 2010.

Lands D (2010b) Legal Advisory and Conveyancing Office Circular Memorandum No. 63, Lands Department Consent Scheme, Legal Advisory and Conveyancing Office, Lands Department, 1 September 2010.

Lands D (2016) Legal Advisory and Conveyancing Office Circular Memorandum No. 72C, Lands Department Consent Scheme, Legal Advisory and Conveyancing Office, Lands Department, 28 June 2016.

Lee, A. and Goo, S. H. (2008) Regulating Sale of Uncompleted Flats in Hong Kong, The International Conference *The Judicial Reform of Macau in the Context of Globalization*, the Faculty of Law, the University of Macau.

Lin, D (2012) The New Rules for Sales of Uncompleted Flats, Law Lectures for Practitioners 2010, Cheng, M. L., Jen, J. and Young, J.Y.K (Eds.), Hong Kong Law Journal & Faculty of Law, the University of Hong Kong, pp. 78–118.

Lo, S. (2008) Limitations in the Regulation of Unfair Marketing Practices in Hong Kong, *Journal of International Business and Law*, pp. 109.

Merry, M. (2008) Protection of Purchasers of Uncompleted Residential Flats – The Hong Kong Experience, *HKU-NUS-SMU Symposium Paper*, Singapore, November 2008.

Nield, S. (1990) The Sale of Uncompleted Buildings, *Law Lectures for Practitioners 1990*, pp. 285–318.

Nissim, R. (2008) *Land Administration and Practice in Hong Kong*, 2nd edn, Hong Kong University Press, pp. 55.

SC (2011) Report of the Steering Committee on Regulation of Sale of First-hand Residential Properties by Legislation, The Steering Committee on Regulation of the Sale of First-hand Residential Properties by Legislation, October 2011.

SCMP (2012) Stamp Duty Good News for First-time Purchasers, *South China Morning Post*, 31 October 2012, Hong Kong.

SCMP (2016) Ground broken: Hong Kong property developer fined HK$200,000 for sales malpractice, 19 July 2016, *South China Morning Post*, Hong Kong. www.scmp.com/

news/hong-kong/law-crime/article/1991764/ground-broken-hong-kong-property-developer-fined-hk200000

SRPA (2013a) SRPA's Response on Sales Brochures and Ordinance, *Press Releases*, the Sales of First-hand Residential Properties Authority, 5 April 2013, www.info.gov.hk/gia/general/201304/26/P201304260683.htm.

SRPA (2013b) SRPA's Response to Media Enquiries, *Press Releases*, the Sales of First-hand Residential Properties Authority, 2 June 2013, www.info.gov.hk/gia/general/201306/02/P201306020468.htm.

Willett, C. and Oughton, D. (2010) *Commercial and Consumer Law*, Michael Furmston and Jason Chuah (eds), Pearson Education Limited 2010, pp. 459–464.

Index

Numbers in **bold** denote tables. Numbers in *italics* denote figures. Numbers relating to notes are shown as page number followed by 'n' and note number e.g. 48n2.